£27.50

LIVES OF THE
LORD CHANCELLORS
1940-1970

The Great Seal

LIVES OF THE
LORD CHANCELLORS
1940–1970

BY

R. F. V. HEUSTON

CLARENDON PRESS · OXFORD
1987

Oxford University Press, Walton Street, Oxford OX2 6DP

Oxford New York Toronto
Delhi Bombay Calcutta Madras Karachi
Petaling Jaya Singapore Hong Kong Tokyo
Nairobi Dar es Salaam Cape Town
Melbourne Auckland

and associated companies in
Beirut Berlin Ibadan Nicosia

Oxford is a trade mark of Oxford University Press

Published in the United States
by Oxford University Press, New York

British Library Cataloguing in Publication Data
Heuston, R. F. V.
Lives of the Lord Chancellors.
Vol. 2: 1940–1970
1. Great Britain. Lord Chancellor's Office
—History
I. Title
354.41065   KD7107
ISBN 0-19-820074-9

Library of Congress Cataloging in Publication Data
Heuston, R. F. V.
Lives of the Lord Chancellors.
Includes indexes.
Contents: —v. 2. 1940–1970.
1. Great Britain. Lord Chancellor's Dept.—Biography.
2. Judges—Great Britain—Biography.   I. Title.
KD620.H48 1987   347.42´014 [B]   86-28496
344.20714 [B]
ISBN 0-19-820074-9 (v. 2)

Set by Joshua Associates Limited, Oxford
Printed in Great Britain
at the University Printing House, Oxford
by David Stanford
Printer to the University

PREFACE

THE general object of this work is the same as that of its predecessor published in 1964—namely, to depict the Lord Chancellors in the thirty years between 1940 and 1970 in their legal, political and personal lives. The previous volume ended with Lord Caldecote, and this starts with his successor in 1940, Lord Simon, and ends with the retirement of Lord Gardiner in 1970. His successor, Lord Hailsham of St Marylebone, is not included. I have provided a lengthy Introduction in which attention is given more to the nature and functions of the office of Lord Chancellor than to the characteristics of the holder of it. (Those who have acquired the previous volume, which the publishers have kindly agreed to re-issue, will find that some phrases have been repeated in relation to such matters as the stipend and pension of the Lord Chancellor. As the earlier account had apparently stood the test of time, there seemed to be no point in altering it just for the sake of elegant variation).

There is one major difference between the earlier volume and the present one. In the 1960s nobody mentioned the topic of length; twenty-five years later the economic position made severe restrictions necessary. When a little more space was made available I decided not to divide it equally, between the six Chancellors, but to devote it all to Lord Jowitt, whose legal and political achievements, especially in the field of law reform, seemed to me to have been seriously under-valued.

My best thanks are due to a number of institutions which provided the rarest of academic gifts—time to write. In particular I am grateful to All Souls College, Oxford, and the University of British Columbia. Mr David Kinley of Jesus College, Cambridge, gave valuable help with proofs.

R. F. V HEUSTON.

November 1986

ACKNOWLEDGEMENTS

I MUST first express my gratitude to Her Majesty the Queen for her gracious permission to have access to the Royal Archives at Windsor and to reprint material from them.

I must also express my sincere thanks to the owners of the copyright in other material of which I have made use.

Many people gave time and took trouble to provide me with oral or documentary reminiscences of the Lord Chancellors. Some did so on condition that they remained anonymous. For this reason, amongst others, I have omitted the customary list of eminent persons who are individually and publicly thanked. My gratitude is none the less sincere.

LIST OF CONTENTS

LIST OF PLATES

Frontispiece: The Great Seal

Between pp. 148 and 149

1. Lord Simon's letter to Lord Atkin in October 1941
2. Lord Simon at the Foreign Office (photograph by Cecil Beaton)
3. William Jowitt in 1907: *Portrait of a Gentleman* by Ambrose McEvoy
4. Lord Jowitt as Chancellor: *The Earl Jowitt* (1946–51) by Sir William Coldstream
5. Lord Simonds on the Woolsack in March 1953 (portrait by Lord Methuen RA)
6. Lord Simonds after being sworn in as Chancellor in October 1951
7. Sir David Maxwell Fyfe KC MP at the Nuremberg trials in March 1946
8. Lord Kilmuir as Chancellor in Procession in October 1955
9. Reginald Manningham-Buller with Winston Churchill at Towcester in June 1945
10. The Conservative Cabinet at Chequers in April 1963
11. Lord Gardiner as Chancellor of the Open University
12. Lord Gardiner at the Lord Chancellor's desk

The reproduction of these plates is due to the courtesy of the following persons or institutions: Courtaulds Limited and the House of Lords Record Office (frontispiece); The Viscount Simon and Gray's Inn (1); Sotheby's London (2); Trustees of the Tate Gallery (3); Dr Peter Rumley and Lady Penelope Wynn-Williams (4); The Lord Methuen and the Yeoman Usher of the Black Rod (5); BBC Hulton Picture Library (6, 7, and 8); the Hon. Elizabeth Manningham-Buller (9); Douglas Weaver (10); The Lord Gardiner (11); Sir Thomas Skyrme (12).

LIST OF LORD CHANCELLORS 1940–1970

Name and Title(s)	Great Seal	
	Date of receipt of[1]	*Tenure of*[2]
SIMON, John Allsebrook (Viscount Simon, 20 May 1940)	13 May 1940	5 years, 2 months
JOWITT, William Allen (Baron Jowitt, 2 August 1945; Viscount J., 20 January 1947; Earl J. and Viscount Stevenage, 24 December 1951)	28 July 1945	6 years, 3 months
SIMONDS, Gavin Turnbull (Baron Simonds (life), 18 April 1944; Baron S., 24 June 1952; Viscount S., 18 October 1954)	30 October 1951	3 years, 0 months
MAXWELL FYFE, David Patrick (Viscount Kilmuir, 19 October 1954; Earl of K. and Baron Fyfe of Dornoch, 20 July 1962)	18 October 1954	7 years, 9 months
MANNINGHAM-BULLER, Reginald Edward (Baron Dilhorne, 17 July 1962; Viscount D., 7 December 1964)	16 July 1962	2 years, 3 months
GARDINER, Gerald Austin (Baron Gardiner (life), 15 January 1964)	17 October 1964	5 years, 8 months
HOGG, Quintin McGarel (Succeeded as 2nd Viscount Hailsham, 16 August 1950, but disclaimed peerage for life, 20 November 1963; 1st Lord Hailsham of St Marylebone (life), 30 June 1970)	22 June 1970	3 years, 9 months[3]

[1] In each case the date of receipt is the same as the date of surrender by the predecessor.

[2] It may be convenient to record here that in the last three centuries the longest tenures have been Eldon (24 years, 10 months, and 23 days); Hardwicke (19 years, 8 months, and 16 days); and Halsbury (17 years, 1 month, and 12 days).

[3] Lord Hailsham of St Marylebone ended his first Chancellership on 5 March 1974. His second Chancellorship, in succession to Lord Elwyn-Jones, began on 8 May 1979.

NOTE ON SOURCES

A. PUBLISHED

The more important works consulted are cited in the footnotes. Full bibliographical details are given on the first citation in each part. The place of publication is London unless otherwise stated. Abbreviations for Law Reports, statutes and periodicals follow the standard practice as set out in, for example, Raistrick, *Index to Legal Citations and Abbreviations* (1985).

B. UNPUBLISHED

Three of the six Chancellors left collections of papers. Those of Lord Simon are in the Bodleian Library; those of Lord Kilmuir at Churchill College, Cambridge. A catalogue or finding-aid is available for each collection. The uncatalogued papers of Lord Jowitt are in the possession of the family.

Before their deaths Lords Simonds and Dilhorne told the author that they had destroyed, or would destroy, all papers. These intentions may not have been fully carried out. So a substantial typescript entitled 'Recollections' is in the possession of Mr Kenneth Simonds, a nephew of the Lord Chancellor. In 1984 Lord Gardiner also assured the author that he had kept no papers. But much information is available in Lady Gardiner's admirable biography of her husband (M. Box, *Rebel Advocate* (1983)), on which very considerable reliance has been placed.

INTRODUCTION

THE Lord High Chancellor of Great Britain,[1] to give him his full official title,[2] occupies a position of great antiquity, much dignity, and considerable importance.

The antiquity of the office is a subject of some dispute. Claims have been made for an initial date of AD 615, but Edward the Confessor (1042–66) was the first English king to have a great seal and a Chancellor to keep it. From Herfast in 1068 to Lord Gardiner in 1970 there have been some 229 Holders of the Great Seal.[3] The word apparently derives from the 'cancelli' or lattice-work screen behind which sat the clerks for the dispatch of clerical business in a court. After the Conquest the Chancellor, then an ecclesiastic, was in charge of the secretarial business of the King's court. Once it was customary to call him simply 'the Chancellor' or 'the King's Chancellor'. The proper title of the office is therefore that of Chancellor, and the office-holder is always so referred to in the older and better usage of Whitehall and Westminster.[4] Thus the Chancellor signs official documents with his peerage title followed by 'C'.[5] The Chancellorship of the Exchequer is a comparatively modern office; it can hardly be

---

[1] The introduction to Lord Campbell's *Lives of the Chancellors* (8 vols.; 1848–69) still contains much useful material. The primary historical account of the office is in W. S. Holdsworth, *History of English Law*, 7th edn. (1956), vol. i, ch. v. An authoritative description by Lord Haldane is in ch. x of the *Report of the Machinery of Government Committee* (1918), Cmd. 9230. Many of the other Chancellors have left short accounts, as have some of those who have been Permanent Secretary to the Lord Chancellor. See Viscount Hailsham, *The Duties of a Lord Chancellor*, Holdsworth Lecture (Birmingham, 1936); and essays with similar titles in the same series by Lord Gardiner (1968) and Lord Hailsham of St Marylebone (1972); Viscount Kilmuir, 'The Office of Lord Chancellor' (1956) 9 *Parliamentary Affairs* 132; Lord Schuster, 'The Office of the Lord Chancellor' (1949) 10 *Camb. L.J.* 175; A. Napier, 'The Office of Lord Chancellor' (1950) 1 *Nisi Prius* 88; G. Coldstream, 'The Lord Chancellor's Office' (1962) *Graya* 13. See also M. Bond and D. Beamish, *The Lord Chancellor* (1977).

[2] The Interpretation Act 1889, s. 12(1), provides that ' "the Lord Chancellor" is the Lord High Chancellor of Great Britain for the time being'. But his functions in Scotland are non-existent (see 332 H.L. Deb. col. 431), though the Table of Precedence for Scotland ranks him after the Lord-Lieutenants of Counties but before the Moderator of the General Assembly of the Church of Scotland.

[3] The most authoritative list is in Royal Hist. Soc., *Handbook of British Chronology*, 2nd edn. (1961).

[4] Thus in a Royal Commission for the Opening of Parliament he will be referred to as 'Chancellor of Great Britain'. 'Mr Gladstone would have been horrified if you had called him "The Chancellor" ': 170 H.L. Deb. col. 313, per Viscount Simon.

[5] But he is described in the law reports as e.g. 'Sir Frederick Smith LC' before, and 'Lord Birkenhead LC' after, enoblement. The modern practice of writing e.g. Lord Lane CJ is to be deprecated: Lord Lane holds the office of Lord Chief Justice of England: see J. L. Montrose, 'L.C., L.C.J., L.J.' (1963) 79 *LQR* 187. As the Lord Chancellor is a special kind of Chancellor, the proper plural is 'Lord Chancellors' (like 'Lord Mayors'). But as a Law Lord is a special kind of Lord, the proper plural here is 'Lords of Appeal in Ordinary' (like 'courts-martial'). But Lords Justices of Appeal are an exception because Parliament has so decided (Supreme Court Act 1981, s. 2(3)).

traced back beyond 1714, and did not attain its present importance until the first quarter of the nineteenth century. The 'Lord' and the 'High' are honorific marks of respect as in the titles of Lord Chief Justice and Lord Chief Baron, which date in usage from about 1485 and 1589 respectively.

The dignity of the office is great.[6] Its holder is the first subject in the realm after the Archbishop of Canterbury, and immediately before the Archbishop of York and the Prime Minister.[7] By the House of Lords Precedence Act 1539, s. 4, the Lord Chancellor is given a precedence which, in Kilmuir's words, is 'temporary but immense'.[8] The section provides that 'the Lord Chancellor, Lord Treasurer, Lord President of the Council, and Lord Privy Seal, being of the Degree of Barons of Parliament, or above, shall sit and be placed, as well in this present Parliament as in all other Parliaments hereafter to be holden, on the Left Side of the said Parliament Chamber,[9] on the higher Part of the Form on the same Side, above all Dukes . . .'. Of the three other 'Great Officers of the Realm' expressly mentioned in the section, the Lord President of the Council and the Lord Privy Seal still survive: the office of Lord Treasurer has been in commission since 1714.[1] But the Lord Chancellor outranks them all. In the words of the greatest English legal historian: 'His position is as singular as it is splendid.'[2] It is older than democracy, older than Parliament, older than Magna Carta, older than the Norman Conquest. The office of Keeper of the Great Seal, the powers but not the dignity of which were identical with those of the Chancellor, was formerly used when for various reasons it was expedient to confer the greater dignity. Its holder was customarily a commoner at first; so the last Lord Keeper, Sir Robert Henley, was appointed in 1757 and not made a peer until 1760 and Chancellor until 1761.

The antiquity of the office also explains why the Lord Chancellor is the Speaker of the House of Lords, and why he can discharge his functions as Speaker without being a peer, and therefore not a member of the House. (Down to 1837 the Deputy Speaker was often a judge: today there are four

---

[6] There is much about the ceremonial side of the position in J. Derriman, *Pageantry of the Law* (1955), pp. 154–64.

[7] So when the Prime Minister (Harold Wilson) was late for a dinner-party, nobody liked to sit down until Lord Gardiner suggested it. 'That is one advantage in having a Lord Chancellor to dinner. He can make a protocol decision for you' (Marcia Williams, *Inside No. 10* (1972), p. 287).

[8] Earl of Kilmuir, *Memoirs* (1964), p. 234.

[9] i.e. looking from the Throne.

[1] The statute refers to six other 'Great Officers of the Realm': the Lord Great Chamberlain; the Lord High Constable; the Earl Marshal and Lord High Admiral; the Lord High Steward; the King's Chamberlain; and the King's Secretary. The Lord Great Chamberlain and the Earl Marshall still function; the office of Admiral was in commission, but has been revived and vested in the monarch; the Steward has not officiated since 1935, when the office was called out of abeyance for Lord Hailsham (see R. F. V. Heuston, *Lives of the Lord Chancellors 1885–1940* (Oxford, 1964), pp. 482–3). These Great Officers of the Realm (now usually called Great Officers of State) should not, of course, be confused with the three Great Officers of the Household—the Lord Chamberlain, the Lord Steward, and the Master of the Horse.

[2] F. W. Maitland, *Justice and Police* (1889), p. 14.

Deputy Speakers—all peers.) As was said by an eminent authority on constitutional history:

Parliament is still the highest Court in the land, and the Lord Chancellor sits in Parliament by a better prescriptive title than anyone else. It is he who summons all the rest, but *qua* Lord Chancellor he sits without a summons at all, and therefore he presides. It is true that as a peer he receives a summons, but a peerage is a modern and meretricious adornment of the Lord Chancellorship.[3]

But as the Speaker, by an English paradox, cannot speak in debate unless he is a member of the House,[4] every Chancellor of modern times has been created a peer, unless, as with Haldane, Maugham, Simonds, and Gardiner, he already held that rank.

Qualifications for Position

There are none. This great office can, as a matter of strict law, be conferred on any person, male or female, who is capable of swearing the oath of allegiance and the official oath. No legal knowledge or professional qualification is required. As Salisbury mordantly observed in 1897, 'Perhaps it is not an ideal system—some day no doubt the Master of the Rolls' (he might have added the Lord Chancellor and the Lord Chief Justice) 'will be appointed by competitive examination in Law Reports, but it is our system for the present; and we should give our party arrangements a wrench if we throw it aside.'[5] In practice it is indispensable that the Lord Chancellor should not only be a supporter of the party in power, but also a lawyer of first-class ability, capable of evoking the respect, and even fear, of lawyers, politicians, and civil servants. Indeed the paradox is that the Lord Chancellorship is the only Cabinet office which cannot possibly be held by an amateur. He cannot rely on his officials, however gifted, as can a Secretary of State. The necessity of being a Government supporter is interpreted very widely: two twentieth-century Chancellors (Maugham, Simonds) were personally unknown to the Prime Minister of the day (Chamberlain, Churchill) when given the Great Seal. It has sometimes been said that the requirement that the Lord Chancellor should be a member of the government of the day has produced men of less than first-rate ability. It may have been so once. In 1473 Chancellor Booth, formerly Bishop of Durham, 'wore himself out doing nothing',[6] and had to be appointed Archbishop of York after ten months. Hatton (1587–91), and Shaftesbury (1672–3) were generally

---

[3] A. F. Pollard, *The Times*, 12 Dec. 1916.

[4] Although F. E. Smith (characteristically) broke this rule by delivering a speech in an appeal four days before he became a peer—see (1919) 88 *LJ*(Ch.) 304.

[5] Heuston, *Lord Chancellors 1885–1940*, p. 52.

[6] So the *Hoyland Chronicle* puts it. It also states that in the House of Lords 'he never ventured to open his mouth'.

regarded as men of fashion: they certainly had no legal qualifications.[7] But in modern times this has not been so. As Peel said in 1850: 'The political advantage of a Lord Chancellor to a government would be entirely relinquished if he were not a man of the highest eminence in the profession.'[8] Each of the Chancellors in our period had a substantial professional record, in some cases one of real distinction, at the date of his appointment. The need for the highest legal qualifications was recognized clearly by the only man who is known to have refused the Great Seal for the sake of conscience—Sir Henry James. When he received the offer from Gladstone in 1886 he refused, partly because he could not accept the policy of Home Rule, but partly because he thought that 'before a man accepted it he ought to search his conscience and determine whether he was fit to review the decisions of all the judges who had spent their lives as lawyers'.[9]

Like other Cabinet Ministers, the Lord Chancellor holds office at the pleasure of the Prime Minister. The Lord Chancellor has never enjoyed the protection given by the Act of Settlement to the High Court judges whom he appoints. This became the constitutional practice after the dismissals of Thurlow (1792) and Loughborough (1801). Indeed, two of the Chancellors in our period, Simonds and Kilmuir, were dismissed with peremptory abruptness for reasons which seemed good to the Prime Minister of the day.

On three occasions in this century (1938, 1951, and 1984) it has been considered whether the office could be granted to a member of the Scottish Bar, and the names of past or present Lord Advocates (Macmillan, Reid, Mackay of Clashfern) have been mentioned. There is no legal objection to such an appointment. There is no requirement that the Lord Chancellor, unlike the judges whom he himself appoints, should have a professional qualification in English law. Such judicial functions as the Presidency of the Court of Appeal and the Chancery Division are his by statute (the Supreme Court Act 1981, s. 5) in virtue of his office. It is true that one possible candidate, while conceding that such an appointment was legally possible, commented that 'it is manifest that such an appointment would be contrary to constitutional convention and both incongruous and inconvenient'.[1] But the highest appellate tribunals have gained too much from their Scottish members in the past for this opinion to be regarded as final for the future.

---

[7] Hatton had other claims on the monarch's benevolence, as mentioned in Gray's poem 'A Long Story':

> His bushy beard, and shoe-strings green,
> His high-crown'd hat, and satin doublet,
> Mov'd the stout heart of England's Queen,
> Tho' Pope and Spaniard could not trouble it.

[8] *Report of the Select Committee on Official Salaries* (1850), C. 6617, p. 28.
[9] Lord Askwith, *Lord James of Hereford* (1930), p. 161.
[1] Lord Macmillan, *A Man of Law's Tale* (1952), p. 156.

One possible restriction on the appointment of a Lord Chancellor existed until 1974, and so must be mentioned—namely, that it was thought to be uncertain whether a Roman Catholic could be appointed. The highest authorities differed. Simon liked to recount the story, told to him by the second Lord Russell of Killowen, that when the latter's uncle was appointed Lord Chief Justice in 1894, Rosebery, who as Prime Minister had made the appointment, rode over from Epsom to Tadworth Court in order to congratulate Lady Russell. She said 'Well, Prime Minister, I had hoped that my husband would be the first Roman Catholic Lord Chancellor since the Reformation.' Rosebery replied that, though the Woolsack was a dignified position while it lasted, the Lord Chief Justiceship was a far more enviable post, for its occupant did not change with changing governments, 'whereas an ex-Lord Chancellor is nothing but a shabby old gentleman with £5,000 a year'.[2] But all these doubts were swept away by the Lord Chancellor (Tenure of Office and Discharge of Ecclesiastical Functions) Act 1974. Introduced by Lord Hailsham of St Marylebone (when in opposition) it had all-party support. It might have benefited Lord Rawlinson if his political career had taken a different turn.

A paragraph may be added here about the peculiar concept that the Lord Chancellor was 'keeper of the king's conscience'. Nobody has been clear as to what this phrase, apparently first used by Hatton in 1587,[3] meant. Some thought it had a connection with the ecclesiastical character of many medieval chancellors, and that it was therefore the Chancellor's duty to act as the King's confessor or attend him at the Chapel Royal;[4] others thought that it had something to do with the equitable jurisdiction of the Court of Chancery;[5] others that it had its origin in Thurlow's opposition to Catholic Emancipation.[6] Two Lord Chancellors have said the phrase is now meaningless.[7] The matter may rest there.

Method and Date of Appointment

The office of Lord High Chancellor is conferred by the Sovereign delivering or granting the Great Seal to the person chosen. It is customary today for the Sovereign also to address the recipient by the title of his office, but high authority and precedent doubt whether this is necessary. Nottingham,[8]

---

[2] Viscount Simon, *Retrospect* (1952), p. 286. See also 127 H.C. Deb. col. 463.

[3] D. E. C. Yale, *Nottingham's Chancery Cases* (1957), p. xi.

[4] Campbell, *Lives*, vol. iv, p. 286.

[5] Lord Hailsham of St Marylebone, 352 H.L. Deb. col. 432 and in (1975) 1 *Poly L. Rev.* 2.

[6] Sir H. Slesser, *Judgment Reserved* (1942), p. 191.

[7] Hailsham, *Duties of a Lord Chancellor*, p. 12; Simon, *Retrospect*, p. 251.

[8] D. E. C. Yale (ed.), *Prolegomena* (Cambridge, 1965), p. 179. Nottingham adds (p. 182) that the Seal should never be taken out of the realm.

Blackstone,[9] and Haldane[1] all state that the delivery is sufficient without any words spoken. And when in 1850 Langdale, together with Shadwell and Rolfe, was appointed a Commissioner of the Great Seal (the last occasion on which this was done), he objected to receiving the Great Seal as First Commissioner until the commission itself had been sealed on the ground that the unqualified delivery of the Seal would make him Lord Chancellor and not Commissioner. Today the delivery is constructive or notional: no physical transfer takes place, the monarch just touching 'it on the table before her in the gesture of handing it into my care'.[2] This practice may have originated when the monarch was female, for that which is delivered is not the wax seal but the two silver plates or discs which constitute the matrix for the Great Seal.[3] These plates are 6 inches in diameter and weigh 18 lb.[4] In 1801 George III took the Great Seal from under his coat on the left side and handed it to Eldon, saying, 'You see it comes from my heart'.[5] And in 1904 it was observed that when Halsbury received the new Great Seal of Edward VII from the hands of the monarch, 'the vivacity and agility of the octogenarian Chancellor in performing his genuflexions and supporting the weight of the two Seals was astonishing'.[6] It is usual for the Lord Chancellor to kiss hands, which seems to be no more than the customry practice when any Cabinet Minister receives the seals of his office.

Immediately after delivery, actual or constructive, the oath of allegiance and the official oath are tendered to the Lord Chancellor by the Clerk of the Council in accordance with the Promissory Oaths Act 1868, s. 5, which requires these two oaths to be taken by a new Lord Chancellor 'as soon as may be after his acceptance of office'. Once he has taken possession of the Great Seal, and taken the oath of allegiance and the official oath, the Lord Chancellor leaves the Privy Council and returns to the Palace of Westminster, fully entitled to discharge those functions of his office which are of an administrative or legislative character—for example, if the Council has been held, as is usual, in the forenoon, he can sit Speaker in the House of Lords in the afternoon, even if he is still a commoner, while his patent as a peer is being prepared. (The Chancellor does not himself carry the Great Seal from the Council at Buckingham Palace to Westminster. That task is performed by a Messenger, who meets the Chancellor outside the Council Chamber, takes from him the Great Seal, and

---

[9] Sir William Blackstone, *Commentaries on the Laws of England*, 17th edn. (1830), vol. iii, p. 47. The same authority adds that he becomes a Privy Counsellor by virtue of his office. All the Chancellors in this volume were in fact Privy Counsellors before their appointment—except Gardiner, who was sworn of the Privy Council on the day on which (and a few minutes before) he received the Great Seal.

[1] *Higher Nationality* (1913), pp. 15–16.

[2] Lord Elwyn-Jones, *In My Time*, (1983), p. 261.

[3] For the mechanics of using the Great Seal, see below, pp. 14–15.

[4] Bond and Beamish, *Lord Chancellor*, pp. 21–2.

[5] A. V. Lincoln and R. McEwen (edd.), *Lord Eldon's Anecdote Book* (1960), p. 5.

[6] A. Fitzroy, *The History of the Privy Council* (1928), p. 306.

hands to him the keys of the Cabinet boxes and of the Seal box.) Although a Chancellor cannot act until he has assumed office by receiving the Great Seal, so long as he has it in his possession, and has not surrendered it, or been required to surrender it, he is in office although his party is not. This happened in the case of Jowitt in October 1951.[7] The surrender may be as constructive as the delivery—for example, again in the case of Jowitt, the Great Seal was sent back to Buckingham Palace by the Messenger, as George VI was too ill to receive his outgoing Ministers. Much earlier, when Eldon went out in 1806 he was told by an affected monarch to leave it on a chair ('I will not take it from you').[8] Today the surrender of the Seal takes place on the same day as the new Chancellor receives it, although if there has been some personal bitterness in the change-over (as in 1954) the surrender may take place in the morning and the receipt in the afternoon, to avoid the embarrassment of a personal confrontation.

Finally the date of receipt of the Great Seal is the critical one for the purposes of the computation of time in relation to all relevant matters, such as the amount of his salary. It seems necessary to stress this obvious point, for some books of reference give the date on which it was announced in *The Times* that the appointment would be made or has been made—dates which may vary significantly from the date of the appointment itself.

The statute also (s. 6) requires a new Lord Chancellor to take the oath of allegiance (again), and the judicial oath, 'as soon as may be after his acceptance of office', and 'in the manner in which such oaths were taken before the Act'. So law and common sense unite in making a distinction between the second and third oaths.[9] The judicial oath should be taken in public to signalize the fact that in England all judicial proceedings, save in a few exceptional cases, should be open to all. But even today in England administration is still the secret garden of the Crown. So as an administrator the Chancellor takes the necessary oaths at Buckingham Palace *coram consilio secreto domini regis*:[1] as a judge the necessary oaths are taken *coram publico* at the Royal Courts of Justice. This delay causes no public inconvenience, for it is in the nature of things impossible to list an appeal before the new Chancellor in the few days which will elapse between taking the official oath before the Sovereign in Council and the judicial oath before the Master of the Rolls at the Law Courts (usually in the Master of the Rolls's Court).[2] The order of that ceremony is as follows. Four chairs are placed on the

[7] See below, p. 124.   [8] Lincoln and McEwen, *Lord Eldon's Ancedote Book*, p. 5.

[9] For the statutory forms, see below, Appendix of Documents. In 1912 Haldane took the oaths 'swearing in Scottish fashion with uplifted hand' (Heuston, *Lord Chancellors 1885-1940*, p. 167).

[1] So a Privy Counsellor to be sworn is carefully instructed that the oath, in its splendid Elizabethan English, 'will be read by the Clerk of the Council, and the Privy Counsellor will mentally repeat the words after him'.

[2] The account which follows is based on personal observations of the ceremony on 17 July 1962 (Dilhorne) and 23 June 1970 (Hailsham of St Marylebone). Heuston, *Lord Chancellors 1885-1940*, pp.103, 337-8, contains accounts of the ceremonies in 1886 (Herschell) and 1916 (Finlay).

Bench in such a fashion that the largest chair ('the central place') is left vacant
for the Lord Chancellor. Starting from the left (facing the Court), the President
of the Family Division occupies Chair 1, the Master of the Rolls occupies
Chair 2, the Lord Chancellor Chair 3, and the Lord Chief Justice Chair 4. For
two reasons it is important to ensure that the Master of the Rolls does not
occupy the central place, as he is normally accustomed to do when presiding in
his own court. First, protocol requires that he surrenders his precedence to the
Lord Chancellor and the Lord Chief Justice if (exceptionally) they are present in
his court. Secondly, the function of the Master of the Rolls at this ceremony is
not a true judicial function, but a ministerial one. It is a survival of his position
as the first of the twelve Masters in Chancery, as is shown by the fact that if the
Master of the Rolls is absent the senior Chancery Master holds the book.

In 1964 Sir George Coldstream, the Permanent Secretary to the Lord
Chancellor, gave thought to the problem, but his reasons for adhering to the
traditional practice seem conclusive.

It would be possible to get things right by placing a fifth chair on the Bench (to be
occupied by the senior Lord Justice) which would enable the Lord Chancellor to take
the central place, the Lord Chief Justice on his right, the Master of the Rolls on his left,
and the President on the right of the Lord Chief Justice. But I am far from clear whether
there is enough room, practically speaking, for it is a crowded affair: the Mace is brought
in and as many Lords Justices and Judges as possible squeeze in behind the chair
occupied by the Lord Chancellor. Moreover, all stand while the Oaths are being
administered by the Clerk of the Crown, which means that the chairs have to be pushed
back and the narrow space between the Bench and the wall still further confined. It
follows that the fewer chairs there are on the Bench the more convenient, and possibly
seemly, the arrangements are likely to be. An alternative would be to leave the President
out of the ceremony altogether but I doubt whether this would be an acceptable
suggestion![3]

These arrangements having been made, the Lord Chancellor enters, in his
black and gold robe of State, with his Train-Bearer, and preceded by his Mace-
Bearer and Purse-Bearer. He takes his place on the right hand of the Master of
the Rolls, as explained, who hands to him a New Testament. The Clerk of the
Crown then administers to him the judicial oath, which the Chancellor
publicly repeats after him, sentence by sentence.[4] It is customary for the Clerk
of the Crown also to administer the oaths of allegiance and office, which have
already been taken at the Privy Council.[5] The function of the Master of the
Rolls in this ceremony is described in some older authorities as 'holding the
book'. In practice today this means simply that he hands over and receives back

[3] To the author.
[4] For their terms, see below App. of Documents
[5] In 1962 all three oaths were taken; in 1970 only the oath of allegiance and the judicial oath.

the Testament: in no sense does he hold it, other than momentarily. Finally, the Attorney-General moves that the proceedings be recorded by the Queen's Remembrancer (an office usually held by the Senior Master of the Queen's Bench Division), who is present wearing a tricorn hat on top of his full-bottomed wig. The Lord Chancellor (not the Master of the Rolls) replies, 'So be it'. The Lord Chancellor then leaves, equipped for the discharge of all his functions so far as the law and custom of England can provide.

The Peerage

Although, as explained, it is not necessary to be a peer in order to hold the Great Seal, every Chancellor in modern times has been made a peer as soon as possible after his appointment,[6] unless he already held such a dignity, as with Haldane, Cave, Simonds, and Gardiner. Simonds had been a life peer since he was made a Law Lord in 1944. He received a hereditary barony in 1952, and a viscountcy on retirement in 1954. (Both his sons had predeceased him, so in a sense the honours were meaningless: but he may have taken the view that it was his duty to the office to claim its traditional honours.) Dilhorne was also created viscount on his retirement. Gardiner had been created a life baron some months before his appointment as Lord Chancellor—and was not promoted to a viscountcy either during his tenure or on his retirement, no doubt because no hereditary peerages had been created under the Wilson government. As Simon and Kilmuir had held the office of Secretary of State which traditionally carries a viscountcy, that was the grade in the peerage to which they were appointed on being given the Great Seal.[7] Kilmuir was promoted to Earl on his retirement, as also was Jowitt (who had previously been promoted to Viscount in 1947). The only Chancellors in modern times, until 1970, who had not been promoted to Viscount on retirement were Herschell and Buckmaster. The reasons for this cannot now be ascertained, but in the case of Buckmaster the omission gave rise to so much difficulty under the rules which then governed the precedence of former Lord Chancellors when sitting judicially that he was promoted in 1933.[8] As those rules have now been altered, the difficulty cannot recur, and whether for that reason or another, Gardiner and Elwyn-Jones have remained life peers after giving up the Great Seal.

Quintin Hogg, later Lord Hailsham of St Marylebone seems to have been the only Chancellor to have taken the oath as a commoner dignified only by a

[6] The interval may be very brief. So Hansard (242 H.L. Deb. col. 527) records that on 17 July 1962 at 2.30 p.m. 'The Rt. Hon. Sir Reginald Manningham-Buller, Honorary Major in the Army, sat Speaker', and that at 2.34 p.m. the House was informed, by the Lord President of the Council, that the Lord Chancellor had been created a peer. He was then introduced (see below, n. 1). But Elwyn-Jones received the Great Seal on 5 Mar. 1974, sat Speaker as 'the Rt. Hon. Sir Frederick Elwyn-Jones' on 6 and 7 Mar., and did not receive the letters patent until 11 Mar., on the afternoon of which day he was introduced.

[7] Haldane and Cave had each achieved a viscountcy some years before becoming Lord Chancellor.

[8] See Heuston, *Lord Chancellors 1885–1940*, p. 301.

Privy Counsellorship: Erskine in 1801, and before him Charles Yorke in 1770, had borne the courtesy title of Honourable, as the younger sons of Earls, but all the others (if not peers) had knighthoods when taking their seat on the Woolsack. Hogg had disclaimed in 1963 the peerage which he had inherited from his father.

Decorations were possessed by only two of the six Chancellors in our period: Simon and Kilmuir were entitled to wear the dark blue sash of the GCVO; Gardiner was appointed CH, but not until five years after his retirement. In the earlier period only Halsbury, Hailsham, Maugham, and Caldecote were undecorated.

The Introduction

When the letters patent for the peerage have passed the Great Seal it is necessary for the Lord Chancellor in his new status to be introduced to the House of Lords. When Jowitt was introduced on 2 August 1945, having received the Great Seal on 28 July, the *Journals of the House of Lords* [9] described the ceremony as follows. The Leader of the House, Lord Addison, reported that the Lord Chancellor has been created a peer

Whereupon his Lordship, taking in his hand the Purse with the Great Seal, retired to the lower end of the House, and having there put on his robes, was introduced between the Lord Winster and the Lord Goddard (also in their robes); the Gentleman Usher of the Black Rod, and Garter King of Arms preceding: His Lordship laid down his Patent upon the Chair of State, kneeling,[1] and from thence took and delivered it to the Clerk, and the same was read at the Table.

After setting out the letters patent verbatim, the *Journals* record that the writ of summons 'was also read at the Table'. (It too is set out verbatim.) The *Journals* then continue:

---

[9] *Journals* vol. 178, cols. 21-2.

[1] This is 'rather a beautiful variation' (Kilmuir, *Memoirs*, p. 234) on the normal practice, which is that the new peer, kneeling, offers his writ of summons, and the Herald, standing, offers the peerage patent, to the Lord Chancellor, wearing his tricorn hat, 'at the Woolsack', as the *Journals* put it. The Lord Chancellor then touches each document with his forefinger to signify their validity, before they are handed to the Reading Clerk to be read. This procedure is impossible if the new peer is the Chancellor himself, or is the Chancellor receiving a step in the peerage, as with Jowitt (Viscount, 1947) or Simonds (Baron, 1952); so the variation set out in the text is followed. (The Chancellor should hold the Purse in his left hand and the patent in his right.) When Jowitt had been created an Earl in the Resignation Honours List of 1951, his introduction on 30 Jan. 1952 necessarily followed the normal practice, although his taste for pageantry was satisfied by the presence not only of two sponsors of the appropriate rank (the Earls of Listowel and Longford) but also of two of the Great Officers of State—the Earl Marshal and the Lord Great Chamberlain—as well as the Gentleman Usher of the Black Rod and Garter King of Arms. It needed all the Earl Marshal's skill in organizing a procession to secure that this retinue of six persons were able, manœuvring in a confined space, to deposit Jowitt 'on the Earls' Bench next below the Earl Mountbatten of Burma' (*Journals*, vol. 184, col. 67). Surprisingly, the *Journals* for 17 July 1962 (vol. 194, col. 341) record that the normal and not the special procedure was followed when 'Baron Dilhorne, of Towcester, in our County of Northampton' was introduced. It is incredible that the procedure was changed by, or for, such a Chancellor: the Clerk may have made an error. The traditional ceremonies were observed in 1970 (Hailsham of St Marylebone) and 1974 (Elwyn-Jones).

Then his Lordship, at the Table, took and subscribed the Oath, pursuant to the Statute; and was afterwards placed at the lower end of the Barons' Bench, and thence went to the upper end of the Earls' Bench, and sat there as Lord Chancellor, and then returned to the Woolsack.

The contemporary account in *The Times* adds a few significant details. First, Jowitt 'walked out of the Chamber' to put on his peer's robes, and a 'few moments later re-entered . . . wearing his full-bottomed wig and carrying the Purse'. No doubt the Tudor House of Lords had no retiring room, and changes had to be made at 'the lower end of the House'. Secondly, he and his sponsors sat at 'the lower end of the Barons' Bench',[2] and 'rising three times, bowed and raised, the Lord Chancellor his three-cornered hat, and the other two their cocked hats, to the empty throne'. This is still the practice punctiliously followed today. But when the procession moved 'to the upper end of the Earls' Bench' (i.e. that referred to in the Act of 1539), the sponsors remained standing, while 'the Lord Chancellor sat and rose three times, bowing and raising his hat to the Throne'. That difference was perfectly correct: only the Lord Chancellor, by virtue of 'his temporary but immense precedence' was entitled to sit on that Bench above all Dukes. Thirdly, the *Journals*, read literally, imply that Jowitt sat on the Woolsack wearing his Baron's robes—something which would be contrary to all precedent. Rather, having made his three bows, he 'withdrew from the Chamber to return almost immediately in the normal black gown and wig of his office'.

After Simon had gone through this ceremony on 21 May 1940 Garter (Sir Gerald Wollaston) wrote to congratulate him 'on the extremely dignified way you did your part in the ceremony'.

I have no hesitation in saying that it was the most effective ceremony which it has been my privilege to conduct in the House; and if I am spared in happier times to look back on the event of a not uneventful life, I shall always remember as outstanding the occasion when, in the midst of the greatest anxieties, the House of Lords maintained the traditional ceremonies of the Introduction of its Lord Chancellor.[3]

The same might have been said when the Lord Chancellor of a Labour Government was installed at the end of the war.

The Dress of the Lord Chancellor

On a State occasion, the Lord Chancellor wears a black velvet court suit with knee-breeches, silk (over black cotton) stockings, and buckled shoes, lace stock[4]

---

[2] When Gardiner was introduced on 16 Jan. 1964 the *Journals* specify that he was 'placed on the Barons' Bench next below the Baroness Northchurch'.

[3] Simon papers.

[4] In modern stocks the lace flows over the top of the collar as well as from the bottom. Earlier stocks were less ornate—e.g. the stock of Hailsham (worn by his son in 1970) had only the lower layer of lace.

(without bands) and cuffs, and white gloves. Over all is a black and gold State robe of flowered damask. This is similar to the State robes of other dignitaries— for example, the Chancellors of Universities. The Lord Chancellor never wears the scarlet robe which laymen associate with English justice—indeed, the Apparel Act 1553 specifically prohibited him from wearing purple silk or satin.[5] On ordinary occasions (for example, when on the Woolsack) the Chancellor wears a black silk gown over a court suit of black cloth, and the ordinary judicial bands. When sitting as one of the commission to signify the royal assent to Bills, he wears his peer's robes. A Lord Chancellor always wears a full-bottomed wig, occasionally (when in commission for royal assent or swearing in a new peer) surmounted by a black tricorn hat. After 1945 the robe cost about £1,200 and the wig £75.

The Procession

On Tuesdays and Wednesdays when Parliament is in session, and the Lord Chancellor has not been dispensed by the House from his duty to sit on the Woolsack, a procession leaves his office at exactly 2.27½ p.m.[6] First,[7] there is the official who holds the combined offices of Permanent Secretary to the Lord Chancellor and Clerk of the Crown in Chancery; then the Mace-Bearer;[8] then the Purse-Bearer;[9] then the Lord Chancellor himself; then his Train-Bearer; and lastly the official who holds the (now) combined offices of Gentleman Usher of the Black Rod and Serjeant-at-Arms. In his latter capacity it is his duty to carry the mace before the Chancellor; but in practice today the duty is often

---

[5] It is the Lord Chief Justice whom Kipling's poem *Gehazi* describes as:

> So reverent to behold,
> In scarlet and in ermines
> And chain of England's gold.

[6] On Thursday at 2.57½ p.m.

[7] On special occasions, such as the Opening of Parliament, the whole procession is led by a tipstaff. His staff is surmounted by a silver-plated crown, of rather pinchbeck appearance, but the gift of Lord Chancellor Selborne.

[8] There is only one Mace-Bearer, though there are two maces, each over 5 ft. in length, and 22 lb. in weight. Neither is used when the sovereign is present; both may be used on special occasions outside Westminster—e.g. the Lord Mayor's Banquet. Gray's poem 'A Long Story' shows two maces in use by Hatton (1587-91) on a festive occasion:

> Full oft within the spacious walls,
> With fifty winters o'er him,
> My grave Lord Keeper led the brawls
> The seal, and maces, danc'd before him.

[9] The purse used to hold the matrix of the Great Seal. Today it is normally empty, except at the State Opening of Parliament, when it holds the text of the Gracious Speech, which is handed to the Sovereign by the Lord Chancellor. Further information: Heuston, *Lord Chancellors 1885-1940*, pp. 480-1; Bond and Beamish, *Lord Chancellor*, pp. 34-5. The purse used to be renewed annually; but that provided in 1940 lasted until 1984.

delegated to the Yeoman Usher and Deputy Serjeant-at-Arms. The Mace-
Bearer and Purse-Bearer are normally Messengers. When the procession enters
the Chamber, Black Rod takes up his duties in his box. In our period the procession was usually an impressive spectacle, as each of the Chancellors (except
Kilmuir) was over 6 feet in height. Jowitt followed the military maxim that one
should never smile when wearing uniform; and Gardiner, with an actor's sense
of occasion, always looked straight ahead.

The Woolsack

On arrival in the Chamber the Lord Chancellor takes his seat on the Lord
Chancellor's Woolsack, passing on his way the Clerks' Table and the Judges'
Woolsacks.[1] The Lord Chancellor's Woolsack is in the gangway between the
Throne and the Table. The Woolsack is a large square bag of wool covered with
red cloth inside a wooden frame: it has no formal back or sides, but a small
temporary back-rest provides some comfort during a long debate. There is
nothing really exceptional in the term Woolsack: sacks of wool were provided
for important persons at meetings of medieval Parliaments—for example, the
benches on which the judges sat were so covered. It is commonly said that the
term was adopted in recognition of the great commercial achievement of the
English wool trade.[2] A simpler view is that those who had to sit long hours on a
wooden bench were anxious to be comfortable.

The Lord Chancellor, with his purse beside him, and the mace, presides as
Speaker over the parliamentary proceedings of the day, which normally begin
at 2.30 p.m. His attendance is required by a standing order which goes back to
1660. The duty is taken seriously: some modern Chancellors, for example,
Gardiner, have 100 per cent attendance records throughout one or more
parliamentary sessions, and it is the practice to seek the leave of the House if
absent for more than one day.[3] The Chancellor does not have the same powers
of discipline as the Speaker of the House of Commons. It is the custom for the
peers to address not him but each other ('My Lords'), because the maintenance
of order is in the hands of the House itself. The Woolsack, and presumably the
space in front of it, is technically outside the limits of the House, so that its
occupant cannot do more than fulfil the function of a chairman by putting the
question at the end of a debate. If, as a member of the House, he wishes to take

---

[1] Used only at the Opening of Parliament. Lord Atkin told his son that 'as a judge, especially in the Court
of Appeal, one had the best seat in the House. . . . It is a great comedown to sit on the back benches as a junior
baron' (Atkin papers).

[2] A claim by the Worshipful Company of Woolmen to supply the wool has not been admitted: 275 H.L.
Deb. col. 237. In 1966 the Woolsack was restuffed, 16 countries in the Commonwealth, including the
Falkland Islands, providing wool. A small admixture of horsehair has been found desirable for comfort: 269
H.L. Deb. col. 115. In 1986 another restuffing was required, as wool, when sat on continuously, turns into
felt.

[3] For an example, see 241 H.L. Deb. col. 104—Kilmuir was granted leave for three days to go to the USA.

part in the debate, he moves to the left side of the Parliament chamber 'above all Dukes', as the Act of 1539 stipulates, and speaks as a peer. Otherwise his communications would be treated as advice to the peers, and not formally recorded in the journals.[4]

The Great Seal

There is some confusion between the Great Seal as a wax seal and the Great Seal as a matrix seal. Since the Conquest at least, State documents of importance have been authenticated by affixing in the Chancery (now the office of the Clerk of the Crown in Chancery) a wax seal, the obverse of which (the Great Seal proper) shows the monarch on horseback and the reverse (the counter-seal) the monarch enthroned, holding the sceptre and the orb.[5] This wax seal is properly described as the Great Seal of England. The term has, however, come to be applied to the matrix, or strictly speaking, matrices, which produce the wax seal. In this sense, which is bears in these pages, the Great Seal consists of two heavy silver (now alloy) plates or discs. So the disc of wax bears the obverse and reverse impressions of the two silver plates, and this disc is appended to the document by a hanging cord or tag embedded in the wax. Originally when a seal was required a large chunk of red-coloured wax was first softened in hot water (hence the official in charge was called the Chaff-Wax (*chaufe-cire*)), and then cooled in cold, after which it was pressed between the two plates, emerging in the above-mentioned shape.[6]

This traditional process has been modified in two respects in the twentieth century.[7] First, as wax has been found to be a relatively fragile material, granules of cellulose acetate plastic are used. They are softened in an oven; the matrix itself is also heated. Then the granules are placed in the matrix with the hanging cord of the document laid centrally in the matrix (see Pl. 1). The two halves of the matrix are locked in a steel collar and, with the aid of a pump, pressure is brought down upon the seal held within the collar. After the matrix and granules have cooled the seal is gently tapped out of the matrix. Colours used for Great Seals have varied; nowadays dark green is used for peerage patents: scarlet is used for most other patents as, for example, for the royal assent to the election of a bishop or for a Supreme Court judge's patent of appointment.

---

[4] As under the obsolete practice when the judges were summoned to advise the Lords on a difficult appeal: see Heuston, *Lord Chancellors 1885-1940*, p. 146.

[5] The Great Seal of Elizabeth II, obverse and reverse, was designed in 1953 by Gilbert Ledward, RA. The designer avoided the mistake made by some of his predecessors of forgetting that finicky detail does not reproduce well in wax. A collection of over 60 Great Seals was made by Jowitt, and later deposited in the Public Record Office.

[6] This was the task of another official, the Sealer. The Chaff Wax and the Sealer were abolished by the Great Seal (Offices) Act 1874, s. 7.

[7] The account given by Bond and Beamish, *Lord Chancellor*, p. 23, is followed here.

Secondly, as a result of rules made under the Crown Office Act 1877, royal proclamations, commissions for royal assent, writs of summons to Parliaments, Commissions of the Peace, and many other documents, which were hitherto handwritten on parchment with the wax seal appended to them, are now authenticated by the use of a new wafer (single-sided) Great Seal which can be impressed upon documents prepared on paper. The impression is that of the obverse of the Great Seal, i.e. the Queen depicted on horseback, and measures 3 inches in diameter.

Usually only one Seal is made during a reign, unless, as in the case of Victoria, the reign is exceptionally long. (New Seals were made in 1860, 1878, and 1900.) . It used to be customary for the old matrices to be rendered useles by being broken into several pieces. Now it is usual to deface, or damask,[8] them with several taps from a hammer with a special indented head. In 1938 Hailsham observed 'two gentle taps from the King, which are carefully calculated to do no possible damage',[8] but in 1953 Simonds recorded that the Queen 'hit the old seal some hefty blows'.[1] The dents so made are supposed to make the wax flow unevenly if the Seal should be used again. One half of the matrix, or both halves, may be granted by the Sovereign to the Lord Chancellor as a family heirloom.[2] This was done in 1948 and in 1953.

The Six Chancellors

All, with the exception of Dilhorne, were born in the nineteenth century. In both educational and social background the subjects of the present volume are more homogenous than those of the previous one. In that volume, two of the Chancellors had not only been born but also been educated abroad (Cave, Maugham); two had been to European universities (Herschell, Haldane), and one (Hailsham) had never been to any university—though his social background was superior to that of any of the others, and his son once intervened in a debate on higher education to remind the peers that a university degree was not a prerequisite to success.[3] In this volume, four (Dilhorne, Gardiner, Simonds, Jowitt) were at schools which are indubitably in the first rank—Eton, Harrow, Winchester, and Marlborough. The other two (Simon and Kilmuir) were at Scottish schools (Fettes, George Watson's) which are certainly members of the Headmasters' Conference, and so entitled to be called public schools, but which

---

[8] Pronounce da-másk.

[9] Heuston, *Lord Chancellors 1885–1940*, p. 480.

[1] Private letter to author in 1964.

[2] The other half may be granted to a seal-less predecessor, as in 1830 and 1860. It was not done in 1948, when only the Great Seal, as distinct from the counter-seal, was renewed, and Jowitt, reasonably enough, claimed the old one. In 1930 Sankey claimed both halves, as did Hailsham in 1938 (he also acquired the hammer), and Simonds in 1953. So the Simon family are without a seal. The seal acquired by Simonds has been deposited with the British Museum.

[3] 499 H.L. Deb. col. 843.

might not be recognised, outside Scotland, as the equal of the four English schools. The two Scottish schools and Marlborough had never before educated a Lord Chancellor. But Dilhorne was the fifth Etonian Chancellor (the others being his great-uncle Bathurst, Talbot, Camden, and Hailsham); Simonds was the fourth Wykehamist (the others being Wiliam of Wykeham himself, Cranworth, and Hatherley); and Gardiner the second Harrovian (Cottenham the first). All six went to the same university, Oxford, and to one of the better colleges. Jowitt and Simonds were at New College; Dilhorne and Gardiner at Magdalen; Simon at Wadham, and Kilmuir at Balliol. Three got Firsts in their final examinations (Simon, Jowitt, Simonds); two Thirds (Kilmuir, Dilhorne); and one a Fourth (Gardiner). Three read for the Law School (Jowitt, Dilhorne, Gardiner); two read Greats (Simonds, Kilmuir); and one Mathematics (after Honour Moderations) (Simon). Simon, Dilhorne, and Gardiner joined the Inner Temple; Kilmuir Gray's Inn; Simonds Lincoln's Inn; and Jowitt Middle Temple. In his youth Gardiner had trained as an actor, but none of the other five pursued any career other than the Bar (except for military service), though earlier Finlay had been a doctor and Hailsham a sugar-planter. On the other hand, two of the six moved in social and intellectual circles unknown to their predecessors—Jowitt amongst writers and painters, and Gardiner amongst actors.

The similarity between the social backgrounds of the six Chancellors is noticeable. This has not always been so. Lord Hailsham of St Marylebone once remarked that 'Legal practice was for many years a *carrière ouverte aux talents* which enabled many persons of relatively low . . . origin to achieve the highest honours in the State'.[4] In 1824 it was said, even more vividly, by Canning, that it 'was one of the noblest and most valuable prerogatives of the Crown of England, that it could take from the walks of Westminster Hall the meanest individual—and when he used the term meanest, he used it not with reference to talents and intellectual endowments, but to birth and original station in society—and place him, at once, in the head and front of the peerage of England; and he never wished to see the day when the Crown was deprived of that beautiful prerogative.'[5]

This rotund piece of snobbery may have had some justification in earlier periods (Eldon was the son of a provincial coal-merchant, St Leonards of a London barber), but it is only partially true of the twelve Chancellers in *Lord Chancellors, 1885-1940*. Of these, the fathers of three (Halsbury, Loreburn, Birkenhead) had been barristers, even if not very successful in that profession; two (Maugham, Caldecote) were the sons of solicitors, and one (Haldane) the son of a Writer to the Signet. The father of Cave was an MP; that of Hailsham a

---

[4] (1983) *LS* 227.
[5] R. Therry, *The Speeches of the Rt. Hon. George Canning*, 3rd edn. (1836), vol. v, p. 181. Canning's mother was an actress, but her family was 'among the oldest in Mayo' (M. Maclagan, *Clemency Canning* (1962), p. 2).

merchant philanthropist; and that of Finlay a doctor. But three came from a
dubious social background. Herschell was the son of a non-conformist minister
who was of Polish-Jewish extraction; Buckmaster's father was originally an
agricultural labourer, but rose to be an inspector of schools; and Sankey's father
was a provincial draper and undertaker.

But in this volume Simon alone came from the area of the English middle
class which is inhabited by non-conformist ministers (but, unlike Herschell, he
had been to a public school and Oxford). Kilmuir's father was a not very
successful schoolteacher, but that is a profession which has always been
regarded more highly in Scotland than in England. Still Kilmuir was justified
when he wrote: 'To have become Lord Chancellor of Great Britain with no
advantage of wealth, station, or influence, is something of which I am proud
and of which I hope my children are proud'.[6]

Jowitt's father was not rich but he was a gentleman and able to send his son to
a good school. The father of Simonds was a wealthy Hampshire brewer; that of
Gardiner, a wealthy shipping magnate of respectable West Country lineage,
who was given a knighthood by Lloyd George, and sent his three sons to
(respectively) Wellington, Harrow, and Eton. To Jowitt, Simonds, and Gardiner
the word of Trollope, in one of his lesser novels, can be applied:

Sir William Patterson was a gentleman as well as a lawyer, one who has not simply risen
to the legal rank by diligence and intellect, but a gentleman born and bred, who had
been at public school, and lived all his days with people of the right sort.[7]

Dilhorne did not spring from the middle classes. He had a patrician background
more splendid than that of any other Chancellor in English history, except
perhaps Talbot (1733–7).[8]

With a peerage the Herald's College will provide a coat of arms if necessary.
Those of Simon, Jowitt, and Simonds (and their twelve predecessors included in
Lords Chancellors, 1885–1940) are depicted in a stained-glass window in the
Queen's Building at the Royal Courts of Justice. (The reason why the series
stops in 1954 is simply that there were no more spaces to be filled. Of the
building (1969) itself, in comparison with the Law Courts, or even the Old
Bailey, the Master of the Temple has remarked that it 'is destitute alike of
biblical allusion and the fancies of allegory. Comfortable and convenient, no
doubt, it yet entirely lacks significance of form and seems almost to exult in
being plain, ordinary and down to earth'.[9]) Each coat of arms had supporters.
Jowitt's showed ingenuity: 'On either side a spaniel with a Chancellor's Purse

---

[6] *Memoirs*, p. xi.
[7] *Lady Anna*, World's Classics edn. (1936), p. 182.
[8] See below, pp. 183–4.
[9] *The Times*, 31 Mar. 1984.

proper.' As Kilmuir's coat of arms was registered in Edinburgh his supporters were granted by Lyon and not by Garter.

With a coat of arms there is a motto, and some of those chosen are revealing. Simon (*J'ai ainsi mon nom*) reveals the late-Victorian liking for a pun. Gardiner's (*In deo confide recte age*) and Kilmuir's (*Decens et honestus*) expressed impeccable sentiments. Jowitt's *Tenax et fidelis* caused some wry comments amongst those who recalled the events of 1929. Simonds gave a Wykehamist answer to those who accused him of being naïve in politics: *Simplex munditiis*. Dilhorne's reflects an aristocratic hauteur: *Aquila non capit muscas*.

With a peerage, a coat of arms, and a motto, goes a country house. In the eighteenth century this was on a splendid scale. Yorke at the age of thirty-five paid £24,000 for Hardwicke in Gloucestershire; Eldon at the age of forty-one £22,000 for the estate in Co. Durham from which he took his title.[1] But in the nineteenth-century Erskine was obliged to sell his Hampstead mansion and live on his pension; Loughborough bought a villa at Slough. None of their successors attempted to live on the scale of the eighteenth century until we reach Simon and Jowitt. Each of these before the age of forty was able to buy a substantial property. Simon acquired Fritwell Manor, near Banbury—suprisingly near F. E. Smith at Charlton, who converted a cottage on 4 acres into something more substantial. But Simon showed little interest in country life, and gave offence during the 1932 recession by cancelling his annual subscription of 10s. 6d. to the Oxfordshire Historical Society. Jowitt was a keen gardener and farmer of his 350 acres near Wittersham in Kent. Simonds had inherited a substantial property at Sparsholt, to the west of Winchester. Kilmuir was a poor man, whose practice was not in the same bracket as those of Simon, Jowitt, or Simonds, and he had to be content with a converted cottage on Lord De la Warr's estate at Withyham, in Sussex. But Dilhorne had an entirely suitable place at Horninghold, deep in the grass country of Leicestershire. Gardiner lived in or near London throughout his life.

In religion none emulated the piety of Cairns or Hatherley amongst the Victorians, or Sankey or Caldecote amongst the Georgians. The religion of Simonds, Jowitt, Dilhorne, and Gardiner was that which is by law established. Kilmuir moved quietly from the Presbyterian Edinburgh of his boyhood to a memorial service at St Margaret's, Westminster. Simon moved decisively in the opposite direction from a similar starting-point. The son of a Congregational minister, he used to read the lessons at Fritwell Parish Church when a young silk. But in 1927 he sent Sir Thomas Inskip (later Lord Caldecote) an immensely long letter[2] supporting his Low Church opposition to the proposed new Book

---

[1] For an interesting judicial reference to Eldon's houses, see *Frost* v. *Feltham* [1980] 1 WLR 452, 455 (Nourse J.).

[2] Heuston, *Lord Chancellors 1885-1940*, pp. 582-4.

of Common Prayer ('I distrust the priestly element in our national life so much'), and by the end, it is thought under the influence of his second wife, specified that he should be cremated without any religious ceremony or memorial service.[3]

Simon and Gardiner each made a happy second marriage. The domestic lives of Jowitt, Simonds, Kilmuir, and Dilhorne were uneventful. Two died knowing that their honours would be inherited in the male line (Simon, Dilhorne); one (Simonds) had to bear the pain of being predeceased by both his sons. Three (Jowitt, Kilmuir, Gardiner) left daughters only—one of Kilmuir's three daughters died young in tragic circumstances.

In one curious respect three of our Chancellors have something in common—each was for a major part of his career unpopular, either with his own profession (Dilhorne), or with both his profession and the politicians (Simon and Jowitt). In Dilhorne's case the unpopularity was of a surface kind, due to a touch of arrogance in his dealings with others; in Jowitt's case it was a (largely undeserved) reaction to a certain insensitivity in his relations with others; in Simon's case it was due to a coldness of disposition and his close association with the appeasement policy of Chamberlain. Gardiner, essentially a private man, was deeply respected but not popular in the sense of having the rather back-slapping affability of Kilmuir, who was probably on first-name terms with more people at Westminster and the Temple than any of the others. But perhaps the English value popularity too highly: when their country had to be saved in 1940 the leader chosen was one who had never been popular with most of his contemporaries.

The Stipend and Pension

The stipend[4] was fixed at £10,000 per annum in 1851. Of this £6,000 was paid to the Chancellor in his capacity as Lord Chancellor and £4,000 in his capacity as Speaker of the House of Lords. The former sum (but not the latter) was charged upon the Consolidated Fund by the Courts of Justice (Salaries and Funds) Act 1869, s. 12, and so does not come up for annual review in the House of Commons. It seems odd that the salary of the Speaker of the House of Commons should be charged upon the Consolidated Fund by statute (2 & 3 Wm. IV, c. 105, ss. 1, 3) but not that of the Speaker of the House of Lords. It is also odd that the proportion between the two parts of his salary should have been settled as it was: in view of the ever-increasing amount of time that a

---

[3] Yet in Dec. 1942 he had marked the silver jubilee of his marriage, which had been before the British Consul-General in Paris, by going through a religious remarriage in the Congregational church at Walton-on-the-Hill.

[4] There is an authoritative paper on this topic by J. C. Sainty in the H.L. Record Office. See also the *Report of the Committee on the Remuneration of Ministers and MPs* (1965) Cmnd. 2516, paras. 130-3; and Samuels (1966) 116 *LJ* 689.

Chancellor spends on legislative and executive duties, the proportion might well have been 80 per cent as Speaker and 20 per cent as judge. Gardiner certainly thought it was his public duty to earn his salary as Speaker by presiding over debates as often as possible. But the tendency has been the other way—in 1983 Lord Hailsham of St Marylebone was paid £31,680 as a judge and £6,400 as Speaker.[5] But the hyper-inflation of the 1970s is outside our sphere. It is enough to remark that Simon and Jowitt were paid the same as their predecessors in 1851. Simonds, Kilmuir, and Dilhorne were paid £12,000 per annum. Gardiner, after 1965, had a salary of £14,500.

The Lord Chancellor's non-contributory pension derives from the Lord Chancellor's Pension Act 1832, fixing the sum at £5,000 for life. The sum was reduced in 1950[6] to £3,750 in return for the payment of a lump sum on retirement equal to twice the annual amount of the pension and for a pension for the widow of one-third. In 1959[7] the figure was restored to £5,000, the lump sum and the widow's pension being correspondingly enhanced. The widow's pension ceases on remarriage—a fact which caused difficulties when Lady Kilmuir's second husband (Earl De La Warr) predeceased her.

In our period the practice was as follows. Simon drew a pension of £5,000 from leaving office in 1945 until his death in 1954. Throughout this period he was active both judicially and politically. Indeed Simon, like Dilhorne, sat on an appeal a few weeks before his death, but died before judgment was given; each, conscientious as ever, had left a final draft of his opinion, which was then adopted by one of the surviving Law Lords.[8] Jowitt drew his pension at the rate of £3,750 from leaving office (30 October 1951) until his death (26 August 1957). During that time he performed judicial duties when requested, and acted as Leader of the Opposition in the House of Lords from 1951 until 1955. Simonds on leaving office in 1954 became a Lord of Appeal in Ordinary once again, and on his retirement, on 1 April 1962, he was granted the pension of a Lord Lord at £4,500 and his contingent right to a pension as an ex-Lord Chancellor was revoked. Kilmuir left office on 16 July 1962 and drew his pension at the rate of £5,000 until 31 August 1962, when he ceased to do so until his death. He did not perform judicial duties. Dilhorne left office on 17 October 1964 and drew his pension of £5,000 until he was appointed a Law Lord on 9 June 1969. Until that date he performed judicial duties when requested, and was Deputy Leader of the Opposition in the House of Lords. Gardiner was active politically, but not judicially, after 1970.

[5] A further increase in 1984 (to £66,000) was voluntarily waived by Lord Hailsham of St Marylebone.
[6] Administration of Justice (Pensions) Act 1950.
[7] Judicial Pensions Act 1959. See also 614 H.C. Deb. cols. 1411–31; 716 cols. 67–8.
[8] Simon's appeal was *Inland Revenue Commissioners* v. *Wilson's (Dunblane) Ltd.* [1954] 1 WLR 282; Dilhorne's appeal was *British Steel Corporation* v. *Granada Television Ltd.* [1981] AC 1096.

Should the ex-Lord Chancellor receive a pension at all? If so, on what basis should it be computed? Although the usage of modern times describes this payment as a pension, it is worth noting that this term is nowhere used in the Act of 1832 or in the letters patent[9] as a description of this sum, which might better be described as a retiring allowance or annuity. Historically it is quite clear that the payment was by way of compensation for the abolition of certain valuable patronage hitherto vested in the Lord Chancellor. The object of Parliament in 1832 in providing an annual payment of £5,000 upon retirement from the Woolsack was almost certainly not to establish a pension contingent upon the performance of certain services. The long title of the Act states that its object was 'to abolish certain Sinecure Offices connected with the Court of Chancery and to make provision for the Lord High Chancellor on his retirement from Office'. It is worth noting that the short title of the Lord Chancellor's Pension Act was only conferred by the Short Titles Act 1896. In 1832 the sinecures which the Act abolished, amounting in value to £24,000, were intended to provide for the family of the Lord Chancellor. The parliamentary debates[1] make it plain that by way of compensation for the abolition of these offices his 'retiring allowance' was to be increased from £4,000 to £5,000 per annum. Section 3 of the Act makes this perfectly clear. After reciting that 'Whereas by reason of the abolition of the said offices the Lord Chancellor ... will be deprived of patronage' it goes on to provide that 'it is therefore just and equitable that more ample provision should be made for the Lord High Chancellor'.

The sum of £5,000 is paid quarterly by the Paymaster-General under letters patent issued under the authority of the Act. The first payment is made on the first quarter day after the Lord Chancellor resigns the Great Seal, and the payments are suspended while he again occupies the office of Lord Chancellor or any other office of profit under the Crown. Therefore if any ex-Lord Chancellor should wish to abdicate his right to the whole or any part of his pension, all he has to do is to give notice to the Paymaster-General of his intentions. Otherwise the payments would seem to be secured upon him by statute and to be just as much his property as the Post Office pension secured upon the Duke of Marlborough by Parliament in the reign of Queen Anne. The true character of the payment is clearly seen from the fact that the letters patent granting it are issued as soon as possible after the Chancellor has received the Great Seal. This ensures to the Chancellor that, if the changes and chances of political life should compel his retirement, or even his dismissal, his financial future is reasonably secure. He is also spared the disagreeable necessity of relying upon his political opponents, now come to office, to make provision for

---

[9] Reproduced below, App. of Documents.
[1] See Hansard's Parliamentary Debates, 3rd Series, vol. xiv, col. 1296.

the payment of his allowance. Under no other terms could a Government expect to secure the services of a leading member of the Bar.[2] It is worth noting that over a century ago it was denied that £5,000 per annum was an unreasonable sum.

What prodigious efforts are necessary for a lawyer to realise, by his own individual exertions, an amount which would produce an income of five, four, or even three thousand a year! And let anyone of common-sense and ordinary knowledge of the world ask himself whether the highest of these amounts be more than barely sufficient, without undue economy, to provide for a dowager peeress and a young family.[3]

Finally, although the letters patent describe the payments as being 'free from all taxes and deductions whatever', since 1919 they have been subject to income tax.[4]

But the fact that the payments made under the Act of 1832 are not in strict law a pension conditional upon the performance of services does not conclude the matter, for a constitutional convention has grown up requiring such services. The practice of the past century has undoubtedly been for an ex-Lord Chancellor to sit judicially when asked to do so.[5] Conversely, if he should wish neither to sit nor to draw his pension, it was once said that there was no reason why he should not be entitled to act in this way, whatever views might be held as to the propriety of the means which he had adopted to supplement his income.[6] But this is to overlook an argument cogently made by Simonds in his unpublished 'Recollections':

I am not sure that too much emphasis has not been laid on the question of pension. I should regard it as wholly objectionable if (for example) a judge who had been accustomed to sit in the Commercial Court retired from the Bench and accepted directorships in commercial companies and my objection would be the same whether he sacrificed a pension or not.[7]

Simonds lived long enough to see this 'wholly objectionable' procedure followed in 1970 by a judge of the Queen's Bench Division appointed by Gardiner in 1968. The incident remains an isolated one—perhaps because the Lord Chancellor's Department instituted the practice of giving a homily to new judges in which they were told that their irremovabilty was a reason for

---

[2] See Peel in 1850: C. 6617, p. 27.
[3] S. Warren, *Miscellanies* (1856), vol. i, p. 80.
[4] 112 H.C. Deb. 5s. col. 1480, and 220 H.L. Deb. 5s. col. 104.
[5] Sankey seems to have been an offender: see Heuston, *Lord Chancellors 1885–1940*, p.531.
[6] See Heuston, *Lord Chancellors 1885–1940*, p. 389. Buckmaster (very briefly), Birkenhead, and Kilmuir all went into the City: Buckmaster and Kilmuir surrendered their pensions; Birkenhead did not (see Heuston, *Lord Chancellors 1885–1940*, pp. 302, 396–7; and 667 H.C. Deb. 5s. col. 999).
[7] Simonds added: 'It is in truth a pity that the wisdom and experience in the law that a Lord Chancellor must be presumed to have should be lost in the wastes of the City.'

treating their career as permanent. It may well be that the obli
judicially is in practice less onerous today than at the beginning of
when there were only three to five Law Lords as compared with
today, and the Treasury was less willing than it has since become
judgeships. Also the modern practice of appointing an ex-Lord Cl
vacant Law Lordship (begun in the case of Dilhorne in 1969, and followed in
that of Elwyn-Jones in 1979) avoids all these difficulties—and the awkwardness
of paying such a dignitary less than the Law Lords over whom he may be called
upon to preside. This practice may properly be said to have begun with
Dilhorne, and not with Maugham or Simonds, for each of these had been a Law
Lord before being appointed to the Woolsack, and thus might reasonably have
stipulated that he should not be in a worse position on being obliged to resign
the Chancellorship.

The Duties of a Lord Chancellor

Brevity of treatment is imposed, but is almost impossible to achieve. Those
duties which arise from the fact that the Chancellor is Speaker of the House of
Lords, and the chief spokesman for the Government in that Chamber of the
Legislature, have already been outlined. There is a general obligation, of an
indefinite character, to advise the House on legal problems, but there is 'no
obligation to help a party to a dispute who has painted himself into a corner and
cannot get out'.[8]

In the Chancellor's capacity as a member of the executive, some distinctions
are necessary. It is often said that he is chief legal adviser to the Government.
This is true in the sense that he may be asked to undertake tasks which do not
fall clearly within the sphere of the Law Officers, or of some other departmental
minister—for example, in 1942 Simon had to consider whether a peer suspected
of a breach of the Official Secrets Act had to be tried by his fellow peers.
Another example, of a more controversial kind, of the Lord Chancellor acting
as chief legal adviser is his use to investigate, and report on, the conduct of
another member of the Cabinet, or of the Government. So in 1949 Jowitt had to
inquire into the conduct of a junior Minister (Belcher), and in 1962 Dilhorne
into that of a Secretary of State (Profumo). Gardiner was asked by Wilson to
investigate a problem involving an indefinite number of Cabinet Ministers—
unauthorized leakages to the media. Gardiner's successor stated emphatically
that it was quite inappropriate for the Lord Chancellor to be employed on such
tasks,[9] so perhaps the practice has ceased.

On the other hand, it would be wrong for the Lord Chancellor to advise a
specific Government department on a legal problem, partly because to do so

---

[8] 212 H.L. Deb. col. 1314. See S. Shetreet, *Judges on Trial* (1976), pp. 374–6.
[9] Lord Hailsham of St Marylebone, *The Door Wherein I went* (1975), p. 204.

would be inconsistent with his position as head of the judiciary, and partly because that is the function of the Law Officers—and in our period they had to remind one Lord Chancellor of this division of functions on several occasions.

To the legal profession one of the most important functions of the Lord Chancellor is that of recommending to the Crown barristers (male or female) of ten years' standing for appointment as High Court judges. Attempts to widen the area of selection to include solicitors have so far been unsuccessful, but in May 1986 the Lord Chancellor's Department responded to the pressure for open government by publishing a booklet setting out the policies and procedures followed in selecting candidates for judicial appointments. Most of the Lord Chancellors of our period have testified to the gravity of this task.[1] In earlier periods there was a belief, often much exaggerated, that political experience or connections were advantageous to a candidate for judicial appointment.[2] In our period the belief has been proved to be quite unfounded, largely as a result of the scrupulously impartial stand of Jowitt during the Labour Government of 1945–50.[3] Indeed, during the seventies and eighties a different tendency has become noticeable—leading barristers have been reluctant to add to their burdens by adopting a parliamentary career, and many constituency parties have become reluctant to select barristers as candidates.[4] If this tendency should continue, as it seems likely to do, the effect on the Bar, and on the Law Officers of the Crown (including the Lord Chancellor), may be considerable. In practice the Lord Chancellor is also consulted by the Prime Minister as to judicial appointments falling within the latter's gift, for example the Lord Chief Justice, the Lords Justices, and the Master of the Rolls. He also has responsibilities in relation to various minor appointments in the Courts and in relation to the Rules Committee of the Supreme Court. He also appoints circuit judges and has considerable duties in relation to the proper administration of that branch of Judicature.

He also appoints and removes Justices of the Peace other than those in the Duchy of Lancaster, not merely for England and Wales but also for Scotland. The advisory committees instituted under Loreburn have saved the Lord Chancellor some, but not much, work in this department. During this period there were sixty-two counties and 222 boroughs with their own separate Commissions of the Peace in England and Wales, and thirty-seven counties in Scotland. There is also administrative work in connection with the office of the Public Trustee and the Land Registry.

---

[1] e.g. Lord Gardiner, *Trials of a Lord Chancellor* (1968), p. 9.
[2] The subject was fully investigated in Heuston, *Lord Chancellors 1885–1940*, pp. 36–66, with particular reference to Halsbury.
[3] See below, pp. 118–21.
[4] See Lord Hailsham of St Marylebone, *The Office of Law Officer of the Crown, and the Office of Lord Chancellor*, Child Lecture (1978), p. 11.

He also has considerable ecclesiastical patronage, almost three times as much as the two archbishops together. As the livings in question are those valued at less than £20 in a year in the reign of Henry VII they are mainly the poorer benefices of the Church, so that the task of filling them is often difficult. They amount to twelve canonries and nearly 500 benefices. The Crown livings (more valuable) are filled by the Prime Minister's office, but Dilhorne prevented overlapping by securing that the same official was in charge of both lists.

During the past twenty years the scope of the Lord Chancellor's duties has greatly widened with the coming of the Welfare State. It has been recognized that he has a general responsibility for the exercise of judicial functions by special or administrative tribunals. In 1961 these were some 420 in number. There are also considerable new responsibilities connected with law reform, legal aid, and the Public Record Office. There has also been an increase in the political and legislative burdens of the office. In view of this vast range of duties it is surprising to find two areas in which, formally, the Lord Chancellor has no function—the organization of the legal profession itself as distinct from the courts, and legal education. Contacts with the Bar and the Law Society are close, but at an unstructured level. Legal education might seem to be within the jurisdiction of the University Grants Committee—but that body seldom deals with education, as distinct from administration, and two twentieth-century Lord Chancellors, Sankey and Gardiner, have felt a concern about this.

Again, complaints from members of the public about the legal profession make up a large part of the mail of the Lord Chancellor's Department. In the nature of things these relate largely to solicitors, as these are more exposed to the public than barristers. But it is not for the Lord Chancellor to interfere in the internal disciplinary procedures of a self-governing profession, especially when, as with the Law Society, there has been evolved an elaborate procedure, which includes lay participation, for dealing with the matter.

On the judicial side the Lord Chancellor presides over judicial sittings of the House of Lords and occasionally over appeals to the Judicial Committee of the Privy Council. Under the Supreme Court Act 1981, s. 5, the Lord Chancellor is President of the Chancery Division of the High Court, and the senior court-room in the Chancery Division is known as the Lord Chancellor's Court, but within living memory no Lord Chancellor has sat at first instance. The Vice-Chancellor is the Vice-President of the Chancery Division. The Chancellor is also understood to be responsible for manning the final appellate tribunals. The selection of the appropriate Law Lords to hear an important appeal may be a difficult task. In practice much discretion seems to be given to the Permanent Secretary.[5] An even more junior official may perform the task: in the 1970s it was often done by the Fourth Clerk at the Table (J. V. D. Webb). Before 1945

---

[5] See A. Paterson, *The Law Lords* (1982), pp. 86-7.

the normal day of the Lord Chancellor was to preside over the hearing of judicial appeals from 10.30 a.m. to 3.45 or 4 p.m., with half an hour for lunch. After leaving the Woolsack in his judicial capacity the Lord Chancellor returned to it almost immediately at 4.15 p.m. for the dispatch of legislative business, which occupied him until 7.30 or 8 p.m., after which there might be an official dinner, as well as the Cabinet papers of the day to be read. Cabinet meetings (usually weekly, but in a crisis more frequently), had also to be fitted in, as well as the mass of administrative business.

After 1945 the judicial side of the Lord Chancellor's work became much less noticeable. The reason for this is curious. The House of Lords has always adopted the theory that at any of its sittings business of a legislative or a judicial character may be transacted. It is for this reason that the judgments were, until recently, known as speeches (delivered standing, as in a debate), and that a motion is made at the end of the proceedings for the affirmation or reversal of the judgment which is under appeal. As legal decisions in the House of Lords are the result of previous speeches which persuade the House to take the course which the speeches recommend, it follows that an appeal cannot, properly speaking, be allowed before those speeches are delivered. This has caused a problem when the House has decided to allow an appeal against a conviction for a criminal offence and a consequential sentence of imprisonment, but time is required to formulate the reasons. The proper procedure is for the Appellate Committee to intimate to the House that the appeal will be allowed for reasons to be given later, and for a representative of the Home Office, or the gaoler, to be present at the event so that the executive (over whom the Law Lords have no powers) can, if so minded, order the immediate release of the prisoner. So, too, it is no more than a convention of the Constitution, although since 1884 a well-established one, that lay peers do not attend the hearing of judicial appeals. Therefore until the 1940s the hearing of appeals took place on the floor of the House itself, although for reasons of convenience the Chancellor and the Law Lords moved down towards the Bar of the House.[6] After the war, rebuilding operations made it impossible to sit in the Chamber during most of the day. It was therefore resolved to commit the hearing of all appeals to an Appellate Committee which met in one of the Committee Rooms.[7] Another factor also affected the position. As a result of war-time difficulties the House began its sittings at 2.30 p.m. and not at 4.15 p.m. and the Lord Chancellor was in effect

[6] See the admirable cartoon in *Punch*, 14 Feb. 1891.
[7] See 162 H.L. Deb. 5s. col. 1326; 166, col. 33; 169, col. 19; L. Blom-Cooper and G. Drewry, *Final Appeal* (1973), pp. 100–3; and Paterson, *Lord Lords*, pp. 97–109. The Committee reports back to the House. Conversely, when the House is not disposing of legislative business (e.g. in the parliamentary recess), the Law Lords still sit in the Chamber itself. The Appellate Committee must be distinguished from the Appeal Committee, which considers applications for leave to appeal, and tersely gives its decision without any reasons.

faced with the choice between sitting in committee to hear appeals from
10.30 a.m. until 4 p.m. and sitting on the Woolsack from 2.30 p.m. except for a
fortnight in January and in October, when the Courts were sitting but
Parliament was not. In practice most Lord Chancellors have taken the latter
course, so that a judgment by a Lord Chancellor is now much rarer in the Law
Reports than it used to be. This temporary device undoubtedly facilitated the
progress of both judicial and legislative work, but it has also meant that the
functions of the Lord Chancellor have become less obviously judicial. This has
several important consequences—not least that the Chancellor's knowledge of
leading members of the Bar has lessened at a time when he has to fill an
exceptional number of judgeships. During the period 1951-70 the Lord
Chancellor presided over no more than thirty-nine appeals—Simonds six,
Kilmuir twenty-four, Dilhorne seven, and Gardiner two.

Another important change is illustrated by a reform of practice in 1963
under the Chancellorship of Dilhorne. He calculated that up to three weeks of
parliamentary time was taken up by the Law Lords reading their speeches—a
process which changed the minds of nobody, as the speeches had already been
circulated in draft. He persuaded the peers to adopt the practice which had been
followed since 1922 in the Privy Council without public or professional
criticism.[8] So the visitor to the highest appellate tribunal in this country can no
longer hear the reasons for judgment delivered openly. Instead the written
opinions of the Lord Laws are made available, free, to the legal advisers to the
parties one hour before the House meets to consider the report of its Appellate
Committee, and afterwards, for a fee, to the public.[9] (As the speeches of the Law
Lords are now unspoken, the term 'opinions' is preferred.)

The attenuation of the Lord Chancellor's judicial functions can be illustrated
from a change in the rules governing the chairmanship of the Appellate
Committee made in May 1969, one month before the appointment of Dilhorne
as a Law Lord. Until then the rules—purely conventional in origin—were that, if
present, the Lord Chancellor presided, whatever his rank in the peerage. But if
the Lord Chancellor was absent, then any ex-Lord Chancellor invited to sit on
the appeal was entitled to preside, unless there was also present any Law Lord
(including another ex-Lord Chancellor) of higher rank in the peerage. So, to
take an example from the 1920s, Buckmaster, an ex-Lord Chancellor but only a
Baron, was liable not only to be presided over by Finlay, Birkenhead, Cave or
Hailsham, each of whom was junior to him in the office of Lord Chancellor,
but senior in rank in the peerage, but also to be ranked below Dunedin and

[8] See 253 H.L. Deb. col. 447.
[9] There are critical remarks in *The Times* for 18 and 27 Oct. 1984. *The Times* now prefaces its Law Report
with the words 'speeches sold the — day of — '. Yet the C.A. has reprimanded a trial judge for sending his
undated judgment to the parties by post (*The Times*, 5 Sept. 1986).

Sumner, each of whom had been promoted to Viscount. One change was
certainly desirable in view of the fact that the Appellate Committee had
developed into a body entirely distinct form the hereditary peerage: seniority
amongst the Law Lords should be governed by the date of their appointment
and not by their rank in the peerage. There would have been little difficulty in
changing the rules along these lines, but Dilhorne happened to be both an ex-
Lord Chancellor and a Viscount. (No other ex-Lord Chancellors were then
living, and no Law Lord had held a rank higher than Baron since the retirement
of Radcliffe.) It was represented to Gardiner that some of the Law Lords were
not entirely happy at the prospect of Dilhorne automatically presiding—
particularly as Gardiner himself had in effect ceased to sit judicially.

Some of the Queen's Bench judges also made representations through the
Lord Chief Justice that, as criminal appeals were now reaching the Lords more
frequently, they would be happier if the presiding Law Lord was someone who
might have had recent experience of the problems of trial judges. Gardiner
wrote later about Dilhorne's appointment as a Law Lord, 'As soon as he said that
if he were a Law Lord he didn't care two hoots whether he was to take the chair
or not, the solution seemed to me clear.'[1] This was to make precedence depend
entirely on seniority of appointment as a Law Lord.[2] (This worked until 1984
when the principle of allocating work according to seniority was thought to
cause difficulty, and elaborate changes were made to enable the monarch to
designate some Law Lord as the senior and so entitled to take the chair.)[3]

These changes were not a mere matter of protocol. They are important for
two reasons. First, research has demonstrated what was hitherto not fully
appreciated—that the presiding Law Lord has much control over the pace and
direction of an appeal, and so has a material influence on the reputation of the
tribunal.[4] Secondly, the implications of the changes for the office of Lord
Chancellor are serious. For if an ex-Lord Chancellor is unfit to preside over the
Appellate Committee at the end of his period of office, then logically a new
Lord Chancellor is even less fitted to preside at the beginning of his period. If
this argument is coupled with the undoubted fact that some recent Lord
Chancellors (Kilmuir, Gardiner) have, for one reason or another, not sat
judicially as often as their predecessors, then some fundamental changes in the
role of the Lord Chancellor may occur. One result already is that the Law Lords

[1] To the author in 1984.
[2] See 302 H.L. Deb. col. 469.
[3] For details, see 453 H.L. Deb. col. 918.
[4] See Paterson, *Law Lords*, pp. 66–83. So Thankerton was often sent to the Privy Council to preside over
Indian appeals because, as Schuster admiringly remarked, 'experience has shown that he can get through
them, not indeed in indecent haste but with advantageous celerity' (G. Lewis, *Lord Atkin* (1983), p. 212).
When in 1984 Lord Diplock retired after 23 years in the appellate tribunals, 9 of them as presiding judge, he
told the peers that 'this taught me that the task of presiding over a plurality of judges in such a way as to
promote an efficient and expeditious way of dealing with appeals is not the same as producing judgments
which clarify and develop the law' (453 H.L. Deb. col. 918).

have become a tightly knit professional body, distinct from both the hereditary peerage and from the link with the Cabinet supplied by the chairmanship of the Lord Chancellor. But the most recent figures show a reversion to the former practice—between 1974 and 1984 Lord Hailsham of St Maylebone delivered thirty-eight judgments, and Lord Elwyn-Jones twenty-six.[5]

The Lord Chancellor is chairman of many committees—for example, the Supreme Court Rules Committee. A foreign observer might be pardoned if he concluded that the Lord Chancellor and four others could prescribe the whole of English civil practice and procedure. In practice this is not what happens. The Chancellor has only one vote, and must work through persuasion rather than dictation. A foreign observer might also conclude that there was much significance in the statutory duty laid on the Lord Chancellor to summon an annual meeting of the Supreme Court judges (the Council of Judges) to discharge the statutory duty to report annually to the Secretary of State about any provisions which it would be expedient to make for the better administration of justice.[6] This provision may have been sensible when the number of such judges was twenty-eight; but the steady increase in judicial numbers (now just short of one hundred) has made it unworkable, and it has been many years since the Council of Judges submitted an Annual Report. 'All Lord Chancellors respect the law, but some are more respectful than others.'?[7] The identification and solution of the problems of law reform are now performed better by other agencies.

The burden of work is heavy: Haldane cited with approval Herschell's remark that no man could, or should, hold the office for more than three years. But Lord Hailsham of St Marylebone has put it in perspective:

Reading my father's and Lord Gardiner's addresses I am sure one would gain the impression that a Lord Chancellor's life is unduly busy. I would to some extent like to correct that impression. Most lawyers, including myself, have acquired the habit of working hard and fast to the limit of their capacity. Perhaps they even enjoy doing it. But whether they wish to do so or not, so do most Cabinet Ministers. I simply do not believe that any Lord Chancellor in my life-time has worked harder than, and some may not have worked as hard, as the Chancellor of the Exchequer in the same Government, or the Foreign Secretary, or, perhaps, a number of other senior colleagues. In particular, the Lord Chancellor does not suffer the constant lack of sleep or time for reflexion which is occasioned to the holders of those portfolios which involve the reading at all hours of the night and day telegrams from countries where the time of day differs by anything up to twelve hours from our own.[8]

---

[5] A. Bradley, 'The Changing Face of the House of Lords' (1985) *JR* 178, 186.
[6] Supreme Court of Judicature Act 1873, s. 75 (re-enacted by the Supreme Court of Judicature (Consolidation) Act 1925, s. 210).
[7] Lord Devlin, *The Judge* (1979), p. 53.
[8] *The Problems of a Lord Chancellor* (1972), p. 2.

At the close of Gardiner's Chancellorship one may glance ahead to the 1970s and indicate a few of the problems which he was spared, but with which Hailsham and Elwyn-Jones had to deal. In each case the paperwork increased at an exponential rate—and so did the staff to deal with it. The number of silks increased—the total in 1972 was over 500, although only 200 were in practice. The annual number of creations varied between eleven (1956) and forty-five (1972). In 1966 the procedure was as it had been since 1866—the candidate applied, in a handwritten letter, to the Lord Chancellor, including such personal and professional details as seemed good to him.[9] He also informed all his seniors on the circuit. By 1980 a six-page printed form of application had to be completed. The English Bar has always asserted its independence of the Government: it is strange that it sees nothing inconsistent in entrusting to the uncontrolled discretion of a senior Cabinet Minister the advancement of its members within the profession by the granting of silk. Perhaps the system works because each Lord Chancellor has taken so much trouble over applications (there are usually three times as many unsuccessful as successful candidates) in the period between Christmas and Easter each year.

Another post-Gardiner development was the growth of the expectation, at least on the part of the media, that the Lord Chancellor should be able to give instant comment to the merits of a decision of any tribunal anywhere in the country. With instant comment went instant law reform. A judgment of the House of Lords at 10.30 a.m. has been followed by a question in the Commons at 3 p.m. the same day asking the Prime Minister to introduce legislation to reverse it.[9a]

After the Beeching Report[1] there was a remarkable change, which has been vividly described.

Before the Courts Act 1971 the Lord Chancellor appointed Judges but was otherwise able to interfere little in the administration of justice. Judges were sent on Assize by the Lord Chief Justice and the High Sheriff was responsible for their reception and lodging. The Assize Courts were organised by an Assize staff who also provided the Clerk of the Court and dealt with the allocation of cases. Quarter Sessions were either run by a County Council, or by certain Local Boroughs and were organised by the respective Clerks to those Authorities and they also sat as Clerks of the Court. Juries in all cases were summoned by the Under-Sheriff. This diversification made the chances of any corruption virtually nil.

The Lord Chancellor's Department is now one of the major 'empire building' concerns of the Civil Service. Even at this moment it is in the process of extending its

[9] Sir Harold Morris's book *The Barrister* (1930) provided a model letter of application which was copied for many years. It was half-a-dozen lines in length but advised that 'a statement of my pretensions' was enclosed. This 'should set out the date of birth, details of education, and date of call to the Bar and particulars of practice'.

[9a] 17 H.C Deb. 6s col. 1124 (11 Feb. 1982).

[1] *Report of the Royal Commission on Assizes and Quarter Sessions* (1968) Cmnd. 3799. See below, pp. 227-8.

power still further by assuming responsibility for the last remaining function, namely the execution of High Court Writs. The Lord Chancellor as before appoints Judges of all ranks but his department now also organises all the old Assize Courts and all the old Quarter Sessions in the form of the first, second, and third tier Courts of the High Court. It also summons all juries. Thus the Department now decides who shall form the jury, where a case shall be held, who shall try it, and who shall be the Clerk of the Court.[2]

The strains and stresses on the law produced by the vast technological changes of the twentieth century—industrial espionage is one example of the new problems—did not really affect the Lord Chancellor's Department before the 1970s. Gardiner recognized that they existed, but no more. The single-purpose pressure group was also unknown. In 1985 it was noted that single-purpose pressure groups, often opposed to each other, had hindered the work of statutory consolidation and codification.[3]

The task of presiding over the legislative work of the House became, paradoxically, more difficult under Edward Heath and Margaret Thatcher. The House was capable of taking an anti-Government line, sometimes on important matters.

Staff

In 1381 the House of Commons complained that the Chancellor's clerks were 'too fat in body and in purse, and too well furred'.[4] But this complaint referred to the administrative staff of the Court of Chancery (a well-known target for reformers), and not to the staff of the Lord Chancellor's Department, who, until the 1980s, have been remarkably few in number, and paid on established Civil Service scales.

Before 1885 the Lord Chancellor's Secretaries of Presentations and Commissions were entirely personal: not merely did they have no office space at Westminster, but they went out of office with their master, dc•roying the files as they did so. Under Halsbury the office of Permanent Secretary to the Lord Chancellor was combined with the distinct office of Clerk of the Crown in Chancery, who was assisted by the Deputy Clerk of the Crown and the Clerk of the Chamber. Twenty years later there was no typewriter in the office which has been newly acquired in the Palace of Westminister, and Halsbury's Private Secretary, R. C. Norman[5] (paid for by Halsbury himself) wrote all letters in his own hand.

---

[2] F. H. Alsop, 'A Ministry of Justice', *Law Soc. Gazette*, 29 Jan. 1975.
[3] Lord Hailsham of St Marylebone, 'Addressing the Statute Law' (1985) *Stat. L.R.* 1.
[4] N. Underhill, *The Lord Chancellor* (1978), p. 37.
[5] A brother of Montagu Norman, the banker, he later rose to be Chairman of the BBC.

There was no time, except at lunch, to get at the poor man and he showed amazing patience.... I have been into his room and found him dictating a judgment. He showed not the slightest irritation at being interrupted; turned to me, heard my point, and decided it and went back to his judgment. He never had time to read any of the letters I wrote for him—scores and scores of them he 'topped and tailed'—i.e. he wrote 'My dear someone' at the beginning and 'Halsbury C.' at the end, without ever reading or hearing what I had said. I think I very seldom, if ever, betrayed that wonderful confidence and got him into a mess. ... One thing I did feel hard was that, being the only private secretary for ordinary business, I never had a complete holiday except for four days after my wedding. Every day a pouch full of letters arrived from the House of Lords and, wherever I might be, these I duly answered as from the House of Lords, sending them back again in the same pouch, to be posted in London. I feel sure we ought to have arranged that better.[6]

In 1960 there were still only thirteen in the office (apart from typists), but each had a legal qualification. However, a century after Halsbury's reorganization, the staff of the office, which had become the Lord Chancellor's Department (LCD in the usage of Whitehall), had risen to the staggering figure of 10,000, largely administering legal aid in a building some distance away. It is a remarkable fact that this very large department has been specifically freed from the scrutiny of any of the twelve Select Committees estbalished in 1979—apparently because the Government thought that judicial appointments might be criticized.

Whether the office was small or large, its efficient operation would depend on the Civil Servant in charge of it—the Permanent Secretary.[7] Here fortune has favoured the Great Seal. There have been only six holders of the office since 1885 and each was a man of quality, fully comparable to his fellow Whitehall mandarins in charge of larger establishments—and also from a background somewhat 'grander' than normal. Sir Kenneth Muir Mackenzie (Charterhouse and Balliol), the fourth son of a baronet, held the post from 1880 to 1915,[8] when he was succeeded by Claud Schuster (Winchester and New College), who for twenty-nine years was at the centre of English legal administration, serving ten successive Chancellors. Schuster and Muir Mackenzie were created peers on retirement. As his successor, Sir Albert Napier, wrote, 'Schuster was always alert,

<hr/>

[6] Private communication to the author.

[7] As D. Karlen noticed. His dedication to *Appellate Courts in the United States and England* (New York, 1963), p. v, runs: 'To Sir George Coldstream, whose titles of "Permanent Secretary to the Lord Chancellor" and "Clerk of the Crown in Chancery" obscure the central and vital role which he plays in the administration of British justice.'

[8] One of Lady Muir Mackenzie's two sisters was the mother of the 1st Viscount Hailsham. The Assistant Secretary (later Private Secretary) in the office throughout this period (1886–1915) was A. G. S. Liddell (Eton and Balliol), related to Lords Ravensworth, Harewood, Strathmore, and Stair. In 1919 he was succeeded as Private Secretary by R. W. Bankes (Eton and University College), a son of Bankes LJ, and a direct descendant of Lord Eldon LC.

his reaction to the news immediate, his course of action soundly planned and quickly put in train.'[9] It so happened that only one of his Chancellors (Birkenhead) showed initiative and willingness to control events rather than respond to them. One cannot help wondering what would have happened if Schuster had served Jowitt or Gardiner. Jowitt was served by Napier,[1] who was extremely efficient, but perhaps more of a brake than an accelerator. He also had, as he himself said of Schuster, 'many of the prejudices common amongst Englishmen of his class, and he often gave pungent expression to his dislikes'.[2] In 1954 Napier was succeeded by Sir George Coldstream (Rugby and Oriel), and he in 1968 by Sir Denis Dobson (Charterhouse and Trinity, Cambridge), who held office until 1977. His successor was Sir Wilfrid Bourne (Eton and New College), a great-grandson of Lord Chancellor Cairns. A custom which goes back to the 15th century permits the Clerk of the Crown in Chancery to subscribe his name to formal documents (for example, a writ of summons to Parliament (see Appendix)) in the same style as if he were a peer.

[9] *DNB, 1951-1960*, p. 868.
[1] The Hon. Sir Albert Napier (Eton and New College) was the ninth son of a Victorian military hero, Lord Napier of Magdala. His wife was the daughter of another, FM Sir George White, VC.
[2] *DNB, 1951-1960*, p. 868.

LORD SIMON

JOHN ALLSEBROOK SIMON was born at 16 Yarborough Street, Manchester, on 28 February 1873. He was the only son and elder child of the Revd Edwin Simon, a Congregational minister, and his wife, Fanny,[1] daughter of William Pole Allsebrook. Edwin Simon's parents came from south Pembrokeshire—the father had been a stonemason, the mother a dairymaid. They talked Welsh when in private; to the end of his life there was a touch of Wales (or was it Scotland?) in their grandson's voice, and when he was granted a viscountcy in 1940 it was 'of Stackpole Elidor', the name of the Cawdor seat in Pembrokeshire. The Allsebrooks were a more settled rural family from Worcestershire. A connection with Cardinal Pole was claimed, and a likeness of character has also been detected.[2]

After a period at Bath Grammar School John Simon obtained a scholarship to a small, recently founded Scottish public school—Tettes College near Edinburgh. Here he rose to be head of the school and had a respectable academic and athletic career.[3] Another scholarship, in classics, enabled him to go up to Wadham College, Oxford, in 1892. Wadham was then remarkable for a number of gifted young men—F. E. Smith, C. R. Hone, C. B. Fry, H. M. Giveen, A. A. Roche, and F. W. Hirst. Their characters and achievements are fully described in the latest biography of F. E. Smith,[4] and need not be retold here. But it may be permissible to quote at length from the autobiography of Sir Maurice Bowra. As Fellow, and subsequently Warden, of Wadham, he knew well both Birkenhead and Simon, and was also an exceptionally shrewd judge of character.

The antithesis of Birkenhead in many ways was his contemporary, and in some sense rival, Sir John Simon. Simon was equally tall but less heavily built and quite bald; he was equally ambitious, but less frank about it; he was never exuberant, never indiscreet; even when he told you something that 'must not go beyond these four walls', it was usually common knowledge; he allowed his wineglasses to be filled but hardly tasted of them. He was an excellent speaker, clear and persuasive, with an apt taste for words and some

---

[1] His mother was an object of devotion, as is shown by Simon's *Portrait of a Mother* (1937). This book, and C. E. Bechofer Roberts, *Sir John Simon* (1938) (the proofs of which were corrected by Simon), are much more revealing than the flat and uninteresting *Retrospect* (1952). See below, p. 132.

[2] Hugh Ross Williamson, *The Walled Garden* (1956), p. 12: 'There is the same isolation and indifference to public opinion; the same intellectual liveliness; the same rectitude; the same unpopularity with the mass balanced by the devotion of the few; the same scrupulous refusal to use a permitted maximum of worldly wisdom to secure the highest office open to them—Pole the papacy, Simon the Premiership'. As Sir John Simon (1816-1904) (no relation) pronounced his name in the French style, it may be recorded that the Lord Chancellor's family always used a long English 'i'.

[3] 'Edinburgh air, combined with Fettes traditions, made a boy as hard as nails for the rest of his life', Simon later recorded in his diary.

[4] J. Campbell, *F. E. Smith, First Earl of Birkenhead* (1983).

well-chosen touches of sentiment, but he was not provocative, and his few jokes lacked
frivolity. Birkenhead liked him as an old friend, but could not refrain from teasing him.
He usually managed to speak before him and to put in some mocking touch. At a
college dinner, when Simon was making large sums at the bar and Birkenhead was
temporarily out of office, he began, 'Sir John Simon, whose presence here this evening is
costing him a thousand pounds . . .' and on another occasion, 'The law is an arid but
remunerative taskmistress. In me you see an example of its aridity, in Sir John Simon of
its remunerativeness.' He went further than this in ragging the eminently respectable
Simon, 'My dear Simon, when you came here, you were an innocent boy. When you
were here, you learned things that you now prefer to forget.' Poor Simon, who lacked
humour, could not imagine what these things could be but felt that there must be
something somewhere. Birkenhead treated Simon in this deflating way, partly because
he was an old friend, partly because Simon's combination of righteousness and success
was not altogether to his taste. He felt that there was some humbug somewhere, and he
took a shot at it. Simon accepted it politely, but was not happy. He was not without
vanity, and he disliked ridicule. So when Birkenhead made fun of him, he had to
pretend to like it and think it characteristic of an old friend, but it took the edge off such
pleasure as he hoped to get.[5]

As Churchill put it tersely, at the mention of F. E.'s name, 'Simon wore his
marble smile'.[6]

Simon obtained Second Classes in Mathematical[7] (1893) and Classical
Moderations (1894). Then the line on the graph of worldly success moved
steadily upwards—in 1896 a First in Greats, and also the presidency of the
Union, where he first met his future political leader and friend H. H. Asquith.
Then in 1897 he was elected a Fellow of All Souls. Simon's habitual reserve
('shyness has always been my trouble, though I have learned to conceal it') was
absent when he spoke or wrote of what the companionship of All Souls, as
exacting intellectually as undemanding emotionally, meant to him in life.

In 1899 he was called to the Bar at the Inner Temple. He became a pupil first
of A. J. Ram,[8] and then of (Sir) Richard Acland. He joined the Western Circuit,
and earned 27 guineas in his first year. His first brief was at Bristol Quarter
Sessions. The customary journalism and authorship supplemented his income.
In 1902 he revised the chapter entitled 'Self-governing Colonies' in Sir Henry
Jenkyns' *British Rule and Jurisdiction beyond the Seas*.[9] Forty years on, Simon
recalled his days as a young circuiteer:

---

[5] Sir M. Bowra, *Memories 1898–1939* (1966), pp. 140–2.

[6] *Sunday Pictorial*, 8 Nov. 1931.

[7] Simon attended the mathematical lectures of the Revd C. L. Dodgson at Christ Church, and was
sometimes entertained to dinner by him (something which in Oxford then could be done without attracting
comment). In later life Simon enjoyed recalling the bizarre conundrums of a mathematical character which
the author of *Alice* used to put to the company.

[8] Son of Revd Canon A. J. and Lady Jane Ram, of Clonatin, Co. Wexford, and father of (Sir) Granville
Ram, the famous parliamentary draftsman.

[9] A book much relied on by Manningham-Buller A.-G. in *Ex Parte Mwenya* [1960] 1 QB 241.

Then there was the most remarkable and vivid personality of Willie Mathews, who later on, as Sir Charles Mathews, became Director of Public Prosecutions.[1] If you saw and heard him in action on the Circuit or at Hampshire Sessions you did not need to be told that he was the son of an actor. No advocate I have ever met conveyed so overpowering a sense of the drama of life. I was his Junior here in Winchester in the Crown Court in a terrible trial for murder years ago—it was known as the Aldershot Murder. Ernest Charles, I remember, made a fine speech for the defence; we were for the prosecution. Two soldiers and a civilian were charged with murdering a woman of the town at a little distance outside Aldershot. Never shall I forget how Mathews started his opening in that case to the stolid, serious-faced Hampshire jury. There were none of the conventional sentences about the seriousness of the charge. In the silence which followed James Read's recital of the indictment to the jury, ending 'it is your duty to inquire whether they be guilty or not guilty, and to hearken to the evidence'—the little figure rose and began his rather high-pitched vibrating tones, 'At 10 o'clock on the morning of Midsummer Day, the driver of a four-wheeled cab who had just deposited his fare at his destination, was returning towards the town, when he observed, near the side of the road, under some bushes in a little wood, something lying which attracted his attention. He got down to look. What was it?' (almost in a whisper) 'The body of a woman—dead—barely cold. What was there which attracted the special attention of this cabman as he examined this poor creature? On her feet, there were no sh-o-o-es.' This last word was a long drawn-out croon. There followed a pause, while a cold shiver ran down one's spine. And then, in a brisk matter-of-fact voice, Mathews resumed, 'At five o'clock that morning Private X and Private Y who are in the dock behind me' (with a jerk of his thumb over his shoulder) 'entered Malplaquet Barracks after a night's leave. One of them was carrying something. What was he carrying? A pair of women's sh-o-o-es.' The echo was exact, and there was not much good in arguing after that, that circumstantial evidence did not amount to proof.[2]

Briefs in London began to pour in, and he soon moved into the highest class of civil practice, taking silk only nine years after call. He never gave a clear explanation of his decision to appear once a year in the divorce court. His chambers were at 2 Hare Court. In 1909 he became standing counsel to Oxford University.

Simon was much indebted for his London success to R. L.Hunter, a City solicitor then in his forties. Years later he recalled the exciting days.

[1] From 1908 to 1920: 'He was a modest man: he was once offered a brief before the Privy Council: he crept in to watch that tribunal at work, and then asked the solicitors to allow him to decline the brief, as he did not consider himself equipped for the task' (*DNB 1912-21*, p. 370).

[2] Simon, *Memoirs of the Western Circuit* (1942), reprinted in *Retrospect*, app. B. Simon added: 'I had no notes for my speech, but I dictated what I could remember of it, with a little embroidery here and there.' He enjoyed exercising his power of total recall. In 1951 he insisted on proposing the toast at the marriage reception of a young peer. He spoke for ten minutes without using notes. Some weeks later the groom expressed gratitude but also regret that no record of the speech had survived. Simon summoned a secretary and instantly dictated what all agreed to be a flawless reproduction of his remarks.

Do you remember the day when you first sent me to a Parliamentary Committee (I think, if my memory serves me, for Colonel Raleigh Gray who owned the coal below Cockett Tunnel) and I had, in the absence of my leader, to cross examine Lawrence the Mineral Manager of the G.W.R.? You told me, I remember, that Mr. Nelson, the Great Western solicitor, asked you 'who I was'. As in later years I held the general retainer of nearly every Railway Company in England, I feel that it was your kindness which opened the way for me.[3]

Simon did not rate the law as one of the highest of human achievements, and he expressly refused 'to revive the memory of ancient encounters in Court, which may have created a sensation at the time, but have now passed into an oblivion which to some concerned may be welcome'.[4] The Bar has more than enough rules of etiquette: but might it not enforce a rule that retired barristers did not retail their memories of cases in which they had been profesionally engaged without the express consent of their clients, or their families? In this respect at least Simon gave good advice to the elderly barrister. Less well known is his advise to the young barrister that: 'You must cultivate the faculty, in your early days, of giving professional advice, when consulted by people older than yourself, with firmness and without either pomposity or apologies.'[5] In court Simon was elaborately polite, especially to his juniors. Slesser recorded approvingly that whenever he made an acceptable suggestion Simon would say, 'I am indebted to my learned friend for this argument.'[6] Advocates more intellectually gifted than Slesser cynically dismissed this as 'Simon's soft-soap', and expressed dislike of his habit, perhaps unconscious, of glancing round a court-room after he had made a good point, as if seeking applause. At the Old Bailey 'Simon's gambit' referred to the question 'Was this an ordinary transaction?' in a prosecution for fraud. Whatever the answer, the subject of the cross-examination saw trouble calling. It was also noted that, like some other Englishmen of his generation (for example, Buckmaster and Maugham), he could be blisteringly rude in public to those whom he regarded as his inferiors, such as solicitors' clerks.[7] Again like others of that time, he could be charming to those, like children of the upper classes, who could not be his rivals.[8]

In 1906 Simon had been returned, naturally as a Liberal, for Walthamstow, with a majority of nearly 4,000. His maiden speech, on 3 August 1906, was in support of the proposal to reverse the decision in the Taft Vale case. In September 1910 when Asquith appointed him Solicitor-General, Simon was

[3] Simon papers.

[4] *Retrospect*, p. 11.

[5] Ibid., p. 48. The Earl of Kilmuir (*Memoirs* (1964), p. 31) gave similar advice, stressing the psychological fact that the client is under strain, and wishes to unload his burden on the barrister.

[6] Sir H. Slesser, *Judgment Reserved* (1942), p. 73.

[7] In 1953 Simon attended Encaenia: there was some problem at the door over tickets for his companions, and a pro-proctor went forward to help. He was rebuffed with a withering snarl.

[8] See Lord Egremont in the *Spectator*, 8 Apr. 1966.

aged 37—only two others have been appointed younger (Philip Yorke, Follett).
Asquith received a grateful letter.

> You have a natural sympathy with lawyers who care for politics, and you won't mind
> my saying that it is the political, rather than the legal, side of things which attracts me; I
> should feel inclined to remain a private member if did not think that even to a Solicitor
> General, political opportunity sometimes offers . . .[9]

The customary knighthood followed—and in 1911 a KCVO as a mark of
royal favour after the successful prosecution for criminal libel of Mylius, who
had alleged that the King had committed bigamy. In 1912 he was made a Privy
Counsellor, and in October 1913 Attorney-General in succession to Sir Rufus
Isaacs. Like Isaacs, Simon was a member of the Cabinet. This arrangement was a
mistake, as he frankly confessed later.[1] It was a confusion of deliberative and
executive functions, and made it difficult for the Attorney-General to preserve
the requisite degree of legal impartiality on issues which he had heard discussed
politically.[2] In one small way Simon was able to repay what he owed to the
Asquith family.[3] In 1914 he appoined Raymond Asquith junior counsel to the
Inland Revenue in place of William Finlay, who had just taken silk. The
appointment delighted Asquith,[4] and seems to have escaped the criticism which
had greeted Finlay's own appointment (by his father) in 1905.[5] Simon was
always generous to the young. Some contemporaries found their sons' fees at
Fettes being paid for them. And when Wilfrid Greene was in financial trouble,
Simon insisted on making an interest-free loan ('I feel for you not only great
admiration and goodwill but a real affection'). Junior barristers in Simon's
chambers found themselves invited to golfing holidays at Gleneagles with all
bills met by their host. But then, during his four years as Law Officer his fees for
contentious business came to a total of £55,000, in addition to his annual salary
of £6,000.

In appearance in the prime of his life Simon's face was curiously unlined and
youthful, 'constantly broken by the dazzling smile of a boy of twenty well
content with himself and life'.[6] But ten years later the editor of the *Manchester
Guardian*, interviewing the Foreign Secretary, was disconcerted to find that he
had 'a determined, hard, and sometimes sneering or bullying face . . . his eyes

---

[9] Simon papers.   [1] *Retrospect*, p. 89–90.
[2] It is 60 years since (Sir Douglas Hogg in 1924) any Attorney-General was given a Cabinet seat. If anyone
should in future receive this honour, he should remember, when summoned to a Court at Buckingham
Palace, to wear a black damask tufted gown and lack stock: his costume as a Queen's Counsel is not appropriate, as it is the mourning costume of an 18th-cent. gentleman.
[3] Even Simon made a mistake when, as President of the Union, he first met Asquith, and asked whether
he had been up at Balliol with Matthew Arnold. 'The reaction was considerable' (Simon papers). But he was
forgiven: within a few weeks Margot had invited him to tea at 20 Cavendish Square.
[4] H. H. Asquith, *Letters to Venetia Stanley* (1983), p. 271.
[5] R. F. V. Heuston, *Lives of the Lord Chancellors 1885–1940* (Oxford, 1964), p. 332.
[6] 'Serjeant Buckram' in (1925) 60 *L.J. Newsp.* 548 (a perceptive article).

(which are blue and rather prominent) remain entirely unmoved when he is smiling'.[7] Simon aged remarkably little: when over eighty he could consult the telephone directory without the aid of spectacles.

So on his fortieth birthday Simon's achievements deserved all the traditional adjectives such as 'brilliant'. It was Oliver Wendell Holmes, another lawyer of passionate ambition and determination, who said that 'if a man was to do anything he must do it before forty'.[8] Simon certainly passed this test. But the war brought a halt to the dizzy tale of success, after first offering even further advances.

In July 1914 the speed and ruthlessness of Germany's actions against probable opponents, possible opponents, and innocent bystanders alike shocked the British Cabinet into firm decision. On Friday, 31 July Loreburn, the ex-Lord Chancellor, who had always been a strong opponent of Grey's foreign policy,[9] thought a majority of the Cabinet was against war.[1] On Saturday, 1 August Ramsay MacDonald dined with George (later Lord) Riddell, and recorded briskly his impressions of his fellow guests: 'Masterman jingo, George ruffled, Simon broken.'[2] With Morley and Burns (who eventually did resign), Simon had earlier that day been persuaded to withdraw his resignation from the Cabinet. On the morning of Tuesday, 4 August C. P. Scott, summoned south by an early train, hurried to No. 10, and found that Simon 'was looking terribly worn and tired. He began at once by saying that he had been entirely deceived about Germany.'[3] But in the end he did not resign, telling his supporters that he remained 'solely in order to prevent the appearance of disruption in face of a grave national danger. ... He is, as it were, an unattached member of the Cabinet and sits very lightly.'[4] Some of the traits of character disclosed by this incident—for example, the unwillingness to face difficulties and assume responsibility for awkward decisions—were to reappear in the thirties.

(In later life one of Simon's conversational 'set pieces' was his description of how, on the evening of Wednesday, 5 August, he had been one of the first in England to hear of the famous phrase 'a scrap of paper' which the German Foreign Minister, Bethmann-Hollweg, had flung at the British Ambassador, Goschen, when the latter had justified his country's actions by reference to her treaty obligations.)[5]

   [7] A. J. P. Taylor (ed.), *W. P. Crozier, Off the Record* (1973), pp. 33–4.
   [8] M. de Wolfe Howe, *The Proving Years* (1963), p. 8.
   [9] See Heuston, *Lord Chancellors 1885–1940*, pp. 173–5.
   [1] T. Wilson (ed.), *Political Diaries of C. P. Scott* (1970), p. 93. But he warned Scott against 'elements on the wrong side'.
   [2] D. Marquand, *Ramsay MacDonald* (1977), p. 164. C. F. G. Masterman (1874–1927) was Chancellor of the Duchy of Lancaster.
   [3] Wilson, *Diaries of C. P. Scott*, p. 96.   [4] Ibid., p. 103.
   [5] Modern research has confirmed that Bethmann-Hollweg used the phrase (in English): see C. Howard (ed.), *The Diary of Edward Goschen* (1980), app. B.

Asquith did not abandon Simon. Obliged under Conservative pressure in May 1915 to reconstruct his Government, he offered Simon, aged just forty-two, the Woolsack. The offer was refused, possibly on the advice of Asquith himself, who may have thought of 'the Impeccable' as a future leder of the Liberal Party. To Buckmaster, Solicitor-General, aged fifty-four, who was eventually appointed, Simon wrote after an evening driving round the roads of Hampstead discussing the offer:

I will not go to the Lords on any account—the sack rather than the Woolsack! Such qualities as I have are, I think, those of the House of Commons. I shall gladly give up the Attorney-Generalship and its emoluments so long as I get *real* work to do![6]

In the event Simon went to the Home Office in place of McKenna. But he held that great office for just over six months, for in December he expressed doubts about the policy of conscription which led him into resignation in January 1916. Later he realized that this decision had been a mistake from all points of view—not least in that it resulted in his exclusion from ministerial office for fifteen yers. But at that time he was able to find some traditional Liberal arguments in support of it—at any rate from the sillier wing of the party. (From Oxford, Professor Goudy wrote: 'To attempt to force compulsory service on a nation in the middle of a War ... cannot be justified.')[7] Today, after all have become accustomed to compulsory national service even in peace-time, the 1915 dispute seems futile. But at the time there was much correspondence, especially with the monarch and the Prime Minister, each of whom showed a pardonable testiness at his departure from a senior Cabinet office in circumstances which would only give encouragement to the enemy. Simon was prudent enough to foresee this hostility. On leaving office he at once volunteered for military service, and rose to the rank of major in the Royal Flying Corps, serving in France, obtaining the OBE, and being mentioned in despatches. At first Trenchard, the commander of the RFC, was hostile ('I had not asked for him, nor did I want him'), but soon they became close friends.[8]

An old Oxford friend, Leo Amery,[9] sent some advice in January 1916:

I am afraid you have been going through a bad time lately and I have felt much sympathy for you. I think you were right to resign and will be glad of your decision some day. But may I, as an old friend, add somehting more? You and the political principles and traditions you most cherish have come up against the facts of a new world which is incompatible with them. Whatever their intrinsic truth they have no

[6] Heuston, *Lord Chancellors 1885–1940*, pp. 264–9.
[7] Simon papers.
[8] See A. Boyle, *Trenchard* (1962), p. 259. Simon put an end to any doubts over his physical courage by flying (as a passenger) over enemy lines.
[9] They had been elected at All Souls on the same day.

real relation to the facts of today—or of many years past. The peculiar conserving effects of our party system have kept them politically alive for more than a generation after their time. But the last ten years have been, not the herald of some great advance but the last backwash of a tide that has run out and may not come back for generations. You were brought up in the Liberal, Gladstonian tradition—I don't believe you even realised the possibility of thinking in any other, and in the conjuncture of events it carried you almost to the summit of political power and influence before the war came. Now the ground has given under your feet and you are too honest to jump across, like Samuel and others, on to a very different ground and pretend you are still where you were before.

Now for the moral of this disquisition. Don't be tempted by your feelings to throw yourself henceforward into a campaign of opposition, and waste the rest of your life in vain opposition to all the inevitable changes that the new order of things will bring with it during the war and after the war, universal service, Protectionism and the like, things that you have been accustomed to call reaction—as they were in 1850, and as they may be again in 1950. You can do no good and you can only make life miserable for yourself—and I can speak with some experience of what it means to have all one's hopes and ideas deferred even for ten years, and to see the coming of the disasters one had wished so much to prepare against. Sit down and think the world out for yourself anew. Become for a few years a dispassionate student of the Empire's and the world's affairs— or of the affairs of a single factory or back street. Then come back again, five years hence or ten years hence, with a new view and a new message. You will still be young, you will still have the prestige of all you achieved before the war, and above all you will be in the position of being able to get something real done instead of merely striving for the rest of your days to fight against the whole main stream of the nation's life and thought.[1]

Simon was indeed out of things. Not holding Lloyd George's 'coupon', he was defeated at Walthanstow in 1918, and did not get back to the House until he was returned for Spen Valley (by only 787 votes) in 1922 as a Liberal National. He returned, as Amery predicted, 'five years hence', but unfortunately without 'a new view and a new message'. Perhaps Amery should have realized that this was impossible.

These bleak years in Simon's life were marked by one personal event—his remarriage in 1917. On 24 May 1899 he had married Ethel Mary Venables, then Vice-Principal of St Hugh's College, Oxford. In September 1902 she had died shortly after giving birth to his only son and the third of his children. A widower with three young children while still under the age of thirty, he became increasingly moody and reserved. The tragedy 'broke him up terribly', to quote the words of Bishop C. R. Hone,[2] who had introduced them. Thereafter, to quote one of his pupils at 2 Hare Court, 'he appeared to be no longer in need of sympathy, but only of admiration, and this, not because he was

---

[1] Simon papers.
[2] Private communication to author.

unduly vain, but because it helped him to do his work to his own satisfaction'.[3]
The pupil found himself summoned to listen to Simon dictating opinions in
difficult cases. 'Though I never opened my mouth he told me that I helped him,
and in the sense that I provided him with an admiring and, I hope, reasonably
intelligent audience, I suppose this was true.' There is no record of any female
relationship until March 1914, when the Asquith house party at Sutton
Courtenay, made miserable by rain and the lack of smart company,

were reduced to motoring to Sir Sympne's at Fritwell.[4] We found him returning from a
father's Sunday walk with his two girls and the family deerhound. He has an Irish
governess whose name I forget,[5] but who rules the whole establishment. She had been
hunting (!) with the Bicester on Saturday in the company of F. E. Smith, who had told
her which of my colleagues in the Cabinet were loyal, and which (a large majority) were
otherwise.[6]

Mrs Manning, a widow with one son, Brian, later left the Simon household but
invoked its aid when Brian, serving with the Irish Guards, became a prisoner-
of-war. The revived relationship led to marriage in December 1917. To quote
Bishop Hone again, 'she cheered him up greatly, and encouraged his self-
confidence', but her breezy extrovert manner sometimes caused colleagues and
civil servants to run for cover. In the words of her *Who's Who* entry, she was
'devoted to the cause of freedom everywhere; to Ireland, to Zionism, to assisting
backward and oppressed peoples'. In the 1980s this would have made her a
television personality: in the twenties and thirties it caused embarrassment,
particularly when she made her husband embark on public speeches attacking
the Black and Tans in 1921. But Simon was devoted to her, and secured her
promotion to DBE, refusing for himself the peerage offered for his work on the
Indian Statutory Commission.

Three major events in Simon's life during the twenties were the Campbell
case (1924), the General Strike (1926), and the Indian Statutory Commission
(1928). The first showed him to be a master of destructive House of Commons
tactics; the second also showed him in a negtive or destructive light, but gave
him what had hitherto eluded him—a major parliamentary success; the third
gave him a constructive opportunity to achieve greatness on an imperial, as
distinct from a merely national, scale. He just failed to do it.

The downfall of the 1924 Labour Government was largely due to the
controversy caused by the withdrawal of a prosecution against J. R. Campbell,

---

[3] J. W. Scobell Armstrong, *Yesterday* (1955), p. 120.
[4] The Asquiths had the irritating Edwardian habit of conferring nicknames on their circle. Simon was
usually 'the Impeccable', but was also 'Sir Sympne' on the analogy of Lympne (pronounced 'Lim').
[5] It was Kathleen Manning (née Harvey), who came from Kyle, on the Slaney north of Wexford.
[6] Asquith, *Letters to Venetia Stanley*, p. 53.

acting editor of the *Workers' Weekly*.[7] The Prime Minister and the Attorney-General gave dissimilar and confusing accounts of how the prosecution had been instituted and then withdrawn, and presented the Opposition with a golden opportunity to assert that there had been an infringement of the basic constitutional principle that the Attorney-General is not subject to political control in his public duty of enforcing the criminal law. As the Opposition had, in Simon and Hogg, two ex-Attorneys who were in legal and political skill infinitely more experienced than the unhappy Patrick Hastings, they did not lose a trick in the debate, and the Government came out badly mauled. 'The petty and sneaky spite of Sir John Simon and the personal triumph that beamed from Sir Douglas Hogg were humilitating to behold', the Prime Minister confessed.[8] Hastings, whose integrity was untouched, was so disgusted that he abandoned politics—thereby opening the way for Jowitt in 1929. The long-term moral of the Campbell case for the Labour Party was that they must equip themselves with first-class legal advisers.

On 6 May 1926 Simon told the House of Commons that the General Strike was illegal at common law. Supported in his view by a judgment of Astbury J., though not, then or later,[9] by other lawyers, Simon's speech was generally thought to have had a significant role in ending the dispute. An observer commented that 'the Simon–Astbury intervention in 1926 shows the remarkable respect for the law amongst English people, specially the working class'.[1]

In 1927 Parliament decided that there shold be a Statutory Commission to investigate Indian constitutional development since the Montagu–Chelmsford reforms of 1919, and to report on future prospects. The Commission was to consist solely of English parliamentarians: there were to be no Indian represen-tatives because, it was decided after much discussion, it would be impossible to secure proper representation of all points of view in India without making the Commission too large to be effective. Looking back, it can be seen that this was a serious psychological blunder, deeply offensive to Indian sensitivity. Simon accepted the post of chairman. He announced that he would give up practice at the Bar—a decision which, as Birkenhead wrote to the Viceroy, Lord Irwin, 'will be regarded as a great proof of earnestness in the task he has undertaken, and of

---

[7] The case has been exhaustively considered in recent years: see J. L. Edwards, *The Law Officers of the Crown* (1964), pp. 177-225; Edwards, *The Attorney General, Politics and the Public Interest* (1984), pp. 310-18; Marquand, *Ramsay MacDonald*, pp. 364-78. The conclusion is that there was muddle and misunderstanding on a scale exceptional even for MacDonald.

[8] Marquand, *Ramsay MacDonald*, p. 372.

[9] The Attorney-General (Hogg) was very careful not to express agreement with Simon's proposition of law; and Arthur Goodhart always complained that Simon could never be induced to state the exact nature of the illegality.

[1] O. Kahn-Freund in M. Ginsberg (ed.), *Law and Opinion in England in the Twentieth Century* (1959), pp. 226-7. That comment could not be made of England in the 1980s as distinct from the 1920s.

his own realization of its difficulty and importance. He is, of course, a rich man, and I suspect that he was becoming weary of eternal forensic conflicts . . .'.[2]

Simon himself took the decision very seriously. He wrote to Hogg on 13 January 1928:

I have come to the conclusion, in view of the Indian Commission and of the complications it creates, that my best course is to give up the Bar, and I finished my last case yesterday. It is a great wrench, and most of all in that it parts me from daily contact with so many friends. Twenty-nine years, twenty of them in Silk, has meant a lot of work, some quarrels, and many pleasant memories. I think, looking back, I have enjoyed my times with you as much as anything. So I am starting to India on Thursday as a person without a profession to come back to.[3]

The Cabinet has, as Birkenhead's letter to Irwin continued, the highest opinion of Simon's 'extraordinary suitability for this particular task . . . with which his clear, penetrating mind is eminently qualified to deal'. (As Simon rather acidly noted, his own restraint and courtesy would also be more acceptable in the East than the 'rather bullying' style which F.E. adopted towards Indians who visited him in London[4] (he had never set foot on the subcontinent for the good government of which he was responsible to Parliament).) Two years of unremitting public service followed. In June 1930 the Simon Report was published in two volumes. Today they are unread. But they entitled Simon to a place amongst those who were honoured in the cloisters of Westminster Abbey by a plaque carrying the simple phrase: 'They Served India'. Volume i was a masterly survey in four hundred pages of Indian constitutional history. Only the Chairman of the Commission had the analytical power and the clarity of style for such a mammoth task. It is a great State paper of which he was rightly proud. (The Stationary Office made a substantial profit on it. The price of each volume was 3s. (15p).) Volume ii was not so successful. It proposed the abandonment of diarchy, and instead the introduction of responsible government in the provinces, but not at the centre, where the Governor-General in Council would retain control of defence. The Legislative Assembly was to be reconstituted on a federal basis. The Viceroy was quick to put his finger on the flaw.

'The fundamental omission of all his Report, as I read it, is his very obvious and deliberate refusal to take the bandage off his eyes and admit the existence of the Dominion Status claim in terms. The thing seems to me very much to lack imagination.'[5]

[2] Heuston, *Lord Chancellors 1885-1940*, p. 395.
[3] Simon papers. [4] Ibid.
[5] Earl of Birkenhead, *Halifax* (1965), p. 287. Irwin had in Oct. 1929 publicly announced his support for dominion status: this was seen by many as an attempt to torpedo the report. Simon treated it with dignified silence.

Irwin added a comment about the difference between the views of a Harley Street specialist and those of a family doctor who knew all the foibles of a patient. While not many would have compared the great Yorkshire aristocrat, reared in all the smiling goodwill of pre-1914 England, with a family doctor, the comment is perceptive. But though perceptive it is not just: Simon did not have the gift of imagination, so it is no fairer to blame him for not displaying that quality than it is for a critic to blame an author for a book which he has not written.

Within months the tide of history had swept the Simon Report away. At the round table conference in November 1930 not one of the eighty-seven Indian delegates supported it. Events were in the saddle. Soon the elaborate structure set up by the Government of India Act 1935 was itself submerged. India has now been a republic for just forty years. Simon did not complain. Indeed, he had scarcely been released from India when, at the urgent request of the Government, he undertook yet another public service—an inquiry into the disastrous loss of the airship R101. This did not call for any qualities of imagination or perception, but for patience and analytical skill. On this topic the report by Simon (and two expert assessors) has never been criticized.

Simon returned to the Bar. In February 1930 he had consulted his former clerk, Ronald Pocock, who had been a faithful friend since Simon had first taken chambers in the Temple, about his prospects. He put two questions to him: (i) how his resumption of practice at the Bar would be received by the two professions; (ii) what income would probably result from such resumption of practice? As to (i) Pocock said that both branches of the profession would welcome his return, although there might be a few at the Bar who would adversely criticize his action in announcing his retirement and then returning as a competitor, but they would be very few in number and their grievance would be founded on selfish considerations. 'The few who would object would be the jealous ones, and as you know, jealousy does exist to a certain extent in the Temple.'

With reference to (ii), until the recent promotion of Mr. Macmillan to the House of Lords, the great proportion of the work which you used to do has been shared by him and Mr. Wilfrid Greene, and there is no doubt if you returned, you and Mr. Greene would share this practice as you used to share it with the then Mr Douglas Hogg. Of course there is not such a large amount of this class of work at the moment as there used to be, but I think a very fair and perhaps moderate estimate of your income would be £35,000. If you decide to return, my own opinion is that you should devote yourself to the big cases and leave the smaller ones alone. In other words, when you have a big case on hand devote yourself to that almost entirely and not attempt to do smaller cases at the same time. My experience is that clients would be quite prepared to pay you large fees if they knew that they would get your almost undivided attention.[6]

[6] Simon papers.

There was also a return to party politics. The position in 1931 was confused. The Labour Party had been split when Ramsay MacDonald had formed the National Government, and at the resultant general election its vote declined by one and a half million, and in seats it was no stronger than in 1918—a disaster not to be equalled until 1983. The Liberal Party was divided into those who followed Lloyd George, and those who did not. The latter were themselves divided into Samuelite free traders,[7] and Simonites, who supported the tariff policy of the Conservatives, and were to the world indistinguishable from them. (The official name of the party was Liberal National, later changed to the National Liberals.)

The Government had eleven Conservative members out of twenty (though 80 per cent of the backbenchers were Conservatives); four National Labour; three Samuelite Liberals; and two Simonites (Walter Runciman was the other). Simon was appointed to the Foreign Office on 9 November 1931. At 11 a.m. on that day he received a telegram: 'Cordial congratulations on your great office after all these years of political exclusion. Winston'. Endorsing it 'the very first I received' Simon filed it away.[8]

MacDonald usually left his Ministers alone, but his control of foreign policy, at least on the most important questions, was almost as complete in this period as it had been in 1924.[9] Though Simon's 'silky urbanity' grated on him as much as it did on other people,[1] he kept a close eye on him.

I am not a little troubled about the effect upon your health of the strain and worry that has been imposed upon you, and I want you to take care of yourself. I had not seen you for some days until yesterday, and you did not look at all robust. The Assembly of the League is not going to meet until September, and I really think you ought to take advantage of Anthony Eden's steady presence in London to take a sea voyage during July and August. It would really pay you. Eden and Van[2] together can take temporary charge in your absence. The House of Commons, I am told, is pretty dead, and even difficult corners can easily be got round. So far as I can see the coming winter is going to be a heavy one and, once we get back to work in September, we will all be required to stay here on the spot, so that I am afraid the results of a successful voyage will soon be taken out of you on your return. Pray consider this, because you must get back to your usual fine form.[3]

Simon had to face the rise of the dictators in Germany and Italy. One document illustrates his policy. It is a letter to the Prime Minister on 27 July 1934:

[7] Their leader was Geoffrey (later Lord) Samuel.
[8] Simon papers.
[9] Marquand, *Ramsay MacDonald*, p. 704.
[1] Ibid., p. 706.
[2] (Sir) Robert (later Lord) Vansittart, Permanent Under-Secretary at the FO.
[3] Simon papers.

You will like an abbreviated report on things international. The assassination of
Dollfuss, of course, overhangs the whole scene. I enclose what I said in the House yesterday. I thought it wiser to confine myself to the objective facts without going into
remoter causes and of course I abstained entirely from any hint of *action*. The last
sentence stating that our attitude remained the same as we expressed last February refers
of course to the joint declaration that we, in common with France and Italy, desired to
see Austrian independence continued but this involved nothing military.... Our own
policy is quite clear. We must keep out of trouble in central Europe at all costs. July
twenty years ago stands as an awful warning, and indeed I should not be surprised if the
date selected for this assassination was inspired by some memory of twenty years ago in
this very week. We must keep in friendly touch with Austria without going beyond our
previous declaration of general policy. Italy and France will be very well satisfied with
that declaration. All this may draw France and Italy closer together. Our own ties with
Italy are now so good that I do not think there is any risk of their being weakened.
Mussolini's position is quite different from ours. There are circumstances in which Italy
might move troops into Austria. There are no circumstances in which we should ever
dream of doing so.[4]

'I abstained entirely from any hint of action': this one sentence summarizes the
whole of Simon's foreign policy.

The ambition of 'keep[ing] out of trouble in central Europe at all costs' was
not achieved. It is strange that neither Simon nor anyone else seemed to
remember that in July 1914 he had made a fundamental miscalculation about
German ambitions. As late as March 1935, when Simon and Eden met Hitler in
Berlin, 'Simon's approach was to adopt a generally passive attitude in the face of
complaints from Hitler ... Eden inevitably had to follow this low-key lead'.[5]

Those who were responsible for British foreign policy in the thirties have
had great difficulty in obtaining justice. The policies pursued so nearly brought
the country to total disaster, and were swept away so completely in the
Churchillian gale of 1940, that an impartial judgement is difficult. But there
was much to be said in their defence. Without military strength to back his
policy,[6] the Foreign Secretary was expected to reconcile the French demand for
security with the German claim for equality of status, and also to persuade fifty
states at Geneva to accept a plan for disarmament. He was also expected to keep
Italy and Japan quiet. At first Simon's task was aided by a Parliamentary Under-

    [4] Ibid.
    [5] D. Carlton, *Anthony Eden* (1981), p. 62. But Ralph Wigram, of the FO, gave Virginia Woolf a different
impression. 'Wigram and the rest frightened. Anything may happen at any moment. Here in England we
haven't even bought our gas masks. Nobody takes it seriously. But having seen this mad dog, the thin rigid
Englishmen are really afraid' (A. O. Bell (ed.), *The Diaries of Virginia Woolf* (1983), vol. iv, p. 304).
    [6] The strength was denied by those who were the strongest critics. In March 1936 (after Abyssinia and the
Rhineland), Dalton, Labour Spokesman on Foreign Affairs, said: 'It is only right to say bluntly and frankly
that public opinion in this country would not support, and certainly the Labour Party would not support,
the taking of military sanctions or even economic sanctions against Germany at this time' (310 H.C. Deb. col.
1454).

Secretary aged only thirty-four, whose personal glamour and diplomatic skill evoked European admiration. 'The man who really has *the* international position here is Anthony Eden. Somehow or another Anthony has got the confidence—nay the adulation—of all these strange animals that live in this zoo. Simon can never get it': so wrote Ormsby-Gore to Baldwin from Geneva in October 1933.[7] But as Eden's ambition was comparable to, and his vanity greater than, that of Simon, their relationship became more difficult—at least on Eden's side. Simon seems to have retained for his Parliamentary Under-Secretary an affection of a paternal kind, which sometimes was expressed in a manner which in someone else might have been called 'skittish'.[8] But by 1938 Eden's attitude to Simon had become one of hostility.[9] With more senior colleagues, doubts had arisen much earlier. In January 1934 Neville Chamberlain noted that 'Simon's weakness has given rise to much criticism . . . his manner inspires no confidence'.[1] By December the Chief Whip, Margesson, warned the Prime Minister that the Foreign Secretary was one of his biggest problems: on the back-benches dislike had intensified.[2] But it was not until June 1935 that MacDonald and Baldwin exchanged places. Simon went back to the Home Office after twenty years, being also made Deputy Leader of the house ('to soften his fall'). Sir Samuel Hoare became Foreign Secretary.[3]

The Home Office always has a few draft Bills in its files which will enable its Minister to gain some parliamentary reputation as a reformer, and Simon thus got credit—for example, for the Money Payments (Justices Procedure) Act 1936 and the Factories Act 1937. Civil Servants were much impressed by the trouble he took to find reasons for exercising the prerogative of mercy in capital cases.[4]

[7] Carlton, *Anthony Eden*, p. 33. W. G. A. Ormsby-Gore, later Lord Harlech, was a junior minister and a strong opponent of the Nazis.

[8] 'Dear Anthony, meet me at Geneva. Yours Cleopatra', was how the Foreign Secretary informed his junior that he had been appointed a British delegate to the League Assembly (Simon papers).

[9] J. Harvey (ed.), *The Diplomatic Diaries of Oliver Harvey 1937-1940* (1970) contain several examples of this.

[1] K.Middlemas and J. Barnes, *Baldwin* (1969), p. 804.

[2] Ibid., pp. 804, 807. But even some of these back-benchers sent letters of congratulation when in 1933 Simon recovered judgment for libel against the Revd J. Whitaker Bond, an eccentric non-conformist clergyman, who had alleged that Simon's foreign policy was based on his financial interests.

[3] Hoare was the only senior British politician who was a fluent speaker of Russian. During the previous 4 years he had been totally immersed in the affairs of India, often missing Cabinets for weeks at a time. Six months later he had to resign office: he had shown too much imagination and initiative in making a deal with the French Prime Minister, Laval, over Abyssinia.

[4] Terence FitzGerald of the Home Office, now deceased, wrote: 'In modern times the Home Secretary whose decisions in capital cases stand high is John Simon. If all Home Secretaries had shown his judgment capital punishment might have gradually withered on the vine and we might have been spared the 30 years of uncertainty. I think I can accurately outline Simon's approach to capital cases, and distinguish it from the more traditional line, as follows. Before his term in office the view taken in general by Home Secretaries and their senior officials was that as death was the penalty laid down for murder there had to be some mitigating circumstances to justify setting that penalty aside and substituting life imprisonment. Opinions might well differ on what amounted to an adequate mitigating circumstance, but not on the need for its existence if a reprieve were to be granted. Simon's approach seems to have been different. He evidently took the view that since a substantial proportion of those sentenced to death were in practice reprieved it followed that the

The abdication of Edward VIII found Simon one of the inner circle in Government: his talents as a staff officer were exerted to the full in the complex administrative arrangements which were required. 'It was all a matter of modalities', to use one of Simon's own favourite phrases, which sometimes infuriated his juniors when used on an occasion which struck them as inappropriate—for example, the invasion of the Rhineland. But as the King made no real or sustained effort to keep his throne instead of Mrs Simpson the term was here quite appropriate. An answer to a parliamentary question from Attlee about the prospect of a morganatic marriage was 'brilliantly drafted by Simon'.[5] Nobody could have doubted where Simon stood on such an issue, or on the proposal emanating from Fort Belvedere that in return for abdication Parliament should provide legislation to make the Simpson divorce decree absolute at once, instead of after the six months which the law then required. On one day Baldwin and Simon were together for seven hours; when an exhausted premier returned from Fort Belvedere to London he found that all the 'modalities' had been smoothly arranged by Simon and two All Souls colleagues, Gwyer (formerly Treasury Solicitor, and now first parliamentary draftsman), and Somervell (Attorney-General).[6]

In May 1937 Simon surrendered the Home Office to Hoare and became Chancellor of the Exchequer. The Czech crisis of 1938 found the same Cabinet inner circle round the Prime Minister, Chamberlain. At Lanark on 29 August Simon delivered a speech to which the Government attached importance, warning Hitler that, once begun, any war would eventually involve Britain. But to Eden and his followers, 'The Lanark speech was not nearly enough and coming from Simon was immediately discounted'.[7]

On Wednesday, 14 September Chamberlain told the Cabinet about his plan to fly to Germany to meet Hitler (Plan Z). Sir Thomas Inskip left a mordant picture of the meeting.

John Simon finished by his usual shower of compliments to P.M.—all fully deserved, but somehow or other coming from John Simon's lips they give an impression of soapiness and flattery which they do not deserve. 'Brilliant'—his absence 'grievous' even for 48

community expected, or were at any rate prepared to acquiesce in, a practice policy under which the death sentence was carried out only for the worst murders: and he looked for some aggravating feature before putting a case into that category—it might be pre-meditation, it might be the use of a knife or firearm, or poison, it might be the fact that the murder was committed in the course of some other crime, e.g. bank robbery, or it might be that the victim was e.g. a policeman. But in default of some aggravating feature he was prepared to reprieve. The proportion of reprieves under Simon's policy and under the more traditional policy might not be all that dissimilar, but the difference in approach is nevertheless important.'

[5] Middlemas and Barnes, *Baldwin*, p. 1007.

[6] Two more were helpful behind the scenes in the House of Lords: Lang (Archbishop of Canterbury) and Halifax (Lord Privy Seal). Another, G. Dawson, as Editor of *The Times*, guided the formation of public opinion.

[7] Harvey, *Diaries of Oliver Harvey 1937–1940*, p. 172.

hours. If he came back with seeds of peace with honour 'a remarkable achievement' and so on. I don't think the P.M. relishes such butterings, but he was plainly touched—as he said—by the confidence placed in him.[8]

Chamberlain flew to Germany for two meeetings with Hitler—at Berchetes-gaden and Godesberg. The French also had to be kept in line. On Sunday 25 September the French premier and his Foreign Minister flew to London for their second visit within ten days. It was a painful meeting. Chamberlain and Simon pressed Daladier and Bonnet very hard. The French found themselves at the receiving end of a cross-examination by a master of the art. Were the French public prepared for immediate German bomber raids? Was the French army capable of doing more than holding the Maginot line?

On Wednesday, 28 September Parliament met to hear Chamberlain's account of events. A microphone at the dispatch-box relayed his speech to the House of Lords—the first time any proceeding in the House of Commons had been broadcast. After Chamberlain had been speaking for an hour a sheet of what was observed to be Foreign Office paper was hurriedly passed along the Treasury Bench to Simon who was seated next to Chamberlain. It was a message from Hitler inviting Chamberlain to meet Mussolini, Daladier, and himself at Munich the next day. A man with less self-control than Simon might have interrupted Chamberlain at once.[9] Simon, however, recorded in his diary, that 'the problem was how and when to let the speaker know this encouraging and indeed vital fact without disturbing the flow of his discourse'. At what he judged to be the right moment Simon handed the paper to Chamberlain: as he read it, 'he appeared ten years younger and triumphant'. 'Shall I tell them?' he asked Simon, who answered, 'Yes'. Pent-up emotions produced a scene of hysterical support for the Prime Minister, who returned from Munich on Friday the 30th.

In his calm way Simon analysed the afternoon of high tension. 'It was incomparably the greatest piece of real drama the House of Commons has ever witnessed ... [previous scenes] must have been dramatic enough—but they lack[ed] the element of surprise provided by a vital intervening event, unknown to the chief actor himself until it was told him as he was on his feet.'

Simon's support for Chamberlain seems to have wavered only once—surprisingly, on Saturday, 2 September 1939. Hitler had invaded Poland the previous day. The House of Commons met at 6 p.m. in the belief that they would hear from the Prime Minister that war would be declared at midnight.

---

[8] Heuston, *Lord Chancellors 1885-1940*, p. 593. Inskip was then Minister for Co-ordination of Defence. A year later he succeeded Maugham as Lord Chancellor. 'I spoke a couple of sentences on behalf of us all', was Simon's own diary entry.

[9] Lord Dunglass (later Sir Alec Douglas-Home), the bearer of the message, thought that Simon 'took a second or two to absorb it' (*the Way the Wind Blows* (1976), p. 62). One of the quickest minds in England had absorbed the message at once: it was simply contemplating the most effective mode of delivering it.

Two hours later, Chamberlain entered: he gave an irritated assembly the impression that the Cabinet was weakening. There had been difficulties in securing the synchronization of the British and French ultimatums. 'I have never seen such a revulsion of feeling in my thirty years experience in the House', Simon recorded in his diary. Some members of the Cabinet 'in a state of semi-revolt' met in Simon's room, and he was deputed to put their case, which Hore-Belisha said he did 'very forcibly'. There were two more meetings of the dissidents. One of these, Reginald Dorman-Smith, later recalled how under the strain 'all of us were getting back to our natural selves. I became more Irish, and Hore-Belisha more Jewish—talking of rights and indignities and so on.'[1] Eventually an exhausted Cabinet agreed that the ultimatum to German should expire at 11 a.m. on the Sunday. The incident certainly shows Simon playing a role very different from that which he had played in September 1938—or August 1914. Perhaps he thought that as war was inevitable it would be prudent for him to try to recover his reputation with the anti-Chamberlain forces.

In the debate on the conduct of the war on 8 May 1940 the Government's majority fell to 81 out of a possible 213. Before the division Dunglass had indicated to the rebels that in order to save himself Chamberlain was prepared to sacrifice Simon and Hoare. But it was too late. Chamberlain wrote to his sister Ida given the reasons: 'and finally the personal dislike of Simon and Hoare had reached a pitch which I find it difficult to understand, but which undoubtedly had a great deal to do with the rebellion'.[2] Churchill went to No. 10. Hoare was sent to Madrid and Simon to the Woolsack. Simon received the Great Seal on 13 May. Chamberlain, mortally stricken, retired to the country. On 3 October Simon wrote:

This is a sad loss to the country at so critical a time. You have been most unfairly attacked, largely by those who at the time of Munich were throwing up their hats, and as for the period of the War when you were still P.M., I shall to my dying day maintain that there was *no* substantial difference of view between Winston and yourself and that your wise guidance saved us from many errors. For Winston's leadership since then I have the greatest admiration, and I am sure he will miss your counsel immensely. However, changes there must be. You have the priceless consolation that you have spent yourself in the country's service and have done more than any man alive to improve the conditions of life of humble folk, as well as leading a united nation into war when your struggle for peace finally failed.

Chamberlain replied on the 6th:

---

[1] Sunday Times, 6 Sept. 1964.

[2] H. Montgomery Hyde, *Neville Chamberlain* (1976), p. 163. In September 1939 a department of the Foreign Office informally 'discussed the politicians who were criminally responsible for the war and should be hanged on lamp-posts in Downing Street. Not many candidates. Nearly everyone agreed that sinner No. 1 was Simon' (Kenneth Young (ed.), *The Diaries of Sir Robert Bruce Lockhart 1939-45* (1980), p. 42).

It gave me particular pleasure that in your letter you remembered my efforts for social improvement. Of course I can't and don't expect journalists who are accustomed to deal only with the affairs of the moment, to recollect the past. But it was the hope of doing something to improve the conditions of life for the poorer people that brought me at past middle life into politics, and it is some satisfaction to me that I was able to carry out some part of my ambition, even though its permanency may be challenged by the destruction of war. For the rest I regret nothing that I have done and I can see nothing undone that I ought to have done.[3]

The public image—a phrase which they would have detested—of Chamberlain and Simon was that of cold, grey, stiff, humourless men. Simon, like Chamberlain, resisted all attempts to cultivate the public—for example, by appearing at the Derby. Ice-skating was an interest shared with Hoare, but by no means a popular sport.[4]

Simon was like Jowitt in that he was unable to shake off the reputation for unpopularity which had been attached to him. At times he did not seem to be able to do anything right—or what he did was interpreted in the worst way. One example from his League of Nations days may be enough. In 1932 he had the task of arguing in theory in favour of sanctions against Japan for her invasion of Manchuria, while in practice preserving an isolationist stance in case the weak position of Britain in the Far East should be endangered still more. For such a delicate task Simon did not, as usual, rely on his superb memory, but committed the heads of his argument to correspondence cards, which he shuffled in his hands as he spoke. He was immediately accused by some of his audience of behaving like Uriah Heep.[5]

His inability to reach a decision has two related explanations. First, his mind was in many ways academic or scholarly (though he would not have regarded this as a compliment); he did not like to decide until he had read all the material. But on the major issues of policy the Foreign Office had files going back to the Congress of Vienna; and so while the Secretary of State was reading the documents, his Civil Servants waited for their licence to act and the country slid towards Munich. Yet Balfour, a pure intellectual, could be ruthless and rapid when required to reach an official decision. Secondly, it has been said that Simon had the advocate's reluctance to ask a question to which he does not know the answer–as nobody knew the answer to the problem of the dictators, the Foreign Secretary could not bring himself to raise the question. But not all legal intellectuals have had these failings. Simonds and Cyril Radcliffe were New College intellectuals, with Firsts in Greats, and mandarins at the Chancery

[3] Simon papers.
[4] It is strange that two of the four members of the inner Cabinet should have shared a taste for solitary gyrations on a frozen surface. Simon was also a competent golfer, but he infuriated both partners and opponents by insisting on a meticulous observance of the rules of the game.
[5] B. Liddell Hart, *Memoirs* (1965), vol. i, p. 205.

Bar. Yet when called to public service each exhibited a vigour in debate and a promptness in decision which made them admired by those who had the duty of executing the decisions.

The conclusion is that the defects of Simon as a politician, as distinct from his strengths as a judge, related not so much to any characteristics of the advocate's profession, but to some inherent weakness in his personality which had not yet been fully explained. 'Why then at the end of a life filled with such extraordinary success and activity does one feel a certain sense of inadequacy and frustration?' This was the question which Arthur Goodhart asked after Simon's death.[6] Ten years later Bowra tried to explain this strange, lonely, difficult man.

Whereas Birkenhead seemed not to care what duties tomorrow might bring and was prepared to give himself wholly to the present moment, Simon seemed always to be looking ahead and economising his strength. In conversation he could be most interesting, especially in set-pieces like an account of Curzon lecturing the cabinet on the dangers of retreat from the Dardanelles and quoting at length from Thucydides' account of the disastrous Athenian retreat from Syracuse—only to be told that the greater part of our forces had already been safety evacuated. Simon was something of an artist with words and quoted poetry with feeling, but he never gave the impression of being spontaneous. He seemed, despite his obvious politeness, to be preoccupied with something else, and this impression was enhanced by his habit of calling by the wrong name even people whom he knew quite well.[7] In concentrating on success Simon repressed his more human side, with the result that in the end he never won the success which he desired so avidly. He held most of the high offices of state, but he was never Prime Minister, nor was there any likelihood that he would be. He was thought to be a cold fish and, worse, to have no very strong convictions. . . . Simon longed to be thought a strong man, and struck powerful gestures when he read a lesson in chapel or prepared to drive from a golf-tee, but, though from a safe position he was capable of a formidable pose, he lacked real conviction. Perhaps, like other gifts, it had been dried up by ambition, or perhaps his experience at the Bar meant that he saw problems from too many angles and was not able to decide which was really right. For many years I found him a little difficult to talk to. All would begin promisingly, but then, as his fine turns were exhausted, there was nothing more to say. In his last years I got to know him better. After he ceased to be Lord Chancellor in 1945, there was very little more that he could reasonably want, though he approached me in 1948 about becoming High Steward of the University on the death of Lord Sankey, and was duly appointed. In old age he paid more attention to others. Despite his placid exterior he had a certain pathos. He longed to be liked, to be admired, to please, but somehow he failed, and he knew it.[8]

[6] (1954) 70 *LQR* 177, 178.

[7] 'He was not possessed of sufficiently automatic good manners to enable him to conceal his passing moods. When he was worried or his mind was concentrated on some knotty problem I do not think he even visualised those who approached him, and his icy reception of them after previous cordiality caused frequent offence' (Scobell Armstrong, *Yesterday*, p. 120).

[8] Bowra, *Memories*, pp. 141-2. Two factors which Bowra omitted (perhaps because he could have had no personal experience of them) were the ingrained reticence of one brought up in a household of a non-conformist minister, and the numbing effect of being left a widower with three children while still under 30.

A postscript may be added about the office of High Steward. When Sankey had been appointed in 1930 the claims of Simon, as a lawyer of far greater distinction, were naturally considered. But the then Vice-Chancellor, Dudden of Pembroke, found Simon to be so unpopular that he agreed, reluctantly, to put in a Labour Lord Chancellor.

The war-time years were relatively quiet for Simon. He was not a member of the War Cabinet, and a party truce ensured that there was a minimum of acrimonious debate. There were only ten High Court appointments. N. Birkett (later a peer) was the only new judge in the King's Bench Division. In the Chancery Division, besides H. Vaisey, there were four distinguished appointments— A. A. Uthwatt, L. L. Cohen, R. Evershed, and M. L. Romer. In the Probate, Divorce, and Admiralty Division there was G. St C. Pilcher in place of Langton J. ('mysteriously drowned in the Bristol Channel'), and in 1944, to deal with the expected post-war divorce business, H. Wallington, H. Barnard, and, at the age of forty-five, one who was to become the best known English judge of the twentieth century—A. T. Denning. The war provided an excuse for not undertaking a task for which Simon had no aptitude—the reform of the legal system. But his scholarly taste for intellectual coherence led him to secure the passage of two statutes which made necessary reforms in areas of lawyers' law— the Law Reform (Frustrated Contracts) Act 1943 and the Law Reform (Contributory Negligence) Act 1945. Each Act was preceded by lengthy correspondence with the leading academics at Oxford and Cambridge— Arthur Goodhart and Percy Winfield. But Simon firmly adhered to the traditional policy of excluding academics from judicial appointments. In 1941 he said, 'I do not want to see the judicial bench filled with people who are no doubt terrifically learned but are living in complete seclusion and have no contact with the world.'[9]

As a judge in the highest tribunal Simon was superb. Although it was war-time the accidents of litigation brought before the House of Lords a series of appeals raising juristic questions of the greatest importance. Simon also had the assistance of an unusually distinguished body of Law Lords— Atkin, Wright, Porter, Romer, Russell of Killowen. Even so it is impossible to open any volume of the Appeal Cases from 1941 to 1946 without being struck by the scale and distinction of his achievement—an achievement accomplished in spite of the fact that he had not been a practising member of the Bar for a dozen years before his elevation to the Woolsack. To take only the volumes for 1941 and 1942, there are reported judgments which every lawyer would at once recognize to be of the highest importance, dealing with waiver of tort and quasi-contract;[1] damages for loss of expectation of life;[2] unlawful

[9] *Report of the Select Committee on Offices or Places of Profit under the Crown* (1941), p. 97.
[1] *United Australia Ltd.* v. *Barclays Bank Ltd.* [1941] AC 1.
[2] *Benham* v. *Gambling* [1941] AC 157 (now reversed by statute).

arrest;[3] manslaughter;[4] frustration in contract;[5] the scope of the tort of conspiracy;[6] vicarious liability in tort;[7] and the scope of Crown privilege in the law
of evidence.[8] All are phrased in the English style which is characteristic of
Simon—as transparent and cold as a mountain stream.

In 1942 Lord Dunedin died at the age of ninety-two: he had pleaded before
four Lord Chancellors, and been the judicial colleague of nine more. He was
generally regarded as possessing to the highest degree the judicial gift of open-
mindedness and suspension of judgment until all the evidence had been heard.[9]
Simon published a tribute, which also contains such an interesting picture of
the work of an appellate judge that a lengthy quotation from the unread
columns of *The Times* is permissible.

> The contribution made to our legal development by a great judge has to be measured
> not only by the language in which he expresses his final conclusions but also by his
> contributions while the debate is going on. Arguing a complicated case which has
> already been considered by courts below is rather like rowing on tidal water: you may
> reach your desired haven with the assistance of prevailing wind and stream (curiously
> enough, the weather in supreme tribunals sometimes seems at first to favour the
> appellant), or you may have to round a dangerous point in opposition to gusts and
> currents—but what is quite certain is that you cannot wisely navigate on a pre-
> conceived plan without watching closely the changing conditions and noting the
> reaction of each argument on the members of the tribunal.[1]

For Simon his judicial duty did not end with the day's arguments: he was
active in the weeks which followed, pursuing his own researches and ready to
engage in correspondence about difficult points. He kept a close eye on the
preparation of opinions, and was always ready with a courteously phrased
amendment or correction to a colleague's draft. One attempt to secure a
rephrasing of a well-known passage in Lord Atkin's speech in *Liversidge* v.
Anderson[2] has caused discussion.

To some Simon's intervention passed over the line which marks the
boundary between a permissible intervention by a Lord Chancellor in his
capacity as presiding judge and an impermissible interference by a Lord

---

[3] *Barnard* v. *Gorman* [1941] AC 378.   [4] *Mancini* v. *DPP* [1942] AC 1.
[5] *Joseph Constantine Steamship Line Ltd.* v. *Imperial Smelting Corporation Ltd.* [1942] AC 154.
[6] *Crofter Hand Woven Harris Tweed Co. Ltd.* v. *Veitch* [1942] AC 435.
[7] *Century Insurance Co. Ltd.* v. *NIRTB* [1942] AC 509.
[8] *Duncan* v. *Cammell, Laird & Co. Ltd.* [1942] AC 624. This is the only decision which the House of Lords
has refused to follow: see *Conway* v. *Rimmer* [1968] AC 910. It is worth noting that Simon was a strong
adherent of the pre-1966 view that the House was bound by its own previous decisions: see his little-known
Holdsworth Lecture, *The Limits of Precedent* (Birmingham, 1944), pp. 6–9.
[9] Jowitt regarded Dunedin as the greatest judge before whom he had appeared.
[1] *The Times*, 26 Aug. 1942.
[2] [1942] AC 206. Simon did not preside over the appeal, because in 1915 as Home Secretary he had signed
internment orders the validity of which were upheld in [1917] AC 260—'the only place where my name
appears in the Law Reports otherwise than as counsel or judge' (*Retrospect*, p. 104).

Chancellor in his capacity as Cabinet Minister.[3] If there had been such an interference with the principle of judicial independence, then, in the words of Sankey in 1932, 'a situation of the utmost gravity would have developed'.[4] As Sankey continued: 'No court would ever dream, after giving judgment, of altering it so that the decision should go the other way, nor would a court alter the language of a judgment which is part of the reasoning upon which the decision proceeds'.

This careful statement clearly does not exclude the possibility that a judgment might be altered while still in draft, either because the author of it had second thoughts of his own, or because he had been convinced by the arguments of colleagues, or others, who had seen the draft. Did Simon infringe the Sankey principle? It is best to start by repeating the question at issue in *Liversidge* v. *Anderson*, although it is very familiar to all lawyers. Regulation 18B, made under the Emergency Powers Act 1939, authorized the Secretary of State to intern without trial 'if the Secretary of State has reasonable cause to believe any person to be of hostile origin or associations'. Such an order was made in respect of Robert William Liversidge, alias Jack Perlzweig. Could the courts review Sir John Anderson's statement that he had reasonable cause to believe Liversidge had the qualities specified? A majority of the House of Lords, Lord Atkin dissenting, held that on a proper construction of the statutory regulation there was no such power.

Lord Atkin's dissent was written in passionate terms which attracted much attention then and later. After stating that the views of the majority showed them to be 'more executive-minded than the executive', he remarked: 'In this case I have listened to arguments which might have been addressed acceptably to the Court of King's Bench in the time of Charles I.' He concluded by citing *Alice through the Looking Glass* to ridicule the attitude of the majority.[5] Simon wrote to Atkin in worried terms on Friday, 31 October 1941:

My dear Atkin,

I *do* hope you will not resent it if I write this private and friendly note.

I asked Proby[6] this morning to let me see, in confidence, the speeches prepared for the 18B judgments on Monday. They, of course, call for the closest study and I have not had time for more than a glance.

[3] R. Stevens, *Law and Politics* (1979), p. 333, describes Simon's action as 'most sinister'.
[4] Quoted in A. V. Lowe and J. R. Young, 'An Executive Attempt to Rewrite a Judgment' (1978) 94 *LQR* 255, at 272.
[5] 'I know of only one authority which might justify the suggested method of construction. "When I use a word", Humpty Dumpty said in rather a scornful tone, "it means just what I choose it to mean, neither more nor less." "The question is," said Alice, "whether you can make words mean different things." "The question is," said Humpty Dumpty, "which is to be master—that's all." (*Through the Looking Glass*, c. vi.) After all this long discussion the question is whether the words "If a man has" can mean "If a man thinks he has." I am of opinion that they cannot, and that the case should be decided accordingly.' [1942] AC 206, at 244.
[6] The Law Lords' judicial clerk.

But my eye catches your very amusing citation from Lewis Carroll. Do you really, on final reflection, think this is necessary? I fear that it may be regarded as wounding to your colleagues who take the view you satirize, and I feel sure you would not willingly seek to hold them up to ridicule. I am all in favour of enlivening judgments with literary allusion but I would venture (greatly daring I know) to ask you whether the paragraph should be retained. Of course it is entirely for you. But I have gained so much from occasional suggestions of yours (mostly, it is true, in cases when we have been sitting together) that I trust you will forgive this query. I at any rate feel that neither the dignity of the House, nor the collaboration of colleagues, nor the force of your reasoning would suffer from the omission.

Yours ever,
John Simon[7]

The reproduction of this letter, to a generation intensely suspicious of any flavour of authoritarianism, may be received by some with cynical laughter. Others may feel that it was a legitimate request for loyal co-operation in a difficult situation, phrased in courteous and moderate language. For it should not be assumed too readily that Lord Atkin was entirely right in his use of what may be called 'the Humpty-Dumpty quip', or the 'Charles I jibe'. It is possible that in effect, although not in intention, Lord Atkin was unfair to honest men trying to do their duty in a grave national emergency. A removal of the sneer, quip, or jibe (whichever term is preferred) would not detract from the solid merits of the judgment, and would have avoided giving unnecessary offence. Yet on the other hand it might be said that it is just these phrases which give the judgment its peculiar force and lift it into the category of greatness.

What is certain is that Simon bore no grudge against Atkin. Eighteen months later, when Atkin was very ill, Lord Thankerton produced a draft speech which contained what Simon called 'a little jibe' at some dicta by Atkin. Simon persuaded Thankerton to omit it, on the ground that 'sick men are sometimes sensitive to criticism'.[8]

Simonds later paid a discerning tribute to Simon's judicial work:

A long and wide experience in the law, a scholar's passion for accuracy, and a compelling sense of the judicial oath drove him to sustained and unremitting efforts in the preparation of judgments which will be his most enduring monument. I sometimes thought that in that work he found his greatest happiness.[9]

---

[7] See R. F. V. Heuston, 'Liversidge v. Anderson in Retrospect' (1970) 86 LQR 33, at 45–6, where Lord Atkin's reply, and other relevant material, can be found, and also arguments to support the decision of the majority. Forty years on, the courts have begun to supervise more closely the decisions of government ministers, and some Law Lords, in obiter dicta, have expressed a preference for Lord Atkin's opinion: see e.g. R. v. Secretary of State, ex parte Khawaja [1984] AC 74, 110. But that does not affect the issue of whether Lord Simon acted constitutionally in 1941.

[8] The case seems to have been Knuppfer v. London Express Newspapers Ltd. [1944] AC 116.

[9] 185 H.L. Deb. col. 275 (19 Jan. 1954).

Simonds added, in his 'Recollections':

But he appeared to me to have one defect—and a very curious defect it was in view of his eminent qualities. He was strangely lacking in confidence in his own judgment: he would always before committing himself seek the approval of a colleague on whom he relied. I got to know well the sidelong glance which followed a tentative suggestion. In a word, he did not lead or seek to lead.

There is one glimpse of Simon off-duty in the war. In January 1943 Harold Nicolson

had an appointment to conduct some American doughboys round the Palace of Westminster. In they slouched, chewing gum, conscious of their inferiority in training, equipment, breeding, culture, experience and history, determined in no circumstances to be either interested or impressed. In the Chamber we bumped into another party, of Dominion heroes this time, being shown round by no less a person than the Lord Chancellor of England. I have never cared for John Simon, but I must confess that on this occasion he displayed energy and even charm. Embarrassing he was, to be true. For having stood at the Prime Minister's place and lifted up the dust-cloths from the box and table, he asked me to go opposite to show them the relations between the Government and the Opposition benches. . . . Fifty blank faces, their jaws working at the gum, turned in languid interest in my direction. 'Now Harold . . .' But I was firm, 'No', I said, 'I am no good at amateur theatricals'. So then we went into the House of Lords [*then sitting in the Robing Room*] and Simon sat on the Woolsack and showed them how the Lord Chancellor behaves.[1]

One curious incident must be noted. Simon opposed the trial of the major German war criminals: he preferred the solution recommended by Henry Morgenthau, the US Secretary of the Treasury, which was the complete de-industrialization of Germany together with the summary execution of the Nazi arch-criminals. Although Simon referred to 'the Napoleonic precedent' as justifying this scheme, he apparently contemplated execution, and not exile. Under pressure, especially from the Foreign Office and the Americans, he conceded that there might be 'a document of arraignment'. Eventually the Cabinet decided on a trial after being told that this was the preference of Truman and Stalin—the latter (of all people) saying to Churchill that a trial was 'absolutely essential'.[2] Before the arrangements for the trial had been completed Simon had surrendered the Great Seal to Jowitt. By November 1945 Simon felt able to publish an article in which he asserted that the Nuremberg trial was 'the greatest vindication of the force of moral justice in international relations that the world has every seen'.[3]

[1] H. Nicolson, *Diaries and Letters 1939–45* (1967), p. 275.
[2] See B. F. Smith, *The Road to Nuremberg* (New York, 1981). Perhaps Simon, like so many intellectuals, saw himself as a man of action. He used to recount with pride how, as Home Secretary, he employed men with hammers to break up a seditious printing-works rather than go through the legal formalities.
[3] *Sunday Times*, 25 Nov. 1945.

As an ex-Lord Chancellor Simon was never idle. The Law Reports show that he sat often both in the House of Lords and the Privy Council; Hansard shows that he was skilful and pertinacious in annoying Jowitt. (By 1945 Simon was in effect a member of the Conservative Party: he caused annoyance to old Liberal friends by supporting Tory candidates at by-elections.) But he was also constructive: much time and effort went into the measures which became the Crown Proceedings Act 1947 and the Defamation Act 1952. There were also frequent visits to Oxford. Whatever debts were owed to All Souls from his youth were handsomely repaid: there were gifts to refurbish the fabric, and when the wardenship was vacant (twice) within one year, he was active as Senior Fellow in supervising the electoral process which produced John Sparrow as Warden.[4] There were visits to the Oxford Union, and Presidents who escorted him back to All Souls were entertained by perfectly phrased discourses on the architectural, social, and literary history of Oxford.[5] He also took seriously his duties as supervising editor of one of Butterworths' encyclopaedic productions. *Simon's Taxes* achieved its third edition in 1984. So it could truly be said that on his eightieth birthday Simon had many more friends than on his seventieth.[6] A few weeks before his eighty-first birthday he died peacefully in a London hospital (11 January 1954),[7] and, in accordance with his express instructions, was cremated in his DCL gown without any religious ceremony or memorial service. His estate was sworn for probate at £93,000.

---

[4] Sparrow had once held the fashionably unkind view of Simon, and published a wounding epitaph on him. Later he made amends by publishing an appreciative obituary notice in the *Oxford Magazine* (Mar. 1954), and by placing Simon's coat of arms on the Hawksmoor towers. Simon's speech in praise of the college at a Gaudy in 1951 was pronounced to be one of the best things of its kind ever heard.

[5] See J. Thorpe in *The Times*, 17 Jan. 1954.

[6] No fewer than 216 friends of Simon gave him a dinner in Middle Temple Hall on 20 Oct. 1953.

[7] Characteristically, he left behind a draft speech in a Revenue appeal from Scotland over which he had presided in November. It was complete down to the last comma, and was, under the then practice, adopted by Lord Normand as his own: see *Inland Revenue Commissioners* v. *Wilsons (Dunblane) Ltd.* [1954] 1 WLR 282.

LORD JOWITT

CHAPTER I

WILLIAM ALLEN JOWITT was born at the Rectory, Stevenage, Hertfordshire, on 15 April 1885, the first son but tenth child of the Revd William Jowitt by his wife Louisa Margaret, the third daughter of John Allen, of Oldfield Hall, Altrincham, Cheshire. The boy's grandfather, John Jowitt, of Leeds, behind whom were four generations of Yorkshire ancestors, married on 29 January 1829 Mary Ann, daughter of Thomas Norton of Peckham Rye, Surrey. Their son William Jowitt (1834–1912) was educated at St John's College, Oxford, which he left without taking a degree, and University College, Durham. He was ordained and, after being headmaster of what was then called the City of London Middle Class School, spent the remainder of his life from 1874 as the Rector of Stevenage. The Rectory, now renamed Stevenage Priory, but otherwise littled changed, still survives on the northern edge of the new town of Stevenage built after the Second World War.

The pronunciation of Jowitt's name has given rise to doubt. In Yorkshire the name spelt Jowett or Jowitt is generally pronounced so as to rhyme with 'cow-it', but the most famous representative of the family was probably the Revd William Jowitt, the late-Victorian Master of Balliol, whose name, as pronounced in Oxford, always rhymes with 'joe-it'. Of him there is a well-known rhyme, which runs in its best version:

> First come I; my name is Jowett.
> There's no knowledge but I know it.
> I am Master of this College.
> What I don't know isn't knowledge.

On 27 August 1954 Jowitt wrote to *The Times* to state that he had first learnt this rhyme from his father, to whom, despite the difference in spelling, the Master of Balliol was always 'cousin Benjamin'. Jowitt added: 'I have always set great store by the rhyme—in whatever form—in the vain hope that people would pronounce my name correctly. I desire in this, as in other respects, to follow the example of the former Master of Balliol.' 'How he hated to be called "jow-it" ', Lord Simonds, his successor as Lord Chancellor, once said.[1]

In 1892 Jowitt went to school at Northaw Place, then at Potters Bar, Hertfordshire, where he was placed under the protection of a small boy born two years before himself, Clement Attlee. 'Nice bright, clever little chap', was

---

[1] 264 H.L. Deb. col. 1185.

Attlee's judgement. 'Never gave me any trouble.'[2] The Attlee parents lived in Portinscale Road, Putney, next door to a family called McIntyre, whose daughter Jowitt was to marry. 'I recall', Attlee wrote after he had ceased to be Prime Minister, 'quite clearly sitting next to them at a big service in St Paul's Cathedral and thinking how surprised my mother would have been if she could have seen what had happened to these three children.'[3] From Northaw Jowitt went to Marlborough, after the future Lord Goddard (born 1877) and before the future Archbishop Fisher (born 1887). Jowitt does not seem to have left any definite mark on the minds of his contemporaries at Marlborough. Archbishop Fisher remembered him as rather an individualist (he taught himself Russian), and perhaps also as rather lazy and irresponsible.[4] After Marlborough Jowitt went up to New College in the Michaelmas term of 1903. His rooms were no. 6, staircase 11, in the New Buildings along Holywell. Jowitt read for the Law School. This was not then generally done by the outstanding undergraduates. The Law Faculty was then more distinguished than it had been in the previous few decades, but not as distinguished as it has since become. On the whole the old tradition still survived that an able man should read Greats or History, and then pick up his law in the Temple after he had gone down. Jowitt's tutors were J. B. Moyle and F. de Zulueta, both of whom were distinguished as Roman lawyers, particularly de Zulueta. For his Final Examination in 1906, Jowitt received extra tuition from W. S. Holdsworth, the great legal historian, who had been Lecturer in Law at New College since 1900 and a Fellow of St John's College from 1902, and also from D. C. Cousins, then a well-known coach, who lived long enough to see his pupil made Lord Chancellor. Jowitt was placed in the First Class in the Final Honour School of Jurisprudence, the only First in that subject from New College that year. Only one other Lord Chancellor has obtained a First in the Oxford Law School, F. E. Smith in 1895.

Jowitt remained a loyal Oxonian. When Lord Chancellor, he helped to preserve the vanishing amenities of Oxford by pressing for the completion of the by-pass system. In 1947, he was elected an Honorary Fellow of his College, and was proud of the fact that in the early 1950s New College counted two Chancellors (Jowitt, Simonds) and four Law Lords (Oaksey, Tucker, Radcliffe, and Cohen) among its members. The University, a little belatedly, Jowitt thought, made him an honorary DCL in 1949. After 1906, Jowitt read for the Bar, and on 23 June 1909 he was called at the Middle Temple after being placed in the Second Class in the Bar Final Examination. He joined the set of chambers at 2 Mitre Court Buildings of which A. J. Ashton KC of the Western Circuit, author of a book of legal reminiscences, *Pie-powder*,[5] was the head. Amongst

---

[2] K. Harris, *Attlee* (1983), p. 8.
[3] C. R. Attlee, *As It Happened* (n.d.), p. 180.
[4] In an interview with the author.
[5] (1911).

Jowitt's fellow pupils was Ernest Charles, later a High Court judge. Jowitt's pupil-master was Holman Gregory, later Recorder of London. Gregory wrote to the Revd William Jowitt: 'Any success your son has will be entirely due to himself. I have never known such a worker.'[6] At first Jowitt, who joined the Western Circuit, seems to have had the normal practice of a young barrister. (Yet it is striking that on 9 November 1910 Jowitt, with Leslie Scott KC as his leader, had persuaded the House of Lords to reverse both the Court of Appeal and the Divisional Court, and uphold a pauper's appeal from the Whitehaven County Court in a case in which a miner had been injured by the defendant's stallion while lawfully crossing a field.[7] Jowitt was always proud of the fact that as a barrister of one year's standing he had induced the 87-year-old Lord Halsbury to change his mind, and ascribed this largely to the effect produced by the photographs of the plaintiff's injuries.)

But Jowitt soon gave up circuit work and found enough to do in London. William Joynson-Hicks, later to achieve some fame as a Conservative Cabinet Minister, was then a well-known London solicitor who helped Jowitt. The Revd William Jowitt wrote to his daughter Molly on 25 October 1911: 'I feel grateful to him because as solicitors to the London General Omnibus Company he puts many small briefs in William's way, and though they are mostly small cases of compensation for accidents, etc. they make up the guineas which few younger barristers of William's standing yet get many of.'[8] In 1913 Jowitt felt secure enough to marry, on 19 December, at St Columbas's, Pont Street, Lesley, second of the four daughters of J. P. McIntyre, now of 45 Princes Gardens. They lived first in a flat in Cadogan Place, later at 23 St Leonard's Terrace, Chelsea, moving thence to 35 Upper Brook Street. There was one child of the marriage, Penelope, who married in 1943 George Wynn-Williams, a surgeon and gynaecologist.

After war broke out in 1914 Jowitt wore the King's uniform: he served as an Able-bodied Seaman in the Royal Naval Air service before being declared medically unfit to serve, for reasons which cannot now be discovered, on no fewer than nine ocassions. He then spent some time doing voluntary work of various kinds. But the fact that he did not undergo normal military or civilian service contributed to the critical atmosphere which surrounded him in life. In Jowitt's case the failure to serve was, simply because he had been rejected on medical grounds. It was characteristic of Jowitt that he never troubled to make this fact known.

It was also characteristic of him that he did not attempt to deflect unfavourable criticism by service in one of the Ministries. He devoted himself

[6] Jowitt papers.
[7] *Lowery* v. *Walker* [1911] AC 10.
[8] Jowitt papers.

to his practice. He may have thought that it was a form of public service to make available to litigants in war-time advocates of high quality. Whatever the reason, his conduct was not forgiven or forgotten. A generation which exists under the shadow of nuclear disaster may find it hard to appreciate the depth of this hostility, but Lord Simon of Glaisdale sympathized with Jowitt's contemporaries:

When I was myself struggling to get back my practice after the 1939–45 war, I felt considerable resentment at those who had built up substantial practices during those war years, even though they hastened to assure me that they had volunteered for and been refused service in the armed forces on the grounds of health. I knew that many whose health was far more fragile had spent arduous years in the various Ministries concerned with prosecuting the war effort. I sympathize with those who held it against Jowitt that the foundation of his practice was laid at a time when so many of his contemporaries were being slaughtered in Flanders.[9]

Hostility of this kind had to be endured by others besides Jowitt. So F. T. Barrington-Ward suffered acutely from the knowledge that a cruel rhyme was being whispered behind his back: 'For many kept watch, and the Bar kept Ward'. His practice failed, and he had to accept the position of a metropolitan magistrate (the only Fellow of All Souls who had held such an office). In Jowitt's case the resentment was increased by the fact that his practice had prospered so exceedingly that he was able to adopt a lofty, indeed rather grand, life-style. It was infuriating for his contemporaries in 1919 to find him on the way to acquiring a house in Upper Brook Street (then a fashionable locality) and a large farm in Kent.

The only person who did not have these feelings was Maj. C. R. Attlee of the Inner Temple. Attlee had the simple patriotism which was rare amongst those who controlled, as distinct from those who voted for, the Labour Party. He had served with his regiment in Gallipoli, Mesopotamia, and Flanders, and a few days after the Armistice returned quietly to the Haileybury Boys' Club in Stepney, where he had lived for seven years before the war, after he had been forced to abandon the Bar. (In three years he had earned £50.) Attlee's loyalty to Jowitt reflects credit on both men.

In 1919 H. Bensley Wells, later a County Court judge, entered Jowitt's chambers as a pupil, and later recalled his impressions.

By the beginning of 1919 he had already acquired a very large practice as a junior, mostly in commercial cases of the highest quality. I think what impressed me most in those days was the rapidity with which he dealt with his paper work in Chambers, especially pleadings. He would read through a heavy bundle of papers in a very short

---

[9] To the author. In 1969 it was calculated that 90 out of 117 judges had served in either the First or the Second World War: H. Cecil, *The English Judge* (1972), p. 33.

time and would grasp the essential points in the case so quickly that he was able to dictate the pleadings straight away. When his instructions were 'to advise' he was naturally not quite so quick as often points of law were involved and various decided cases had to be looked up, but once had had considered the authorities he never seemed to have any difficulty in making up his mind what his opinion should be. In court, even in those comparatively early days, he was most impressive. This was due to some extent to his appearance and manner. He was endowed with all the physical attributes which a man might need to enable him to succeed at the Bar. He was tall and well built with a fine head and 'legal' face. In addition he had a magnificent voice, sonorous and full without being harsh. His speech was unhurried but never over-deliberate. His choice of words was invariably apt. His mind worked very quickly when he was on his feet and he always seemed ready with the answer to any point put to him by the Court. His arguments were lucid and, to my mind, were enhanced by the fact that never took a bad point. He was at his best before a judge alone or before the Court of Appeal or a Commercial Arbitrator. I confess that to hear him argue a case fascinated me. I would only add that I never once heard him lose his temper or even become ruffled in court.[1]

It was not only in commercial cases that Jowitt made a name. He also had a fair admiralty practice, and was often briefed in cases of libel and slander. In 1917, with E. Hume-Williams KC as his leader, he persuaded Darling J. and a special jury to distinguish the well-known decision of the House of Lords in *Hulton & Co.* v. *Jones*[2] in an action against the novelist George Moore, who was a personal friend, with common interests in literature and shooting.

All accounts of Jowitt at the Bar pay tribute to his magnificent appearance, which is well caught in the fine portrait by Ambrose McEvoy, painted (1908) when the subject was twenty-three and the artist forty.[3] Any actor would have been grateful for his superbly sonorous voice.[4] As Lord Radcliffe wrote, 'He had some superb points of equipment for an advocate, and it is as one of our great advocate "performers" that I shall always think of him.'[5] When Jowitt entered the House of Commons in 1923 he was, together with (Sir) James Cassels, regarded as the 'handsomest man in the House of Commons'.[6] But Jowitt's intellectual equipment was superior to that of other fashionable silks (to use a description now obsolete): in a heavy appeal involving detailed analysis of a transcript of evidence, he was clearly the master of either (Sir) Norman Birkett or (Sir) Patrick Hastings. The latter could be reduced in stature to a fussy little man when up against Jowitt. But a few contemporaries, such as Simonds,

[1] Jowitt papers.
[2] [1910] AC 20.
[3] But Virginia Woolf (*The Diaries of Virginia Woolf*, ed. A. O. Bell, vol. iv, pp. 72, 293) thought Jowitt's eyes were too small for his face. There are other portraits of Jowitt by William Coldstream (1946), Gerald Kelly (1957), and Andrew Freeth (1957).
[4] Well reproduced on a tape in the possession of the family.
[5] To the author.
[6] I. Adamson, *A Man of Quality* (1964), p. 132.

noticed one weak point—he was easy to knock off his perch if he had a difficult position to maintain.

In 1921 Jowitt moved to chambers of his own at 1 Brick Court, Temple, and in the following year was given silk by Lord Birkenhead. In 1925 R. A. Wright KC became a King's Bench judge, and thereafter Jowitt was the undisputed head of the commercial Bar.

In November 1926 Louise Owen, a former secretary of Lord Northcliffe, unsuccessfuly sued the trustee of his will. The substance of the claim was that certain shares had been sold at an under-valuation and that the plaintiff, who alleged that she was a beneficiary, had suffered loss. Jowitt appeared for the plaintiff, with F. D. Morton as his junior. Numerous allegations of fraudulent conduct were made by the plaintiff, and strenuously denied. Eventually Jowitt settled the case, stating that he was satisfied the plaintiff's allegations were unfounded. The plaintiff then alleged that Jowitt had acted without authority. Proceedings were brought to have the settlement set aside; the plaintiff insisted that Jowitt should give evidence on oath, and refused to accept his unsworn statement at the Bar of the court. Astbury J. dismissed the motion, saying: 'I am satisfied that Mr Jowitt has told the truth clearly and literally, and that the plaintiff's evidence to the contrary is absolutely false.' The plaintiff later published privately a full account of the case interspersed with her own critical comments on the judge, counsel, and the various parties concerned.[7]

Although it is probably true that Jowitt, in the words of The Times obituary of 17 August 1957 'neither sought nor obtained wide popularity at the Bar', his standing among members of the solicitor's profession was undoubted. Those who retained him were impressed by the painstaking attention which he paid to his briefs and the courtesy with which he considered his client's suggestions in conference. The lack of popularity which The Times attributed to Jowitt was due not only to his failure to serve in the 1914–18 war, but also to the peculiar circumstances in which he was appointed Attorney-General in Ramsay MacDonald's second Labour Government, formed in June 1929. As the events of that month undoubtedly had a major influence on Jowitt's career they must be dealt with in some detail.

[7] Northcliffe: the Facts (1931).

CHAPTER II

Jowitt's first venture into politics was in 1910, when he took an active part in both general elections of that year, speaking in various constituencies on behalf of the Liberal Party. When Lord Chancellor, he liked to recall that he had been particularly emphatic about the need for reform of the House of Lords.[1]

Some time after 1918 Jowitt was adopted as prospective Liberal candidate for the Hartlepools. At the general election in October 1922 the result was:

W. A. Jowitt, Liberal	18,252
W. G. H. Gritten, Conservative	17,685
Liberal majority	567

This was a distinct triumph for Jowitt, as Gritten had been sitting member for the constituency from 1918 to 1922, with a majority of 5,356 (and was re-elected for it in 1929, sitting until his death in 1943). He was a member of the Northern Circuit who, in all, fought nine contested elections in the same constituency from January 1910. (It is notable that this loyalty to his party did not result in either political or legal promotion.)

Looking back we can see that the war of 1914–18 marked the beginning of the decline of the Liberal Party. The war itself was a disaster for a party which was pledged to preserve peace and conciliation in international affairs and was devoted to free trade. The Irish transferred support to Sinn Fein, which was pledged not to take its seats at Westminster. Labour in its turn was now an independent political entity, the pacifists were discredited, and the wing of the Liberal Party represented by Churchill (always an uncertain factor) was moving rapidly to the right. Meanwhile Jowitt was a loyal supporter of Asquith. Jowitt's ties with Asquith were close and deep. Although a son of the rectory, Jowitt had to confess himself beaten by Asquith's remarkable memory on an occasion when the pair had a friendly contest in hymn-quoting. Challenged to repeat the third verse of 'Lead Kindly Light', Jowitt had to mutter the first two verses under his breath before clearing the hurdle. But Asquith, on being asked to give the fourth verse of 'Onward, Christian Soldiers' did so immediately and accurately. Jowitt was often to be found at The Wharf, Sutton Courtenay, the small country house near Oxford where the former Prime Minister entertained agreeable company. When, years later, an allegation was made that Asquith had been found playing bridge before luncheon at a critical stage of the war in June

---

[1] 152 H.L. Deb. col. 70.

1916, Jowitt, amongst others, protested from personal knowledge of life at The Wharf that the story was impossible.

My wife and I were constant visitors to The Wharf for several years from the end of 1918 and we very often played bridge with him. Never in any circumstances in winter or in summer, whatever the weather might be, would he ever play bridge until after dinner. He was a man of iron habit, and it seems improbable that a rule so firmly fixed after the War—as to which I can speak with absolute certainty—would not have prevailed during the War.

I was never privileged to meet any man of greater courtesy—the suggestion that he asked a colleague, who had specially come down to visit him on public business, to wait until he had finished a game of bridge with three ladies (whether in the morning or evening) is to me, and I feel sure to all who knew him intimately, utterly impossible.[2]

Jowitt did not speak in the debate on the Campbell case in October 1924, but it was noted that he went into the lobby in support of the Labour Government when Asquith threw the votes of the Liberal Party against Ramsay MacDonald.

At the general election in the autumn of 1924 Jowitt lost his seat to Sir Wilfred Sugden, who had been Conservative Member for Royton from 1918 to 1923. Some of the swing away from Jowitt must undoubtedly be attributed to the intervention of a stronger Labour candidate, C. M. Aitchison, who became Lord Advocate for Scotland in 1929, having been returned for Kilmarnock in that year. (It is a paradox that he should have been Jowitt's colleague as Law Officer in the Ramsay MacDonald government. In 1933 Aitchison was appointed Lord Justice-Clerk, an office which he held until his death in 1941.) But the 1924 election was a disaster for the whole Liberal Party. In 1922 it had obtained 116 seats; in 1923 it had obtained 158 seats; in 1924, although it contested 346 seats, it obtained only 43, and of these no fewer than 21 were former Coalition–Liberal members or candidates. The Asquithian wing of the party was almost wiped out. (Asquith himself was defeated at Paisley, and retired to the House of Lords in the following year.)

In 1929 the election was a genuine three-cornered contest. Each party managed to put 500 candidates in the field, the Liberals largely with the support of Lloyd George's money. The result was Labour 288, Conservative 240, Liberal 59. This may have been an increase of 16 in the number of Liberal MPs over those returned in 1924, but it put an end to the prospect of the Liberals being able to influence the formation of, let alone form, a Government, although 23 per cent of the electorate had voted for them. The rest of the electorate was split almost equally between Labour and the Conservatives. Inevitably all those who remained in the Liberal Party had to consider whether there was any political future in belonging to such an organization. The process of disintegration had been noticeable every since the 1918 election had signalled the end of

[2] *The Times*, 10 Jan. 1956.

Asquithian Liberalism. In 1919 N. E. Noel-Buxton and J. C. Wedgwood (each later created a peer) made the transition to Labour. In 1920 Patrick Hastings resigned from the Liberal Party, which had selected him as a prospective parliamentary candidate, and was returned as Labour Member for Wallsend in 1922. That year also saw the transition of Christopher (later Viscount) Addison, a Coalition Cabinet Minister who had been dismissed by Lloyd George, A. Ponsonby, C. P. Trevelyan, C. R. Buxton, Edward Hemmerde, and H. B. Lees-Smith. (Four of these held office in the second Labour Government.) In 1923 Haldane himself deserted his oldest political and personal friend to become first Labour Lord Chancellor: his obligations to the Liberal Party were far deeper than those of Jowitt, but the move aroused singularly little criticism. In the same year Lord Parmoor, who had been raised to the peerage by Asquith after some years as a Conservative MP, accepted office in MacDonald's Cabinet.

In 1926 J. M. Kenworthy (later Lord Strabolgi) crossed over, and in 1927 W. Wedgwood Benn (later Lord Stansgate). The case of Wedgwood Benn is particularly interesting. He wished to make the same move as Jowitt—from the radical wing of the Liberal Party to the right wing of the Labour Party, but as his widow explained, he played his cards with much more political skill.

in his own case he thought it right to sit in Parliament for only one day—February 8— just long enough, that is, to be welcomed by his new colleagues and to take his seat on the Labour back-benches. This done he neither spoke nor voted but took his leave. Within a week he had received notice of his appointment to the nominal office of 'Steward and Bailiff of the Manor of Northstead'. Nineteen months later at a by-election he was duly returned to the House of Commons as a properly adopted and elected Labour MP. It was always a personal satisfaction to him that his new political allegiance, which he maintained with enthusiasm until his death 32 years later, should have been established from the first in this direct and clear-cut fashion.[3]

Amongst those who followed Jowitt in 1929 were (Sir) Alexander Living-stone, and F. Martin. Some, such as G. M. Garro-Jones (later Lord Trefgarne) delayed their transition until 1935. Another was Rex Fletcher, later Lord Winster, who had a sensational victory at Nuneaton in the 1935 election. His background and character were very like Jowitt's.[4] By 1930 it was no longer a shocking thing for a member of the middle class to support the Labour Party. (It is worth noting that in the second Labour Government the Lord Chancellor (Sankey) and both Law Officers (Jowitt and Sir Stafford Cripps) had been educated at a public school and Oxford.) The reason was that after 1922 Labour was by no means a one-class party. At the 1918 general election all but one of its members or candidates were nominees of trade unions, but in 1922 only 80 out of 142 were trade unionists. After the 1923 election the trade unionists were less

---

[3] *The Times*, 17 July 1974.
[4] See *DNB, 1961-70*, p. 366.

than half of the party—98 out of 191. A number of middle- or even upper-class people had begun to support Ramsay MacDonald—for example, C. P. Trevelyan, Arthur Ponsonby, Attlee, Haldane, Christopher (later Lord) Thomson, and Frederic Thesiger (later Lord Chelmsford).

It is now time to return to Jowitt's own position in a declining party. He had been out of Parliament since 1924, but in 1929 he was returned for Preston, in Lancashire, together with Thomas Shaw, who had been a member for that constituency since 1918 and was to be appointed Secretary of State for War by Ramsay MacDonald. In those days Preston, like many other boroughs, was a two-member constituency. The result was:

T. Shaw, Labour	37,705
W. A. Jowitt, Liberal	31,277
A. B. Howitt, Conservative	29,116
C. E. G. Emmott, Conservative	27,754
S. L. Holden, Independent	2,111

It will be noted that the Liberal fight was against the Conservatives and not against Labour. Indeed, during the election Jowitt enjoyed much Labour support.

The sequence of events after the election was as follows. On Thursday, 30 May Jowitt was declared elected Member of Parliament for Preston as a Liberal. On Tuesday, 4 June he was invited to be Attorney-General in the new Labour Government. On Thursday, 6 June the appointment was announced. In the words of *The Times* on the 10th, 'the rapid conversion of Mr Jowitt continues to be a topic of recrimination and ribaldry among members of all parties'. On 14 June Jowitt received the customary knighthood. Jowitt stood again at Preston at a by-election on 31 July 1929 and was triumphantly returned with the largest majority (6,440) which he obtained in the course of his whole career. The decision to submit his conduct to the verdict of his constituents was a voluntary one, for the legal obligation on newly appointed Ministers to submit to re-election had been abolished by the Re-election of Ministers Acts 1919 and 1926. The Chairman of the local Liberal executive, together with the Chief Whip, Sir Archibald Sinclair, felt bitter disappointment at Jowitt's action, for Preston was regarded as a safe Liberal seat which had been allocated to Jowitt at his own request. But they behaved very well, only extracting from Jowitt a promise that 'when the next election [came]' he would not stand at Preston as a Labour candidate.

So whatever comment might be made amongst politicians or barristers in London, the electors of Preston clearly demonstrated that they approved of Jowitt's action. Indeed, it is a notable fact that during the period 1900–68 only seven MPs for English constituencies voluntarily resigned their seats on changing their party or their opinions, and of these only two were returned at a subsequent contested by-election—Kenworthy in 1926 and Jowitt in 1929.

Jowitt's severance from his former colleagues in the Liberal Party naturally gave rise to difficulties with Lloyd George. There was a painful interview at Churt before the appointment was finally announced.[5]

Some of the criticism of Jowitt's action in 1929 ignores the fact that the Labour Party was as anxious to secure him as he was to join it. For example, as early as 6 January 1927 Charles Ammon, then Labour MP for North Camberwell, wrote to Jowitt:

A day or so ago at the meeting of the National Executive of the Labour Party we adopted a King's Counsellor as a candidate for one of the Scottish divisions. That took my mind back to a conversation which we had together in your motor-car on the way home from the Richmond cricket match a year or two ago, from which I gathered that only your allegiance to Mr. Asquith (Lord Oxford) held you to the Liberal Party.

I suppose you will agree that it is beyond dispute that for good or ill the only alternative government to the Conservative one is the Labour Party, and as you know we were in difficulties the last time through lack of competent lawyers of standing.

I wonder whether you have given any further thought to the matter, because if you do intend to come over it would be far wiser to do it some time before a General Election appears on the horizon, as it would serve to counter any criticism. I know you will pardon my thus writing, and I wish you would think the matter over.

I should say, in conclusion, that I have not consulted anyone on the subject, neither have I discussed you in this respect with any other person, and it is only the coincidence mentioned above that brought the matter to my mind and prompted me to write this letter.[6]

After the Labour Government's downfall in the autumn of 1924 over the handling of the Campbell Case the leaders of the party were certainly anxious that when it returned to power it should have the best legal talent available as its Law Officers. Hastings would in any event have been unacceptable as a result of the Campbell case, even if he had not already resigned from the party in disgust in 1926. Slesser was too weak to carry the burdens of office. In April 1929 Herbert Morrison had specifically invited Cripps to join the Labour Party. Informal approaches were made to a number of other leading members of the Bar who might be sympathetic to Labour, in particular Wilfrid Greene and D. N. Pritt. But eventually the choice of Ramsay MacDonald settled on Jowitt. MacDonald and Jowitt had been personal friends for some years and Attlee later ascribed much importance to this friendship as being the source of the offer in 1929.[7] So if, in Birkenhead's characteristic phrase, 'Jowitt hurled himself upon

---

[5] Countess Lloyd George, *The Years That Are Past* (1967), pp. 121-2.
[6] Jowitt papers. The writer was later Lord Ammon, and Government Chief Whip in the Lords, 1945-9.
[7] Interview with author.

the Socialist omnibus as it was turning at full speed into Downing Street',[8] it can
at least be said that the omnibus first offered to stop to pick up a hesitant
prospective passenger. Indeed, the pressure which was put upon Jowitt to help
the Labour Party with his professional skill can be compared to that put on
Hartley (later Lord) Shawcross in 1945.[9] MacDonald may have expected to
secure competent English law Officers as easily as he had secured H. P. (later
Lord) Macmillan as Lord Advocate for Scotland in 1924. Macmillan was a
Conservative but agreed to serve in the public interest: his action seems to have
aroused no criticism.[1] It is significant that as early as January 1924 Jowitt felt
obliged to deny newspaper reports that he had been offered a peerage, without
or without a Ministry, in the first MacDonald Government.[2]

When Jowitt received MacDonald's offer he thought it his duty to accept. 'I
thought then, and I think now', he told the electors of Preston in his by-election
address in July, 'that if the Prime Minister was right in his judgment—and this
was a matter for him to decide—I ought not to reject the opportunity of assisting
the Government in the great task that lies ahead of them'. But in June Jowitt did
no more than release for publication a rather dry and formal letter to
MacDonald. The controversy over Jowitt's appointment flourished throughout
the following weeks. On 12 June a letter appeared in *The Times* under the
signature 'K.C.'. It read:

As one of the oldest practising members of the Bar I should like to be allowed to
express what I believe to be the universal feeling of the Bar.
The profession very strongly deprecates the action of Mr. Jowitt. The Attorney-
General is the official standard of honour in the profession. His authority and power for
good in this regard cannot but suffer if he has weakened his position by conduct open to
criticism as not conforming to the highest standards of honour and sincerity. I have met
no member of the Bar who is prepared to approve Mr Jowitt's action or to accept the
justification or excuse put forward in his published letter.

The following day 'Historicus' drew a parallel with the unfortunate Charles
Yorke in 1770, who deserted his political friends in order to obtain the Great
Seal but, overcome by remorse, died three days later. But 'Another K.C.' wrote
to say that he knew many barristers who understood and approved Jowitt's
conduct on one or other of three grounds—that he was always a left-wing
radical; that the parties were in a state of transition; and that he had been elected
by the same people who elected Tom Shaw, the Labour Secretary of State for
War. Then 'Solicitor' wrote approving the appointment on the ground that it
was essential for the Attorney-General to be a lawyer of distinction.

[8] *Britannia and Eve* (1930).
[9] So Lord Shawcross informed the author.
[1] Lord Macmillan, *A Man of Law's Tale* (1952), pp. 81-4.
[2] *Newcastle Jour.*, 3 Jan. 1924.

On 14 June the attack was resumed by the defeated Conservative candidate for Preston, Charles Emmott (Christ Church and the Middle Temple, brother of the first and last Lord Emmott) who wrote, hoping not to be thought guilty 'of presumptuous immodesty if I subscribe this letter with my own name', to point out (i) that the leader of the Liberal Party had said that Labour's proposals were disastrous; (ii) that the fact that Jowitt did not specifically criticize Labour policy and was elected on Labour votes was a reason for standing as a Labour but not as a Liberal candidate.

Fortunately for Jowitt his friends supported him. Letters of congratulation and support came from persons as different as Lord Merrivale, Lytton Strachey, Donald Somervell, Norman Birkett, John Simon, and D. N. Pritt.

Emphatic approval was also expressed by Lord Buckmaster, the former Liberal Lord Chancellor.[3] Buckmaster had once been an ardent Asquithian, but in later years his radicalism had become more pronounced, and he had in fact been informally approached before June 1929 to inquire whether he would accept the Great Seal in a Labour Government. Buckmaster declined the offer, which was then accepted by Sankey, whose place in the Court of Appeal was filled by Slesser. (MacDonald was determined to get Slesser out of the way: he offered him Sankey's place within hours of returning from the Palace.

Normally a change of party produces criticism from only one quarter. Jowitt weas criticized from several quarters—by the Conservatives on the ground that he was a traitor to his class;[4] by the Liberals on the ground that he was a traitor to his party; then after 1931 Ramsay MacDonald himself, with Jowitt, was expelled from the Labour Party in circumstances of great bitterness. So Jowitt found himself disliked by the supporters of each of the three political parties. It is not surprising that the file in the Jowitt papers for these years is labelled 'The Difficult Years'.

It is noticeable that Jowitt made no serious or sustained public effort to justify his conduct. His letter to MacDonald supplied reasons for joining Labour, but not for leaving the Liberals, which was really what had to be justified. It might be said that Jowitt did not regard the decision as being quite as important as other people seemed to find it. An unsought opportunity of devoting his abilities to the public service had been offered. Why should he not accept the offer? If the decision was right in itself the failure to provide an acceptable explanation indicates only a lack of prudence and is hardly a subject

[3] See R. F. V. Heuston, *Lives of the Lord Chancellors 1885–1940* (Oxford, 1964), pp. 295–6.

[4] Lord Dilhorne commented on this point in a letter to the author: 'I think that your statement that Jowitt was criticised by Conservatives on the ground that he was a traitor to his class is not right. I never heard any criticism of him on that account. The Conservatives are not concerned with class but they are often concerned with conduct, and it was his conduct in accepting office from a party against which he had been fighting only a few days before that led to condemnation by members of all parties. The case of Lord Macmillan really was quite different because the Lord Advocate is not a political figure of the same character as an Attorney and in fact takes little part in party politics.'

for censure. Some later ascribed this silence to arrogance or pride; others to a distaste for public controversy; others to a feeling that if he kept silent the storm would blow over sooner; others to a certain insensitivity to the feelings and reactions of other people; others to the fact that he was in many ways simple, 'uninstructed',[5] or even naïve, in his approach to politics. All are agreed that he never foresaw or understood, and was deeply hurt by, the depth of the reaction amongst professional politicians to his action.

Jowitt's detached attitude to political questions, which he retained until the end, certainly made his conversion difficult to accept. The ordinary man found it easier to understand Cripps (not otherwise a sympathetic figure), as he clearly had a crusading zeal for social justice. Little in Jowitt's manner or way of living suggested a similar zeal on his part. Hence it was easy to assign to him the role, perhaps more familiar in fiction than in fact, of the cynical legal careerist, and to refuse to give him credit for a natural desire to do the State some service. But Jowitt was never a mere careerist. His radicalism was sincere, if unostentatious. Even *The Economist*, which was critical of his decision, conceded that he 'was a left-wing man with left-wing sympathies'.[6] The motives for his conversion in 1929, though not easy to interpret, were simple and genuine.

The main criticism of Jowitt must be, not that he made a change or made it earlier than others, for in fact there were many precedents for such a move from Liberal to Labour, but that he made it within a week of having been returned by his constituency as a Liberal. This criticism can be answered by the fact that the constituency returned him with a clear majority at a by-election in the succeeding month. But neither politicians nor barristers felt able to accept this decisive verdict of Jowitt's own constituents, and continued to maintain an attitude of hostility.

No doubt there were faults on all sides in this affair. The politicians do not seem to have recognized that lawyers as a class have a flair for divorcing their personalities from their work. When they are in court, or preparing for court, full attention is given to the matter in hand. But when the court adjourns the shutters come down. About their own affairs lawyers are the last people to be legalistic. Jowitt not merely had this characteristic of his profession fully developed: he was also, as all who knew him testify, incapable of taking himself too seriously. If there was a task to be done, he devoted his full professional talents to it: but he did not suppose that he had the final answers to the country's problems. However, no professional politician can afford not to take himself entirely seriously. Jowitt, who had, after all, been in the House of Commons for two years, should perhaps have recognized that his decision called for a full explanation. As *The Economist* said:

[5] 'Uninstructed' was Attlee's word for Jowitt. 'But he had a happy life,' he added briskly.
[6] 15 June 1929.

Except when a new issue emerges, conversion must observe the law of the inevitability of gradualness. The change-over must be effected with dignity, must be adequately explained, and, we may add, should be coupled with an offer to the constituency in question to resign and fight an election under newly-adopted colours.[7]

Jowitt fulfilled the first and third, but not the second, of these requirements. The whole episode shows a certain failure of communication between lawyers and politicians.

Jowitt might also, with some justice, have complained of his treatment by his own profession. The English Bar is a curious body. It was, then more than now, a small, highly centralized, and homogeneous profession.

It is exactly like a great public-school, the boys of which have grown older and have exchanged boyish for manly objects. There is just the same rough familiarity, the same general ardour of character, the same kind of unwritten code of morals and manners, the same kind of public opinion expressed in exactly the same blunt, unmistakable manner ... They are a robust, hard-headed, and rather hard-handed set of men, with an imperious, audacious, combative turn of mind, sometimes, though rarely, capable of becoming eloquent ... [but] with a most sagacious adaptation to the practical business of life.[8]

It might be added that, like the boys at a public school, the members of the Bar can show an unthinking hostility to those who offend against the conventional taboos or standards of conduct, and maintain this hostility despite changed circumstances. It was Jowitt's misfortune to encounter this attitude and never to be able to rehabilitate himself completely with his contemporaries. There is a streak of vindictiveness and jealousy in the Bar's treatment of Jowitt which is not too pleasing.

The Bar even repeated unsubstantiated rumours as fact. A story achieved wide circulation that all but one of the men in Jowitt's chambers left him. When Dilhorne, as an ex-Attorney-General, was asked by the author to comment, he replied:

In my day and in Jowitt's day on appointment as a Law Officer you left your chambers and occupied the Law Officers' Chambers at the Law Courts. So there can be no question of the members of Jowitt's chambers leaving him. He left them, and I suspect that what really happened was that he took a member of his chambers with him to act as devil.

But although anxious to be fair, Dilhorne also remarked:

I myself do not think that there has been an unjustified slur on Jowitt's reputation. It deserved condemnation and I hope that if anyone did the same today, the same response

---

[7] Ibid.
[8] L. Radzinowicz, *Sir James Fitzjames Stephen* (1957), p. 7.

would be provoked. To treat such conduct as permissible would be to lower the standards of public life and decency below the level to which they have now sunk.

From time to time in later life Jowitt had to face remarks which showed that the events of 1929 had not been forgotten. Thus, on the day on which a general election was announced in February 1950, Jowitt entered the dining-room at the House of Lords and took his seat at a table with some younger peers—Lords Mancroft, Tweedsmuir, and Fairfax of Cameron. Jowitt remarked that their future was brighter than his. Their political careers would not be seriously affected by the outcome of the election, whereas if Labour lost, he would lose his position and with it his flat in the Palace of Westminster and be obliged to find another residence. 'I wonder whether there is any room in the vicarage at Bray', remarked Lord Mancroft to his neighbour in an audible aside. Jowitt did not pretend to be amused, and thereafter, whenever Lord Mancroft spoke, Jowitt left the Chamber.

Perhaps the last word may rest with Churchill. In his youth he had crossed the floor, and when asked about Jowitt's conduct he replied genially: 'He did it in the wrong way. If he had come to me I could have explained to him the technique of tergiversation'.[9] Years later, 'Somebody criticised a Labour member of the Cabinet because he had once been a Liberal. "A man who doesn't change his mind with new evidence is no use", was Winston's verdict.'[1]

---

[9] H. Macmillan, *Winds of Change* (1966), p. 247.

[1] Lord Moran, *Winston Churchill: The Struggle for Survival* (1966), p. 188. The events of 1929 are discussed more fully in R. F. V. Heuston, 'A Lawyer in Politics: An Episode in the Life of Lord Jowitt' (1974) 5 *Cambrian L. Rev.* 12.

CHAPTER III

Jowitt's first colleague as Solicitor-General in the MacDonald Government was (Sir) James Melville KC, who had been elected Labour Member for Gateshead with a majority of 17,000. MacDonald apparently offered the position first to Norman Birkett KC MP whose position at the Bar was far superior to that of Melville, but Birkett was unwilling, then, to desert his Liberal colleagues. Melville's appointment as Solicitor-General caused little surprise, but it was unfortunately not a success.

He was too clever a man to make bad mistakes, but he was completely strange to the work, and the class of case to which he had been accustomed was not exactly the best training for Law Officership. He sometimes seemed overweighted, especially in revenue cases, and his health not being robust, it was rumoured in the Temple that he contemplated the acceptance of judicial office should the opportunity arise.[1]

Melville resigned in October 1930, when he was succeeded by Sir Stafford Cripps, though Birkett was again considered for the position. Another person who was apparently considered was D. N. Pritt KC. Pritt, according to his own account, had an inteview with Jowitt during which Pritt was asked to stand for Parliament with a view to becoming Law Officer when Jowitt took another (unspecified) Government post. Pritt inquired what the position of Cripps would then be, and Jowitt replied, 'I will resist pressure to appoint him and will appoint you'. Pritt heard no more until Cripps was appointed Solicitor-General in Melville's place. Later Pritt had another interview with Jowitt in the course of which Pritt stated that he did not wish to be a Member of Parliament without an office, to which Jowitt replied, 'As I appointed Cripps I shall appoint you.' Again Pritt heard no more.[2] In the political life of the House of Commons Jowitt was a success and much relied on by a Government which was not noticeably strong in debating talent. Governments tend to rely on their Law Officers in times of crisis if the Law Officers have a good parliamentary manner, and the pressure on Jowitt during those years was acute. Attlee and Walter Citrine both regarded Jowitt and Cripps as the strongest pair of Law Officers they had known.

The work of the Law Officers' Department saw some changes.[3] In 1929 Melville informed the House of Commons that the Attorney-General and the Solicitor-General did not in future intend to exercise their right of reply in

[1] *The Times*, 2 May 1931. See also Lord Chorley in (1965), 21 *MLR* 489, 490.
[2] D. N. Pritt, *From Right to Left* (1965), pp. 27–8.
[3] J. L. Edwards, *The Law Officers of the Crown* (1964), pp. 41–58.

criminal cases. This right has since been abolished by the Criminal Procedure (Right of Reply) Act 1964. In 1931 Jowitt obtained Treasury sanction for the appointment of a Legal Secretary and an additional clerk in the Law Officer's Department. Until then the department had been almost absurdly under-manned—in 1907 the staff was increased from two to three, but the Treasury resisted all requests for further increases. Indeed, in 1931 permission was given largely because the Law Officers agreed to a reduction in their salaries in the financial crisis of that year. In order to get through the work Jowitt had to employ two young barristers as 'devils'—Colin (later Lord) Pearson and Patrick (later Lord) Devlin. The work was entirely unpaid, though immensely rewarding in practical experience. The only form of remuneration came when the Attorney-General exercised such patronage as he had in the distribution of Government briefs. At that time there was a good deal of derating business arising out of the 1929 Act, and Pearson found himself travelling from one Quarter Sessions to another and thence through the elaborate appellate structure of those days—Divisional Court, Court of Appeal, and House of Lords. In February 1931 a Supplementary Estimate of £22,000 to cover these had to be approved by the House of Commons, and Jowitt provided the House with elaborate statistics to show that the Crown was justified in bringing so many appeals.

Jowitt himself regarded as one of his main achievements during his time as Attorney-General the encouragement of the practice of permitting prosecutors in blackmail cases to be described as 'Mr X'.[4] Jowitt's statement that 90 per cent of the blackmail cases which he had to deal with arose out of homosexual offences was quoted with effect during the debates on this problem in the 1950s and 1960s.

Amongst the major criminal prosecutions of the period were those of Lord Kylsant, the Chairman of the Royal Mail Steamship Company, and H. J. Morland, one of the company's auditors, for the offence created by the Larceny Act 1861, s. 84, of publishing a statement known to be false in any material particular with intent to induce any person to entrust property to the company. 'Of all the cases with which I have been concerned, none has ever caused me more anxiety', wrote Jowitt later.[5] The anxiety arose in part from the position of the defendants, one a peer well-known in the City, the other a senior partner in an eminent firm of chartered accountants, and in part from the difficulty of establishing that the defendants had made in a prospectus a statement which was false, known by them to be false, and intended to deceive. In substance the allegation was that although the company's accounts disclosed a profit for each of the relevant years, it was not diclosed that that profit had been made, not out

[4] See Jowitt, 'Medicine and the Law' (1954), Journal of Mental Science 351; and 187 H.L. Deb. col. 745 (1954).
[5] Jowitt, Some were Spies (1954), p. 104. See also C. Brooks, The Royal Mail Case (1933).

of the previous year's trading, but by the transfer to the trading account of a substantial sum from a secret reserve built up from war-time profits. This transfer was concealed by the formula which the auditors had appended to the accounts: 'Subject to adjustment of taxation reserves'. This fact was known to Kylsant and Morland: but was it false, was it intended to deceive, and whom had it deceived? These were the difficult questions on which the Director of Public Prosecutions sought instructions from Jowitt in his room at the Law Courts. The Director is appointed by the Home Secretary, but he is obliged to act under the general superintendence of the Attorney-General. After the Director had gone, Jowitt contemplated with dismay the massive pile of documents—and the still more gloomy prospect of the results which might follow an unsuccessful prosecution. Jowitt was keenly aware of the difficulties which had overtaken Hastings and the Government in 1924 when the prosecution of Campbell had broken down. He was also conscious of his own uncertain political status. He realized that he could not afford to make a mistake. So, conscientious as always, he sought the best possible professional advice before giving his instructions to prosecute. (During his time as Attorney-General, Jowitt, no doubt with the example of Hastings in mind, never asked the advice of his political colleagues on the question whether the public interest demanded a prosecution.) First, Jowitt consulted Lord Plender and Sir William M'Lintock about the signific- ance of the mysterious phrase 'Subject to adjustment of taxation reserves'. What did this mean to an auditor? (Jowitt placed peculiar value on Plender's opinion, because he had advised Jowitt, when a struggling junior, to master the structure of commercial accounts: Sir Douglas Hogg was, he said, the only member of the Bar who had really studied the problem, and Jowitt might take his place.) Secondly, Jowitt instructed the Director to place the papers before a common law leader, a Chancery leader, and a junior practising at the Old Bailey. All these concurred in Jowitt's tentative view, and Kylsant and Morland were placed on trial. Morland was acquitted, but Kylsant was convicted and sentenced to twelve months' imprisonment. His appeal was dismissed.[6] The trial judge, Mr Justice (later Lord) Wright, vindicated Jowitt's decision by stating that the prosecution was of benefit to the whole commercial community. Shareholders were entitled to be told the truth. Parliament has since approved the doctine in *R. v. Kylsant*, for the Companies Act 1948, s. 46, provides that a statement shall be deemed untrue if it is misleading in the form and context in which it is included.

In January 1930 Jowitt had to deal with an allegation that the *Daily Express* had revealed in advance of official publication the main proposals of the Indian Statutory Commission presided over by Simon. It appeared that a serious breach of the Official Secrets Act 1911 had been committed. Jowitt got in touch with

---

[6] *R. v. Kylsant*, [1932] 1 KB 442.

R. D. Blumenfeld, the Chairman of the *Daily Express*. Jowitt told the House of Commons what followed: 'On my pointing out to him the serious public interests involved, he placed himself unreservedly in my hands', and it was ascertained that the whole story had been concocted by a penniless Indian journalist.[7] Later Law Officers have not been so fortunate in their dealings with Fleet Street. An even more remarkable example of a robust attitude on the part of the law occurred in May 1930, when a newspaper published a story that Gandhi was about to be arrested. The Government took a serious view of this 'leakage', and Jowitt used the powers given by the Official Secrets Act 1911 to interrogate the journalist as to the source of his information. 'He was merely asked to comply with the duty which the Statute imposes on him, namely, to give the source of his information'.[8] No prosecution took place.

In June 1930 there was some correspondence with Sandringham about a proposal that Jowitt should to go Canada in August as an official guest of the Canadian Bar Association for its annual meeting. The King was at first apprehensive that the visit would prevent the Attorney-General preparing himself properly for the important Imperial Conference in October which was due to consider the proposals which led eventually to the Statute of Westminster 1931. The correspondence shows clearly that the monarch's approval for a Minister leaving the country is not a formality to be assumed. Ramsay MacDonald wrote to the King from Lossiemouth on 7 June 1930:

I saw the Attorney-General before I left London and told him how solicitous your Majesty is regarding his visit to Canada in the autumn. He was most gratified and happy to know that your Majesty appreciates what he is trying to do to serve your interests. Both he and I are aware that his days and thoughts will be pretty well filled up in Canada but he begs your Majesty to allow him to carry out his promises for two weighty reasons. He *has* promised, and to cry off at this late hour would entail much inconvenience and some awkward consequences; this visit is only an incident in the general policy I am developing regarding both the United States and Canada (which I want to take more interest in the unity aspect of the Empire than it has shown). Some of us have had a good deal to do in getting the last Canadian Budget so favourable to us, and the Attorney is going over as an apostle in the same mission. I am thinking of the coming Imperial Conference, and his great ability and delightful charm of manner will, I hope and am sure, give the Government here increased influence. The problems which we have to face are very hard and some of them discouraging and we must all spend ourselves in trying to overcome them. The Attorney shares to the full all our sentiments and is heartily with me in my policy and plans. He therefore begs, and I support him, your Majesty to allow him to undertake this bit of work as he now wants to do it, as a service to you and the State. I am making arrangements that his creature comforts will be well

---

[7] 234 H.C. Deb. col. 583.
[8] 238 H.C. Deb. col. 1451.

looked after, and that, in spite of a formidable array of conferences and menu cards, he will have a holiday as well.[9]

Jowitt followed this up with a three-page submission to the monarch in his own handwriting restating the arguments in favour of going to Canada.[1] He pronounced that he felt it his duty to go and that he had no intention of being unduly rushed or of preventing himself from being properly prepared for the Imperial Conference. The Prime Minister himself wrote to Jowitt on the same day as to the King:

I have written to the King about Canada in terms which truthfully set forth the great regard I have for you and your wonderful service to all of us. I asked him to agree to your going because I want you to help our U.S. and Dominion policy, and of course he will do so. I must take this opportunity of putting into writing an expression of my great regard. You are a comfort and a joy, a rock in a weary land, a star in a dark night, God knows what consoling thing . . . I am so glad that you have won the absolute confidence of H.M. I have taken the liberty of saying things to him to show how highly I approve of his judgment. It may stand you in good stead.[2]

Jowitt had fortunately been able to obtain the help of Thomas Jones, the Deputy Secretary to the Cabinet, in preparing the necessary after-dinner speeches—over a hundred in number. On 28 July he invoked the aid of Jones: 'Notwithstanding—or perhaps because of–my training to talk to a particular point, I'm utterly incapable of an after-dinner speech . . . If you should be willing to dictate a speech, or better still speeches, for me I should be most grateful and I would promise perfect reproduction!'[3]

Some of Jowitt's work had to be done at weekends at Budd's Farm, near Wittersham, in the country behind Rye known as the Isle of Oxney, a property of 250 acres whch Jowitt extended and developed. At one time ten gardeners were employed in the grounds. Jowitt also farmed with enjoyment and skill, but without much profit. Jowitt was still under forty-five when he acquired this substantial property—a striking testimony to the financial success which could then be achieved at the Bar. Today it would be impossible to maintain both a house in Upper Brook Street and a large farm in Kent on the income of a leading barrister. Jowitt took an unaffected pleasure in country life; he was an acknowledged expert in forestry and ornithology, a fair judge of cattle and pigs, a good shot, and a keen supporter of village cricket. Jowitt's devils, Pearson and Devlin, would come down to help him with his work—and also to relax amid the congenial company, in some ways strikingly similar to that which could be found at Sutton Courtenay a decade earlier. Jowitt, like Asquith, found stimulus

[9] RA Geo. V, K. 2263/1.
[1] RA Geo. V, K. 2263/3.
[2] Jowitt papers.
[3] T. Jones, *Whitehall Diary* (1969), vol. ii, p. 273.

and relaxation in the social world where Mayfair and Bloomsbury met. As Johnson said of Mansfield, he was 'not a mere lawyer . . . he drank champagne with the wits'.[4]

Jowitt's closest, perhaps his only intimate, friends were St John Hutchinson KC, who had been up at Magdalen when Jowitt was at New College, and Hutchinson's wife Mary, who was always treated with respect and affection by the formidable ladies of Bloomsbury. With the Hutchinsons there were brief excursions to Paris, where Jowitt deepened his appreciation of modern French art. Jowitt 'possessed a number of very good things, including an excellent Sickert and a Matisse . . . and had, at any rate as a younger man, mixed a good deal with artists and had had a good deal of practice in looking at pictures'.[5] At the date of his death, Jowitt's collection included several Sickerts, three Boudins, two Matisses, two Roger Frys, three Dufy water-colours, and miscellaneous pictures by Courbet, Bonnard, Duncan Grant, Steer, and Derain.

The Jowitts, together with some of their circle, are depicted in a mosaic pavement by a friend, Boris von Anrep, which is in the vestibule of the National Gallery—of which Jowitt was later a trustee for seven years. Under the title 'Open Mind' Jowitt is depicted in his Lord Chancellor's robes. At the back there is the figure of Justice, and also a three-headed Janus, signifying circumspection and wisdom. Under the title 'Awakening of the Muses' Lesley Jowitt is shown as Thalia (Comedy), next to Mary Hutchinson, who is depicted as Erato (Erotic Poetry), which Bloomsbury regarded as a sly reference to her relationship with Clive Bell. Another mosaic by von Anrep, which was formerly in the Jowitt house in Upper Brook Street, was given by the Jowitts to the Birmingham Art Gallery. Other friends in England were Arthur Rubinstein, George Moore, Aldous Huxley, Duncan Grant, and Lady Aberconway, who was a member of Jowitt's house party when a visit was paid to Lord Beauchamp at Walmer Castle, but the party was obliged to withdraw in embarrassment at the sight of their host's entourage.[6] The Jowitts also had two close friends among Continental politicians, each of whom was to meet a violent death in defence of freedom in his own country—Albrecht Bernstorff and Jan Masaryk.

Jowitt's success as Attorney-General was marked in the Birthday Honours List in June 1931 in which he was appointed a Privy Counsellor. At the end of the previous year MacDonald had also seriously considered him as a possible Viceroy of India in succession to Irwin. Jowitt's fees during his time as Law Officer were the subject of parliamentary discussion. In the twenty-one months

---

[4] J. Boswell, *The Life of Samuel Johnson*, Everyman edn. (1949), vol. i, p. 416.

[5] Sir William Coldstream to the author. But Sir John Rothenstein was more critical: Rothenstein, *Brave Day, Hideous Night* (1966), pp. 235–84.

[6] C. Aberconway, *A Wise Woman?* (1966), p. 127. The Jowitts often entertained Aldous Huxley in the 1930s and 1940s, but that notoriously ungrateful guest complained about the Victorian Gothic architecture of the Lord Chancellor's flat: Grover Smith (ed.), *Letters of Aldous Huxley* (1969), p. 629.

of the Labour Government he received a total of £39,218 in fees in addition to his salary of £5,000 per annum. In the economic crisis of 1931 the Law Officers voluntarily offered to reduce their joint fees by £10,000 in return for a reorganization of the Law Officers' Department. Eventually it was decided to reduce the salaries of the Law Officers to £2,000 each per annum. (The full amount was restored in July 1934.) But the Attorney-General also received the following fees during that period: 1931 £12,235, 1932 £9,520. As had been remarked, these are sums 'which, although heavily taxed, enabled the recipient to forego the maximum of hardships'.[7] Yet if the Attorney-General has been successful in obtaining judgment for the Crown, costs will normally be awarded against the unsuccessful party, so that the size of the fees is not a true indication of the amount which has been paid out of the Exchequer.

The crisis of August 1931 which broke up the Labour Government found Jowitt a supporter of MacDonald, as also was the Lord Chancellor, Sankey, who wrote to Jowitt on 30 August 1931:

This is just a line to send you my heartiest congratulations. No one has such a difficult task as you had and forgive me saying so but you played the man and the hero. You have put the country and personal loyalty before everything else, and your future is safe for you now and everyone will soon recognise that you did the right thing.[8]

Apart from Sankey and Jowitt, the only members of the Government who stood by MacDonald were his son Malcolm, Lord Amulree and (Sir) G. Gillett. Cripps, the Solicitor-General, being to the Left of the party and not being under the same personal obligation to MacDonald as Sankey and Jowitt, left the Government. Jowitt himself, like MacDonald, was expelled from the Labour Party at the end of 1931.

When MacDonald formed the National Government at the beginning of September, Jowitt was appointed Attorney-General. Moves were made to appoint Birkett as Solicitor-General, and on this occasion, as distinct from 1929, Birkett would have been pleased to accept the offer. But the Conservatives claimed that one of the Law Offices must be held by one of their men, and in the end Sir Thomas Inskip KC MP was appointed Solicitor-General. Inskip was willing to serve in the junior position although he had been Attorney-General in the 1928-9 government. His decision was the source of some disgust to Birkett, who thenceforward ceased to look on the House of Commons as a stepping stone in his career.[9]

The general election took place on 27 October. The Labour Party was almost destroyed. The electorate returned 556 supporters of the National Government, of whom 472 were Conservatives, and an opposition of 56. Only one of

[7] Edwards, Law Officers, p. 109. See also 290 H.C. Deb. col. 574.
[8] Jowitt papers.
[9] H. Montgomery Hyde, Norman Birkett (1964), pp. 325-7.

MacDonald's Cabinet, Lansbury, was re-elected. Jowitt shared his party's humiliations. It was impossible for him to stand again for Preston, which in any event returned two Conservatives. He was obliged to be a candidate for the Combined English Universities—a two-member constituency whose Members were elected by post on the principles of proportional representation. (Another oddity about the constituency was that it did not, despite it title, include Oxford and Cambridge, which were separate constituencies.) One of the other candidates was Harold Nicolson, who was standing for Oswald Mosley's ill-fated New Party. Nicolson made the 'happy discovery that Sir William Jowitt . . . had supported the proposal to abolish University representation only a few months before'. Sir William was enraged by Nicolson's description of his candidature as 'brilliant adaptability'. 'A man votes against the construction of a bridge over a river', wrote Sir William to the *Manchester Guardian*. 'Notwithstanding his opposition, the proposal is carried and the bridge is built. Is he guilty of brilliant adaptability if he makes use of it to cross the river?' But Jowitt was unwise to cross swords with an acknowledged master of urbane controversy. 'Sir William', replied Nicholson promptly, 'had at his disposal no less than 615 bridges. Why should he have chosen the one bridge which eight months ago he condemned as unsound? I fear I must stick to my word "adaptability". But after reading Sir William's letter, I readily withdrew the epithet "brilliant".'[1]

But no ill-will survived the election, at which both Jowitt and Nicolson were unsuccessful. On 14 August 1932 Nicolson recorded in his diary:

> Go over to Rottingdean to lunch with Roderick Joneses. As we arrive a rich car containing Sir William and Lady Jowitt draws up. I have not seen him since the unfortunate incident of the Combined Universities Election. Instead of bearing me a grudge he is as decent as possible both to me and the boys. A good mark.[2]

Unfortunately Jowitt's efforts to obtain another seat were unsuccessful. In December he attempted to obtain nomination for a Scottish seat—Montrose Burghs. The Liberal Executive met on the 7th to hear statements by Sir Robert Hutchison, the Liberal National sitting Member, and Jowitt. Hutchison read out a letter which he had received from the Prime Minister: 'I simply must have Sir William Jowitt in, and that as quickly as possible, as I need him on the Front Bench, and as soon as we come back after Christmas I shall need him still more.'[3] A letter from Baldwin was also read, stating that it was important for the National Government that Jowitt should be returned to Parliament. Simon wrote in similar terms. But the Liberal Executive refused to commit itself

---

[1] H. Nicolson, *Diaries and Letters 1930-39* (1966), p. 95.
[2] Ibid. p. 121.
[3] Jowitt papers.

beyond deciding to get in touch with the local Unionist Association to see whether they would hear Hutchison and Jowitt.

But the Montrose Unionist Association, despite pressure from London, 'emphatically refused to have anything to do with the candidature of Sir William Jowitt or any other Socialist candidate' and expressed 'a strong feeling of resentment' at the attempt to dictate their choice from headquarters.[4] The result was that on 26 January 1932 Jowitt resigned as Attorney-General, being succeeded by Inskip, who in his turn was succeeded as Solicitor-General by Sir Boyd Merriman KC MP.

For a brief period Jowitt was uncertain whether his career had come to a halt or whether a new opportunity had appeared. The Lord Chief Justice, Hewart, had for several weeks been unable to attend to his official duties. On 4 January Sankey wrote to Jowitt:

I have had a very disquieting letter from the Lord Chief Justice. He still suffers from insomnia and says he cannot come back 'at the beginning of the term'. I fear it is the end. I hope you will not hastily refuse any offer. To be Lord Chief Justice of England under 50 and for 25 years would be a unique record and a lasting public service for the public good.[5]

Sankey's letter appears to reflect the older tradition under which an Attorney-General, or ex-Attorney-General, was entitled to an offer of the Lord Chief Justiceship. The prevalent view today is that he is merely entitled to be considered for the position.[6] Since 1946 there have been four holders of the office of Lord Chief Justice (Lords Goddard, Parker of Waddington, Widgery, and Lane). None of them had held any political office, or even sat in Parliament. When Lord Goddard retired in 1958, not only was the Attorney-General, Sir Reginald Manningham-Buller, passed over, but so also was a former Law Officer Sir Walter Monckton, although Churchill had given him a written promise that he would be appointed Lord Chief Justice on the next vacancy. There were also 'influential voices which favoured Sir Hartley Shawcross, Attorney-General in Mr. Attlee's Government of 1945 but by 1958 going pretty footloose politically'.[7] But in any event no decision was required in 1932, as Hewart retained his office until 1940.

Jowitt rejoined the Labour Party in 1936 and in October 1939 was fortunate enough to secure an unopposed return to the House of Commons. The Labour Member for Ashton-under-Lyne, F. B. Simpson, a Railway Trade Union Member, died on 23 September 1939. His majority at the 1935 general election was only 114, but the party truce carried Jowitt triumphantly back to

---

[4] The Times, 8 Dec. 1931; Glasgow Herald, 10 Dec. 1931.
[5] Jowitt papers.
[6] Edwards, Law Officers, pp. 286–308.
[7] Sir J. E. S. Simon, (1965) 81 LQR 289, 295.

Westminster at the end of October, although there was a momentary fear of trouble from a crank Independent candidate who eventually failed to find the £150 deposit. Jowitt was adopted as Labour candidate for the constituency on 13 October, the writ was moved on the 24th, and he took the oath on the 29th. Jowitt's election agent, R. Radcliffe, later wrote:

In view of the prevailing party truce, to secure nomination was virtually to be elected. As a consequence of this the selection committee choosing the candidate met in an atmosphere more tense than would normally be the case. One candidate seemed to seek rejection by his pacifist line: one of the other candidates was A. J. Dobbs who was to be so tragically killed the day following his election at Smethwick in 1945. The usual pattern was followed at the selection meeting: each candidate spoke briefly and then answered questions. After this they retired to another room to be brought back when a decision had been made. The Chairman of the local Party had the task of conveying the verdict to the 'would be's'. To say that this particular Chairman was a long-winded bore is not to be uncharitable. He went on at great length without revealing the slightest indication as to how the voting had gone. The aspirants were on edge straining for some indication as to who might be the lucky one … eventually the Chairman ran out of words and had to come to the point, which he did by announcing 'we have unanimously chosen *Sir Stafford Cripps*'; the meeting exploded in laughter in which Jowitt joined, knowing of course the real name intended. Making this incident more hilarious was the fact that the Chairman did not realise the gaffe he had committed and looked around as if to ask 'why do they laugh'?[8]

In 1934 the House of Lords gave a second reading to a Bill for the recognition and registration of osteopaths. The British Medical Association decided to fight the Bill. Its assistant medical secretary, Dr Charles Hill, later Lord Hill of Luton, took a prominent part in the struggle. It was decided to brief Jowitt before the Select Committee of the House of Lords which was to consider the measure.

Jowitt was a dominating figure. Despite an academic stoop he was tall and handsome, with a tendency to look down his nose with a slightly contemptuous expression. He looked every inch a top-ranking lawyer. He cannot be said to have begun his task with any noticeable enthusiasm. At our first conference with him, he began by describing at considerable length the manipulative treatment he received each morning from an osteopath. He could not, he told us, get through the day without it. The rubbing was as efficacious as it was delicious. The opening gambit hardly pleased the B.M.A. representatives. Indeed, as we departed from Jowitt's chambers, our chairman, Sir Henry Brackenbury, murmured to me that we had chosen the wrong leading counsel.[9]

The anxiety of the BMA representatives increased as the day of the Select Committee hearing approached. Jowitt exercised to the full the right of counsel to control the way in which he would present his client's case. Jowitt not only

---

[8] Mr. R. Radcliffe to the author.
[9] Lord Hill of Luton, *Both Sides of the Hill* (1964), pp. 71–3.

refused to accept the BMA's suggestions as to how its case should be presented to the laymen who made up the Select Committee, but refused to indicate the line of argument which he proposed to pursue. He also reiterated his belief that there must be some merit in osteopathic treatment if it had done him so much good. When the Select Committee began its hearings Jowitt exercised again the privileges of a leader—he was often absent with business before some other tribunal, and when he was present he treated with languid disdain the suggestions which Charles Hill placed before him.

Then the time for cross-examination came. I have never before seen leading counsel like Jowitt or Cyril Radcliffe or W. H. Thorpe[1] in action, and it was a fascinating experience. When Jowitt's cross-examination of the first osteopath witness began, it swiftly became apparent that for all his scorn Jowitt had absorbed not only the material we had prepared for him, but a good deal more. I can still remember his superb cross-examination of the then Principal of the British School of Osteopathy, whose prospectus for one year described him as possessing a certain high degree (no university mentioned but presumably American) but whose prospectus for a later year did not. It was an odd little error. Soon Jowitt was probing the wound. My guess was that he began his questioning knowing this one fact about the witness (which I had put under his nose a few minutes before) and little more. Courteous, urbane, and patient through his cross-examination, the discomfiture of the witness grew visibly as Jowitt added to his knowledge by interrogation. He was the innocent searcher after truth, so anxious to learn how degrees in medicine and philosophy were acquired in the United States. He was astounded—at least, he looked astounded—when the witness admitted he had forgotten the names of his teachers, his old masters, at medical school. He was so gently surprised when the witness did not know where the University of Texas was, though he said he was a graduate of it. So devastating was his cross-examination of this gentleman that it seemed to me that this alone was enough to make it certain that the Select Committee would report against the Bill. It was undoubtedly that, more than anything else, which led the promoter of the Bill to try to withdraw it. I began to forgive Jowitt— and to realise that he was worth the 1200 guineas plus 100 guineas a day which we were paying him.[2]

In May 1940 Churchill formed his Coalition Government in succession to Neville Chamberlain. At that moment the Labour Party was holding its annual conference at Bournemouth, and Jowitt, who was present, told Walter Citrine that he was willing to accept any office which he might be offered. Citrine passed the message on to Attlee, who apparently intervened with some effect when Churchill proposed that both the Law Officers should be members of the Conservative Party.[3] In the end the Attorney-General was Sir Donald Somervell, who had held the position since 1936, Jowitt being his junior as

[1] *Sic*. The reference should be to J. H. Thorpe KC (1887–1944), father of the Rt. Hon. Jeremy Thorpe.
[2] Hill of Luton, *Both Sides of the Hill*, p. 73.
[3] Information from Lord Citrine. See also Citrine, *Men and Work* (1964), p. 261.

Solicitor-General. The appointment dated from 15 May. It is curious that Jowitt should have been involved on the only two occasions in English legal history when a former Attorney-General agreed to act as Solicitor-General—the previous occasion being in 1931 when Inskip was appointed Solicitor-General under Jowitt.

On 19 May 1940 Jowitt wrote to the sister to whom he was nearest in age, Mrs Mollie Pearce, the wife of a rector in Cornwall:

All one wants today is to have one's time fully occupied and to feel that occupation is being of service. And both these things I can feel about the present position—of course it is not quite ideal and will call for not a little tact—but I'm quite determined to make it go.

I never remember four more dreadful days—and it may be more still to come. We seem to live from 'news' to 'news' . . .

I can only hope that out of all this welter there will arise a better and nobler England—and it may well be that, though it will certainly be a much poorer one.[4]

At this period of the war Jowitt had the misfortune to be convicted before the Canterbury magistrates and fined £15 for an offence under the rationing regulations. Some wheat stolen from the London docks had been fed to livestock on his farm. The moral responsibility lay with an unsatisfactory bailiff to whom Jowitt had delegated the supervision of the farm, but on the advice of his counsel, (Sir) L. A. Byrne, he pleaded guilty.[5] Several eminent persons, including Lord Burleigh and Sir George Courthope MP were convicted at the same time as Jowitt, but only the *Evening News* broke the voluntary censorship which the Press imposed on itself in relation to the matter.

Meanwhile Jowitt's political career had seen some development. In March 1942 there was a ministerial reshuffle following on the vote of confidence of January of that year and Jowitt was appointed Paymaster-General on 4 March in succession to Lord Hankey. It was understood that he was to be responsible for the problems of reconstruction after the war. As Paymaster-General Jowitt made his first speech on the second reading of the Minister of Works and Planning Bill on 29 April 1942. The object of the Bill was to transfer to the new Minister functions previously exercised by other Ministers, for example, the town-planning functions of the Minister of Health. (In 1943 the title of the Ministry was changed to that of Town and Country Planning, and Jowitt steered the necessary Bill through the House.) On 21 May 1942 a parliamentary question revealed that Jowitt had a staff engaged on reconstruction problems consisting of nine officers of the administrative grade with appropriate clerical assistance. Special inquiries were carried out by bodies such as the Royal Institute of International Affairs. But essentially Jowitt's task was one of co-

---

[4] Jowitt papers.
[5] C. S. L. Du Cann, *Miscarriages of Justice* (1960), p. 15; and letter to the author.

ordinating the work of the individual departments. As matters of policy arose they were submitted to a committee of which Jowitt was chairman.

The entire work of Jowitt's department came under review in the debate on the Address on 1 December 1942.[6] But the debate had an unreal air, for the Beveridge Report was being published that very day, and Members had had no opportunity to read it, let alone to digest its arguments. Jowitt emphasized that he was not a Minister of Reconstruction—only a co-ordinator. Hence the smallness of his staff was not very important because problems were dealt with first in the department primarily concerned. But if there was no appropriate department, Jowitt took on the task. So he busied himself with questions of housing, water, and forestry. (This proved unexpectedly rewarding: the Chairman of the Forestry Commission, Sir Roy Robinson, for whom Jowitt procured a peerage in 1947, was delighted to find a Minister taking a constructive interest in his work.) For a time Jowitt also dealt with demobilization, but thankfully surrendered this formidable task to Ernest Bevin at the Ministry of Labour when requested to do so.

On 30 December 1942 Jowitt was appointed Minister without Portfolio. This office had been vacant since the retirement of Arthur Greenwood in the ministerial reshuffle the preceding March. There was to be no change in Jowitt's functions. The Prime Minister asked him to continue with his work on reconstruction. The change seems to have been made mainly because the Prime Minister was anxious to give a Government post to Professor Lindemann, Later Lord Cherwell, who succeeded Jowitt as Paymaster-General. Jowitt held the position of Minister without Portfolio until 8 October 1944 when he was appointed Minister of Social Insurance. In fact this Ministry was never established under that name, which was later thought to indicate unnecessary support for the doctrines of the Labour Party. The Ministry was officially established in November under the title of Ministry of National Insurance.

Much of Jowitt's work during this period related to the Report of the Inter-departmental Committee on Social Insurance and Allied Services, set up in June 1941 with Sir William Beveridge as Chairman. The Beveridge Report was published in December 1942 and received an enthusiastic welcome from a war-weary country. The ideas which it embodied were not very new, and the Government had already in May 1942 accepted a proposal for family allowances. But somehow to the ordinary man the report came to represent all that he was fighting to obtain, an impression which its author did little to diminish. In November 1942 Beveridge 'received a severe letter on behalf of the Cabinet by Sir William Jowitt against premature publicity, to which I sent a suitably firm rejoinder, denying the facts which he had assumed without asking me'.[7] In February 1943 a three-day House of Commons debate revealed that the

---

[6] 385 H.C. Deb. col. 1075.   [7] Lord Beveridge, *Power and Influence* (1953), p. 315.

Government was lukewarm in its acceptance of the many implications of the report. An expensive war was still far from being won. Jowitt had received a memorandum from Churchill to this effect in December 1942.[8] But a national undercurrent of resentment at this attitude was revealed. Beveridge himself was dissuaded from standing at one by-election, but Independent candidates made a good showing at others. (Beveridge was returned for Berwick-on-Tweed in 1944, but lost his seat in 1945—the only Conservative gain at that general election.) The Prime Minister decided to act. He asked Lord Woolton, who had been a very successful Minister of Food, with a talent for public relations, to be Minister of Reconstruction with a seat in the War Cabinet.

Jowitt, whose position was clearly in peril, was offered 'another and higher position, free from politics'.[9] (It is almost certain that this was the Chief Justiceship of India, vacant on the retirement of Sir Maurice Guyen, but Jowitt would also have been a natural Labour candidate for the Speakership, which became vacant in March 1943 by the death of the Speaker FitzRoy.) In any event, the offer was refused; Jowitt stated that he was willing to work under Woolton. Hugh Dalton's contemporary comment on this ministerial reshuffle, with which it is hard to disagree, was that Jowitt had an 'unfailing capacity to accept impossible jobs under undignified conditions'.[1]

The spring of 1945 was taken up with work on the Family Allowances Bill, which received its second reading on 8 March 1945. Jowitt was in charge of the Bill. (In the public gallery was a young naval Lieutenant, F. E. Dowrick, who later became an academic lawyer. Jowitt's speech made such an impression on him that he left the next day for the Far East invigorated and encouraged.) In effect the Bill proposed to give a sum of 5s. for every child except the first in a family. It was expected that over 2,500,000 families would benefit. The allowance was to belong to the father but—a controversial point—could be cashed by either the father or the mother. As befitted the son of a large clerical family, Jowitt made a suitable reference to the Vicar of Wakefield and the Revd Mr Quiverful. The Bill received the Royal Assent on 15 June 1945, just before the dissolution of Parliament, although the first payments under it were not made until 6 August 1946. A draft Bill on industrial injuries was also prepared. As the clauses were drafted they were considered, in convenient groups, at an apparently endless series of conferences presided over by the Permanent Secretary to the Ministry of National Insurance, Sir Thomas Phillips, and attended by representatives of all divisions in the department. 'In addition, the Minister frequently called conferences himself, at which he reviewed the

---

[8] W. S. Churchill, *The Second World War* (1951), vol. iv, p. 812.

[9] *The Memoirs of the Earl of Woolton* (1959), p. 264.

[1] H., Pimlott (ed.), *The Second World War Diary of Hugh Dalton* (1986), p. 668. Earlier Dalton had told Attlee that Jowitt as Minister of Reconstruction was 'no damned good at all, and that his staff was lousy' (p. 646).

arguments for and against the course suggested, considered alternatives, and finally gave his decision. In this way, or in consultation with the Secretary, the Deputy Secretary, or other officers, he covered every clause of the Bill.'[2] Jowitt's Parliamentary Private Secretary, Evelyn Walkden (MP for Doncaster 1941–50), also testified to Jowitt's careful chairmanship: 'His morning conferences were the essence of perfection in co-partnership consultation with all his principle officers and colleagues. Each in turn were asked, "now have you any questions to put to me", at the end of the meeting—a gesture which, as an old Trade Union negotiator, I very much admired.'[3] The Bill was ready for the approval of the Cabinet on 18 May 1945, but that was the last day on which Parliament met before the recess, during which Jowitt, together with all the other Ministers in Churchill's Coalition Government, resigned. (He held no office in the Caretaker Government which Churchill formed to carry the country through until the result of the general election was known.) So it was left to Jowitt's successor as Minister of National Insrance, Hore-Belisha, to introduce the bill which Jowitt had prepared.

Jowitt had not entered politics with the intention of introducing major reforms: it was paradoxical that events had put him in charge of no less a task than the reconstruction of the British system of social security. When Churchill offered the Ministry to Hore-Belisha on 24 May, 'He said he attached great importance to this office, particularly from an electoral point of view. The scheme wanted humanising and purging of its present traces of Socialism . . . He wanted me to go into the office on Saturday and take over from Jowitt, or as soon as I can take the oath.'[4] So on Saturday 26 May Jowitt handed over the Ministry to Hore-Belisha. On 31 May Jowitt wrote to Mrs Pearce:

I'd been Minister of National Insurance for almost exactly six months—and had enjoyed working at a really great job. My time as a Minister before that had been disappointing—I had no department of my own—I had been a sort of Ministerial Office boy doing all sorts of odd jobs, but with no authority of my own.

But all that was altered when I moved to Carlton House Terrace and started my own department. I'd built up a really good staff and was getting on with the task in three stages (i) Family Allowances, (ii) Workmen's Compensation, and (iii) the largest of all, the general scheme.

We'd launched (I)—we had stormy passages, during which we had to jettison some deck cargo—but we'd got once more into calmer waters, (II) was just ready for launching—in fact I missed it by two days; and (III) would have been ready by the Autumn. Now it's all ended so far as I'm concerned.

[2] H. V. Rhodes, *Setting up a New Government Department* (1949), pp. 22–3. (This is an almost unknown, but most interesting, account of the formation of the Ministry.)
[3] Mr E. Walkden to the author.
[4] R. J. Minney (ed.), *The Private Papers of Hore-Belisha* (1960), pp. 299–300.

I was rather touched and proud to see how sorry my staff were at my going. They were so obviously sad that I felt I can't be as bad as I'm sometimes painted.

However, I've learned to take my rebuffs and though I'm disappointed I'm by no means heartbroken—but I do loathe all the vulgarities and distortions of a General Election.

I think myself the Tories will get back—but with a substantially reduced majority—and the smaller the majority the better I shall like it.

I confess to an inherited love of peace and to a dislike of acerbity and controversy—and the peace at home has made up for some of the horrors of war.

I think it's a good thing for a lawyer to escape from the law for some time—I think these four years away from it have broadened my outlook and indeed my sympathies.

I was offered a high place on the Bench—but I declined because I wanted to carry this scheme through—now that that's not to be I realise I was probably unwise to refuse—but it's no use crying over spilt milk.[5]

I think I shall get in again for Ashton but I'm 15 years older than when last I had an election and this time I don't much mind what happens.

If I come back to the Bar I may be able to cope better with the wolf whose hot fangs are getting unpleasantly close.[6]

Jowitt's pessimism about his political future was apparent outside his family. His Parliamentary Secretary, Harold Peat, wrote:

I remember talking to him just before the 1945 General Election at the end of the Caretaker Government. He said to me 'I am glad you will be taking over the Ministry after the election.' Greatly surprised, I said 'Why do you think that will happen?' He answered, 'Because I am quite sure the Conservative party will win the Election with at least a majority of 50 over all other parties.' I asked him under those circumstances, what future he saw for himself. He said 'My great ambition is to be Lord Chancellor, but I suppose if the Conservatives win I shall have to content myself by being one of the Lords of Appeal.'[7]

On 24 July 1945 Harold Nicolson recorded that 'William Jowitt is at the Beefsteak. He says he had no idea at all how the Election has gone. Some people feel that there has been a wide swing to the left and that a Labour Government will be returned. Others imagine that Winston will be back with a fifty-seats majority'.[8] In the event, the electorate returned 392 Labour MPs—of whom no less than 253 had never sat in Parliament before. Jowitt himself was returned for Ashton with a majority of 3,394 over Captain F. H. Goodhart, the Conservative candidate. Jowitt polled 14,998 votes and Goodhart 11,604. The election cost just over £300—a very small sum even in 1945. R. Radcliffe recalled the day:

---

[5] See above, p. 94.
[6] Jowitt papers.
[7] Mr H. Peat to the author.
[8] *Diaries and Letters 1939–45* (1967), p. 477.

The counting of the votes was delayed to allow the Services vote to come in. Jowitt came up for the count and though one could smell victory in the air he was far from confident whilst the votes were being counted. If he saw a batch of votes for his opponent he was very downcast.

To the Tories' dismay and before the votes had been even cast we had advertised our 'victory' meeting and also a motor 'victory' tour of the town on counting day. For this tour I had secured a smart open coupé with an attractive lady driver and together we set off to thank the voters. A banner carried the words 'Thanks, Ashton'. It was a gloriously sunny day. I don't think Jowitt relished the bally-hoo but he sat back and acknowledged the handshakes and congratulations. From time to time we stopped in some quiet spot to hear the B.B.C. election announcements of mounting Labour gains. About 3.30 p.m. an overall Labour majority was assured. As soon as this was announced I detected a change in his mood. He suggested we pack up the tour. It seemed to me that the Woolsack was calling.[9]

Jowitt's majority was more decisive than that obtained on some previous occasions in Ashton's electoral history. At the general election of 1880 both Conservative and Liberal candidates polled exactly the same number of votes, and the Returning Officer gave his casting vote to the Conservative. In October 1928, at a by-election, Ashton went Labour for the first time, and the excitement was so intense that the turn-out was 89.1 per cent (the highest ever recorded in England) and the result was made known by the firing of coloured rockets (yellow for Labour) from the Town Hall.[1]

[9] To the author.
[1] F. W. S. Craig, *British Parliamentary Election Statistics* (Glasgow, 1968), pp. 103–4.

CHAPTER IV

O N THURSDAY 26 July 1945 Attlee kissed hands as Prime Minister, and at once and without hestitation offered the Woolsack to Jowitt, who was now in his sixty-first year. No other candidate was considered.[1] Jowitt's claims to the office rested almost entirely on his position at the Bar and very little, if at all, on the fact that he was a former Law Officer. Indeed, the claims to the Woolsack of those with such a status have been exaggerated.[2] Only one in three holders of the office of Attorney-General have reached the Woolsack, and of the former Attorneys-General who were appointed Lord Chancellor in the period 1801–1984, only three (Westbury, Birkenhead, and Dilhorne) were in fact the senior Law Officer at the moment of elevation. Jowitt's position, as an ex-Attorney-General, was really comparable only to that of Inskip in 1938: each had returned to the Bar after being Attorney-General, but each had also then accepted ministerial office and ceased to practise. Loreburn, Finlay, and Elwyn-Jones were in a different position as ex-Attorneys-General who had simply resumed practice at the Bar and continued in practice until the offer of the Woolsack had arrived. In the confusion in July 1945 it was not made clear whether the new Lord Chancellor would be entitled to his traditional seat in the Cabinet (for different reasons Simon had been excluded from the War Cabinet in May 1940, and from the Cabinet in May 1945), and at the Palace on Saturday 28 July, when Jowitt received the Great Seal, he was obliged to inquire of his colleagues what his position was. He was indeed a Member, and regarded as a valuable one, although, or perhaps because, he spoke little.

The Jowitt's moved quickly into the Lord Chancellor's Flat, displacing (in a rather peremptory way) Black Rod, Sir G. Blake, who had established some kind of squatter's rights during the war. The flat was redecorated with their accustomed artistic skill, and parties there were notable for their glitter in the sombre atmosphere of post-war London. Under the Jowitt regime the flat was very different from what it had been under the Caves twenty years before, when a visitor found that the 'official private room of the Lord Chancellor of England was filled with furniture which a second-hand dealer would have treated as scrap. It was a debased and dingy form of Early Victorian, rich no doubt in memories of a long historic past, but economically valueless'.[3]

---

[1] Information from Lord Attlee. Others had favoured Cripps ('a perfect Lord Chancellor': H. Nicolson, *Diaries and Letters* (1984), p. 229), but Attlee disregarded their views.

[2] Edwards, *Law Officers*, pp. 312–13.

[3] G. B. Grundy, *Fifty-five Years at Oxford* (1944), p. 144.

On Wednesday, 1 August Parliament was opened by Royal Commission, Jowitt being one of the Commissioners. On the following day the House of Lords met at 2 p.m., and Hansard records that 'Sir William Jowitt sat Speaker'.[4] Jowitt had hardly received the Great Seal when he was confronted by the problems arising out of the proposed trial of German war criminals at Nuremberg. Several important details relating to the composition and procedure of the tribunal had been left over for decision from the previous Government, and urgency was necessary. On 30 July Attlee, by now in Potsdam, asked Jowitt to try to resolve the outstanding points. On 31 July Jowitt accordingly saw the Treasury Solicitor, and also David Maxwell Fyfe (later Lord Kilmuir), who had been in charge of the negotiations for some months, and discovered that the questions were largely of a drafting nature. On 1 August Jowitt saw the United States representative, Mr Justice Jackson, and still further reduced the points at issue. By now Britain's Allies, who had understandably felt some doubts during the election period, were convinced that the new government meant business. The result was that when the delegates met on Thursday, 2 July the agenda could be disposed of quickly in the midst of a busy day. In November 1951, just after he had left the Woolsack, Jowitt had to deal with an accusation by Lord Maugham that the charter had been drafted with undue haste, and in particular article 6 which conferred jurisdiction on the international Military Tribunal, and article 8, which provided that superior orders would not be an admissible defence to those accused of war crimes. After consulting Sir George Coldstream, Jowitt sent a firm reply.[5]

At the end of an exciting and exhausting day Jowitt found time to write to his sister:

Dearest Moll:

Thanks so much for your letter.

I became a peer today: 'Lord Jowitt, of Stevenage in our county of Herts'—but of course don't use anything but the 'Jowitt'.

All this afternoon I've been signing documents with the familiar 'William A', which was quite out of order, but it doesn't matter, as no one could tell they hadn't been signed this morning.

I'm on the shelf now, but it's a comfortable and gilded shelf and there's some work to be done.

I don't think people need fear any violent revolution—I think we're more likely to be too timid.

All my love
Jowitt![6]

---

[4] 137 H.L. Deb. col. 3. For Jowitt's introduction as a peer, see above, pp. 10–11.
[5] See Heuston, *Lord Chancellors 1885-1940*, pp. 569-90.
[6] Jowitt papers.

At the end of August 1945 Jowitt asked Sir Norman Birkett to act as President of the Nuremberg Tribunal.[7] Birkett travelled up to London to see the Lord Chancellor but discovered that an unfortunate hitch had arisen. The Foreign Office wished the tribunal to be presided over by a Law Lord and were unwilling to accept a King's Bench judge. But Jowitt, who felt obliged to accept this request, was willing to nominate Birkett as the British Alternate Judge. Birkett accepted reluctantly. Birkett discharged his duties at Nuremberg with great success and was understood to have been responsible for drafting a large part of the judgment. But necessarily most of the limelight fell on the President of the Tribunal, Lord Justice Lawrence. When Birkett read in the New Year Honours List of 1947 that Lawrence had been made a peer while he had received nothing, his ultra-sensitive soul revolted. He was not helped by receiving a somewhat uneasily worded letter of commiseration from Jowitt (who had himself been promoted to Viscount in the same Honours List).[8]

In the next Birthday Honours List Birkett was created a Privy Counsellor but he still felt that he had not achieved the position to which he was entitled. In 1949 he personally asked Jowitt whether he could be considered for promotion to the Court of Appeal. Jowitt with reluctance indicated that he thought that Birkett's talents were more suited for trial than for appellate work. Birkett was not satisfied with this decision. 'I must acknowledge that I cannot give myself to a life which consists of reading Law Reports and cutting myself off from the main current of living. I have a mind which I can apply to any case which comes before me, and in this respect have much more judgment than either Jowitt or Simon.'[9]

In 1950 Jowitt offered to obtain for Birkett a peerage without any judicial office, but the office was refused on the ground that Birkett's finances could not stand the strain. These episodes weakened the friendly relationship between Birkett and Jowitt. Birkett reflected in his diary on his achievements: 'King's Counsel, Judge, Bencher, Honorary Fellow, Master, Privy Counsellor—not a bad achievement really, but yet I cannot feel content. John Simon thought it failure to be made Lord Chancellor when he wanted to be Prime Minister: and now of course he has lost even that! Jowitt has become Lord Chancellor, but I would like to know his inmost thoughts.'[1]

Another candidate for a peerage who caused Jowitt some embarrassment was Harold Nicolson, who had lost his seat at West Leicester, which he held under the title of National Labour, at the general election in 1945. Nicolson, like Jowitt, was passionately anxious to be in Parliament, not from any selfish

---

[7] Montgomery Hyde, *Birkett*, p. 494.
[8] Ibid., p. 530.   [9] Ibid., p. 541.
[1] Ibid., p. 531. One can understand why Rupert Hart-Davis wrote: 'I wish I liked Lord Birkett. He is that frightful thing, a professional after-dinner speaker, full of smug clichés. He is much disliked by his brother judges' (R. Hart-Davis, *The Hart-Lyttleton Letters* (1982), vol. iv, p. 96).

reason, but because he had many friends in politics and knew that he had talents which he could devote to public life with advantage to his country. As he was repelled by certain aspects of the Conservative Party, his conscience led him to support Labour. In a sentence which might have been used by Jowitt himself, Nicolson recorded that 'I hate uneducated people having power: but I like to think that the poor will be rendered happy'.[2] In the autumn of 1945 there were negotiations for peerage. Jowitt himself said that he expected Nicolson's name to appear in the New Year Honours List. But apparently Addison vetoed the proposal on the grounds that Nicolson was an intellectual and not a member of the Labour Party. In April 1946 Nicolson swallowed his pride and told Jowitt that he would accept the Labour whip.

He said he thought that a wise thing to do. I said I was heart and soul with the Government in its foreign policy and that I also agreed with its domestic policy. What worried me were the Left-wing elements who seemed to me too revolutionary. 'They are what worry all of us', he said. I did not feel that all difficulties would be solved by my joining the Labour Party—nor did William.[3]

The prophecy was only too true. Nicolson, having joined the party, was given to understand that if he worked his passage he would be given his peerage. So he fought a by-election at North Croydon in March 1948, but was heavily defeated. Unfortunately he then described the impact of electioneering on an urbane and sensitive man in an article in the *Spectator* which was deeply resented in Labour circles. The offence given was so great that Nicolson dropped out of political life. Jowitt was not as upset by the manners and customs of his party as was Nicolson, who felt 'ill at ease, self-conscious, insincere, unauthentic, in their presence. I have none of the histrionic capacity of Hugh Dalton and William Jowitt. I cannot act parts.'[4]

On 18 February 1946 there was a debate on the Rushcliffe Report on Legal Aid, which Jowitt said the Government accepted in principle. The committee had been appointed in 1939 by Maugham with Mr Justice Hodson as chairman, but in 1944 Simon had appointed Rushcliffe in place of Hodson. Neither in 1946 nor in 1947 could a place for the necessary Bill be found on the Government's over-crowded programme. But the King's Speech of 27 October 1948 forecast legislation on legal aid and on Justices of the Peace—the first time that Jowitt had been able to secure a place for his department's proposed reforms.[5] The recommendations of the report were eventually enacted, with minor modifications, in the Legal Aid and Advice Act 1949, of which Jowitt later published a brief account.[6]

[2] H. Nicolson, *Diairies and Letters 1945–62* (1968), p. 30.
[3] Ibid., p. 57.   [4] Ibid., p. 178.
[5] 152 H.L. Deb. col. 79; 159 H.L. Deb. col. 80.
[6] 'Legal Aid' (1949) 24 *N.Y. Univ. L. Rev.* 757.

It was under Jowitt's Chancellorship that the first sustained effort was made to bring the poor as well as the rich within the scope of the protection of the law. In substance the Act made provision for free or assisted legal representation for all who required it in nearly all forms of proceedings before the ordinary courts. It also provided for virtually free legal advice on matters unconnected with court proceedings, although financial stringency prevented this part of the Act being brought into effect until 1959. Legal aid in criminal cases did not exist until 1967.

In civil cases the Act provided that aid would be granted once a legal-aid certificate had been obtained. It was decided to make the issue of such a certificate entirely independent of State control, even though the scheme was being financed by the Treasury. As the trade-union representatives pointed out to the Rushcliffe Committee, much modern litigation involved the State as a party, and a citizen refused a legal-aid certificate by a public authority in such a case might not be convinced that justice had been done. So the entire administration of the scheme was entrusted to the legal profession itself. The responsible body was the Law Society, whose Legal Aid Committee was reinforced by representatives of the Bar.

The Act gave the Lord Chancellor power to extend—or, cautiously, to curtail, if granted—legal aid to proceedings before administrative tribunals such as National Insurance Tribunals. It was decided to be careful about such an extension. 'If the sphere of the lawyers' work were to be increased to these tribunals, there is, we think, a very real danger that there will be too few satisfactorily to absorb the work.'[7] There were then only 13,000 barristers and solicitors in England, and not all of these undertook litigious work. In any event plaintiffs were often represented by trade-union officials. In order to avoid swamping the administrative machinery with claims of a trivial or blackmailing kind, it was also decided to exclude actions for defamation or breach of promise of marriage. 'Unfortunately it is often quite impossible to distinguish between the blackmailing action and the deserving actions until both sides have put their case to the court.'[8] Twenty years later the Lord Chancellor's Advisory Committee on Legal Aid repeated that it would be unwise to bring defamation actions within the scope of the scheme because of the risk of unmeritorious proceedings.[9] Jowitt in October 1949 estimated that 40,000 people would annually receive legal advice, and 100,000 legal aid, and that the scheme would cost about £2,000,000 annually. In 1960 the Exchequer grant amounted to £1,800,000, and in 1965 to £5,325,000, after matrimonial cases and County Court cases had been brought within the scheme.[1]

Jowitt, having dealt with legal aid, turned his attention to the procedure of the courts. In April 1947 he appointed a strong Committee on Supreme Court

[7] Ibid., at 762.   [8] Ibid., at 763.   [9] (1968) Cmnd. 373.
[1] The problems caused by the hyper-inflation of the 1970s are outside the scope of this work.

Practice and Procedure under Sir Raymond (later Lord) Evershed, one of the more distinguished of the Chancery judges, but perhaps insufficiently brisk and decisive as a chairman. The terms of reference were very wide. The committee worked hard for six years and produced three interim reports, and a bulky final report.[2] Radical reforms were proposed, particularly in relation to fixed dates for trials, but singularly few of these had been carried into effect by the time Lord Gardiner started his great era of reform in 1964. The subordinate staff at the courts were also not forgotten. Before he left the Woolsack, Jowitt had begun work on the measure which became the Supreme Court Officers (Pensions) Act 1954.

Jowitt also considered Justices of the Peace. In June 1946 he appointed a Royal Commission under Lord du Parcq with wide terms of reference covering the selection and removal of magistrates, chairmen of Benches, stipendiary magistrates, payment of Justices of the Peace, and juvenile-court panels. (Another committee under Lord Roche had been set up to consider magistrates' clerks.) All appointments of new magistrates, save for urgent cases, were suspended until the Royal Commission had reported in July 1948, and the necessary amending legislation followed in the Justices of the Peace Act 1949. It is noteworthy that all the associations and all the individuals (save one) who gave evidence to the Royal Commission were in favour of the system of lay magistrates, and did not wish to replace them by stipendiaries. The Royal Commission itself, with one dissentient (Lord Merthyr) accepted this view.

The session of 1946/7 was exceptionally heavy. Some of the Government's major proposals were by now through the Commons and had to be considered by the Lords. So Jowitt and Addison had to persuade the peers to accept the Exchange Control Act, the National Health Service Act, the Local Government Act, the Agriculture Act, the Transport Act, the Electricity Act, and, above all, the massive Town and Country Planning Act. All this had to be done with the help of no more than forty Labour peers. The strain was very great. So when Inman, who had become Lord Privy Seal only in April, collapsed the weekend before he had to introduce the mammoth Transport Bill, the task had to be assumed by Addison, who was in his eightieth year. Behind the scenes a major dispute was building up within the Cabinet over the proposal to nationalize fully the steel industry. In April 1947 a small majority of the Cabinet authorized a Bill prepared by John (later Lord) Wilmot, who was Minister of Supply from August 1945 to October 1947. Wilmot's successor, G. R. Strauss, then took up the task. Later, Strauss gave an emphatic negative answer to the question 'which often used to be asked in Left circles whether a Socialist Government would be thwarted by the Civil Service'.[3]

[2] (1954) Cmd. 8878.
[3] *New Statesman and Nation*, 3 Nov. 1954. The article gives an interesting picture of the daily life of a Minister in the Attlee Government.

Jowitt hoped to travel to North America in mid-August for the annual meetings of the American and Canadian Bar Associations. Before he left, a fresh economic crisis arose. The American credits which, it had been hoped, would see the country through until 1949 were in sight of exhaustion. In addition, the pound, which had been freely convertible into dollars from 15 July 1947, in accordance with American insistence the previous year, was coming under great pressure. An anxious August was passed by all members of the Government—curiously like the August of 1931. The Government introduced the Bill which became the Supplies and Services Act 1947. It conferred on the Government the widest power to legislate by way of Order in Council so as to defend the economy. Jowitt on 12 August attempted to secure the passage of the Bill by stating that it was a purely legal necessity to fill certain gaps in the Act of 1945. But in the Commons a wider significance had been attached to the Bill by members of all parties. It was said that traditional English liberties were in danger of being eroded by ministerial decree.

The divergence between Jowitt's statement and that of other politicians induced the King to write a worried letter to the Prime Minister on 26 August. A reply, in length much greater than Attlee's usual laconic style, reached Balmoral a few days later. It emphasized that although Jowitt himself thought that the 1945 Act conferred powers in terms sufficiently wide to deal with the economic crisis, 'it was also possible for a lawyer honestly to hold a contrary view', and so the Government had decided that the correct constitutional course was to seek legislation to put the matter beyond doubt.[4]

Eventually Jowitt was given leave to go to America despite the crisis. He wrote to Attlee on 18 August, three days after India and Pakistan became independent members of the Commonwealth:

Just a line before I leave for America to wish you good luck and—in spite of all worries—a good holiday.

You've stood up to an enormous amount of work, and your handling of the Indian situation alone will ensure you a place in the Hall of Fame.

It maddens me to see and hear praise being dealt out to all and sundry—whether on the B.B.C. or in the press—for the part they played in bringing about this achievement and not to hear you acknowledged as the chief architect.

I shall reach the U.S.A. at a very difficult time, but I shall try to 'sell' the idea that altho' we have great difficulties today, we too shall have our 'tomorrow' and that Britain is not down and out.

As for myself I've greatly enjoyed my work and look back with some pride on having been able to conduct the Insurance Bill, Industrial Injuries, Health, Coal, Electricity, Town and Country Planning and in large measure Transport and Agriculture—a mixed bag.

[4] J. W. Wheeler-Bennett, *King George VI* (1958), pp. 663–5.

I confess I'm devoutly hoping that Iron and Steel won't come to the next programme—for if it does I should feel bound to go.

It would seem to me so obvious that by doing it as things are today we should be rightly accused of fiddling with politics whilst the nation is burning.

I was quite prepared to accept Herbert's compromise—next to that for it to be left out of the next programme—or at least a scheme on a 50/50 basis temporarily—a partnership between the State and the Industry, giving the State a power of control.[5]

If large schemes of reconstruction were practicable I can see that the 50% outstanding shares might give rise to difficulties, so that you might have to add to the 50/50 scheme a right to acquire the outstanding balance in any particular case after holding a public enquiry.

But as at present advised I couldn't conscientiously stand for more than this—and I think you should know how I feel tho' I hate adding to your worries.[6]

The Prime Minister replied the same day:

Thank you very much for your very kind letter. India is really a cause of much rejoicing. If we had kept Wavell we should now be slinking out with our tail between our legs or struggling with an anarchic situation. Mountbatten was, I think, the only man who could have saved the situation and it was lucky that I thought of him.

You have done a wonderful job in the Lords and we owe you and Christopher [Addison] a good deal for the way you have managed that difficult 'other place'.

I can understand your feelings about Iron and Steel. We shall see more clearly next next month as to how the position unfolds—so will the Party.

Meanwhile I have intimations of resignation whichever course we take—frankly I don't like them. We shall get through our present difficulties, but only if we stick together.

All good wishes for a successful, interesting and not too exacting tour in the U.S.A.[7]

On the following day, 19 August, Jowitt wrote to Addison, who was in Calcutta on his way to Australia, reviewing the entire political situation:

Tomorrow I leave for America on the *Queen Mary*. I am due to come back on the *Queen Elizabeth* on the 3rd October. Clem is sending Listowel[8] to Burma and he will not be back until after the 12th September. In the result, all our three Cabinet Ministers will be away for the meeting on the 9th September. Herbert has pointed this out to Clem and suggested that it may be necessary to get Listowel back.

In the meantime, the situation in regard to the loan is developing with giant strides. In five days of last week no less than 175 million dollars were converted. At this rate what is left of the loan—about 600 million dollars—will be gone in two or three weeks.

We decided on Sunday at a specially convened Cabinet to send instructions to Eady[9]

---

[5] Morrison's compromise was to 'leave the steel industry *un*nationalised but bring it under public supervision' (K. Harris, *Attlee* (1982), p. 342).

[6] Jowitt papers.   [7] Ibid.

[8] The 5th Earl of Listowel, Secretary of State for India and Burma until the offices were abolished in Jan. 1948.   [9] Sir Wilfrid Eady, Joint Second Secretary to the Treasury, 1942-52.

telling the Americans that we were forthwith going to suspend convertibility. Hugh [Dalton] was to broadcast tonight after the nine o'clock news announcing this fact. Eady and Cobbold[1] of the Bank of England were anxious not to be confronted with the necessity of announcing a *fait accompli* but we all thought that the situation was so grave that we must stop convertibility forthwith. The danger, of course, is that the Americans may regard this as a breach of our loan agreement—as indeed it is—and may therefore not be forthcoming with regard to the balance of the loan.

I have just heard that a Cabinet meeting has been summoned for 12 o'clock today at which we are going to have circulated a telegram from America. I will add a postscript to this letter after the meeting letting you know the position.[2]

In the meantime, there is an obvious risk that Parliament will have to be summoned—indeed, I regard it as certain that there will be a demand starting tomorrow for this to be done. I am very doubtful, however, whether we shall be able to resist this demand. Herbert, whom I saw yesterday, thinks we shall be driven to give in to it. What will be done if Parliament is going to meet I do not know.

I raised with my colleagues on Sunday the question whether I should, notwithstanding all these developments, go to America and they thought I should continue on, but I pointed out that if they sent me a telegram I would at once book a seat on a 'plane and come back.

I am sorry to leave at such a critical time and had I foreseen what was likely to happen I would never have gone away.

There is, of course, no question of your coming back; the work you are doing is of fundamental importance to our very existence.

The iron and steel difficulty is still very grave. I discussed it yesterday with Herbert. At his suggestion I have written to Clem making it clear that it they go on with the full proposal I should feel compelled to go. Herbert entirely agrees that it would be utterly wrong to go on with it at the present time. His argument is this; next to coal, steel is the greatest bottleneck. If at the moment of time when we want maximum production we proceed with this scheme, even though there will be no sabotage, yet the attention of the management will inevitably be drawn off from their immediate job of production to fighting the Bill.

I regard Herbert Morrison's proposal as by far the best solution; it would give us control of Steel House and we could plan at leisure in the light of knowledge. Alternatively, I would be quite happy if it were left out of next Session's programme. Thirdly, and I like it least of the lot, I would be content with my 50/50 scheme, acquiring only 50% of the shares and thus for the time being running the industry as a partnership between the State and the industry. This would give the State effective control and at the same time would induce the management to stay on and do their best in the interest of their 50% shareholding. I quite realise that if and when big schemes of reconstruction become practical politics, the 50% outstanding would be a nuisance. I would therefore be prepared to agree to a Clause saying that in the event of our desiring to acquire the outstanding 50% of any particular concern we might do so after holding a public enquiry.

[1] C. F. (later Lord) Cobbold, Governor of the Bank of England, 1949-61.
[2] The Treasury view of the problem is presented in B. Pimlott, *Hugh Dalton* (1985), pp. 450-95.

But our practical job now is administration and not legislation, and I feel sure we have got to take drastic and courageous action.[3]

The effect of Clem's speech in the House [*on 6 August*][4] has been most unfortunate in the country, and, I am told, in the United States. It has given the impression of lack of vigour and determination. Whether there is any truth in this view you and I had better not say . . .

P.S. We have decided to postpone action for another 24 hours, but this is final. Snyder[5] was quite willing to help, but Lovett,[6] the Treasury official, was most unhelpful. We hope we may induce the Americans to agree that we are only exercising our rights in accordance with the loan agreement and that they will allow us to have the balance of the loan, but at the present moment they are sticking about these and indicating that if we default we must lose the right to draw on the balance. The drawings over the weekend were 60 million dollars; yesterday only 16 millions; if today is not too bad there will be some 500 millions left. We all agreed to the 24 hours postponement for which our representatives strongly urged, but this is final and whatever the consequence we must announce non-convertibilty tomorrow night.[7]

The result of these discussions was that Dalton broadcast at 9 p.m. on Wednesday, 20 August, making the official announcement that convertibility had been suspended. The pound had been freely convertible for only six weeks. Jowitt left uneasily for America. He was much aware that he left behind him an exhausted and divided Cabinet. Before he returned, Cripps and Morrison had made an unsuccessful attempt to replace Attlee by Bevin. Meanwhile Jowitt faced a heavy programme of engagements on the North American continent.

Jowitt arrived in Ottawa on 3 September, where he gave a number of Press conferences attempting to restore confidence in the British economy. Jowitt discovered that the Chief Justice of Canada, T. Rinfret, was anxious to be made a United kingdom Privy Counsellor, and, after consulting the Governor-General and Attlee, recommended this. On 7 September Jowitt arrived in Chicago. He kept a rough diary of his North American tour.[8]

In *Who's Who* I give 'gardening' as my hobby, and the good people of Chicago, who have obviously read this and are determined that every moment of my time shall be filled in, take me round to see gardens in the broiling heat. In the next edition of *Who's Who* I shall put 'repose' as my recreation.

[3] The controversy over nationalization of steel continued within the Cabinet for another year: it was not until Oct. 1948 that the Bill which became the Act of 1949 received its first reading.

[4] Attlee's speech on the second reading of the Transitional Powers Bill was in essence 'a forthright explanation of the country's difficulties and a call to the nation to recognize "the difference between gravity and panic" ' (Harris, *Attlee*, p. 345).

[5] J. W. Snyder, Secretary to the Treasury, 1946–53.

[6] R. A. Lovett, Under-Secretary of State, 1947–9.

[7] Jowitt papers.

[8] Ibid.

On 14 September he arrived in Vancouver and like all visitors to that city admired the site of the University. 'I cannot think that any University has such a marvellous view as this one.' He also found, as most visitors did, that the structure of the courts was perplexing. 'It is rather confusing about Chief Justices. Each province seems to have two. Sloane is Chief Justice of the Court of Appeal and Farris, brother of the Senator, is Chief Justice of the Trial Court.' On 20 September he was in Winnipeg and attended a dinner given by the Lieutenant-Governor of the province. This was 'an awful ordeal' as the host turned out to be a strict teetotaller and imposed his prejudices on the guests. Jowitt, however, had the prudence to arrive equipped with a small pocket flask.

From Winnipeg Jowitt flew to Cleveland, Ohio, for the annual meeting of the American Bar Association. On Wednesday, 24 September there was a speech by the Chief Justice of Ontario, who 'is followed by a Senator from Wisconsin. The latter rather annoys me. I speak in answer to him.' The Senator in question was not Joseph McCarthy, but the (Republican) Senior Senator, A. Wiley, who had delivered an oration of a conservatively flavoured kind common at meetings of the American Bar Association.[9] Jowitt in reply expressed pride and confidence in the British Constitution, and then uttered some platitudes on Anglo-American co-operation.

Jowitt then moved east and returned to England through Harvard. On 29 September he visited the Harvard Law School and talked to the students. 'It's a very easy audience to talk to; very quick and appreciative and I am quite sorry when it's over.' That evening there was a dinner of the Massachusetts Law Society.

I am warned that my audience that night will consist mainly of the Irish. I change into evening clothes in the club and am waited on by an Irishman. I go to the dinner. There is a large gathering of the notables from Massachusetts, including their Chief Justice and many of their judges. I make my appeal to the Irish at once, telling them some stories of a mild anti-Protestant nature and pointing out that in my Hartlepool days I always had the support of the Irish. This speech goes very well and there is not the slightest anti-British feeling manifested. I wish I could say the same about the Jews.

The economic crisis still existed on Jowitt's return. At the end of 1947 the Exchange Control Act attempted to solve one aspect of the problem. It continued permanently all the war-time powers of exchange control. The Chancellor of the Exchequer, Dalton, had more difficulty getting it through Cabinet than through Parliament. Jowitt

solemnly declared that this Bill took more drastic powers than any other Bill ever presented to Parliament in time of peace. It could only be justified, he thought, by the

---

[9] (1947) 72 *Proc. Am. Bar Assocn.* 83–4. 'Given to back-slapping and wise-cracking, Wiley had a habit of making occasional 20-minute speeches in the Senate on the merits of Wisconsin cheeses and butter' (*The Times*, 28 Oct. 1967).

most serious prospective situation of our balance of overseas trade in the next three years. The Solicitor-General, who wasted weeks of the time of my officials and the official draftsmen, trying to tone down the powers in the Bill, finally put in a paper of his own to the Cabinet drawing attention to the Bill's unprecedented character. He did his best to frighten my more timid colleagues out of their wits. But I refused to make any concessions.[1]

An appeal to the House of Lords in July 1947, *Franklin* v. *Minister of Town and Country Planning*,[2] had caused Jowitt some personal embarrassment. The Minister, Lewis (later Lord) Silkin, selected Stevenage for 'a daring exercise in town planning' under the New Towns Act 1946, which had been passed to relieve the strain on the metropolitan area. The Act imposed a duty to hold a public inquiry before the ministerial order designating the new town was made. Objectors sought to upset the order on the ground that the Minister had not given fair consideration to the report of the inquiry. It was alleged that the Minister was biased, in that before the inquiry was held he had addressed a public meeting in Stevenage at which he defended his decision in vigorous language. He stated that in future people would come from all over the world to visit Stevenage. Jowitt read this speech with mixed feelings, and was careful not to preside over the hearing of the appeal to the House of Lords from the decision of the Court of Appeal that although the law required the Minister to be impartial he had fulfilled this requirement. The leading judgment was delivered by Lord Thankerton and unanimously concurred with by four other Law Lords. The Lords affirmed the Court of Appeal, but went even further in the direction of abdicating judicial control over administrative action. The Lords held that the Minister was under no duty except that of following the statutory procedure, which had been done. Allegations of bias were irrelevant, because he was not under any duty to be unbiased. The decision has been said to endanger 'the basic English of administrative law',[3] and there can be little doubt that in the decades before or after 1948 the law would have insisted on the Minister preserving an open mind in the matter. But at that date the courts were anxious not to seem to hinder the social legislation of the Attlee Government.

On 23 April 1948 Jowitt wrote to Mrs Pearce:

Thank you so much for your nice birthday letter.

I am glad you managed to hear me on the wireless; you are almost the only person I know who can get the Third programme.

How I wish there was some prospect of getting down to see you and Cornwall and its lovely flowers.

---

[1] H. Dalton, *High Tide and After* (1962), p. 169. The Solicitor-General was (Sir) Frank Soskice (Lord Stow Hill).

[2] [1948] AC 87.

[3] H. W. R. Wade, *Administrative Law*, 5th edn. (1982), p. 438.

I knew all the portraits in your card except Bertucci. What a lovely portrait [Augustus] John made of Suggia,[4] and the Jan Steen is very lovely. All my congratulations; what fun it must be to be able to do these things.

I love my work at the Tate and National Gallery.[5] I have had William Coldstream put on to the Board of the National Gallery. He will love it and be very useful.

I have got the Tate to lend me some large pictures for my big room upstairs and I have now got hanging there McEvoy's portrait of myself,[6] Steer's *Richmond Castle* and *The Music Room*. They look absolutely lovely and I dread the day—which will soon come—when they want them back . . .[7]

By chance only a week later Coldstream, accompanied by William Townsend of the Tate, visited Jowitt in his office to work on the portrait which Jowitt had commissioned for the Middle Temple in 1945. Townsend recorded the visit in his diary for 1 May.

I had promised to sit for a couple of hours in the Lord Chancellor's robes, so we went straight on to Westminster, penetrated into the courts of the House of Lords and up to Jowitt's suite. In the corridor the Chancellor himself, on the point of leaving for some appointment, bore down on us bending slightly from his truly majestic handsomeness, arm extended with aristocratic cordiality and invited Bill [Coldstream] to make free of his office. A great room, in modern perpendicular, with three windows giving onto the Thames, decorated with a nice water-colour by Tonks, three larger and vapid ones by Dufy and others by Jowitt's sister. Bill settled me in the robe, stiff black moiré surfaces encrusted with embroidery in wiry gold thread and there I sat for two hours while Bill screwed and stretched his eyes in agonies of penetration and balanced rulers on an extended finger in the search for statements of pure location, and in the course of it put down some fifty touches of yellow ochre and black to establish a fragment of the surface of one of the sweeping panels of the front of the robe.[8]

---

[4] Madam G. Suggia, a leading violinist.

[5] Jowitt was a Trustee of the National Gallery (1946–53) and also of the Tate (1945–53), of which he rose to be Chairman. Sir William Coldstream had a high opinion of Jowitt's artistic knowledge (see above, p. 86).

[6] See Pl. 4.

[7] Jowitt papers.

[8] Unfortunately the portrait (Pl. 5) was not found worthy of acceptance by the Middle Temple—mistakenly, in the opinion of Coldstream's biographer, Dr Peter Rumley, who wrote to the author on 21 April 1986: 'One of the greatest problems with Coldstream's work is that it appears unfinished. Yet this is an aspect which is important. Most painters hide the scaffolding—McEvoy is typical, as are most portrait painters who are commissioned to reproduce a photographic likeness in paint. Coldstream is on a different tack, which makes him quite remarkable and interesting. The Jowitt portrait depicts Coldstream's aesthetic vision admirably—delicate, short, and ultra thin parallel sable brush strokes, in the manner of Degas, of low key pigment, achieved through constant rigorous visual measurement, like a laser, narrow, intense, continually probing the tight area of straight forward objective matter-of-fact painting. I have only mentioned this as looking at a Coldstream, possibly for the first time, you may not know what to extract, and dismiss the portrait as did the Middle Temple. Jowitt's portrait is monumental, powerful and noble, and is a major painting within Coldstream's *œuvre*. It certainly is Jowitt's most important portrait and any biography should include it.'

In June 1948 an Irish Government trade delegation came to London. It comprised the Taoiseach, J. A. Costello, and the Finance Minister, P. McGilligan, who had both been in office in the Cosgrave Government in 1929, and whom Jowitt had met when drafting the Report of the Operation of Dominion Legislation which preceded the Statute of Westminister 1931. Costello pressed the Jowitts to take a holiday in Ireland, and promised to provide a car and two detectives. Thus fortified, the Jowitts accepted an invitation from some friends, Geoffrey and Esther McNeill-Moss, to borrow their house near Drominagh on Lough Derg. (Mrs McNeill-Moss was a daughter of Lord Cushendun who, as Ronald McNeill MP, achieved fame by throwing a book at Winston Churchill in the House of Commons during a debate on Home Rule.) At that particular stage in Anglo–Irish relations, Costello, at the head of an inter-party government, had just replaced de Valera after the latter had been in power for seventeen years. The new Government was anxious to obtain goodwill in London, while British Ministers were glad to spend their summer holidays in a restful and well-fed atmosphere only a few hours from London. Several of Jowitt's colleagues were in Ireland during that summer.

The Jowitts, with a niece, Margot Anderson, left for Dublin on 10 August, and, as usual when on holiday, kept a full diary.[9]

Margot comes to the Residence before 9 a.m. and leaves with us for Northolt at about 9.30 a.m. It is to be her first flight except for a 5/- flight at an airfield. Notwithstanding much correspondence authorising us to arrive late, we arrived long before anyone else. We started our flight at 10.30 a.m. We rise to 8,500 ft. and cannot see any land until we get near the Welsh coast. From this point the weather clears and we soon see the outline of Ireland. The Mourne Mountains stand out quite clearly. I go and sit with the pilot. We land at Collinstown Airport punctually at 12.30, where we are met by Lord Rugby[1] and representatives of the Irish Government. The Press are there and I have a short interview at which I convince them that my visit has no political significance. We drive out to Farmhill where Rugby lives and lunch with him. After lunch, Lady Rugby takes Lesley and Margot into Dublin for shopping. I go with Lord Rugby to write my name in the President's Book. He is out of Dublin. We then make a tour of the town. . . . We return to Farmhill for tea and after tea we find it very cold and Lesley and Margot seek warmth under the bedclothes. I fear judging by the colds they got later that they failed to get it. That night we had a banquet at Iveagh House. Sean MacBride, Minister for External Affairs, suggests to me the following procedure in regard to the formal toasts. He proposes that Mr. McEoin, the Minister for Justice, who is acting as host, should propose the toast of 'The President of Ireland'. I decided to accept this without asking Rugby, as I thought he might feel embarrassed. He was pleased and surprised when it happened. After the formal toasts Sean MacBride, Minister for External Affairs,

[9] Jowitt papers.
[1] Sir John Maffey, later Lord Rugby, held with distinction the difficult office of British Representative in Eire from 1939 to 1949.

proposes my health in a short speech and I reply. I sit between Mrs. McEoin and Mrs. Conor Maguire, wife of the Chief Justice. Frank Pakenham was present at the Dinner and stayed the night at Farmhill, leaving very early next morning. It is a very good party and a lot to drink. We all enjoy it and are sorry when Lesley, urged thereunto by Rugby, tells us it is time to go.

The following day the party set off for Lough Derg. An idle Irish holiday was enjoyed by all. Not much interrupted the placid routine of fishing, visits to neighbours, and excursions to places of interest.

In the autumn of 1948 many legal and political difficulties arose out of the Irish Government's decision to make Eire an independent republic outside the Commonwealth. The decision was announced without warning and Jowitt, who thought he had established friendly relations with Costello and MacBride during the previous summer, felt aggrieved that he had been taken by surprise. It was decided, however, to recognize the special position of Irish citizens in the United Kingdom, and their contribution to its economy, by a provision to the effect that although not British subjects they were not to be treated as aliens. British subjects in Ireland were to enjoy comparable, but not identical, privileges. The task of explaining this complex legislation strained even Jowitt's powers of exposition.

On quite a different topic, Jowitt was much troubled by the Married Women (Restraint upon Anticipation) Act 1949. It arose in a curious way. The old common law gave all a married woman's property to her husband. Equity invented the device of the restraint on anticipation, whereby before marriage her separate property could be put in trust with the result that she would be entitled to the income as it accrued due, but would not be entitled to anticipate those periodical payments, or to alienate the capital. When the equality of the sexes was recognized, the doctrine was no longer needed, and was abolished by the Law Reform (Married Women and Tortfeasors) Act 1935—but only for interests arising under post-1935 settlements. Older settlements were still subject to the doctrine. One such settlement was that made by Lord Mount Temple, the financier, when his daughter married Lord Louis Mountbatten. After the war Lady Mountbatten desired to realize some of her capital but found she could not do so. A private Bill to give her this power met with objections. It was said that the hardship, if it existed, should be removed for all and not only for one. The Government felt obliged to accept this argument and introduced the necessary Bill. It was a strange position for a Labour Government, as its critics gleefully pointed out. The only beneficiaries of the Act would be people of wealth. But the Government pressed on: apart from its obligations to the Mountbatten family for their work in India, it felt that a genuine point of principle was involved: the restraint on anticipation was an obsolete device and should be abolished completely. But Lord Simon opposed the Bill on the grounds that it was retrospective and unequal as between men and women. The composure which had sustained Jowitt through the lengthy nationalization debates deserted him. He lost his temper and exchanged some hot remarks with Simon. Then support for the Government came from an unexpected quarter. Lord Maugham, whose distinction as a Chancery lawyer was equalled only by the depth of his conservatism, intervened to state that Simon had confused the two perfectly distinct devices of the restraint on anticipation and the discretionary trust. It would still be possible for a settlor to protect his spendthrift daughter (or son) by establishing a trust under which payments would be made to the beneficiaries in the absolute discretion of the trustees. Indeed, a discretionary trust had many advantages over the restraint on anticipation, particularly in regard to taxation. Maugham was pleased to say that Jowitt's account of the problem was 'perfectly correct'. Thus supported, Jowitt, by now, in his own words, 'somewhat warm', described Simon's speech as 'wholly lamentable'.[2] Tempers were not improved when, on the committee stage, Lord Simonds gave vigorous support to Jowitt, and appeared to take some pleasure in pointing out the deficiencies in Simon's knowledge of Chancery practice. In a strained atmosphere the Bill passed by 28 to 23.

In September 1949 the Lord Chancellor's function as supreme legal adviser to the Cabinet was well illustrated by the part which Jowitt took in investigating the Sidney Stanley affair.[3] A junior minister at the Board of Trade was alleged to have abused his official position by granting licences improperly to a businessman. Jowitt made a preliminary inquiry 'at the request of the President of the Board of Trade and with the concurrence of the Prime Minister', and as a result recommended to Attlee that there was unfortunately enough suspicion to justify the establishment of a tribunal of inquiry. The Attorney-General, Sir Hartley Shawcross, appeared as counsel for the tribunal, and by his severe cross-examination of his ministerial colleagues showed that the Law Officers could place their duty to the public above their loyalty to their party.

In February 1950 Parliament was dissolved and the Labour Party was returned to power but with a greatly reduced majority. Attlee continued as Prime Minister and invited Jowitt to remain in office. Jowitt replied on 1 March 1950:

Thanks for your letter telling me you want me to go on as Lord Chancellor. I regard this as an honour because it shows that I have your confidence.

I believe that the record of your administration in the field of Law Reform is quite unparallelled—Crown Proceedings, Legal Aid, Criminal Justice, Justices of the Peace— to mention only a few.

[2] 163 H.L. Deb. col. 916.
[3] For an account of this bizarre affair, see S. W. Baron, *The Contact Man* (1966).

Moreover, we've done more in the way of Consolidation and Statute Law Revision than any previous Government, but much though we've done there's still much to do: and the recent Hignett case[4] has demonstrated that the increasing use of Commissioners is both costly and unsatisfactory.[5]

I shall have to ask for power to appoint more Judges. Stafford entirely agrees. The Attorney-General is enthusiastic, and I think that Herbert sees the need—always provided that we don't mix it up with the questions of salary or pensions.

I've enjoyed my work here. Everybody should be happy working under Christopher [Addison]—a very dear and a very wise old thing. Long may he reign over us.

For myself I confess that I shouldn't have been the least bit distressed had you decided to appoint some younger man—by nature I'm afraid I'm lazy—and by circumstance I've never yet had a chance of indulging in that vice—which, perhaps for that reason seems very attractive.

I'm so glad at the greatly enhanced position which you have won for yourself in the country—both by your conduct of affairs over the last 4½ years and not least by your conduct of the recent election.[6]

The appointment of six new High Court judges, bringing the maximum number up from thirty-three to thirty-nine, was duly authorized by the High Court and County Court Judges Act 1950.

Attlee always found Jowitt a loyal Cabinet colleague, although when the question of finding a successor to Bevin as Foreign Secretary was first discussed in 1951 Jowitt favoured Shawcross rather than Morrison, and caused some embarrassment by telling Shawcross prematurely that he had been appointed.[7] Shawcross had for some time been unhappy in his position as Attorney-General. Attlee was unwilling to appoint him Foreign Secretary but instead in March 1951 offered him the judicial vacancy opened up by Lord MacDermott's decision to return to Northern Ireland as Lord Chief Justice. Jowitt wrote urgently to Shawcross. 'Please don't do anything rash. Remember Disraeli's advice. You have only got a few months more of endurance and then the ball is at your feet. I am sure you would be terribly sorry if in the prime of life you gave up the struggle to sit in the silence and obscurity of the upper shelf.'[8] Shawcross refused the offer, but in April became President of the Board of Trade.

Jowitt's detached attitude to political matters was always a source of wonder to friends as well as opponents. Lord Longford wrote of him: 'It was true, of course, that he was short of Party feeling, but he performed prodigies for the Labour Party ... He was a most modest, friendly, unpompous, civilised,

---

[4] Hignett was an ex-solicitor and ex-coroner who had been convicted before Mr Commissioner (later His Honour Judge) Reginald Clark in December 1949. On appeal a new trial was ordered, and this lasted into May 1950.

[5] In 1949 Jowitt had appointed 15 Commissioners, who sat for 283 days (166 H.L. Deb. col. 954).

[6] Jowitt papers.

[7] Dalton, High Tide, p. 360. Lady Jowitt did not accept the accuracy of Dalton's story.

[8] Jowitt papers.

humorous man to sit next to hour after hour on the front bench."[9] To some extent Jowitt's detachment was an advantage in the House of Lords when he had to deal with an overwhelmingly Conservative assembly. But his natural detachment was reinforced by the skill of the successful advocate. He was fond of saying that the secret of advocacy was to discover the worst thing one's opponent could say about one's case, and then to say it oneself. So he managed to give the peers the impression that he found the social legislation of the Attlee Government every bit as distasteful as they did, that it was only with great difficulty that he had succeeded in holding in check yet more revolutionary proposals, and that if the House was unable to accept the present Bill a measure even more disastrous might be put before it. On such legislation Jowitt was accustomed to spend hours behind the scenes negotiating with the representatives of both parties. For example, on the committee stage of the Companies Act 1948 no fewer than 410 amendments were proposed, 360 of which were accepted by the Government. On the Town and Country Planning Bill there were 289 Government amendments and 47 opposition amendments. All this necessitated consultations, some of them lasting late into the night, but Jowitt placed considerable weight on the value of inviting opposition peers to talk over difficulties in his room. Indeed, the importance of the House of Lords in the legislative procedure of those years is illustrated by the fact that in 1946/7 no fewer than 1,222 amendments were moved in the House of Lords by both parties, and only 57 of these, 42 of them on the Transport Bill, were rejected by the House of Commons.[1] By now the Labour Party had fully accepted the value of the House of Lords as a revising chamber.

Much of Jowitt's time as Lord Chancellor was taken up with a sustained effort to improve the form of the statute-book. This was law reform which attracted little publicity or credit, but was of great value to the community as well as to the legal profession. It was a problem with a long history. Under the influence of Benthamite ideas two Royal Commissions were appointed, in 1833 and 1845, with a view to preparing a complete code. The second Commission produced a draft Bill, but it was never submitted to Parliament. Cranworth recognized that the revision of the statute-book by the repeal of obsolete enactments was a process different from that of consolidating the Acts in force. His Statute Law Revision Board of 1853 was succeeded in the following year by the Statute Law Commission, presided over by the Lord Chancellor himself, and including Lyndhurst, Brougham, Pollock, Parke, and Ker among its members. This body produced four useful reports, the Statute Law Revision Acts of 1857 and 1861, and four large Criminal Law Consolidation Acts in 1861. Westbury in the 1860s gave further impetus to the programme of consolidation

---

[9] Earl of Longford, *Five Lives* (1964), p. 81.
[1] 156 H.L. Deb. col. 450; 179 H.L. Deb. col. 531.

and revision. The result was that between 1861 and 1898 no fewer than thirty-two Statute Law Revision acts were passed. In 1870 the first edition of that indispensable tool, the *Chronological Table and Index to the Statutes*, was published. In 1868 Cairns set up the Statute Law Committee to prepare 'an edition of Statutes Revised'. A century later the committee still exists, but with wider functions. The committee also dealt with consolidation, but here progress was slower. the causes were lack of draftsmen, failure to secure the co-operation of the departments, and pressure on parliamentary time. The second edition of *Statutes Revised*, in forty volumes, was published at intervals between 1888 and 1929.

When Jowitt came to the Woolsack and reviewed the position he found that 'It [was] no exaggeration to say that the condition of the Statute Book was a scandal'.[2] He decided that statute law reform should receive a prominent place in Parliament and the Cabinet, and in 1946 secured Cabinet approval for the following recommendations:

1 That the general superintendence of revision and consolitation should remain with the Statute Law Committee, though its membership should be strengthened.
2 That a definite place should be given to consolidation Bills in the legislative programme for each session.
3 That the machinery for enacting consolidation Bills should be improved.
4 That a separate Consolidation Branch should be established in the Parliamentary Counsel's Office.

The Statute Law Committee was reconstituted with Sir Granville Ram[3] as Chairman, and Sir Robert Drayton[4] was appointed Director of the Statutory Publications Office.

The work of consolidation now moved swiftly ahead. The Consolidation of Enactments (Procedure) Act 1949 provided that consolidation Bills should be referred to a joint committee of both Houses which should have power to make corrections and minor improvements for resolving ambiguities and removing doubts or unnecessary provisions or anomalies. If both the Lord Chancellor and the Speaker certified that the corrections were truly minor, and did not require separate enactment, the Bill became law. This Act was an important instrument for the enactment of large measures of consolidation. The Act is also a good example of Jowitt's technique of legislation by consultation. The idea came from the fertile mind of Ram, but Jowitt was careful to secure the consent of all parties, and in particular of Simon, before the second reading. In effect, the 1949

---

[2] Jowitt, *Statute Law Revision* (Birmingham, 1951), p. 13.
[3] First Parliamentary Counsel, 1937-47.
[4] Formerly Attorney-General of Tanganyika, and Chief Secretary of Ceylon.

Act meant that consolidation Bills took a short cut through the ordinary parliamentary procedure. In return for this both Houses required the joint committee's certificate that such Bills made no changes in existing law. On the whole, successive joint committees have taken a very cautious view of the scope of their powers. In particular, the power to remove doubts has been very restrictively construed.

Statute-law revision was an even more difficult task. Because of the arrears which had accumulated during the war, it was decided not to await the enactment of the consolidation Bills already in the pipeline, but to press ahead with the publication of a new edition of *Statutes Revised*, of which all the volumes would be published simultaneously. After the ground had been cleared by the immensely detailed Statute Law Revision Acts of 1948 and 1950, the latter affecting 1,350 statutes and covering 149 pages, the third edition of *Statutes Revised*, in thirty-two volumes, was published in January 1951. (The title-pages are dated 1950, but copies were not available until the New Year.) At the same time there was published a volume of *Church Assembly Measures* and a *Chronological Table and Index* in two volumes. One figure alone shows the scale of the achievement: the statutes were now contained in 28,000 pages, instead of 40,000. The whole series was favourably reviewed in the *Law Quarterly Review* by Sir Cecil Carr QC,[5] the former editor of *Statutory Rules and Orders*, and probably the leading expert in the country on the whole subject of statutes, their draftsmanship, publication, and interpretation.

Unfortunately the edition was a commercial failure. By 1955 fewer than a thousand sets had been sold, and the Treasury lost over £62,000 on the venture. There were several reasons for this. One was that Jowitt's edition was arranged chronologically, whereas the rival edition by Butterworths was arranged by subject-matter, and accompanied by a commentary. The fact that this commentary is often of indifferent quality does not detract from its usefulness in the eyes of the ordinary practitioner. Any commentary is better than none, and psychologically a text broken up by a commentary is easier to read than an unbroken text. Butterworths also had an efficient 'noter-up' system. The Statutory Publications Office prepared annually a 'noter-up' volume for *Statutes Revised*, but the result was ugly in appearance. Also Jowitt in his foreword had stated—most unwisely, as he later admitted—that the third edition might be superseded by a fourth edition. 'Why should a man pay £65 when he is warned that in a few years his purchase will be superseded by something better?' Another reason was that as the edition closed with the year 1948 only four of the great post-war consolidation statutes could be included. It was indeed a disadvantage to have an edition of *Statutes Revised* which omitted the Income Tax Act 1952—indispensable to any practitioner.

[5] (1951) 67 *LQR* 482.

On the other hand, *Statutory Instruments Revised*, which had been published in twenty-four volumes at the same time as *Statutes Revised* had been a success. It was true that the sales of *Statutory Instruments Revised* had been minimal (just over two hundred sets of twenty-five volumes at 55 guineas a set), but it was acclaimed as an indispensable tool by Governments and law libraries. This was partly because the arrangement was by subject-matter and not by date, and partly because statutory instruments lasted for a shorter time than statutes, and once revoked, rarely needed to be referred to again.

Jowitt reformed the substantive law as well as the structure and procedure of the legal system. A major reform was in the field of legal proceedings by and against the Crown. At common law the Crown could not be sued at all in tort, and in contract only by the cumbrous procedure of Petition of Right. By the middle of the twentieth century these immunities were increasingly irksome, for the Crown had become the largest employer of labour and occupier of property in the country. Several Lord Chancellors attempted to solve the problem. Birkenhead in 1921 appointed a committee to consider the question, and Haldane in 1924 gave it his support. In 1927 the committee published a draft Bill, but this was dropped as a result of opposition from the Post Office and service departments. Jowitt decided to act. A comprehensive Bill, based on the draft Bill of 1927, was prepared by the Treasury Solicitor himself, as Parliamentary Counsel were fully occupied with the massive governmental programme of social legislation. This Bill was then examined by an informal committee of Law Lords and others presided over by Simon. So Jowitt's Bill became the Crown Proceedings Act 1947.

Jowitt's judicial appointments are generally regarded as admirable. There was never the slightest suggestion that his appointments to superior courts were in any way influenced by political considerations, though the Labour Whips had a few candidates to put forward after so many years out of office. The disappointment expressed at the paucity of socialist lawyers of High Court calibre ignores the fact that one very suitable candidate, L. Ungoed-Thomas KC MP, expressly refused an offer on the ground that he did not wish to leave his party at a moment when its fortunes were at a low ebb. (He must surely have recalled the events of 1929 when he told Jowitt this, and felt some sly satisfaction. In 1951 Ungoed-Thomas was Solicitor-General from April to October; in 1962 Kilmuir made him a High Court judge.)[6] The only Labour MP in fact to be made a High Court judge, T. Donovan KC (later a Law Lord) in July 1950, had the highest professional standing at the Revenue Bar.[7] One appointment to

---

[6] Ungoed-Thomas was more than a lawyer-politician: he 'was a great master of equity' (*Cornhill Insurance p.l.c.* v. *Improvement Services Ltd.* [1986] 1 WLR 114, at 118, per Harman J.

[7] Almost the only objection Jowitt had to Donovan was that he had been a member of the Haldane Society.

a recordership in Yorkshire may have been due to political pressure, but this is the sole criticism which has ever been made. After he had left office, Jowitt wrote:

I think that I can fairly say that we have established a tradition in which 'politics' and 'influence' are now completely disregarded. The Lord Chancellor selects the man whom he believes to be best able to fill the position. In my own case I had an unusually large number of appointments, and I can only recall appointing two men who were members of my own party.

You must remember these facts which help in establishing the tradition. The Inns of Court are completely independent of any governmental control. The Lord Chancellor has always been a barrister, and must be a barrister, and must therefore be a member of one of the Inns. He is in close touch with all that goes on in his Inn of Court. How should I have felt if I had made a lot of unworthy appointments, when I noticed the cold looks that I should have received when next I went to lunch at the Inn.

Secondly, in practice the Lord Chancellor would always consult with the Head of the Division to which he was called on to appoint a judge . . .[8]

The tradition that judicial appointments should not be influenced by political considerations is not of long duration in England. It certainly did not exist in the Chancellorship of Halsbury, although his appointments are not in truth open to the criticism which has often been levied against them. But under Haldane there was a change for the better, and by the time Hailsham held the Great Seal it was established that appointments should be based on professional merit alone. Jowitt built upon this foundation and established the principle of non-political appointments so firmly that it probably can not be questioned again in England.

In Jowitt's period as Lord Chancellor seven out of nine Law Lords, the Lord Chief Justice, the Master of the Rolls, all eight Lord Justices of Appeal, twenty-five out of thirty-seven High Court judges, and twenty-eight out of sixty-three County Court judges were appointed. The complete list of Jowitt's High Court appointments is as follows:

Queen's Bench Division: Morris, Lloyd-Jones, Byrne, Sellers, Finnemore, Streatfeild, Ormerod, Slade, Pearce, Devlin, Parker, Gorman, Barry, Donovan, McNair, Havers, Pearson.
Chancery Division: Jenkins, Roxburgh, Harman, Danckwerts, Lloyd-Jacob.
Probate, Divorce, and Admiralty: Willmer, Collingwood, Karminski.

Seven of these were not in silk at the date of their appointment—four because they were already on the County Court Bench (Lloyd-Jones, Finnemore, Ormerod, and Collingwood), two because they had been Treasury devils

---

[8] M. Erskine (1953) 39 *ABAJ* 279. Lord Gardiner has stated that Jowitt 'rather leaned over backwards never to appoint Labour men': (1969) *NZLJ* 171, 173.

(Parker and Danckwerts), and one (Byrne) because he had been Senior Treasury Counsel at the Old Bailey. Jowitt also appointed eleven judges who died or retired while he was still in office. The grand total of judicial appointments is, therefore, eighty-two. (England then had fewer judges than any comparable country. In 1871 there were eighteen Queen's Bench judges for a population of twenty-two million; in 1948 there were twenty for a population of forty-three million. When Jowitt left office in 1951 the increase in judges was comparable to the rise in population: there were thirty-nine High Court judges, twenty-one of them in the King's Bench Division.) This large number of appointments naturally cast a great burden on Jowitt, even though only the High Court and County Court judgeships were his constitutional responsibility, for Attlee made it a practice to consult closely with him before making any of the other appointments. For example, it was Jowitt who suggested Mr Justice Asquith to Attlee for promotion, both to the Court of Appeal and to the House of Lords, although at the Bar Asquith had no great practice. But Asquith was known to Jowitt because at the request of his father he had taken him as a pupil. 'Lord Maugham, very wisely, appointed him a judge, and Lord Simon, whose judgment on these matters was of the highest value, told me that he thought Asquith possessed the most distinguished mind of any judge on the Bench— with this view I agreed.'[9] But some law teachers were disappointed that Jowitt expressly refused to consider appointing to the Bench one of their number, although pressed to do so by Arthur Goodhart.[1] Instead, Attlee deserves as much credit as Jowitt for impartiality, for in one month in 1946 he appointed as Lord Chief Justice a former Conservative candidate (Goddard); and to the Court of Appeal a former Conservative Law Officer (D. B. Somervell). In 1948 Attlee appointed a former Conservative Lord Advocate, J. S. C. Reid, to the House of Lords.

The appointment of magistrates is one of the most difficult tasks which any Lord Chancellor has to perform. In a perfect world it would not have been easy to secure a proper balance between the political parties, for in the nature of things those who had the experience and, above all, the time, to enable them to discharge the duties of the unpaid magistracy were more likely to be supporters of the Conservative than of the Labour Party. But the difficulties of an imperfect world had been much increased by Halsbury's consistent refusal to appoint anyone who was not a Conservative. This had produced by 1905 a striking imbalance in the representation of the political parties on the magisterial bench. Loreburn, Haldane, and Sankey had consistently refused to correct this disproportion by the mass creation of Liberal or Labour supporters.

---

[9] *The Times*, 26 Aug. 1954.
[1] Speeches by Goodhart and Jowitt at the Annual Dinner of the Society of Public Teachers of Law in Lincoln's Inn on 14 July 1950 (not recorded in (1950) 1 *JSPTL* 369, but heard by the author).

Their policy had always been to appoint the best candidate. This policy was honourable and praiseworthy, but it had the practical disadvantage of accentuating the built-in imbalance of the system. Successive Liberal and Labour Chancellors were engaged continuously in attempts to satisfy the demands of their political supporters without lowering the judicial quality of the bench.

Jowitt was guided by two main principles, which he expounded in the memorandum of evidence which he drafted himself and submitted to the Royal Commission on Justices of the Peace. First, the overriding duty of the Lord Chancellor was to seek out and appoint those who, whatever their political views, were best qualified to discharge the work of a Justice of the Peace. Jowitt also conceded that only those who lived in an ivory tower could disregard politics entirely. Still, the political allegiance of candidates should be a secondary consideration. Secondly, Jowitt emphasized that the advisory committees in the counties and boroughs established by Loreburn had no independent authority, statutory or otherwise: they were the Lord Chancellor's committees and their sole function was to tender advice when asked to give it. Occasionally Jowitt had to enlighten advisory committees who thought that the Lord Chancellor should accept their nominations without argument—or, worse still, proved obstinate about accepting names he himself put forward. Jowitt was clearly of the opinion that the Lord Chancellor could not share his responsibility for appointments and must remain completely *dominus* of the situation. 'If anybody says that I am seeking to be a pocket Hitler in this matter, it is the only respect in which I desire to emulate Hitler.'[2]

Since Jowitt's day there has been a development which is apparently in the direction of taking political allegiance openly into account in the first instance, instead of only as a subordinate consideration. In 1966 Lord Gardiner sent to all his advisory committees a memorandum which stated that he desired them to have regard to the political affiliations of those nominated in order that 'a proper balance' should be maintained. 'The Lord Chancellor', said Gardiner, 'cannot disregard political affiliations in making appointments, not because the politics of an individual are a qualification or a disqualification for appointment, but because it is important that justices should be drawn from all sections of the community, and should represent all shades of opinion'.[3] Perhaps it is no more than a difference in emphasis, but Jowitt would not have used such definite language.

In August 1951 Jowitt attended the Seventh Legal Convention of the Law Council of Australia.[4] One day Mr Justice Fullagar of the High Court of

---

[2] 164 H.L. Deb. col. 1019.
[3] *The Times*, 3 Dec. 1966.
[4] (1951) 25 *Austr. L.J.* 296–7.

Australia read a paper entitled 'Liability for Representations at Common Law', which was a careful survey of the question whether an action for damages would lie for a misrepresentation which was neither fraudulent nor part of a contract. The value of the paper was not affected by the fact that it had been composed before the report of the decision in *Candler* v. *Crane, Christmas & Co*.[5] was available. In that case the Court of Appeal discussed the question in great detail, and by a majority, Denning LJ dissenting, held that no action lay. Fullagar J. stated that he did not belong to the school which wished to reduce the whole law of torts to the proposition that the customer is always right, but on this occasion he had attempted 'to range [him]self on the side of the heretics' who thought that in some circumstances a duty to take care in making statements might be imposed.

All the speakers to the paper, except Sir John Latham CJ, who cautiously indicated some of the difficulties which would arise if a new tort were to be created, expressed welcome for the idea.

Jowitt then spoke. After indicating the delicacy of his position, in that he might have to preside over an appeal in *Candler's* case, he said:

I do want to tell you quite shortly how the House of Lords would proceed to consider that case, because it seems to me that some of the speakers today have completely lost sight of this. We should regard it as our duty to expound what we believe the law to be, and we should loyally follow the decisions of the House of lords if we found there was some decision which we thought to be in point.

It is really not a question of being a bold or timorous soul: it is a much simpler question than that . . . It is quite possible that the law has produced a result which does not accord with the requirements of today. If so, put it right by legislation, but do not expect any lawyer, in addition to all his other problems, to act as Lord Mansfield did, and decide what the law ought to be. He is far better employed if he puts himself to the much simpler task of deciding what the law is . . . please do not get yourself into the frame of mind of entrusting to the judges the working out of a whole new set of principles . . . Leave that to the legislature . . .

In 1964 in *Hedley Byrne & Co. Ltd.* v. *Heller & Partners Ltd.*[6] the House of Lords reversed the decision in *Candler* v. *Crane, Christmas & Co.* and created a new cause of action in tort for careless misrepresentation, but Jowitt's remarks in 1951 have drawn criticism. One who was present wrote later:

During a discussion of some matters of lawyers' law, it became apparent that a number of Australians were prepared to criticise decisions of the House of Lords on policy grounds, a policy which the Americans present took as a matter of course, but which the Socialist Lord Chancellor felt impelled to oppose; he gave a little lecture on the theme that the House of Lords as a judicial body was never concerned with policy questions,

---

[5] [1951] 2 KB 164.
[6] [1964] AC 465.

and only gave effect to the law. It was the sort of conventional incantation which Jerome Frank[7] would have delighted to hear and preserve. But Evershed M.R., neither a socialist nor a pronounced 'bold spirit' protected the reputation of English legal scholarship by saying[8] that he wished respectfully to dissociate himself from the conservative, the extremely conservative—'of course not in any political sense'—view of judicial function which the Lord Chancellor had expounded.[9]

Jowitt's view of the judicial function may well have been conservative. Indeed, it was certainly more conservative than that of his immediate predecessor, Simon, but not sufficiently so to justify the criticism that he was reactionary. Jowitt's creative energies found release in legislative reform. His achievements in that field were so great as to demand at least respect for his views on the judicial function.

On his return from Australia Jowitt was plunged into an election. In October 1951 Parliament was dissolved and at the general election on 25 October the Conservatives won 321 seats to the 295 of Labour. On Friday the 26th Attlee resigned and was succeeded by Churchill. On Tuesday the 30th Jowitt surrendered the Great Seal, which was then given to Lord Simonds.

Attlee decided to create Jowitt an Earl. Before this was done an investigation was made into the precedents since the time of Hardwicke (1737-57). It was discovered that thirteen of the thirty-three Chancellors of that period had been created Earls, some of them after quite a short period of office (Cairns and Selborne four years, Birkenhead three years). (Cave died before the letters patent for his earldom had passed the Great Seal.) Some of those who had not been created Earls had held office for less than three years—Erskine, Truro, Campbell, St Leonards, Herschell, Buckmaster, Finlay, Maugham, and Caldecote. (Buckmaster had refused the Woolsack and an earldom in 1929.) Some Victorian Chancellors had held office for more than three years without being promoted to an earldom, but an adequate explanation was usually available. Thus Westbury had retired under a cloud; Brougham had been given a peerage with a special remainder; Lyndhurst had refused an offer; Cranworth and Hatherley were undistinguished as lawyers, and unhelpful to their parties in debate; Chelmsford had quarrelled with Disraeli, who dismissed him with the humilitating offer of a GCB. In the twentieth century explanations were also available for those who had served more than three years without promotion—Haldane was unmarried, and had been make KT and OM; and neither Sankey nor Simon, for different reasons, had done much in the way of law reform, while the latter had both the GCSI and the GCVO.

[7] (Judge) Jerome Frank, author of *Law and the Modern Mind* (1930), and a leading member of the American Realist school of jurisprudence.
[8] No remarks by Sir R. Evershed are reported in the *Austr. L.J.*
[9] G. Sawer, *Law and Society* (Oxford, 1965), p. 206.

Churchill had announced the names of some of his Ministers on Saturday, 27 October. But the new Lord Chancellor was not among them, so Jowitt was in the curious position of holding the Great Seal under a new Prime Minister of another party. Although unusual, this was not unprecedented, for in 1905 Halsbury retained the Great Seal until 11 December, although Balfour had resigned on the 4th and Campbell-Bannerman had kissed hands on the 6th.

To his sister Molly, Jowitt wrote on 27 October from West Lodge, Bradfield St George (a modest brick house in an attractive part of Suffolk, which he had acquired after the War instead of Budd's Farm):

I certainly have nothing about which I can complain. I've had 11½ years in office with the exception of the 2 or 3 months of the caretaker government—it's been continuous service, and I've been Lord Chancellor for 6¼ years.

But I must confess just at the moment I fell that the bottom has quite fallen out of my market. I've given myself completely to my office. It's been my life and enshrines all my interests.

I am prevented by convention from going back to the Bar, and I feel a lost soul just for the time being. It's no good prescribing rest, for my brain is going on crying for pabulum—and none comes.

It's a problem of adjustment to new conditions and new circumstances. Ever so many people have faced it and overcome it before, and though I've got to go through a difficult time I shall soon surmount it, and get fresh interests, and, I hope, be able to earn some money, for the jolly old wolf is at the door.

I was told that neither the King nor Queen would receive any of the outgoing Ministers—but that the Great Seal was to be sent round in what the late Mr. Drage would have called 'a plain van'.[1]

However, my successor hasn't yet—so far as I know—been appointed and whilst the aforesaid seal reposes in the office I remain Lord Chancellor: and so I have brought down my official car and chauffeur for the week-end . . .

I think—looking back—that I can be proud of my work as L.C. Circumstances made it necessary for me to take a much larger part in the controversial part of the House than any L.C. has ever taken before or than it is desirable for the L.C. to take.

Old Christopher Addison—he and Ernie Bevin were the only two for whom it was a pleasure to work—is, I fear, failing rapidly and I don't feel much like taking a prominent part in political controversies.

I shall always be willing to lend a hand to further my schemes of law reform and the like—and shall continue to watch them with interest.

It all sounds like the lament of Job from the bottom of the pit. I'm sorry—and in a week's time it will all be different.

I said my farewells at the office this morning.

We've had a wonderful time during our office and though I am called upon to surrender the seals, no one can call upon me to surrender the memories.[2]

---

[1] Mr Drage was a pioneer in supplying furniture to the middle classes on hire-purchase terms.
[2] Jowitt papers.

It was certainly unusual for the monarch not to receive his outgoing Ministers, but in this case there was an adequate explanation. The King had undergone a serious operation at the end of September, and his health would not permit him to receive individually the seventeen Cabinet and sixteen other Ministers. 'They therefore took leave of him collectively, and each received a personal letter of thanks.'[3] It is perhaps surprising that Jowitt did not mention this aspect of the matter, for he had been one of the four Privy Counsellor who had attended the meeting of the Privy Council on 5 October when the King, with great difficulty, had uttered the word 'Approved' to give the force of law to the Order in Council requisite for the dissolution of Parliament. (The Counsellors of State already appointed were expressly debarred by the Regency Act 1937 from dissolving Parliament except on the express instructions of the monarch.)

Jowitt was given a warmer farewell at Westminster than at Buckingham Palace. On 29 October 1951 Sir George Coldsteam wrote:

It is in truth very much a family concern here, and had you known what the state of affairs was before you took office, you would realise still more the measure of your acheivement (and it is mainly yours) in bringing us all together and giving everyone a sense of belonging to a first-class regiment, where the trials and tribulations, or the successes, of each are the concern of all. So far as I am concerned, I shall do my utmost to keep things as they are.[4]

After an interval of two months, and the dropping of some hints, Hugh Gaitskell produced a rather perfunctory letter of congratulations.

I must apologize for not writing before. But I do want to send you my sincere congratulations. I do not know how much becoming an Earl matters these days—but what is satisfactory is that your outstanding contribution in the Lords these last 6 years has been publicly acknowledged.[5]

To the Jowitts the earldom did matter a lot. The promotion was then properly regarded as a reward for outstanding contributions to the Labour Party and the State. It is surprising that this contribution has been ignored by later writers. The major figures in the Attlee Government—Bevin, Morrison, Cripps, Addison, Dalton, Bevan, and Gaitskell—have all been the subject of major biographies. Yet between them they contain fewer than a dozen references to Jowitt. It is entirely characteristic that Attlee himself in his autobiography should have mentioned Jowitt only twice: the pages above show how close they were. But this taciturnity has been imitated by Attlee's biographer: almost his only reference to Jowitt is to record that the Prime

---

[3] Wheeler-Bennett, *King George VI*, p. 798.
[4] Jowitt papers.
[5] Ibid.

Minister brought his family to the Lord Chancellor's Flat to watch a firework display on the Thames.[6] Richard Crossman, on the back-benches, described his experiences in over three million words without once referring to Jowitt.[7] Even the much praised history of the Attlee Government by Dr. K. O. Morgan has only a few fleeting references to Jowitt.[8]

It is time to attempt a summary of Jowitt's achievements and to assess his place in legal history. In appearance and manner Jowitt was a great Lord Chancellor. His superb natural gifts were seen to the best advantage at some State ceremony, such as the Opening of Parliament. But even when he was winding up a debate on some technical point in a thin House his dignity was enormous. Nothing slipshod in procedure or language was ever permitted. Jowitt was also an accomplished parliamentary technician, in part because of his training in the House of Commons, and in part because he was conscientious and went to immense pains to master the business before the House. His speeches were in clear and simple English, unmarred by the prolixity or jargon of the lawyer, and often adorned by some telling quotation from the bible or the standard English authors of the eighteenth and nineteenth centuries.

Although punctilious about maintaining the dignity of his office on formal occasions, Jowitt was too English to insist on ceremony in private life. Lunching at the Beefsteak in October 1945, Harold Nicolson noticed that Jowitt, 'coming in late, had to find a seat at the little side-table which serves in extreme cases for the overflow. "Observe that", said Cartier,[9] "In what other country in the world would a club like this allow the Lord Chancellor to take a seat away from the table? In what other country in the world would this happen quite naturally—without any of us regarding the occurrence as unusual?" "In the United States", I say. "Certainly not", he answers. "If the Chief Justice came into a club in Washington, a place would be found for him at the head of the table".'[1]

Jowitt rendered great service to his party in a House whose members were overwhelmingly hostile to the Labour Party in general and to the legislation of the Attlee Government in particular. To some extent Jowitt was helped by the fact that the Leader of the Opposition, the Marquess of Salisbury, was a constitutionalist who appreciated the perils which lay in wait for a House of Lords which consistently delayed or obstructed the House of Commons. The only issues on which the delaying powers of the House were exercised in

---

[6] Harris, *Attlee*, p. 416. T. Burridge, *Clement Attlee* (1985), has four brief references to Jowitt.

[7] J. Morgan (ed.), *The Backbench Diaries of Richard Crossman* (1981).

[8] K. O. Morgan, *Labour in Power 1945-1951* (1984).

[9] Baron Cartier de Marchienne, Belgian Ambassador in London.

[1] Nicolson, *Diaries and Letters 1945-62*, pp. 37-8. The memoirs of the period contain several references to Jowitt at the Beefsteak Club. Another member (Hart-Davis, *Hart-Lyttleton Letters*, vol. iii, p. 144) found that Jowitt warmly approved his description of 2 Chr. 36:9, as the shortest and saddest biography ever written. ('Jehoiachin was eight years old when he came to the throne, and he reigned in Jerusalem for three months and ten days. He did what was evil in the eyes of the Lord.')

Jowitt's time, namely capital punishment and the nationalization of iron and steel, were those on which Salisbury sensed that the view of the majority in the Commons did not reflect popular feeling in the country. In the case of capital punishment he was probably correct. As, in the last resort, the Conservative peers had absolute trust in Salisbury, Jowitt had reason to be grateful to him. On the other hand, Jowitt had to face sharp opposition from some of the younger Conservative peers, who saw no reason why they should show towards Jowitt and those of his colleagues, such as Listowel and Pakenham, whom they regarded as traitors to their class the measure of polite restraint displayed towards trade-union back-benchers elevated to the peerage. There was also Simon to be reckoned with—aged over seventy, but having lost none of the dazzling speed and power of his mental equipment, and ruthless in exploiting a weak point in the adversary's position. Attlee and his Cabinet were fully conscious of the debt which they owed to Jowitt. No other legal member of the Labour Party would have had the power or the skill to have presided on the Woolsack with Jowitt's success. The Labour appreciation of his talents was increased rather than lessened by a certain baffled wonder at Jowitt's air of weary detchment from the internal quarrels of the Cabinet and the party on points of doctrine or personality.

It is interesting to study the twenty Chancellors who preceded Jowitt in the light of their achievements in reform of the structure and substance of English law. Some were unfortunate in that war-time prevented any display of their powers in this field. In this category are Buckmaster, Finlay, Caldecote, and Simon. Others were men of ability who for some good reason did little in this field—in this category are Herschell, who was overworked, and Maugham, who was Chancellor for only eighteen months on the eve of war. Others appear to have been overwhelmed by the routine duties of their office and done little or nothing for reform—in this class are Loreburn, Cave, Hailsham and Sankey in the twentieth century, Cranworth and Chelmsford in the nineteenth. (Halsbury is in a category of his own: although generally regarded as an Eldonite Conservative, he had two major statutes to his credit, the Land Transfer Act 1897 and the Criminal Evidence Act 1898.)

Three Chancellors in the nineteenth century achieved major legislative reforms—Westbury, Cairns, and Selborne. Westbury was anxious for a Ministry of Justice, and pressed for the revision of the statute-book and the appointment of a commission to prepare a digest of case-law. None of these projects came to anything, nor did his scheme for a legal university to be established by the Inns of Court. But he did procure an Act for Registration of Title to Land, an important bankruptcy Act, and Acts to facilitate dealings with settled estates, to amend the lunacy laws, to confer equitable jurisdiction on the County Court, and to increase the strength of the Judicial Committee of the Privy Council.

Cairns was responsible for the Act of 1858 which bears his name, giving the

Court of Chancery power to award damages in lieu of an injunction. He helped to pass the Judicature Acts which had been framed under Selborne, and, conversely, prepared the Conveyancing Act, the Settled Land Act, and the Married Women's Property Act, all of which went through Parliament during Selborne's second Chancellorship.

Westbury as a reformer (though not in any other way) is comparable to Jowitt. Both were interested in reform by statute of the structure and machinery of the legal profession, though Westbury, unlike Jowitt, was also a considerable jurist, with the particularly Victorian judicial flair for writing an authoritative judgment based on general principles and without the cumbrous citation of precedents which is common today. Jowitt was like Westbury in that each was interested in reform not only *by* statute but *of* statute. In this field Jowitt's achievement is unparalleled amongst English Chancellors. It is indeed rare for one trained in the majesty of the common law, with its peculiar reverence for the decided case as the basis of juristic knowledge, to be interested in the form of the statute-book and the technique of draftsmanship. But Jowitt had this interest.

It is true that much of the preparatory work for Jowitt's reforms had been done by others. The Home Office had the Criminal Justice Bill in draft, and the Acts relating to legal aid and magistrates owed much to the Royal Commissions under Rushcliffe and du Parcq. The Crown Proceedings Bill had been in draft for some years, and the Consolidation of Enactments (Procedure) Bill owed much to the fertile mind of Granville Ram. But all experience shows that between a law reform bill and its enactment lies a shadow. It was Jowitt who found parliamentary time for these proposals in a legislative programme already overcrowded, and who steered them through the Cabinet and Parliament.

Finally, it should be noted that all this was done with a small staff. In Jowitt's time the staff of the Lord Chancellor's office was less than ten. On the other hand, he was able to rely on the unpaid public service which eminent men were then willing to give to Royal Commissions and similar bodies. By contrast, today the Law Commission has seventy on its staff, of whom half are lawyers.

JOWITT had three main occupations after October 1951—as Leader of the Opposition in the House of Lords, as a judge, and as an author. He was also Treasurer of the Middle Temple for 1952, at a time when there was much business in connection with rebuilding. (Jowitt's arms are carved in stone above the entrance to Elm Court from Middle Temple Lane.)

As a judge Jowitt sat on seventeen appeals between his retirement and his death. He did not sit at all in 1954, but sat six times in 1955. Although an ex-Law Officer, Jowitt was apparently not asked to sit on any criminal appeal.

As an author, Jowitt published three books. In *Some Were Spies*, published in 1954, Jowitt collected memories of some of his cases at the Bar—five dealt with spies whom he had prosecuted as Solicitor-General, two dealt with defamation, and the others concerned various criminals (Hatry, Thorne, Fox, and Kylsant). The publishers sold about 5,000 copies of the book—for which Jowitt, unnecessarily, but prudently, had taken out an insurance policy against libel. Another book was the substantial *Dictionary of English Law*, with Jowitt's name on the title-page as editor, published shortly after his death in 1957. The basic material was derived from two earlier works—Byrne's *Law Dictionary* (1923), and Wharton's *Law Lexicon* (1938). Before his death Jowitt had passed the final proofs of the book.

The third book was the most significant and interesting (though it was never a commercial success—a full study of the case of Alger Hiss, the American career diplomat, who in 1950, at a retrial, had been convicted of perjury for swearing before a Congressional Investigating Committee that he had never been a member of the Communist Party. (Much of the evidence disclosed a prima-facie case of espionage—the passing of official documents to the Communists—but as this had taken place before the war, a prosecution was barred by lapse of time. The only offence which could legally be alleged against Hiss was perjury: but in substance the case raised the far greater question whether he was a spy.) The case was one in a series which convulsed the free world at the outset of the cold war and during the later McCarthy period in the 1950s. The complexity of the facts and the curious characters of the chief participants attracted much interest. Even those who were eminent as lawyers and knew the USA well confessed themselves puzzled. Jowitt's volume, published in England on 30 May 1953, certainly illustrates the power which successful English lawyers possess of mastering quickly the transcript of evidence in a lengthy trial. It is remarkable that Jowitt, who had only just retired after six strenuous years as Lord Chancellor, and was Leader of the Opposition in the House of Lords, should have had sufficient time to produce within nine months (the work was sent to the printers in the late summer of 1952) an elaborate analysis of a difficult case.

Jowitt was sceptical about the guilt of Hiss—or, to put it in a way which would be familiar to an English lawyer, he doubted whether it had been proved beyond a reasonable doubt that Hiss was guilty. Jowitt never asserted that Hiss was innocent; he merely raised a doubt as to whether his guilt had been proved with the certainty which a serious criminal charge required.

On the whole Jowitt's book was not well received. Churchill displayed alarm at the possible effect on Anglo-American relations, and when Jowitt explained that matters had gone too far with his American publishers for the book to be withdrawn, he received a bleak one-sentence reply from Downing Street. The American reception was also in general unfavourable. (When Simonds visited the USA a year later he was left in no doubt about this.) Some of the critics were ignorant or malicious. It was easy for them to twist a carefully worded argument that Hiss had not been proved to be guilty into an assertion that Jowitt believed Hiss to be innocent. Other critics fastened on factual errors— which, considering the scale of the work, were surprisingly few, though it was certainly unwise for Jowitt to have described Harry Dexter White, a prominent government official who had committed suicide shortly before the exposure of his Communist affiliations, as 'a witness of truth'. Others took exception to a rather patronizing tone about American institutions which could be detected in places. So Hiss's election to Phi Beta Kappa at Harvard was described as 'an honour which will convey more to an American than an English reader'. The statement is true, and yet it might have been phrased more happily.

But the most serious criticisms were made in England by authorities who knew American—and Communism—well. D. W. Brogan,[1] Alistair Cooke,[2] and G. F. Hudson[3] each argued that Jowitt had displayed a naïve unawareness of the nature of Communist conspiracy, and shown that he was 'quite unable to understand what [was] implied in acts of treason committed for the sake of revolutionary ideology', and was 'benignly unaware of unparalleled wicked-ness'.

Apart from authorship, Jowitt was kept busy as Leader of the Opposition in the House of Lords. With the support of only a small number of peers, Jowitt was obliged to speak constantly on many topics of foreign and domestic policies. In February 1952 Jowitt spoke on the second reading of the Judicial Officers (Salaries) Bill, which increased the salaries of County Court judges and metropolitan magistrates from £2,000 to £2,800 per annum. Jowitt had been

[1] *Spectator*, 1 May 1953.
[2] *Manchester Guardian*, 18 May 1953.
[3] *Twentieth Century*, 104 (1953) 20.

so disturbed by the difficulty of securing suitable men for these positions at the old figure that before he left office he had begun negotiations with the Treasury for an increase.[4] One of the other topics in 1952 was the Schumann Plan for a European army. Jowitt had always shared the distrust of the Labour Party for such schemes.[5]

Jowitt's cautious attitude to the judicial function was again revealed in a debate on the administration of the National Insurance Act in March 1952. It was alleged that the chairman of the local appeals tribunal at Leeds, G. L. Haggen, had not been reappointed by the Minister at the expiry of his three-year term of office. This was conceded, and the official reason given was that Haggen had persistently disregarded relevant rulings of the National Insurance Commissioner. It was argued that the Minister's action was an infringement of the principle of judicial independence. Lord Simonds did not accept this, and Jowitt gave him firm support. After stating that he was largely the father of the national insurance scheme, and was willing to consider any change in it, he said: 'What is entirely wrong is that judges should take it upon themselves to try to strain the words which Parliament has used so as to bring about what they think is a more equitable system . . . that would be the end of the rule of law and the rule of justice.'[6] (The fact that Haggen was Dean of the Law Faculty at Leeds University may have reinforced Jowitt's suspicion of academic lawyers as judges.)

In 1953 the Government decided to increase the salaries of judges of the superior courts. This had not been done for 120 years, and the case for an increase was very strong. Unfortunately the Government proposed to give the salaries a measure of stability in an era of inflation by making part of them tax-free. This was not acceptable to Parliament, and in the following year the Judges' Remuneration Act proposed instead a straightforward increase of £3,000 a year to High Court judges and £2,000 a year to the Lord Chancellor and the Lord Chief Justice. (It was calculated that after tax these would produce net increases of £335 and £284 respectively. The then Lord Chancellor, Simonds, announced that he would not accept any part of the increase, as he wished to be free to advocate the proposal without being charged with self-interest.) Jowitt, who had on several occasions stated that he was worried lest he should be unable to induce suitable men to leave the Bar to become judges, gave the Bill his warm support.[7]

Jowitt's visit to Australia in 1951 led to an intermittent correspondence with Sir Owen Dixon, who had just succeeded Sir John Latham as Chief Justice. On 29 June 1952 Jowitt wrote:

[4] 170 H.L. Deb. col. 322; 171 H.L. Deb. col. 988.

[5] In June 1950 he told Dalton that opposition to European integration would help the Labour Party at a general election.

[6] 176 H.L. Deb. col. 546.   [7] 186 H.L. Deb. col. 1023.

Talking of the Privy Council, I do wish that something had been done to follow up my idea. Either you or Latham or some other distinguished person from Australia ought surely to be over here to help us with some of our cases. Rinfret is here and seems to be enjoying himself very much.[8] I meet him at all sorts of dinners. He is sitting on a case from Mauritius, and as this involves French law and practice, it's right up his street. I sit from time to time in our House of Lords to try to clear up the lists, as one of the Law Lords is presiding over the Divorce Commission[9] and another over the Income Tax Commission,[1] and they are a bit short-handed.

I wonder if you have read John Simon's book called 'Retrospect'?[2] I am afraid it is not very interesting. It suffers from the fact that he can never let himself go, and I don't think he has ever been really enthusiastic about anything or anybody.[3]

Jowitt always maintained his own interest in law reform. Throughout 1952 he was busy not only with his book on the Alger Hiss case but also with the enactment of the Defamation Bill, which had been introduced by Harold Lever, a private Member, to give effect to the recommendations made by Lord Porter's Committee on the Law of Defamation, which had reported in 1948.[4] Jowitt had much experience of libel while at the Bar, and he took a keen interest in the progress of the Bill. He was involved in correspondence with three former Labour Law Officers, Shawcross, Soskice, and Ungoed-Thomas, the new Conservative Attorney-General, Sir Lionel Heald, the former Conservative Lord Chancellor, Simon, who was in charge of the Bill in the House of Lords, and also with two leading academic lawyers, Goodhart of Oxford and Winfield of Cambridge. The Bill triumphantly passed its second reading in the Lords.

On the committee stage Jowitt reaffirmed his belief in the need for the abolition of the distinction between libel and slander, and asserted that the proposed penal sanctions for costs would discourage trumpery actions. He pointed out that very few actions had been brought under the Slander of Women Act 1891, perhaps for this reason. But Lords Simon, Simonds, Tucker, and Oaksey expressed opposition. A letter from Simon took up the points Jowitt had made in committee.

I have gone through the points mentioned yesterday on the Committee Stage, which I promised to look at further before Report. I take it that you will not be further raising the suggestion to assimilate libel and slander (though I agree with you in thinking that the argument against this is not 'overwhelming'). There is an argument both ways, but the Law Lords take the view which had prevailed in Committee and I must say, on balance, that I agree.

On Clause 2, you suggested that we might make a difference between slanders that 'degrade' and slanders which do not. I have been considering whether words could be

---

[8] Rinfret owed his Privy Counsellorship to Jowitt: see above, p. 107.
[9] Lord Morton of Henryton.
[1] Lord Radcliffe.   [2] See above, p. 37, n. 1.
[3] Jowitt papers.   [4] Cmd. 7536.

found which would make this a clear distinction, and frankly I agree with Porter and the draftsman that this does not seem possible. My conclusion is that we should leave this as it is.

Clause 4 about unintentional defamation is certainly not as clear and simple as the language of the Porter Report, but I think the Clause does makes valuable provision against unintentional defamation. Subsection (6) raises, as you pointed out, a problem. Should the publisher forfeit the benefit of the section when publishing what he did not himself write if he himself acted innocently and carefully? Porter's Committee thought that the concealed malice of the actual author should not affect the protection of the publisher. But there is very strong feeling about this, as indeed the Commons' reports show, and Lever tells me that he does not think that the Commons could be got to change their views. And there is this to be said, that in the cases in which hitherto the publisher has been hit for unintentional defamation, evidence was given to prove that the author of the words wrote them without malice (*Artemus Jones*, *Newstead* and *Cassidy*). So I think subsection (6) had better be retained.

The promoters of the Bill are greatly obliged to you for playing up so well to get in on the Statute Book.[5]

It was two years before the House of Lords was asked to consider another measure of law reform, and even then it was again a private Member's Bill and not a Government measure to give effect to the recommendation of the Law Reform Committee to repeal s. 4 of the Statute of Frauds 1677 and s. 4 of the Sale of Goods Act 1893. Jowitt had doubts about the latter proposal. He thought there was some wisdom in the former rule that contracts for the sale of goods should be in writing if the goods were of more than a certain value, although he conceded that the limit of £10 imposed by the 1893 Act was now out of date.

When I was in large practice at the Bar, and had a good deal of money to spend, it used to be my habit to go in and buy pictures, or to visit old curiosity shops to buy china, and so on. I am appalled at the risk you run if you go into a shop now . . . I think it is a dangerous thing when no requirement exists for anything to be in writing. Why have all that uncertainty in a country where nearly everyone writes nowadays, when a simple writing could put the thing beyond all argument and beyond all danger? It does not matter to me, because I am no longer in a position to buy anything, and therefore I shall not go into the shops and look at these attractive things.[6]

In the spring of 1955 Jowitt initiated an important debate, in which many peers took part, on forestry.[7] It was the first debate on the subject since the Forestry Act was passed in 1951. Jowitt recalled how in the war he had fostered the work of the Forestry Commission, and drew attention to the poor progress made by the post-war reafforestation programme. Jowitt also supported the County Courts Act 1955, which increased the jurisdiction of those tribunals. He

---

[5] Jowitt papers.
[6] 187 H.L. Deb. col. 773.
[7] 191 H.L. Deb. col. 370.

also gave vigorous support to the suppression of 'horror comics', and, contrary to practice, used his parliamentary privilege to give the names and addresses of those who imported these publications into England, as 'a little publicity in matters of this sort does no harm at all'.[8]

At the general election on 25 May 1955 the Conservatives were returned with a majority of 26. On 21 June Jowitt wrote to Dixon in Australia:

I was not in the least surprised at the result of our election. Indeed, I anticipated it almost exactly. Had the Labour Party won, I suppose I should once more have been Lord Chancellor, and as things are—for I have now reached the age of seventy—it is very unlikely that I shall ever hold office again. Of course, in a sense I am disappointed, but I should not have been happy had I been serving a divided party with a much stronger pull to the left than I think desirable.

I have always believed in the 'inevitability of gradualness', and I think the real explanation is that after all our reforms—or at any rate alterations—extending over six and a half years, the country wants more time for digestion.

I wish there was some chance of your coming over here and meeting your colleagues of the Middle Temple Bench. But of course I see how impossible it is. Alas, it is equally impossible for me to come out to see you, for although I am master of my own time, yet the expense of travelling is so great that I cannot contemplate it.[9]

In the spring and summer of 1955 Jowitt was much concerned with the future of the work on revision and consolidation of the statutes, which had made such good progress during his Chancellorship. Kilmuir, who had succeeded Simonds as Chancellor in 1954, wrote to Jowitt on 24 February 1955 to tell him that he had received from Sir Alan Ellis, the First Parliamentary Counsel, and Sir John Rowlatt (Ellis's predecessor) a memorandum about the work of the Statutory Publications Office. The memorandum from Ellis and Rowlatt was a remarkable document.[1] Exclusive of appendices, it ran to 15,000 words, and covered all aspects of the subject in a tone of mordant and destructive cynicism. Each of the three topics to which Jowitt had devoted so much effort—consolidation, revision, and the publication of a new edition of the statutes—was riddled with criticism. There was said to be some future scope for consolidation ('though it must be emphasised that there is no prospect whatever of spectacular results') but none for the other projects.

Criticism was also made of the staff of the Statutory Publications Office, both its numbers and its personnel. The office employed eighteen persons—but during the war Sir Cecil Carr had done nearly all the work himself, with the aid of one lawyer, one clerk, and an office boy. Praise was indeed given to Sir Robert Drayton, the Director, but the two Deputy Directors were regarded more

[8] 191 H.L. Deb. col. 270.
[9] Jowitt papers.
[1] Ibid.

coolly. The likelihood of finding a suitable Director from outside was pronounced to be unpromising.

It is extremely unlikely, in view of the paucity of real talent in the Government legal service, that any able member of it would take the job except after his retirement to supplement his pension and, for the same reason, a good man is unlikely to be allowed to retire until his last working days are over. Ex-members of the Colonial Legal Service do, it is true, retire at a period when their powers are not appreciably past their best. They have, however, grave limitations; they may, like Sir Robert Drayton, be men of considerable, or even outstanding, ability (though it is not always so), but they rarely have much familiarity with English conditions or much real feeling for the law.

The non-legal staff were no more satisfactory. 'In the relevant classes [executive and clerical officers] good men and women are all too few and very indifferent men and women are all too many', although it was conceded that 'many of the present staff are not inefficient within their limitations'.

Jowitt was naturally upset. He sent Kilmuir a letter of protest.

I shall take a little time to give a considered answer to your letter with its enclosure on the above subject. In this letter, which is intended *for your eyes only*, I want you to be aware of my general impression concerning certain points.

I have the highest regard for John Rowlatt personally, for his great intellectual ability, and of course, for his complete integrity. On the other hand, his mind is purely destructive. He will give you a thousand and one reasons against any project of law reform: the one may be good, but the thousand will probably be bad.

It is, of course, a great tendency for the legal mind to be negative in its outlook. I remember Ramsay MacDonald once saying to me, a propos of John Simon's failure as Foreign Secretary, that no lawyer ever ought to be appointed as Foreign Secretary. Whilst I would not go as far as that, I do think our training does make it difficult for us, with notable exceptions, to acquire the necessary enthusiasm about any project of law reform.

Ram told me the same thing about John Rowlatt. He derived no help or encouragement from him about our scheme for Consolidation or Statute Law Revision, or about that useful little Bill which enables minor difficulties to be corrected on Consolidation. When I say he received no support, I should make it plain that he received most vigorous though kindly criticism of the whole scheme.

I am by no means saying that it is not most useful to have somebody who will subject to criticism any proposal for alteration. An ideal combination, however, is surely to have somebody with fire in his belly who is not content with things as they are and wants to bring about what he believes to be reforms, coupled with someone who will subject all those proposals to vigorous and well informed criticism. But you must have the accelerator as well as the brake, and if the brake becomes too powerful the machine will stop.[2]

[2] Ibid.

The question was finally settled in October 1955, when Kilmuir sent the Statute Law Committee a memorandum containing his decision. In general it followed the recommendations of Ellis and Rowlatt, but it also attempted to meet Jowitt's arguments.

Shortly before his retirement in December 1955 Jowitt achieved a major parliamentary success—perhaps the most striking of his whole career. Almost unaided at first, he initiated and carried to a successful conclusion a campaign to prevent a Government which had a crushing majority in the House of Lords from banning the manufacture of heroin from 31 December 1955. The Government had come to this decision in the light of the recommendations of an expert committee, and also what it imagined to be its international obligations to suppress the traffic in dangerous drugs. The Government did not appear to have given enough weight to the interests of reputable medical practitioners and their patients. Heroin was undoubtedly a drug of addiction, misuse of which had dreadful consequences. But it was also undoubtedly of the greatest benefit to those suffering from incurable diseases. At first Jowitt seems to have been impressed mainly by the strength of the medical arguments against the Government decision. There was much correspondence with physicians, surgeons, and nurses throughout the country. But the chances of inducing a powerful Government to rescind its decision seemed remote.

Then it occurred to Jowitt to investigate the legal strength of the case for the Government. He discovered in it what appeared to be a fatal weakness. The Dangerous Drugs act 1951, s. 9, provided: 'For the purpose of preventing improper use of . . . drugs . . . a Secretary of State may by regulations provide for controlling the manufacture, sale, possession and distribution of those drugs.' But did a statutory power to *control* authorize the Home Secretary to *prohibit*? It is one of the fundamental principles of public law that a discretionary power must be exercised for the purposes for which it is conferred. The exercise of a discretion must not be beyond the powers (*ultra vires*) granted by the enabling statute. There was authority to support the view that the holder of a discretion could not properly announce in advance that he would always decide in one way—for example, it would be wrong for licensing justices to announce that they would not consider each case on its merits, but would refuse all applications.

The point was a significant one to Jowitt, because, as Lord Chancellor in 1948, he had had the difficult task of answering an argument which he later confessed[3] to be 'unanswerable'—that the then Home Secretary, Chuter Ede, had exceeded the limits of his discretion in announcing that the prerogative of pardon would be used to commute the sentences imposed on all those convicted of murder. However, Jowitt realized that Kilmuir would not be easily

---

[3] 195 H.L. Deb. col. 20.

convinced. He therefore obtained an opinion from B. MacKenna Q.C., which supported his own, and showed it to the Lord Chancellor shortly before the debate. The Government, reluctantly, confessed itself impressed with the strength of Jowitt's case. Lord Mancroft, the Under-Secretary of State at the Home Office, admitted that it had 'more than considerable merit'. At the end of a lengthy debate the Government offered to resume the issue of licences for the manufacture of heroin until the legal point raised had been settled. Jowitt refused to accept this: it was too vague. Hurried consultations between Ministers conscious that the debate had gone against them produced a definite promise that licences would be issued for the year 1956, and on this 'plain understanding' Jowitt, who had never been anxious to divide the House, withdrew his motion. It was a real triumph, and Jowitt received many congratulatory letters and telegrams.

1956 was the year of Suez, and Jowitt took an active part in the critical debates. He travelled from Scotland to attend the special two-day debate on 12 and 13 September. He stated that so far he had no quarrel with what the Government had done, but gave a stern warning that the use of force outside the framework of the United Nations Charter would not be either wise or lawful. The charter contemplated that force could be used either under the authority of the Security Council or in self-defence. Only the second head was relevant here. In the debate on the Address on 7 November Jowitt stated emphatically that self-defence was not permissible on the facts of the Suez situation.[4] By the beginning of December the Government's policy had completely and humiliatingly collapsed. On 12 December Jowitt made a powerful speech.[5] The reputation of Britain as an upholder of the rule of law had been tarnished. Jowitt refused to believe, so he said, that there had been connivance at the Isareli attack: but he asked some awkward questions. On 13 December Lord McNair, who had retired in 1955 from the office of President of the International Court of Justice, wrote congratulating Jowitt on his 'punishing speech of last night. I felt almost sorry for the Government Front Bench. It was plain that they dared not answer your questions. There is some mystery here of a sinister character, and I hope that I shall live long enough to know what it is.'[6] (Lord McNair, born in 1885, did not die until 1975, when the truth about Suez had been revealed.)

In the intervals of this great crisis, Jowitt found time to protest against the regulations issued by the Governor of Cyprus, Sir John Harding, to preserve public order. Jowitt convincingly demonstrated the folly of supposing that a colonial power on the eve of withdrawal could prevent crime merely by

[4] 200 H.L. Deb. col. 75.
[5] 200 H.L. Deb. col. 1037.
[6] Jowitt papers.

announcing severe penalties. It was neither the first nor the last time in British colonial history that such a mistake had been made. Jowitt did not take an active part in debate in 1957, although in May he gave a welcome to the second reading of the Occupiers' Liabilty Bill, an important piece of law reform based on the Tenth Report of the Law Reform Committee.[7] Jowitt's last intervention in debate was on 25 July 1957, when he spoke on the need to support the United Nations.

Out of office Jowitt had time to indulge in his various recreations—tennis (he was Vice-President of Wimbledon), golf, shooting, and cricket. 'I think he seldom missed any of the great festivals of sport, and to be his neighbour on such an occasion, at Lord's, at Wimbledon, or at Twickenham, was a delightful experience, because he understood games as a games player and sportsman.'[8] In the summer Jowitt tried to find occasional free hours in which to slip away to the Oval, often accompanied by James Chuter Ede, the Home Secretary, who carried a score-book and sandwiches. Seated in the front row of the pavilion balcony, they recorded every ball bowled and worked out the averages. 'Then, exactly at 2.50 p.m., off they went to their respective Houses at Westminster with the score-book tucked away in the official brief-case.'[9] Another companion on these occasions was Lord Lucan.[1] When the debate was dull Jowitt would catch his eye and they would slip away together.

Jowitt died on 16 August 1957 at West Lodge, Bradfield St George, near Bury St Edmunds. He was cremated at Ipswich and his ashes were deposited in his parents' grave at St Nicholas's Church, Stevenage. The church and the rectory (now known as the Priory) look today much as they did when Jowitt was young. To the north the gently sloping fields of Hertfordshire run up to the church-yard, but 100 yards to the south an arterial road has been cut through a hill, and beyond it lies the new town of Stevenage. There is no memorial tablet in the church, the parochial church council having refused to permit one to be erected, but there is one in the ante-chapel at Marlborough, with the inscription 'Many shall Commend his Understanding'.[2] Jowitt's estate was sworn for probate at £104,727.

---

[7] 203 H.L. Deb. col. 264.
[8] Earl of Home in 205 H.L. Deb. col. 523 (20 Oct. 1957).
[9] Mr Evelyn Walkden to the author.
[1] The 6th Earl (1898–1964) was Captain of the Yeomen of the Guard in the Attlee Government.
[2] Eccles. 39: 10.

LORD SIMONDS

G AVIN TURNBULL SIMONDS[1] was born on 28 November 1881 at The Point, Bath Road, Reading. The house was so called after that on Long Island, New York, where his father, Louis de Luze Simonds (1852–1916), had been born and spent his early years before returning to the family brewery at Reading. The father of Louis had emigrated to the USA after Waterloo. There he had married a daughter of a French emigré family, Sophie de Luze,[2] and their son, Louis de Luze, married in 1880 Mary Elizabeth (1857–1930), daughter of Surveyor-General Gavin Ainslie Turnbull, of a family once prominent on the Scottish Borders. The marriage was followed by two sons in 1881—in January, Frederick Adolphus, and in November, Gavin Turnbull. In later years there were two more sons and a daughter. Gavin Simonds was accustomed to claim that, like Lyndhurst (1772–1863) before, and the second Hailsham after him, one of his parents had been born on American soil. But generally the Franco–American strain in the ancestry does not seem to have been emphasized. (When the Lord Chancellor visited Paris and Quebec his speeches in French were observed to make his audiences wince.) Kilmuir wrote that his predecessor had 'an appearance more often seen in Bordeaux than in Lincoln's Inn'.[3] But to Lord Pearce there was 'nothing non-English in appearance or outlook. He always appeared a bluff, big, highly educated and very able squire—a typical product of the English gentry'.[4] In later life his recreations were certainly those of the Hampshire gentleman—shooting the pheasants as they came rocketing over the woods at Highclere, or, often in company with Reggie Manningham-Buller, fishing Tommy Sopwith's water on the Test below Stockbridge. The youth of Gavin Simonds was spent at Audley End, a solid house near Basingstoke, not then the ugly dormitory suburb which it became in the 1970s. Although hardly 'brought up rich',[5] as Kenneth Clark described his childhood, the Simonds family 'learned to shoot and ride and were not over-awed by the presence of a butler and footman.'[6]

A scholarship to Winchester in 1894 was followed by an exhibition to New College, where Firsts in Honour Moderations (1902) and Greats (1904) were duly recorded. He just missed obtaining half-blues for soccer and tennis.

[1] The name is pronounced as if spelt 'Simmonds'. Chairmen who displayed ignorance of this fact (and so caused confusion with Lord Simon) would be rebuked with a jocular 'the "i" in my name is short, as will be my speech'.
[2] The firms of Simonds and de Luze, though controlled by others, are still trading under the family names in Reading and Bourdeaux.
[3] Earl of Kilmuir, *Political Adventure* (1964), p. 194.
[4] To the author.
[5] Lord Clark, *Another Part of the Wood* (1974), p. 30.
[6] Simonds, 'Recollections' (unpublished TS).

Simonds was called to the Bar at Lincon's Inn on 19 November 1906. 'I look back on the next two years as the unhappiest of my life.'[7] He had gone into chambers which should have been good but were not—those of G. P. C. Lawrence (a son-in-law of Lord Davey) at 18 Old Square. Then came an invitation to join the chambers of the Treasury devil in Chancery matters, James Austen-Cartmell at 6 New Square. Here he stayed happily until he moved to 9 Old Square on taking silk in 1924, sharing a room with W. J. Whittaker, 'monumental in figure and learning',[8] the editor of Maitland's *Equity*.

Simonds was loyal to the institutions with which he had been connected—Winchester, New College, and Lincoln's Inn. Although only the fourth Wyke-hamist to become Lord Chancellor, he discovered in 1938 that there were seven Wykehamist judges ('never before have so many judges come from one school'), and arranged for a reception *ad portas* of Lords Thankerton and Merriman, and Talbot, Farwell, Crossman, Bennett, and Simonds JJ. 'Thankerton wore Privy Counsellor's uniform; the rest of us (by permission of the sovereign) our judicial robes.'[9]

On 28 March 1912 Simonds married at St Margaret's, Westminster, Mary Hope Mellor, daughter of (Judge) F. H. Mellor KC. The Mellors were a prolific legal dynasty with their roots in the commercial life of Lancashire. (The firm of Gee, Mellor, Kershaw & Co. was a solidly based product of the Industrial Revolution.) Simonds's father-in-law was the tenth son of the Rt. Hon. Sir John Mellor, a judge of the Queen's Bench from 1861 to 1879. (As a young man 'his inveterate repugnance to the subscription to all dogmatic articles of religion'[1] precluded his acceptance of an offered place at Lincoln College, Oxford.) Amongst the bride's nine uncles were Sir John Mellor, Procurator-General and Treasury Solicitor, 1909-23,[2] and Sir James Mellor, Master of the Crown Office, 1908-26.

It was a happy marriage. Lord Pearce recalled: 'We used to dine with them (solo *not* parties) and it was obvious that they loved each other very dearly. It was delightful to see Mary twinkling and poking fun at Gavin in the demurest Edwardian way, and him responding in like style.'[3]

Twin sons were born on 1 August 1915. Each went to Winchester: then the elder to New College, and the younger to Magdalene, Cambridge. Each served in the Second World War. The elder survived, to die, unmarried, of a rare disease in March 1951. The younger was killed at Arnhem in September 1944. Before his death he had married Barbara (Robinson), widow of FO A. J. Willock

---

[7] Ibid.   [8] Ibid.   [9] Ibid.
[1] Ibid.
[2] His successor in that office was A. C. Lawrence (one of the sons of Lord Trevethin LCJ), whose widow married the 1st Viscount Hailsham as his second wife.
[3] To the author.

(who married thirdly Dr Angus McPherson). The death of the surviving twin was a domestic calamity from which the parents never really recovered, though the blow was mitigated by the father's appointment to the Woolsack in October of the same year. Unfortunately the Simonds parents did not feel able to maintain contact with their daughter-in-law.

At the outbreak of war Simonds was aged thirty-two. In 1915 he was gazetted Second Lieutenant in a territorial battalion of the Royal Berkshire Regiment, but fell seriously ill with diptheria just before being posted to France. After convalescence he returned to Austen-Cartmell's chambers, where work for the Government had begun to flow in, especially in the Prize Court and the Mixed Arbitration Tribunals set up under the various peace treaties. The work increased so much that Simonds felt entitled to take silk at the age of 42—although he had some qualms because he had few private clients. 'I never pass the pillar-box at the bottom of Bell Yard without recalling the spasm of regret that I felt as soon as I had posted by application.'[4] But all went well.

The career of a Chancery silk can not be made interesting except to a few devotees in Lincoln's Inn but it is certainly surprising to find from Simonds high praise for Gordon Hewart as an advocate but not as a judge ('It was an intellectual treat to hear him expound his case with equal clarity of thought and felicity of language').[5] Just two cases may be mentioned. In the Portuguese bank-note case[6] Simonds appeared for Waterlows, the printers of the forged notes, who had been adjudged liable to pay £610,000 to the Bank of Portugal. Simonds spoke for twenty-five hours, 'and, if that seems too long, I must plead that I met from first to last with the open hostility of one of their Lordships, who failed to disguise that he had made up his mind before I began'.[7] Simonds lost by three to two. 'I have never been persuaded that the majority were right.'[8] In the König case[9] Simonds appeared for the Administrator of German Property against D. N. Pritt KC, who had to argue unsuccessfully that his German clients were entitled to share property in England. Lord Buckmaster was presiding on the appeal, and Pritt and he were past maters of the sort of arid repartee which was common fifty years ago in English courts. The result was an atmosphere of personal tension unusual in Chancery appeals.

At the end of his time at the Bar Simonds was given the general retainer for the Commonwealth of Australia in Privy Council cases. This was then a fertile source of appeals in constitutional law, thanks in part to the litigious streak in

[4] 'Recollections'.   [5] Ibid.   [6] [1932] AC 452.
[7] 'Recollections'. Three of the Law Lords praised Simonds's argument. The hostility was shown by Atkin, whose judgment was really 'the hard-hitting, driving speech of the advocate' (G. Lewis, Lord Atkin (1983), p. 77).   [8] 'Recollections'.
[9] (1934) 50 TLR 114.

the national character, and in part to the much admired intellectual quality of
the judges of the High Court of Australia—and in particular, Sir Owen Dixon,
with whom Simonds later had much correspondence.

There is no record of any political activity—apart from the secretaryship of
the Canning Club and some Hampshire canvassing at the elections of 1905 and
1910. But Simonds was a member of the Donoughmore Committee on
Minister's Powers, and in fact helped to draft the report, which was published in
1932. One comment on another member, Harold Laski, may be recounted: 'He
did not make any great contribution to our discussions, nor did the quality of
his observations justify the portentousness of his manner'.[1] In 1936 Simonds was
chosen, with Roland Oliver KC, to form a tribunal of inquiry under Porter J.,
into a leakage of Budget secrets. The report of the tribunal[2] resulted in the
resignation of J. H. Thomas, Secretary of State for the Colonies, and the
disappearance from public life of Sir Alfred Butt, a curious figure on the murky
borders of business and politics. Since 1936 the procedure at such tribunals has
been improved. Then the Attorney-General, Donald Somervell, was content to
call the witnesses and leave it to the tribunal to cross-examine them. This was a
procedure of which Simonds disapproved as 'flatly opposed to our idea of the
judicial function'.[3]

In 1937 Lord Hailsham appointed Simonds to the vacancy in the Chancery
Division created by the retirement of Eve J., who had served as puisne judge for
the remarkable period of thirty years. Eve was 'a typical English countryman
with marked limitations. He did not like musicians, cranks or foreigners. He
greatly preferred dogs.'[4] One feels he would have been happy to be succeeded
by Gavin Simonds.

The work of a Chancery judge is as unspectacular as that of a Chancery silk. 'I
did three cases before him as a puisne', wrote Lord Pearce.[5]

He was courteous, attentive, human, quick, with no time to waste on what was *clearly*
rubbish—but *never, never* domineering or overbearing, and *never* discourteous. Masterful? Well, he listened to any points you had, and when he had got them fully he didn't
want repetitions (so like Somervell). I would prefer 'forceful' to 'masterful'. Once I was
trying to get him in chambers in the war in 1940 to send a boy of 10 to the safety of
Canada or U.S.A. I could see I was losing, and he said 'Have you ever talked with a boy of
this age about this problem?' I said 'Yes, last week, with my son.' Gavin said, 'And he
won't go, will he? Wants to stick it out with his parents?' I said 'Yes'. Gavin said, 'Quite
right: and I shan't send this one.' A charming smile to me and out I went—and glad to be
relieved of having to go on arguing vainly, as I should have been encouraged to do, e.g.
by dear old Johnny Morris.[6]

---

[1] 'Recollections'.   [2] (1936) Cmnd. 5184.   [3] 'Recollections'.
[4] Sir G. Hurst, *Closed Chapters* (1942), p. 125.   [5] To the author.
[6] (Sir) John (later Lord) Morris of Borth-y-Gest, a good but notoriously slow judge.

Simonds himself recalled the first case he tried, a relatively simple action for specific performance.

It presented no real difficulty, but I remember to this day the trepidation with which I began to deliver an extempore judgment involving the evaluation of conflicting testimony and the application of the relevant law to the facts as found. I longed to reserve my judgment and write it out. But this would have been a fatal course. Among many letters of congratulation I received on my appointment was one from Lord Warrington, a former Chancery judge, who advised me in the strongest terms not to reserve judgment during my first term. 'Grasp the nettle', he said, 'if you once get into the way of reserving judgement you will never get out of it.'[7]

It may be recalled that Hatherley LC only twice delivered a written judgment as 'I find such writing to be positively injurious to my health'.[8]

Another who practised before Simonds recorded his surprise, 'admittedly not very rational, at finding that such a big man had such a neat and tidy mind'.[9] But to those without the ability or opportunity to answer back, Simonds could indeed seem domineering and not just forceful. When he was Treasurer of his Inn in 1951, a student (later a Labour MP), published an article on that most attackable of targets—catering in Hall. He received a two-page rebuke from the Treasurer, written in his own hand. In the seventies there would have been placards and marches against such 'arbitrary and authoritarian' behaviour: in the fifties a humble apology was sent.

Sir Robert Megarry, who had many opportunities as a practitioner of appearing before Simonds, and, later as a judge, on having his opinions cited to him, wrote that:

In some ways he was an equitable counterpart of Goddard, though a much more profound lawyer. For him, argument was a forthright process. He did not seem to have any particular affection for the niceties of practice; his interest lay in the substance. Of the accepted masters of equity, Cairns was perhaps the nearest to him—certainly not Radcliffe. It is difficult to say whether Simonds will come to be regarded as being in the first rank of equity lawyers, or just as missing it; but on any footing he stands very high.[1]

In 1939 Simonds was chairman of a committee on law-reporting established by Lord Maugham, largely on the prompting of Goodhart, to inquire whether any improvement was possible in the haphazard system of reporting judgments. Although the English legal system depended on the reported judgment, there was no official system for ensuring that the reasoned judgments of the superior

---

[7] 'Recollections'.
[8] J. B. Atlay, *The Victorian Chancellors* (1908), vol. ii, p. 214.
[9] Lord Wilberforce to the author.
[1] To the author.

courts were readily available to the profession and the public. Yet the answer of a witness to the most trivial question in the most trivial case in the High Court was recorded at public expense. The system, such as it was, could be criticized as expensive, inaccurate, incomplete, and also repetitious—one case might be reported in a dozen different series; another might escape the attention of all the reporters. The Simonds Committee was asked a sensible question: there was general agreement at the time that it had produced a sensible answer—namely, that although some valuable judgments remained unreported, the cost of setting up a system to report them would be prohibitive.[2] (The invention of electronic retrieval systems has changed the position completely.) From 1940 to 1944 Simonds was Chairman of the National Arbitration Board, whose task it was to settle industrial disputes. It dealt with over 500 cases.

In March 1944 Lord Romer's resignation created a vacancy for a Chancery Law Lord, and on Lord Simon's advice, Downing Street appointed Simonds, who was then aged sixty-two and the senior puisne judge. Simon had it in mind that the other Chancery Law Lord, Russell of Killowen, was aged seventy-seven, and the only possible rival to Simonds was Luxmoore LJ, who was sixty-eight and in poor health (in fact he died later that year). Simon assured Churchill that Simonds had 'an excellent reputation'.[3] So the position was offered, and Simonds personally dropped his letter of acceptance through the letter-box of No. 10.

He joined a strong team. 'They looked like a Rembrandt, so old and remote and learned, and Gavin (though silent, while Simon, presiding, talked 'clever' stuff) looked like some super-imposed figure painted in by Franz Hals—so eager and vital and robust and down to earth.' So Edward Pearce recalled[4] the lengthy appeal arising out of the loss of the submarine *Thetis*.[5] Readers of the Appeal Cases were conscious of a fresh mind able to express conclusions in an English style which was unusually clear and vivid. Two examples may be given—one Chancery and one common-law. In *Chichester Diocesan Fund* v. *Simpson*,[6] immediately after his appointment, Simonds dealt with a basic point in the law of charities, and 'the speech he gave there set the tone of his judicial career'.[7] He held that a testator who required his executors to devote his estate to 'charitable or benevolent purposes' had failed to establish a valid charitable gift, for the estae might be distributed amongst objects which were benevolent without being legally charitable. It was impossible to read the 'or' as conjunctive rather than disjunctive, and it was a 'rude shock' to hear the Attorney-General argue

---

[2] The committee's report appeared in Mar. 1940—a bad date for attracting attention, which seems to have been given only by C. G. Moran, *Heralds of the Law* (1948), pp. 93–100.

[3] Simon papers.

[4] To the author.

[5] *Woods* v. *Duncan* [1946] AC 401 (an appeal which had been argued over 15 days in Oct. 1945).

[6] [1944] AC 341.

that the bequest was valid. 'Equally irrelevant are the facts which are brought to your Lordships' attention that the estate is a large one, and that the next-of-kin are not near relatives.'

In *Christie* v. *Leachinsky* the House of Lords established that a person who had been arrested was entitled to be told the true reason for his arrest. 'Blind, unquestioning obedience is the law of tyrants and of slaves: it does not yet flourish on English soil.'[8] On the other hand, 'there is no need for the constable to explain the reason of arrest if the arrested man is caught red-handed and the crime is patent to high Heaven'.

Much more could be cited—in particular to illustrate the point that Chancery judges have perhaps contributed more to the development of the common law than their common-law colleagues have to equity. In his eightieth year Simonds restated the law relating to remoteness of damage in *The Wagon Mound*,[9] and also affirmed emphatically in *Shaw* v. *DPP*,[1] that a conspiracy to corrupt public morals was a criminal offence. In fact no further prosecutions for this offence took place until 1965. In the following six years 32 prosecutions are recorded, with 134 individual convictions. The trenchant language of the judgment attracted some criticism, but fifteen years later, after a full investigation by the Law Commission, the principle laid down by Simonds was affirmed in the Criminal Law Act 1977. s. 5.

But the chronological order of events must be observed. Simonds's career as a Chancery Law Lord was about to undergo a change which was not, in the language of the law of torts, reasonably foreseeable. In October 1951 Attlee called a general election. For a year his Government had been struggling to survive with a majority of less than a dozen. By Friday, 26 October it was clear that the Conservatives had been returned in sufficient strength to form a Government. Onthe evening of Saturday, 27 October Churchill released the names of nine members of his new Cabinet. The list did not include the Lord Chancellor, but it did contain the name of the favourite candidate for that office, David Maxwell Fyfe, who was to be Home Secretary. Churchill regarded his presence in the Commons as essential. So if Maxwell Fyfe was not to be Lord Chancellor, who was? In September Brendan Bracken, close to the centre of power, had told Harold Macmillan that Churchill had 'set his heart on getting Cys Asquith as Lord Chancellor, chiefly because he wished his last administration to hold both an Asquith and a Lloyd George'.[2] (It was not held against Asquith that he had been promoted to the Court of Appeal and the House of Lords on the recommendation of Jowitt.) It is certain that Gwilym Lloyd

[7] R. Stevens, *Law and Politics* (1979), p. 346.
[8] [1947] AC 573, at 593.
[9] [1961] AC 388.
[1] [1962] AC 220, at 267–9.
[2] H. Macmillan, *Tides of Fortune* (1969), p. 356.

George became Minister of Food (without a seat in the Cabinet). It is also certain that the Woolsack was offered to, and refused, by Cyril Asquith. His reason was health. His family pleaded with him to accept the offer, but he insisted that Churchill 'mustn't be saddled with a lame duck on the Woolsack'.[3] (In the event Asquith died in August 1954). Churchill then chose Simonds.

On Monday, 29 October Simonds was presiding over a part-heard appeal in the Privy Council

I took my seat as usual, little dreaming what fate had in store for me. In the course of the morning an usher came in with a message that the Prime Minister wished to see me at once. I did not feel justified in interrupting the appeal and said so. It was arranged that I should go round to No. 10 Downing Street at half-past three. I said nothing about it to anyone but wondered. At 3.30 I went round. Mr. Churchill, whom I had met but who did not remember meeting me, asked me at once to join the Government as Lord Chancellor. I was not wholly surprised, for there was a recent precedent in Lord Maugham for the appointment of a Lord Chancellor who had no political experience. And, after all, for what else could a Prime Minister want me so urgently when his mind must be fully taken up with Cabinet-making? Yet I was not so sure of it that I had made up my mind what the answer should be. I was approaching seventy: the office of Lord Chancellor is a very heavy burden and I should be embarking on an unknown sea. Most important of all, I wanted to consult my wife. For her too it meant a great change. We had for many years led a very quiet life and she had lately sustained a crippling blow in Gavin's illness and death. So I told Mr. Churchill that I was greatly honoured but would like a little time to think it over. 'How long do you want,' he said. 'Well', I said, 'I want to talk it over with my wife.' 'Where is she?' 'In the country.' 'When will she be back?' 'About six o'clock.' 'That is too late. I have to tell the King by five o'clock. You must take this fence by yourself'. So I took the fence by myself and said 'Yes'. The die was cast![4]

The Court Circular for Tuesday the 30th announced that at 6 p.m. that day Jowitt had delivered up the Great Seal, which had been given to Simonds. He was a month short of his seventieth birthday—an age exceeded only by Finlay (seventy-four) and Campbell (eighty) in 1916 and 1859 respectively.

It is not clear how the name of Simonds had been brought to the attention of Churchill.[5] There were in the field two Conservative ex-Law Officers with strong claims—J. S. C. Reid (later a Law Lord), and D. B. Somervell (then a Lord Justice of Appeal—a position to which he had been appointed by Attlee). It would have been unprecedented to appoint a Scotsman who was not a member of the English Bar, so the friends of Somervell thought that his claim could not be overlooked. But they were. It may well be that Churchill remembered that Somervell as Attorney-General had threatened Duncan Sandys with prosecution under the Official Secrets Act. He would also have remembered that

---

[3] *DNB, 1951-60*, p. 41.
[4] 'Recollections'.

Oct 31
1941

HOUSE OF LORDS,
S.W.1.

My dear Atkin

I so hope you will not resent it if I write this private and friendly note.

I asked Proby this morning to let me see, in confidence, the observations prepared for the 18B judgments on Monday — They of course call for the closest study & I have not had time for more than a glance. But my eye catches your very amusing citation from Lewis Carroll — Do you really, on final reflection, think this is necessary? I fear that it may be regarded as wounding to your colleagues who take the view you satirize, and I feel sure you would not willingly seek to hold them up to ridicule.

HOUSE OF LORDS,
S.W.1.

I am all in favour of enlivening judgments with literary allusion but I would venture, (greatly daring I know) to ask you whether the paragraph should be retained. Of course it is entirely for you. But I have gained so much from occasional suggestions of yours (mostly it is time, in cases when we have been sitting together) that I trust you will forgive this query. I at any rate feel that neither the dignity of the House, nor the collaboration of colleagues, nor the force of your reasoning would suffer from its omission. Yrs ever John Simon

1. Lord Simon's letter to Lord Atkin

3. William Jowitt in 1907

2. Lord Simon at the Foreign Office

4. Lord Jowitt as Chancellor

5. Lord Simonds on the Woolsack in March 1953 (the Bishop is Rt. Revd H. E. Wynn, Bishop of Ely)

6. Lord Simonds after being sworn in as Chancellor in October 1951

7. David Maxwell Fyfe at the Nuremberg trials in March 1946

8. Lord Kilmuir as Chancellor in Procession in October 1955 (the Mace is carried by the Serjeant-at-Arms, Air Vice-Marshal Sir Paul Maltby KCVO KCB; the Purse is carried by the Head Messenger, Mr Francis; the Train-Bearer is a Messenger, Mr Cokayne)

9. Reginald Manningham-Buller with Winston Churchill at Towcester in June 1945

10. The Conservative Cabinet at Chequers in April 1963 (Lord Dilhorne is second from right, beside Lord Hailsham)

11. Lord Gardiner as Chancellor of the Open University

12. Lord Gardiner at the Lord Chancellor's desk

Somervell had supported the Munich settlement—at Chartwell a sin which was not excused.[5A] It is also possible that Churchill lost interest in the whole matter once his Asquithian scheme had collapsed. But who would have taken the steps necessary to prefer Simonds over Somervell? The answer has been given by Lord Pearce:

Fred Woolton, with whom (and his Maud) we were on very friendly terms, when we were staying with them at Walberton told me that it was he who had suggested Gavin to Churchill after Cys Asquith had refused, and supported him with the backing of Bobbety Salisbury.[6]

This is inherently likely—but it still leaves open the question of how Woolton (and Salisbury) knew that Simonds was *papabile*. Woolton had a slight acquaintance with Simonds, but 'was frankly scared of Churchill and never became intimate either with him, or through lack of social self-confidence, with other leading Tory politicians'.[7] It is most unlikely that he would have imperilled his position as Leader of the Conservative Party by suggesting an appointment which might have proved disastrous. (This is not a factor that would have influenced Salisbury, or members of the Chartwell entourage like Bracken: but to Woolton it would have been important.) So whom would Woolton have asked for advice? It is suggested that only one man fulfils the required qualifications—Sir Albert Napier, who had been Private Secretary to the Lord Chancellor since 1944, and had been an exact contemporary of Simonds at New College. He had already been in contact with Sir Norman Brook at No. 10 to stress the importance of an early appointment to the Woolsack if the writs for the new Parliament were to be sealed in time.

So when Parliament met on 6 November it found Simonds on the Woolsack. He needed no writ of summons or introduction.[8] In another Government it might have been a disadvantage to have a Lord Chancellor who was so inexperienced politically. In the well-known words of Kilmuir, Simonds 'was as innocent of politics as a newly baptized babe, and obviously enjoyed his immersion enormously'.[9] But Salisbury and Woolton were able to control the Lords, and Sir Lionel Heald and (Sir) Reginald Manningham-Buller in the Commons were able to deal with the rather moderate legal talent fielded by the Labour Party.

Simonds was unknown by sight to most of the inhabitants of the Palace of Westminster. So Richard Crossman, although a Wykehamist and the son of a Chancery judge, was surprised to find at a parliamentary reception for Conrad

---

[5] The Churchill Archive contains nothing relevant.
[5A] Somervell was unrepentant. 'Better be a man of Munich than of man of Yalta', he said to the author.
[6] Letter to the author.　　　　　　　　　　　　　　[7] *DNB, 1961–70*, p. 731.
[8] See above p. 3.　　　　　　　　　　　　　　　　　[9] Kilmuir, *Political Adventure*, p. 194.

Adenauer in December 1951 that the visitor was introduced by 'an unknown character in white bands and with odd black eyebrows which must have stuck out a quarter of an inch', who proceeded 'to make a fulsome and boring speech about German democracy'.[1]

Lack of political experience was certainly a disadvantage to Simonds personally inasmuch as Chancery judges are not accustomed to being contradicted, and he was too apt to interpret opposition as an insult to himself or the office which he held. One such incident arose out of proposals to legitimize what was then called commercial television. A White Paper which proposed the breaking of the BBC monopoly was the subject of a debate on 26 May 1952. 'Trust the people', Simonds advised the peers.[2] Some amongst his audience were surprised—but for different reasons. A few of the opponents of commerical television, such as Jowitt ('this evil thing') thought that a Wykehamist should have been more alive to the problem of educating our masters. The former Director-General of the BBC (and in effect its creator), Lord Reith, recorded in his diary:

Sat in the House of Lords from 2.30 till 7.15. Some of the speakers were utterly revolting. And the Lord Chancellor was shocking also—talking like a socialist on the hunt for votes about liberty, Milton's *Areopagitica* and all . . . Very tired and *very, very disgusted*.[3]

Reith's feelings erupted in the *Observer* for 15 June. He wrote:

It is the B.B.C. and its friends who are fighting to preserve the freedom of the ether: Lord Woolton, the Lord Chancellor, Mr. Profumo and his associates who would surrender it to the brute force of money.

In his turn the Lord Chancellor erupted, as he recorded in his 'Recollections'.

What then was my anger when I read in the next issue of a Sunday newspaper an article by Lord Reith in which he questioned my sincerity and in effect charged me with prostituting my high office for party advantage? I will confess that I saw red. The annoyance and self-righteousness of the writer might be forgiven but his insolence in making such a charge against me was more than I could bear.

Reith was not accustomed to apologize or explain, but in Simonds he met his match for tenacity. An opportunity for a counter-attack did not arise until another Lords debate on television in November 1953.

---

[1] J. Morgan (ed.) *the Backbench Diaries of Richard Crossman* (1981), p. 47.
[2] 176 H. L. Deb. cols. 1439–46.
[3] C. Stuart (ed.), *The Reith Diaries* (1975), p. 481.

By that time no doubt the thing for everyone except myself had become rather stale. But I was not inclined to let it go. I gave Lord Reith notice and said what I thought of his attack. He did not attend the debate but next day appeared and made an explanation which I was content to accept as an apology. So ended what was for me the only disagreeable incident in my tenure of office.

The remainder of Simonds's speech was marked by an extraordinary degree of rhetoric. He denied that in art or literature the bad drove out the good. 'Does Shakespeare live? Has that immortal voice been stilled? Is that hand of glory withered? Shakespeare reigns. And why?' Because, Simonds answered, for once almost losing control over the structure of his speech, Shakespeare had been chosen by the British people and not by the BBC.[4]

In 1952 there was a debate on a motion 'to restore and preserve' the liberties of the subject.[5] The mover was Viscount Samuel, almost the last survivor of Asquith's Cabinet. He was naturally given support by Simon. One of the points made was that not all the proposals of the Donoughmore Committee had been carried into effect. Simonds, in a speech which was otherwise rather lukewarm, denied this in his usual trenchant style, and refused 'to be cross-examined' on whether he still held views to which he had subscribed in 1932. Simon slipped in a remark about the Lord Chancellor having signed the report 'before he became a politician'. There was an explosion on the Woolsack. A call was made for the withdrawal of 'a singularly unpleasant observation'—but Simon, with the skill of an old parliamentary hand, avoided this.

Incidents like this gave rise to the impression of Simonds as a domineering or impatient chairman. It is true that Simonds, in part because of his lack of political experience, was not good at concealing his impatience with irrelevant or obstructive speakers. A Chancery judge in his own court also has the advantage that he can cross and uncross his legs in irritation without being observed. On the Woolsack, as the Methuen portrait of Simonds in that position shows, every movement is clearly visible.[6] Mutterings were also audible during the speeches of socialist intellectuals like Chorley;[7] twenty years later there were more peers with fashionably progressive views, and even more muttered comments from the Woolsack.

But as a chairman of the Appellate Committee Simonds attracted the admiration of a critic as a severe as Lord Radcliffe.

Looking back over a long personal experience of the final court (I argued my first case in the Privy Council in 1930), I do think that the actual hearing of appeals has much

---

[4] 184 H. L. Deb. cols. 667–81. So the crowds outside the Albert Hall at Easter 'are not waiting to hear some melancholy crooner mouthing an erotic melody: that they can hear on the B.B.C.'.

[5] 177 H. L. Deb. cols. 1168–1242.   [6] Pl. 6.

[7] R. S. T. Chorley, Professor of Commercial Law at LSE, had been created a peer in 1945.

improved ... A good presiding judge counts a lot here. I have never detected any correspondence between his eminence as a lawyer and his performance as a president. There have been fine lawyers, for instance, such as Lord Blanesburgh and Lord Atkin, themselves the nicest of men, who seemed positively to prefer that a case should go on for ever to the possibility of an argument of which they disapproved remaining on its legs: whereas Lord Simonds, whom many think of (wrongly) as an obstinate and prejudiced judge, was a model in his conduct of a hearing, concise, courteously patient and resignedly fair.[8]

(It should be added that this account was written by one who knew that Simonds disapproved of his frequent absences from the House of Lords to chair Royal Commissions.)

This impression can be checked by reference to *The Times* for 16 May 1963, which devoted two and a half columns to a verbatim report of an application for leave to appeal brought by a Nigerian litigant in person, Chief Enahoro, against a decision by the Home Secretary to deport him to Nigeria to face (he claimed) a trial by his political enemies. Simonds, presiding, treated him with every consideration. On the other hand, when the House conferred after argument, one Law Lord noted that Simonds 'so hated being in a minority that he would have two or three meetings trying to get everybody round to his point of view'.[9]

This is the appropriate point to consider the difficult question of the relationship between Simonds and Denning. In the summer of 1951 the House of Lords had in three different appeals refused to approve the views of Denning LJ—and the refusal was expressed in language markedly different from the elaborately polite phrases normally used when correcting the errors of the lower courts. One judgment was that of Simon in *British Movietonews Ltd.* v. *London & District Cinemas Ltd.*[1] He had appointed Denning to the Bench, and he wrote him a letter 'to soften the blow'.

No such letter was written by Simonds before or after his speeches in *Howell* v. *Falmouth Boat Construction Co. Ltd.*[2] and *Magor & St Mellors UDC* v. *Newport Corporation.*[3] In the latter case, on 25 October 1951, he delivered the leading opinion of a tribunal which also included Lords Goddard, Radcliffe, Morton, and Tucker on a question of local-government law which was of such little importance that the editor of the Law Reports stated, exceptionally: 'it is unnecessary to report the case save as relates to their Lordships' observations as to the construction of statutes'. Denning, in what Lord Morton called 'a vigorous judgment', had said that 'we sit here to find out the intention of

---

[8] (1973) 36 *MLR* 559, 562. Simonds himself 'recalled how the continual interruptions of Lord Blanesburgh used to worry his colleagues almost beyond self-control' ('Recollections'). See also above, pp. 27–8.

[9] A. Paterson, *The Law Lords* (1982), p. 120.

[1] [1952] AC 166.   [2] [1951] AC 837.   [3] [1952] AC 189.

Parliament and of Ministers and carry it out, and we do this better by filling in the gaps and making sense of the enactment than by opening it up to desctructive analysis'. Simonds retorted that 'this proposition . . . cannot be supported. It appears to me to be naked usurpation of the legislative function under the thin guise of interpretation'. Nearly thirty years later Denning was unrepentant: 'So injustice was done'.[4]

In April 1957 Denning himself became a Law Lord. His first speech was a dissent—and it provoked a strong rebuke from Simonds which was concurred in by the other members of the tribunal (Lords Reid, Cohen, Morton, and Tucker).[5] Denning thought that a sovereign state could not plead immunity from suit in England if the transaction in question was a commercial one. This dissentient view has since been approved by Parliament in the State Immunity Act 1978. It is irrelevant now that Simonds and his colleagues thought otherwise on a difficult question. What is still relevant is the reason for their rebuke of Denning—namely that he had considered questions and authorities not mentioned in the argument of counsel.

To Simonds this was an error which went to the heart of the judicial process—although nobody seems to have noticed that it was one which he himself had committed ten years before.[6] It was one thing for a judge to use his background reading and knowledge acquired over a lifetime in the law— indeed, the litigants expected him to use his matured mind and judgment: that was what he was paid to do. But it was quite another thing to decide against a litigant without giving him the opportunity of meeting the results of the judicial researches. On this issue Simonds was surely right. For a judge to do this

has the effect of depriving the parties to the action of the benefit of one of the most fundamental rules of natural justice: the right of each to be informed of any point addressed to him that is going to be relied upon by the judge and to be given an opportunity of stating what his answer to it is.[7]

After *Rahimtoola* Simonds seems to have developed an intense intellectual dislike or contempt for Denning's approach to the law. He seems to have regarded that approach as marked by intellectual dishonesty which imperilled the structure of the law and gave undue prominence to the individual judge. In 1960 there was a debate on the law relating to charities, in which Denning

[4] Lord Denning, *The Discipline of Law* (1979), p. 14.
[5] *Rahimtoola* v. *Nizam of Hyderabad* [1958] Ac 359.
[6] In *National Anti-Vivisection Society* v. *IRC* [1948] AC 31, Simonds based a vital part of his judgment on a passage in an obscure textbook (*Tyssen on Charitable Bequests*) not cited by counsel.
[7] *Hadmor Productions Ltd.* v. *Hamilton* [1983] AC 191, at 233, per Lord Diplock. Paterson, *Law Lords*, pp. 38–43, has a full discussion of this question. The same authority (p. 249) records that in 10 appeals between 1953 and 1961 in which the HL split 3:2, Simonds was in the majority in only 5. So to Simonds dissent in itself was not objectionable.

spoke, and gave a critical account of the Diplock case. Simonds described
Denning's account as 'completely unwarranted'.[8] That was a very strong
statement for one Law Lord to make about another. A year later the climax was
reached in the Midland Silicones case.[9] It raised the issue whether a third party
was ever entitled to sue on a contract which had been made for his benefit.
During the argument counsel noticed some tension in the air after one midday
adjournment. Perhaps conscious of the way the wind was blowing, Ashton
Roskill QC, for the respondents, argued that 'it is more important that the law
should be clear than that it should be clever'. His point was taken. A majority of
the Law Lords (Denning dissenting) emphatically reaffirmed the traditional
principle of privity of contract. The third party was not entitled to sue. Simonds
said:

For me heterodoxy, or, as some might say, heresy, is not the more attractive because it is
dignified by the name of reform. Nor will I easily be led by an undiscerning zeal for
some abstract kind of justice to ignore our first duty, which is to administer justice
according to law, the law which is established for us by Act of Parliament or the binding
authority of precedent. The law is developed by the application of old principles to new
circumstances. Therein lies its genius. Its reform by the abrogation of those principles is
the task not of the courts but of Parliament.

There can be no doubt as to the target of these remarks. Denning later wrote
that he was 'verbally beheaded'.[1]

   It has been debated whether this intellectual antipathy on Simond's part
passed over the boundary into personal dislike. They were certainly men from
very different Hampshire backgrounds, who might not have wished to sit
beside each other at dinner unless obliged to do so—not from dislike, but from
absence of points of contact. Lord Pearce, who often saw both together at
Lincoln's Inn, was confident that there was no personal enmity. (This is also the
opinion of the Simonds family, who recall friendly visits between Sparsholt and
Whitchurch.) But Lord Pearce did not arrive in the Lords until Denning had
left it, and some of those who were there at the time thought he had painted 'a
rosier picture of the relationship than existed'. One said that the tension was
manifest to all, and that there was general relief when in 1962 the Lord Chief
Justice, Parker (also of Lincoln's Inn), produced the happy solution that
Denning and Evershed should exchange places, Denning being appointed
Master of the Rolls, and Evershed going to the House of Lords. Another who
knew all parties very well, recorded simply that 'I am not prepared to write
about what I saw and heard'.

---

[8] 222 H. L. Deb. cols. 530–2.
[9] [1962] AC 446, 459.
[1] Lord Denning, *The Family Story* (1981), p. 202.

There were few judicial vacancies during Simond's Chancellorship—and only one in the Chancery Division, in November 1951, to which Gerald Upjohn QC was appointed. He remained the junior Chancery judge for an exceptionally lengthy period (over eight years) until he was promoted to the Court of Appeal, and then to the House of Lords. There was also only one appointment to the Queen's Bench Division (H. Glyn-Jones QC). In the Probate, Divorce, and Admiralty Division there were two appointments—Arthian Davies QC and E. Sachs QC. In his 'Recollections' Simonds recorded that he was under no political pressure in respect of any of these appointments—and conversely, that the Prime Minister had consulted him in relation to each of the appointments which were in his gift. The highest standards were expected from all judges: twice rebukes were privately administered. Sir George Coldstream informed the author:

I have the clearest memories of G. T. S.'s passionate concern for 'standards' in the conduct and disposition of judicial business in the House of Lords and the Privy Council. He was immensely concerned about 'quality' in all its aspects—and I have used the word 'passionate' advisedly! He really *hated* sloppy advocacy, and sloppy writing . . . In that respect the style (or lack of it) of Raymond Evershed and Tom Denning really irritated him.

As a legislator Simonds was not outstanding: even if he had had more time on the Woolsack, he would not have been interested in, perhaps would even have disliked, the possibility of reforming English law by statute. His creative energies found release in his judgments. In this he differed from Jowitt. But Simonds must be given credit for his revival, in 1954, of the Law Reform Committee, which had been set up by Sankey in 1934, but not revived by Jowitt after the war, because the latter's experience of the Commons made him doubt whether time could be found for any legislation which it recommended. But Simonds 'under pressure from the reformers', took the necessary steps, appointing Jenkins as the chairman. (Its first report recommended the repeal of some obsolete provisions of the Statute of Frauds, which was duly done by the Law Reform (Enforcement of Contracts) Act 1954. The report was one and a half pages in length, and its cost to the Treasury was £10. 7s. 6d. One wonders what the Law Commission would have done with it today.) In 1952 Simonds had set up a similar body to devote itself entirely to the very special problems of Private International Law and—an important point—appointed a member of the Lord Chancellor's Department as its secretary.

Three law reform measures did reach the statute-books under Simonds, but he could not claim the main credit for any of them. The Defamation Act 1952, which was based on the Porter Committee's Report in 1948, was enacted largely through the efforts of Jowitt and Simon. The Law Reform (Limitation of Actions) Act 1954 was based on the Report of the Tucker Committee.

The end of Simonds's Chancellorship came as suddenly as its commence-
ment. In the spring of 1954 all seemed set fair. Walter Monckton, then Minister
of Labour, was anxious to reassert his claim to succeed Goddard as Lord Chief
Justice, and asked Simonds for advice. Simonds did not regard Monckton's
divorce as unfavourably as Goddard was know to do, and replied that, if as was
expected, Lord Porter resigned in the autumn, he (Simonds) would advise that
Monckton should be appointed in his place with the excpectation of the
ultimate desired preferment.[2] Porter, who was aged seventy-seven and in poor
health, was induced to tell Downing Street that he would retire when it was
convenient. In the event this had unexpected repercussions for Simonds.

A minor Cabinet reshuffle in July 1954 passed without incident, but it was
know that Sir David Maxwell Fyfe felt he had done his duty to the party and the
country by serving in the Home Office for three difficult years. Churchill
recognized his claims and was willing to gratify them.[3] By contrast Simonds had
never been personally congenial to Churchill (indeed, few lawyers except
Birkenhead ever had been), as distinct from other members of his Cabinet.[4]
During the summer Woolton had tried to hint to Simonds that his tenure was
insecure, but he did not think the Lord Chancellor had really taken it in.

The axe fell in the second week of October. Salisbury was sent to break the
news. He gave several reasons. One was that Churchill desired to bring Gwilym
Lloyd George into the Cabinet, and this could be done only if Maxwell Fyfe's
promotion opened up a vacancy at the Home Office. On 14 October Porter was
informed by No. 10 that his resignation would be activated immediately. On
Monday the 18th it was announced that Simonds had surrendered the Great
Seal and had been reappointed a Lord of Appeal in Ordinary. (The surrender
took place in the morning: in the afternoon Maxwell Fyfe took delivery. So the
two men did not meet.) On the same day Simonds was granted a viscountcy: 'it
was an honour that I was glad to receive'.[5] The pleasure was somewhat tarnished
by the granting of the same dignity to Maxwell Fyfe. (The announcement was
also made on the 18th, but to avoid the impropriety of exactly simultaneous
creations, the letters patent for Maxwell Fyfe's viscountcy did not pass the Great
Seal until Tuesday the 19th.)

Simonds did not conceal his annoyance at being replaced by one nearly
twenty years his junior for whose attainments as a lawyer he had little respect. (It
is significant that throughout his 'Recollections' he consistently refers to his
successor as 'Fyffe', and that this misspelling alone is left uncorrected). Simonds
never seems to have appreciated that Churchill would be under pressure to
recognize Maxwell Fyfe's services to the party and the Government. Heald, who

[2] Earl of Birkenhead, *Walter Monckton* (1969), p. 303.
[3] Macmillan *Tides of Fortune*, p. 547.
[4] Lord Moran, *Winston Churchill: The Struggle for Survival* (1966), p. 605.
[5] 'Recollections'.

was replaced as Attorney-General by Manningham-Buller, later wrote that Simonds 'made no complaint'.[6] This is a minority view. 'Everybody knows that Gavin felt deeply hurt and affronted by the way in which the change was announced.'[7]

Thus after three years my 'political adventure' ended and once more I was back in the familiar world of law and lawyers. And now, as I write about it nearly ten years later, it sometimes seems like a strange dream. I suppose that at some future date there will be a successor to Atlay and Professor Heuston who will write the Lives of the Chancellors from 1940 onwards and I daresay he will not find much good to say about me. I was at any rate loyal to my colleagues and gave them what help I could.[8]

Naturally these feelings were not allowed to influence the way in which Simonds discharged his duties as Lord of Appeal in Ordinary after 18 October 1954. (Simonds stated in his 'Recollections' that the full title of the office was due to the fact that it was 'ordinarily' held by life peers who sat to hear appeals. But Denning said that it was 'a technical term used in law to describe a judge who has judrisdiction to hear cases by virtue of his office. In contrast to other persons who have jurisdiction only by being peers.'[9] On this point Simonds was, uncharacteristically, wrong and Denning was right.) A steady flow of judgments of the highest quality culminated in two powerful contributions in Simonds's eightieth year—*The Wagon Mound (No. 1)* and *Shaw* v. *DPP*. One month after *Shaw* he was laid low by a stroke, and on 31 March he resigned his office. He had been a judge for twenty-five years in all—seven in the Chancery Division, and eighteen in the House of Lords. Despite his retirement, he was called back to sit on five appeals between 1962 and 1966. In all he sat on 174 appeals between 1952 and 1966—a figure surpassed only by Reid (359). Only six of these were his years on the Woolsack. Beyond his judicial work there was activity at Lincoln's Inn (Treasurer, 1951), Oxford (High Steward, 1954–67), and Winchester (Warden, 1946–51). In the last capacity some annoyance was displayed with those who wished to broaden the investment portfolio to include more than the traditional trustee holdings in land and Government securities. 'Equities? An absurd term': so Simonds would rebuke the reformers. He was delighted to discover that the Chairman of Lazards, Lord Brand, was assuring the Fellows of All Souls that 'If there had been such a thing as equities in the Middle Ages there wouldn't be a College in existence in Oxford today'.[1]

Simonds also fulfilled the duty, traditional to ex-Lord Chancellors, of acting

[6] *The Times*, 2 July 1971.
[7] Sir George Coldstream to the author.
[8] 'Recollections'.
[9] Denning, *Family Story*, p. 184.
[1] G. Rees, *A Chapter of Accidents* (1971), p. 232.

as editor-in-chief of a new (third) edition of Halsbury's *Laws of England*. He took his duties seriously. The editor of the article on powers was sent a list of ten comments, 'nine of which were spot on'.

In his eighty-seventh year Simonds delivered a short but vigorous speech on the committee stage of the Divorce Reform Bill, which in effect proposed that the breakdown of a marriage should be the grounds for dissolving it. After warning the House that 'I am not only old-fashioned but very old!', Simonds opposed the Bill on the grounds of 'justice, decency and honour'.[2] These were certainly old-fashioned words in the England of 1969.

Simonds died at his London flat, 54 Rutland Gardens, on 28 June 1971, and was cremated at Golder's Green on 2 July. Only a few days beforehand he had excused himself from a Lincoln's Inn dinner to mark the retirement of Lord Parker, the Lord Chief Justice. His handwriting was as firm as ever. Simonds's estate was sworn for probate at £305,279—the largest sum left by any Lord Chancellor since Eldon.

[2] 303 H. L. Deb. cols. 1298–1300.

LORD KILMUIR

THERE are three places in Scotland called Kilmuir. The best-known is in Skye, but there are two in Ross and Cromarty—one a small village a few miles east of Inverness, and the other a larger locality east of Invergordon, on the north side of the Firth of Cromarty. The later gave the Lord Chancellor his title, although his father, William Thomson Fyfe, came from Kirkton-of-Echt, west of Aberdeen. But William Fyfe's second wife,[1] Isabella Campbell, came from the parish of Creich, next to that of Kilmuir Easter, and ancestors are buried in the graveyard at Creich, some miles west of the ancient borough of Dornoch, in which she had been born, at Tordarroch, a small house opposite the cathedral. The parents had met at Aberdeen University. Their only child, David Patrick Maxwell Fyfe,[2] was born at 8.40 a.m. on 29 May 1900 at the house then numbered 60 (it is now 72) in Morningside Drive, a good residential quarter of Edinburgh. The father was described as 'publisher' in the birth certificate. Previously he had been headmaster of Aberdeen Grammar School; later he was to be described as 'inspector of schools' and 'author'. (He had written a good book on the Edinburgh of Walter Scott.) David Fyfe went to George Watson's College, one of the famous day schools of Edinburgh.

In the autumn of 1917 Maxwell Fyfe went up to Balliol. It was very unusual for a boy from such a Scottish background to arrive at Balliol without either a degree or a scholarship. But the devotion of his parents, the traditional percipience of the dons, and the chances of war-time, combined to bring this about. His tutor was A. W. Pickard-Cambridge, who was succeeded by A. D. Lindsay. Neither was remembered with affection or respect. The first was recalled as a snob; the latter as 'a grey socialist don'.[3] Maxwell Fyfe was not the sort of undergraduate who would have interested 'Sligger' Urquhart,[4] so his contacts with the senior members of the College (of which he later became an Honorary Fellow) were slight—especially after he obtained a Third in Greats in 1921, following Pass Moderations in 1919. On festive occasions in later life Kilmuir was fond of repeating the dictum that 'a Third [was] the best Class, because it avoid[ed] the blatant ostentation of a First, the pretentious mediocrity of a Second, and the obvious failure of a Fourth'.

Maxwell Fyfe's interests were in his contemporaries: through them he found the entry to the inner circles of English political life, still excitingly romantic

---

[1] One of five children of his first marriage was Sir Sutherland Fyfe, an authority on agriculture. He is not mentioned in his brother's memoirs.

[2] The future Lord Chancellor started using the (unhyphenated) form Maxwell Fyfe in his early days at the Bar, to avoid confusion with another David Fyfe, a Middle Temple barrister. When created Earl of Kilmuir in 1962, he took as his secondary title Baron Fyfe of Dornoch.

[3] Kilmuir, *Memoirs* (1964), p. 18.

[4] F. F. Urquhart was Dean of Balliol 1916-33.

and aristocratic. So time and energy were given to being Treasurer of the Union (he was beaten for the presidency by Cecil Ramage of Pembroke), and President of the Arnold Society.

Maxwell Fyfe and Balliol were contemplating the wisdom of him staying up for a fourth year in which to read for the Law School, when an opportunity arose which was far better for all parties. A vacancy occurred on the staff of a body called the British Commonwealth Union, which did the parliamentary work of the Federation of British Industries. 'It seemed a wonderful chance to earn some money while I read for the Bar and passed my Bar exams.[5] So a year passed in which more friends were made at Westminster, in the City—and in Mayfair. Thirty-five years later the Lord Chancellor could always be persuaded to accept an invitation to dinner if the hostess was notable for birth, beauty, or intelligence. Maxwell Fyfe as a co-founder of the Coningsby Club was naturally a firm believer in the Disraelian dictum that 'A little dinner-party with all the guests clever, and some pretty, offers human life and human nature under very favourable circumstances'.[6] He had few other recreations. He was not interested in field sports or country life, and read little outside his work.

Maxwell Fyfe was called to the Bar at Gray's Inn on 28 June 1922. He became a Bencher in 1936 and Treasurer in 1949. He was only the third Lord Chancellor to come from Gray's Inn (Bacon and Birkenhead were the others). All his ambitions lay in London: but Scottish prudence dictated a start in the provinces. So he entered the chambers of the future Mr. Justice Lynskey at Liverpool, and joined the Northern Circuit. Even Maxwell Fyfe's spirits sank at the sight of Liverpool in January 1923. 'I did not know a soul in this vast, cloud-enshrouded, mushy, and weeping city except the wonderfully kind Judge Dowdall[7] and Philip Rea.'[8] Years later Lord Rea recalled how Maxwell Fyfe had told him he intended to take silk in his thirties, to be a Government minister in his forties, and to be at the top of the legal profession in his fifties.[9]

The note of frank ambition struck some as careerism. This is 'a trait that Scots are particularly quick to spot in each other, and which may be the term which an envious person uses to describe another's success'.[1] To those who had accused John Buchan of this vice, Maxwell Fyfe replied that 'they never understood the living sense of history of the Scot'.[2] To the Celt, looking in from the outside darkness through the windows which framed the splendour of

---

[5] Memoirs, p. 19.

[6] B. Disraeli, Coningsby, World's Classics edn. (1982), p. 26.

[7] This remarkable man combined several careers—Lord Mayor of Liverpool before he was 40 (and as such the subject of a magnificent portrait by Augustus John); draftsman of the York–Antwerp Rules of bills of lading, and President of the Society of Public Teachers of Law.

[8] Memoirs, p. 26.

[9] 242 H.L. Deb. col. 531.

[1] J. Adam Smith, John Buchan (1953), p. 346.

[2] Memoirs, p. 23.

English political life, there was something very satisfying about being on first-name terms with the Cecils and the Cavendishes. So one can explain much in the life-style of John Buchan, Brendan Bracken, Iain Macleod—as well as in that of Maxwell Fyfe himself. In him there were two Scottish characteristics—canniness and moral integrity. But the canniness never gave the impression of deviousness, as it did with Macleod; and in his integrity never lurked 'the indescribable Scottish quality of unction', which Buchan disapprovingly noted in some Scottish lawyer-politicians.[3]

Maxwell Fyfe had one quality which young barristers do not often possess: he looked older than his years. In him the Celtic strain had produced a visage of Middle Eastern pallor and swarthiness. (His great-great-grandfather had been known in Sutherland as Dai Dhu (Black David).) A large head, bald early in life, but adorned with dark, heavy eyebrows, surmounted a stocky, pear-shaped body.

Maxwell Fyfe's first chambers were at 25 Lord Street, Liverpool—an address which had once been that of F. E. Smith. In his first year, Maxwell Fyfe earned £330, but by 1930 the figure had risen to nearly £5,000—a good income for a provincial junior. In part this was due to support from the formidable party machine which the Conservatives had established in Liverpool under Sir Archibald Salvidge. In any case Maxwell Fyfe was able to take silk just before his thirty-fourth birthday—an achievement which not even Simon or Birkenhead had surpassed. In 1935 he set up his own chambers in the Temple (1 Harcourt Buildings), and until the outbreak of war his annual income did not fall below £5,000.

On 15 April 1925 Maxwell Fyfe married Sylvia (Margaret) Harrison, daughter of William Reginald Harrison, a civil engineer of Liverpool. She was a sister of Rex Harrison, the actor, and as ambitious and perspicacious as he was.[4] She gave her husband unremitting support in his career, both in Liverpool and in London. The Maxwell Fyfe's had three daughters. After Kilmuir's death, his widow married the ninth Earl De La Warr, an old friend, on whose estate in Sussex the Kilmuirs had a small house for some years. This house, then called Hardings, had been a wood-keeper's cottage; now, much enlarged and embellished, it is called Kovac's Corner.

Maxwell Fyfe's political career developed a little slowly. In 1924 he had fought Wigan—a hopeless contest, but it won goodwill in the party. In 1929 he was selected to fight Sir John Simon at Spen Valley, but Baldwin personally intervened to secure his withdrawal in view of Simon's responsibilities as Chairman of the Indian Statutory Commission. It was not until July 1935 that

---

[3] Adam Smith, *John Buchan*, p. 182.

[4] 'I think of myself as a self-made man—I had no education to speak of, and inherited no money. My main incentive was to get out and get on, and not hang about like my father' (R. Harrison, *Rex: An Autobiography* (1974), p. 229).

Maxwell Fyfe was returned unopposed at a by-election for the West Derby Division of Liverpool. (He was re-elected for the same constituency at the general election in November, and again in 1945, 1950, and 1951. But on each occasion his majority was slightly reduced,and in 1964 the seat went to Labour.) Simon, reasonably enough, was grateful to Maxwell Fyfe, and did his best to help the new MP—for example, by advising him not to make his maiden speech on a legal subject. When a fortnight later Maxwell Fyfe did just that, Simon showed no resentment, but simply repeated his advice in a letter of 30 July:

I failed to catch you in the Division Lobby yesterday after your maiden speech to congratulate you and tell you how good I thought it was. You must be glad to have taken the plunge and I hope you will choose your opportunity from time to time to build up a reputation as a debater. If an old hand may venture a suggestion, it would be that the next time you should eschew a lawyer's subject. The greatest compliment ever paid to me in my early days in the House was Arthur Balfour's smiling observation, 'Why, I did not know that you were a lawyer.'

It is very difficult for a busy man at the Bar, and especially for a K.C. whose colleagues persist in calling him their 'honourable and *learned* Friend', to do this. And it is out of the frying pan into the fire if a lawyer M.P. takes part in general debate without really knowing the subject from end to end, for the house very quickly detects superficiality, but it is the real way to do it, as the careers of Harcourt and Carson and Asquith show.

I hope that you won't take this as a paternal lecture! I take a very special interest in your Parliamentary debut because of our old associations, and am so glad that you got in without defeating me![5]

From 1935 to 1940 Maxwell Fyfe devoted himself to his legal and political careers. He recorded that 'during the Assizes I was constantly conferring from 9 a.m. until 10.30, in Court (with a short interval for lunch) until 5.15 p.m., then on the 5.25 from Liverpool or 5.45 from Manchester, reaching London at 9. Then in the House until after the 11 o'clock division, then back on the midnight train to the North . . .'. It is not surprising that he was 'envied in politics much more often for my physical stamina than for my brains'.[6]

The strain did not prevent the development of a fairly active London social life. In the words of a Northern Circuit ditty, 'Under the forbidding shell,/He does himself extremely well.'

But after the war even Maxwell Fyfe felt the strain of having a constituency so far from London. He had hopes of being selected for Epsom, but his elevation to the Woolsack occurred before a decision was necessary. His successor at West Derby, A. V. Woollam, recalled how industrious Maxwell Fyfe was in the constituency—he obeyed without hesitation any request from the party agent to attend even the humblest function, and, in the days before MPs came to be

[5] Simon Papers.
[6] *Memoirs*, pp. 38, 224.

regarded as welfare officers, was assiduous in dealing with tiresome requests about housing and pensions, which others might have referred to members of the local authority.

At the Manchester Spring Assizes in 1936 Maxwell Fyfe appeared for the Crown, with Shawcross as his junior in the prosecution for murder of Dr Buck Ruxton, who was defended by (Sir) Norman Birkett—'one of the longest and most horrible murder trials in English criminal history'.[7] Some lessons to be of value at Nuremberg were learnt. The outbreak of war found Maxwell Fyfe too old for active service with his regiment (he had been commissioned in the Scots Guards in 1918). He joined the Judge Advocate General's department, where he found Reginald Manningham-Buller, his successor as Lord Chancellor, as well as six future High Court judges.

In March 1942 Maxwell Fyfe became Solicitor-General in place of Jowitt. Churchill had first thought of appointing 'a very well-known political lawyer'.[8] but Bracken had strongly supported the claims of Maxwell Fyfe. The routine duties of his office did not entirely occupy Maxwell Fyfe's time: at one stage he had a committee meeting each evening. He was made a Privy Counsellor. When he was replaced by Hartley Shawcross (an old colleague from the Northern Circuit), he was permitted to continue with the preparatory work he had done for the Nuremberg trials. Shawcross was the chief prosecutor, but after making the opening speech, he was content to leave the daily conduct of the trials to Maxwell Fyfe.

Once it had been decided to hold the Nuremberg trials, a vast degree of organizational skill was required to bring together the people and the documents needed. All this was satisfactorily accomplished, largely as a result of the efforts of the American prosecutor, Mr Justice Jackson. Unfortunately he was less successful in the court-room. His cross-examination of Goering lasted three days, and threw the prosecution team into deep despair. On the Bench Birkett noted two reasons for this triumph by Goering. First, he turned out to be much more intelligent than anyone had imagined, and had a photographic memory. 'Suave, shrewd, adroit, capable, resourceful, he quickly saw the elements of the situation, and his confidence grew, his mastery became more apparent.' Secondly, Jackson 'had never learnt the very first elements of cross-examination as it is understood in the English courts. He was overwhelmed by his documents, and there was no chance of the lightning question following upon some careless or damaging answer, no quick parry and thrust, no leading the witness on to the prepared pitfall, and above all no clear over-riding conception of the great issues which could have been put with simplicity and

---

[7] Montgomery Hyde, *Norman Birkett* (1964), p. 445.

[8] *Memoirs*, p. 66. It is not certain who this was—perhaps Walter Monckton. Bracken in 1958 made some wounding remarks about the quality and quantity of Maxwell Fyfe's practice: see C. Lysaght, *Brendan Bracken* (1979), p. 327.

power'.[9] There was a good example of this on the first day. Jackson pressed Goering with a document which was alleged to show his knowledge of the liberation of the Rhineland. Not at all, responded the witness—the document dealt with the clearing of the river Rhine from such obstructions as sunken vessels. There were smirks of triumph in the dock, and Jackson was reduced to complaining to the Bench that the witness was 'unresponsive'.

In this depressing atmosphere Maxwell Fyfe rose to begin the cross-examination for the British team. His difficulties were increased by the fact that the tribunal had ruled that further cross-examination could not traverse ground already covered: the trial had already lasted too long. Also he had to begin immediately after Jackson had finished, at the unpromising hour of 4.50 p.m. But he had decided to confront Goering, not on any ideological issue, where he would risk defeat, but on an issue of fact. The issue chosen was the murder, on the orders of Hitler, of fifty RAF prisoners who had escaped from Stalag Luft III. Meticulous as ever, Maxwell Fyfe made his juniors check and recheck Goering's claim that he had been on leave at the relevant time. He thought he could prove Goering's complicity, and he succeeded. He had done his homework: his knowledge of the organizational structure of the German air force was great enough to enable him to correct the answers of its former head. Once the witness had been shown to be fallible, Maxwell Fyfe moved on to other issues—the bombing of Belgrade, the death camps, the use of slave labour. A day and a half later Maxwell Fyfe sat down to general congratulations on a great forensic success. But it had been a close thing. As he recorded later, 'without question Goering was the most formidable witness I have ever cross-examined'.[1] The international reputation gained at Nuremberg was a considerable asset in the post-war years.

Maxwell Fyfe played a prominent part in the movement for European unity centred on Strasbourg. Unusually for a British lawyer, he was a strong advocate of the European Convention on Human Rights, and in fact drafted much of it himself. The United Kingdom eventually acceded to the convention. He was proud of the fact 'that I have done something positive as well as negative in regard to tyranny, which so many of my generation in the twentieth century have accepted without a murmur',[2] and never entirely forgave his seniors in the new Conservative Cabinet for their veto on Britain's entry into Europe. In particular a negative speech by Eden in Rome on the same day as Maxwell Fyfe was speaking in Strasbourg on a possible link between Britain and a proposed European Defence Community was widely seen as an attempt to torpedo that proposal. 'Ineradicable suspicion of London now prevailed in Western Europe capitals',[3] whereas only a few months before, whenever a committee of

---

[9] Montgomery Hyde, *Birkett*, p. 511.
[1] *Memoirs*, p. 114.   [2] *Memoirs*, p. 184.
[3] D. Carlton, *Anthony Eden* (1981), p. 311.

politicians had been set up to discuss any problem the United Kingdom representative had invariably been invited to take the chair, and his views listened to with almost excessive deference and respect. But all that goodwill was dissipated by the apparent duplicity of British conduct in 1951/2, and the humiliating rebuff administered by de Gaulle in 1963 was one of the results.

Back at Westminster Maxwell Fyfe found that the morale of his party was low. Many of the senior Members had not survived the 1945 landslide to Labour, and those who had were often suffering from post-war exhaustion. The task of opposition was taken up vigorously by Maxwell Fyfe—he made 178 speeches on the Tranpsort bill alone in the eighteen months following December 1946. After 1950 there was 'a rejuvenated and frankly bellicose opposition challenging every measure with tenacity and spirit... Our hatred of the Government was deep and sincere, we had many old scores to pay off, and the price which the Labour Party had to pay for their annoyance and abuse after 1945 was a very heavy one.'[4] In October 1951 Churchill appointed Maxwell Fyfe to be Home Secretary.

But Maxwell Fyfe was never content to be purely destructive. There was much work with R. A. Butler, rethinking Conservative policy on industry. Then the Maxwell Fyfe report on Conservative Party Organization was presented to Lord Woolton, Chairman of the Central Office, in 1948/9. One of its main results was the etablishment of a system of professional agents throughout the country. (A minor recommendation, based on some humiliating personal experiences, was that chairmen of local constituency organizations should treat potential candidates with greater civility.) An unexpected, and unwelcome, result was the greater independence of Central Office which the constituency organizations began to display. they showed a tendency to select, or reselect, as it would now be called, local worthies—a tendency hitherto confined to the Labour Party. 'Very few of the new Members who entered the Commons in 1955 and 1959 had achieved a reputation outside Westminster in any field, and far too many of them were obscure local citizens with obscure local interests, incapable—and indeed downright reluctant—to think on a national or international scale.'[5] (Maxwell Fyfe's successor at West Derby, A. V. Wollam, did not make his maiden speech until March 1955. He lost his seat to Labour in 1964.) Maxwell Fyfe died before he had to contemplate those who supported the Heath Government in 1970.

Maxwell Fyfe took his profession as a politician very seriously. He was not only assiduous in his constituency, and later at Central Office, but he also tried to explain why life in the Commons was enjoyable, and what qualities were

---

[4] *Memoirs*, p. 171. Lord Simonds ('Recollections', p. 152) was shocked that any British politician should feel hatred for his opponents.

[5] *Memoirs*, p. 158.

needed for success. 'A man who is not proud to be there has no right to be there … Time and again I have just walked down the book-lined corridors in the evening of a big debate with, in Duff Cooper's wonderful phrase, "causeless exultation in my heart".'[6] 'One vital test of the successful politician is that you can put him in any place and tell him to make a speech, and it would be perfectly attuned to the mood or circumstances of the audience—without losing its own purpose.'[7] Oddly enough, one of his staff at the Home Office thought he did not fulfil his own prescription. He wrote that he was astonished that 'a man who had made his living by speaking could do no more, on any public occasion, in the House or outside, than read out, in a rather halting manner, the exact words that his wretched civil servants had provided for him'. But Kilmuir was indefatigable. At the end of 1956 he made twenty speeches in six weeks outside Parliament, and in January 1957 there were eight. At weekends no party function in the country was too small for the Lord Chancellor to attend if invited by the organizers—or requested by Central Office. His officials sometimes chafed at the expenditure of time and energy which might have been devoted to the work of the office.

One quality which Maxwell Fyfe certainly had was what he himself called 'two o'clock in the morning courage'. When the politician

has come to a decision after the most careful thought and advice he must be prepared for the unpleasant consequences … It is always easy to see convenient and dignified lines of retreat, and the siren voices of well-intentioned friends are always present, but the public man, having reached his decision, and fully aware of the probable consequences must hold his ground.[8]

These qualities were most clearly demonstrated in January 1953 when Maxwell Fyfe refused to recommend the use of the royal prerogative to save from hanging a 19-year-old man, Bentley, who had been correctly convicted of murdering a police officer. (In those days the English police were unarmed.) Bentley's confederate, Craig, who had fired the shot, was aged sixteen and so was legally exempt from execution. Maxwell Fyfe refused to interfere with the due process of the law. An exceptional storm broke out over his head. In the streets there were demonstrations, and the police guard on the Maxwell Fyfe flat in Gray's Inn had to be doubled. But a man who had fought elections in Liverpool was not easily disconcerted by a London 'rent-a-crowd'.[9] Hostility in the House of Commons was another matter. Two hundred MPs, including ten ex-Ministers, signed a motion asking the Home Secretary to reconsider his decision. Maxwell Fyfe decided to give no public reason for the decision, and it

        [6] Ibid., p. 326.   [7] Ibid., p. 27.   [8] Ibid., p. 6.
      [9] 'It is all nonsense that electors sympathise with a candidate who has his meetings broken up. They don't. They think him a cissy' (Memoirs, p. 245).

was his alone, to allow the law to take its course.[1] White-faced and silent, he was a grim sight on the front bench. Only Dilhorne could have displayed similar conviction and courage. Simon and Jowitt would have been careful not to put themselves in such an exposed position; Simonds and Gardiner had never been required to ride out a major storm in the House of Commons. Kilmuir did this, and never lost his nerve or his judgement, as he was to accuse Harold Macmillan of doing in July 1962.

A happier aspect of the Home Office was the close connection with the arrangements for the Coronation in 1953, which brought the award of GCVO (conferred also on Simon for similar services in 1937).

Maxwell Fyfe left a deep impression on the head of the Cabinet secretariat, Norman Brook, who wrote that he was

very conscientious. What I like about him is that if you have a problem he will at once offer help and take any amount of trouble to find a solution. He has good judgment and when his report is ready every aspect is considered. Nothing is left out. It is pretty dull stuff, but when David is done the Cabinet doesn't want to discuss it any further, but is ready to pass on to the next item of the agenda.[2]

The point was put by R. A. Butler in his characteristic way: 'Maxwell Fyfe may have been living proof that Carlyle was wrong to define genius as a transcendent capacity for taking trouble; but he did have a most astounding appetite for and application to paper work'.[3] Yet it is hard not to agree with A. V. Dicey's observation that no lawyer should be appointed Home Secretary; his training does not fit him for the post, in which he is apt to display either rashness or timidity.

On Monday, 18 October 1954 Maxwell Fyfe succeeded Simonds on the Woolsack in circumstances which have already been described. On Tuesday, 19 October he sat Speaker, and was introduced as Viscount Kilmuir, and on Wednesday 20th he was sworn in before Sir Raymond Evershed, the Master of the Rolls. His political role will be considered first: it was that to which he attached prime importance. His judicial duties were not treated with the same seriousness.

In the long-drawn-out final phase of Churchill's premiership little could be done. After Eden's succession in April 1955 the way was clear for a few minor pieces of legal reform. Kilmuir felt a little distant from the new Prime Minister. He disapproved of his 'chronic restlessness' in domestic affairs, which often took the form of telephoning Ministers at unsocial hours. Although Kilmuir had burnt his fingers in 1951 when he intervened in a matter of foreign policy

[1] In 1973 his widow recalled some of his reasons: see F. Bresler, Lord Goddard (1977), pp. 256-7.
[2] Lord Moran, Winston Churchill: The Struggle for Survival (1966), pp. 447, 678.
[3] R. A. Butler, The Art of the Possible (1973), p. 146.

(European unity) on which Eden held contrary views, paradoxically much of 1956 had to be devoted to a defence of Eden's foreign policy over Suez. Kilmuir was not a member of the Egypt Committee of the Cabinet which conducted day-to-day operations, but he was an outright supporter of a policy of Thorough—somewhat to the alarm of his more senior officials. The alarm spread to other Government lawyers: the Solicitor-General, H. Hylton-Foster, was believed to have drafted a letter of resignation; the ex-Attorney-General, L. Heald, actually voted against the Government, and Monckton felt he could not go on as Minister of Defence. The Legal Adviser to the Foreign Office, Sir Gerald Fitzmaurice, was mortally offended that his advice was not sought by Eden. But Kilmuir and Manningham-Buller stayed loyal, even when the policy had to be reversed and the troops withdrawn.

The strain on the Lord Chancellor was considerable. For although the Lords' debates were less passionate than those in the Commons, and Salisbury and Home could always be relied upon for support, the Government's actions raised difficult questions of international law. This was not an area in which Kilmuir could claim to be an expert, and he had a difficult time, especially with McNair, recently retired as President of the International Court of Justice. Kilmuir argued that Egypt's action was forcible aggression against territory marked with an international character which could be resisted by the lawful use of force in self-defence under article 51 of the UN Charter:

For the last proposition I must admit that I could not get any support from international lawyers, except from Professor Arthur Goodhart. I believe that in another ten years no one will be able to understand how anyone could think otherwise.[4]

Twenty years on this prediction has been falsified by the bulk of academic writing, so far as the legal strength of the Government's case is concerned,[5] although it has been cogently argued that an earlier display of force by Britain and France alone would not only have been possible tactically (just), but infinitely more productive, politically, in avoiding American hostility and the charge of collusion with Israel. For it is also unfortunately impossible, in the light of what has since been published, to support Kilmuir's assertion that 'the wild accusations of collusion between the British, French and Israeli Governments which were hurled by the Labour Party had absolutely no foundation in fact'.[6]

The most recent survey concludes that 'if Eden concealed the exact degree of the collusion and the incitement of Israel, he nevertheless involved the whole

---

[4] *Memoirs*, p. 268.
[5] R. Blake, 'Anthony Eden', in J. P. Mackintosh (ed.), *British Prime Ministers* (1978), vol. ii, pp. 106–10.
[6] *Memoirs*, p. 278.

Cabinet in substantial foreknowledge of what was to happen' at the end of October.'[7] On Boxing Day 1956 Eden was sufficiently assured of Kilmuir's loyalty to ask him whether he should stay as Prime Minister. The reply was an unhesitating yes. But early in January a resignation became imperative on medical grounds. Kilmuir and Salisbury were given the task of polling the Cabinet about the succession. All except one favoured Macmillan, who was duly appointed.

Government and backbenchers 'were all emotionally and physically exhausted' early in 1957, and it took some time for the Government, the party, and the country, to recover. Fortunately for Kilmuir, he was then 'in the most active and efficient period of his life'.[8] He was able to devote himself to the task of seeing the Government's legislative programme through the House. Much of it was seriously in arrears as a result of the year of Suez. One example must suffice. In July 1956 there was a two-day debate in the Lords on a private members' Bill to abolish capital punishment. The Cabinet had decided not to produce its own Bill on the subject, but to allocate Government time for the debate. This unhappy compromise eventually produced the Homicide Act 1957. Kilmuir's speech was conceded, even by his opponents, to have been a good performance.

One of a dozen examples can be taken to illustrate Kilmuir's readiness to undertake almost any public service outside Parliament at the request of the Government. Eden asked him to be chairman of a round table conference on Malta which was to begin on 19 September 1955. Kilmuir cut short a holiday at his brother-in-law's villa at Portofino[9] in order to prepare himself for the task. (It was the only holiday he had outside Britain during his eight years in office.) Officials found their own holidays cut short in order to brief the Lord Chancellor. The conference eventually produced the suggestion that Malta should be treated like a French African possession—i.e. as an integral part of the United Kingdom. It was the kind of surprisingly radical proposal which Kilmuir sometimes favoured. He was particularly pleased that he persuaded the Treasury to offer most generous terms to Malta. But in the end Dom Mintoff, the Prime Minister of Malta, refused to accept the offer.

Africa was a subject which occupied much time in the fifties and early sixties. For example, on 29 July 1959 the Lords debated both Nyasaland and the report on the Hola detention camp.[1] Kilmuir was on the Woolsack from 2.30 p.m.

[7] Carlton, *Anthony Eden*, p. 440.
[8] H. Macmillan, *Riding the Storm* (1971), p. 504.
[9] In the 20th cent. show business has been given the rewards which the 18th cent. gave to the Bar. As well as a house at Portofino, where the guests might include the Windsors, Rex Harrison had a Rolls-Royce, which he took with him to California when making the film of *My Fair Lady*, 'feeling that it might, in times of stress, boost my morale' (Harrison, *Rex*, p. 205). Birkenhead might have done this; but he could not have afforded it.
[1] See *Documents Relating to the Deaths of Eleven Mau Mau Detainees at Hola Camp in Kenya* (1959), Cmnd. 778.

until 12.30 a.m. on the following morning, with only the briefest of intervals. In both Britain and France right-wing Governments were intent on rapid disengagement from their responsibilities. When the white settlers in Rhodesia and Algeria realized what was happening to them there was a considerable reaction. In each case they found support from powerful forces within the Government. But in each case they were defeated by superior political skill—combined with much more than a touch of ruthlessness. The Colonial Secretary from 1959 to 1961, Iain Macleod, was thought to display these qualities to a special degree, and in a debate on 7 March 1961 Salisbury (no longer in the Cabinet) sought to destroy Macleod with the phrase 'he has been too clever by half', and depicted the Colonial Secretary as a middle-class card-sharper (he was a bridge player of international standard) outwitting the simple settlers. Kilmuir leapt to the defence of his Cabinet colleague and fellow-Scot. Some rhetoric reminiscent of a Lancashire by-election engulfed Salisbury.[2] But to Kilmuir the speech 'was undoubtedly the most successful I ever made from the Woolsack'.[3] In the sense that it was greeted by applause from peers like Chorley, this was true. But in the long run it did not save Macleod; over-exposed as Colonial Secretary, he had to be moved sideways only six months later, and despite his new positions as Party Chairman and Leader of the House of Commons found himself frigidly ignored by the charmed circle from which Home emerged as Macmillan's successor in October 1963. A happier African event was the establishment of a Committee on Legal Education for African students under Lord Dennning. Thanks to the Chairman's ability to work quickly, and the Lord Chancellor's personal enthusiasm, the recommendations were implemented in a very short time.

No major reconstruction of the legal system took place in Kilmuir's time. But there were useful minor changes. Some of the recommendations of the over-lengthy Evershed Report of 1954 were carried into effect by the County Courts Act 1955 and the Administration of Justice Act 1956, and also by amendments to the Rules of the Supreme Court. In November 1960 the increase in appeals to the Lords required a resolution authorizing the Appellate Committee to sit in two divisions. On the other hand the declining jurisdiction of the Privy Council caused concern: Kilmuir was much attracted by the idea, which had been discussed in the twenties, that the business might be increased if the tribunal became peripatetic. But the practical difficulties—which included the unwillingness of Australian lawyers to give up their trips to London—proved insuperable. Attempts were also made to increase the attractiveness of the Commercial Court. The Administration of Justice Act 1960 provided new methods of appeal to the House of Lords in contempt of

[2] 229 H.L. Deb. cols. 317, 346.
[3] *Memoirs*, p. 316. A fervent letter of thanks on 12 Mar. from Macleod ended 'I still feel bruised by the sheer vulgarity of Salisbury's speech'.

court and habeas corpus cases. It also abolished the requirement that the consent of the Attorney-General must be given before the Lords could hear a criminal appeal.

Important statutory reforms were the Occupiers' Liability Act 1957 and the Tribunals and Inquiries Act 1958—one in the field of private, the other in the field of public, law. Each was preceded by the report of a committee, but Kilmuir was responsible for securing that the necessary Bill found a place in the Government's legislative programme—in some ways perhaps the most difficult aspect of law reform. There was also a great deal of correspondence[4] on the topic of the reform of the statute-book—something on which all Lord Chancellors have set their heart, and from which all have retired defeated.

A reform enacted in the last month of Kilmuir's Chancellorship was the Law Reform (Husband and Wife) Act 1962, which carried out the recommendation in the Ninth Report of the Law Reform Committee that each of the parties to a marriage should have the like right of action in tort against the other as if they were not married. On the other hand, Kilmuir opposed as 'unworkable' Lord Mancroft's Right of Privacy Bill 1961, which had the support of Law Lords as different as Goddard and Denning.

Kilmuir acted with extraordinary speed to consider reform in the very specialized area of the limitation of actions when a decision held that in some cases of personal injuries, which were caused by the secret onset of an insiduous disease, a plaintiff might lose his cause of action before he knew it had arisen. The Lord Chancellor did not even wait for the appeal to the House of Lords to be heard. In January 1961 he set up a committee under Mr Justice Edmund Davies to investigate the matter, and when its report in August 1962 recommended legislation, Kilmuir ensured that the Limitation Act 1963 was enacted in July.

Kilmuir's judicial appointments were surprisingly few in the earlier years of his Chancellorship. In October 1954 he was nominally responsible for the promotion of the Treasury devil on the common-law side, J. Ashworth, to succeed Parker J., who had been promoted to the Court of Appeal. Then there was a gap until January 1956, when Diplock QC was appointed (orally, as was Kilmuir's practice) to the Queen's Bench Division. In 1960 a lengthy freeze in the Chancery Division was broken by a number of deaths and promotions, and eight appointments were made. In January 1961, following increases authorized by the Administration of Justices Act 1960, no fewer than twelve appointments were made. In all Kilmuir was responsible for forty-one appointments to the High Court. But under the accepted constitutional practice of modern times he was invariably consulted by each of his three Prime Ministers (Churchill, Eden, Macmillan) about appointments or promotions to the Court of Appeal and the

---

[4] Preserved in the Jowitt papers.

House of Lords, although in point of law these are made by the Prime Minister and not the Lord Chancellor. So in 1953 Kilmuir was able to record that some sixty out off seventy of the higher judiciary had assumed their offices during his Chancellorship.[5] The complete list of appointments was as follows. All were in silk unless otherwise noted.

> *Queen's Bench Division*: Ashworth, Diplock, Hinchcliffe, Paull, Salmon, Edmund Davies, Elwes, Thesiger, Winn,[6] Atkinson, Nield, Howard,[7] Veale, Megaw, Lawton, Widgery, MacKenna,[8] Thompson, Brabin, Roskill, Lyell, John Stephenson.
> *Chancery Division*: Russell, Cross, Buckley, Pennycuick, Wilberforce, Scarman, Plowman, Ungoed-Thomas.[9]
> *Probate, Divorce and Admiralty*: Melford Stevenson, Lloyd-Jones, Cairns, Baker, Ormrod, Rees, Payne, Wrangham,[1] Hewson, Marshall, Phillimore. (Some of these were later transferred to the QBD.)

At the other end of the scale, Kilmuir in 1957 had to deal with the problem of Hallett J., who had been severely criticized in the Court of Appeal for his conduct of a trial on the ground of talking too much. The Court had reserved judgment for over three weeks as

we realised that it might lead to the end of the Judge's career.. . . Of course [Lord Kilmuir] did not speak to me of the case beforehand, but afterwards he told me that he was grateful to us. He sent for the Judge. It was arranged that he should sit for a little while and then resign. This he did at the end of the summer term.[2]

Kilmuir was also concerned about judicial behaviour off the Bench. In 1955 he recorded his clear opinion that 'as a general rule it is undesirable for members of the Judiciary to broadcast on the wireless or to appear on television'. The Kilmuir Letter (as it is known) is still regarded as authoritative.[2A]

Kilmuir's reported judgments are not remarkable either in quantity or in quality. In his eight years as Lord Chancellor he sat in only twenty-four appeals

---

[5] *Memoirs*, p. 303.

[6] Winn was the Treasury devil (common law). His predecessor in that position was J. Ashworth, and his successor R. Cumming-Bruce.

[7] Howard had never taken silk, but he had been up at Balliol with Maxwell Fyfe and had been a Tory MP from 1950.

[8] MacKenna had once been pressed by Manningham-Buller to enter Parliament with a view to becoming Solicitor-General. He refused. As a QBD judge he was very successful.

[9] Ungoed-Thomas QC MP had briefly been a Labour Solicitor-General, but refused an offer of promotion from Jowitt (see above, p. 118). Kilmuir was impartial in his appointments.

[1] Wrangham had never taken silk, but he was only the sixth County Court judge to be promoted to the High Court. He had been a Balliol contemporary of Maxwell Fyfe.

[2] Lord Denning, *Due Process of Law* (1980), pp. 61–2. Hallett J. had been a judge since 1939. He was aged 68.

[2A] The Kilmuir Letter is printed in (1986) *Public Law* 383.

to the House of Lords.[3] His first reported judgment is in January 1956.[4] That being the year of Suez, it is not surprising to find only three (very brief) judgments reported.[5] In the following years the number increased.[6] The abiding impression is that of a judge who was simply uninterested in the development of legal concepts by analytical reasoning. This is not unusual amongst trial judges, but it is not only unusual but also inappropriate in a Lord Chancellor. The closest comparison is with Loreburn (another Balliol man), whose judgments are perhaps the shortest and most perfunctory of any in the twentieth century. It has been said that Kilmuir's judgments 'revealed something attractive about his commonsense approach to the judicial process',[7] but it might have been better if he had displayed this valuable quality more often instead of leaving the disposition of so many appeals to the Chancery Law Lords (Simonds, Radcliffe, Morton, Cohen, and Jenkins) who were predominant at the end of the fifties.

There is no doubt that Kilmuir's reputation as a jurist has suffered severely from the speech in his name in which the House unanimously restored a conviction for capital murder in *DPP* v. *Smith*.[8] The judgment gave rise to a considerable amount of criticism, because it was understood to lay down an objective test for responsibility for murder—i.e. to reject a defence that the accused did not actually intend to kill or cause grievous bodily harm—by erecting into an irrebuttable presumption of law the maxim that a man is presumed to intend the natural and probable consequences of his acts.[9] The argument of the Crown does not seem to have gone beyond the assertion that it was the likely consequences of the act (as distinct from the act itself) which had to be determined objectively, but some inapt sentences in the judgment were seized upon by the critics as supporting a radical change in the common law.[1] (It

---

[3] R. Stevens, *Law and Politics* (1979), pp. 424–5. Kilmuir's name does not appear in the index to A. Paterson's *The Law Lords* (1982).

[4] *A. V. Pound & Co. Ltd.* v. *Hardy & Co. Ltd.* [1956] AC 588.

[5] *G. Renton & Co. Ltd.* v. *Palmyra Trading Corporation* [1957] AC 149; *LCC* v. *Wilkins* [1957] AC 362; *Vine* v. *National Dock Labour Board* [1957] AC 488.

[6] The more important are *Cade* v. *British Transport Commission* [1959] AC 256; *Wigley* v. *British Vinegars Ltd.* [1964] AC 307. Kilmuir's speech (concurred in by four other Law Lords) in the *Wigley* appeal was literally his last act as Lord Chancellor, for it was read (by Lord Hodson) on Monday, 16 July 1962.

[7] Stevens, *Law and Politics*, p. 424. Kilmuir is also praised because 'he shook the complacency of the system' (p. 425).

[8] [1961] AC 290; Lords Kilmuir, Parker, Goddard, Tucker, and Denning. This was the last criminal appeal brought to the House of Lords under the procedure which required the consent of the Attorney-General. It is believed that Kilmuir insisted on one judgment, which was drafted by Lord Parker of Waddington LCJ (Paterson, *Law Lords*, pp. 93, 184).

[9] See *R.* v. *Moloney* [1985] 2 WLR 648, 666.

[1] One result of the decision may have been 'to bring down the wrath of the academic community' (Stevens, *Law and Politics*, p. 611), but some of these critics failed to state the simple facts correctly. So H. L. A. Hart (*The Morality of the Criminal Law* (1964), p. 49) refers to 'the case of the brave policeman who jumped on to the bonnet of a car to stop a thief driving off with stolen property. The thief drove on with the consequence that the policeman was shaken off and killed.' This omits the vital evidence of three oncoming

has less often been noticed that the Kilmuir judgment defined grievous bodily harm in a way which has been generally accepted.) Whatever the true interpretation of Smith, it is certain that the Criminal Justice Act 1967, s. 8, requires a subjective test to be satisfied both as to the accused's intention to do the acts in question and also as to his foresight of the consequences of those acts.

Kilmuir's lengthy tenure of the Great Seal ended suddenly in 1962. On Friday, 6 July R. A. Butler was told of the Prime Minister's plans. 'I was particularly sorry about the move of David Kilmuir from the Woolsack. He had been with me all my political life and had helped me to reform the Conservative Party; he represented, with the Prime Minister and myself, the only remaining link in the Cabinet with the Churchill era.'[2] On Saturday the 7th the Prime Minister's Adviser on Public Relations noted the substance of the proposed moves in his diary. 'The key to it all is the replacement of Selwyn Lloyd as Chancellor of the Exchequer (he is to be seen next Thursday evening: presumably he can only become Lord Chancellor).'[3] With two such persons in receipt of confidential plans, it is not surprising that rumours began to circulate during the week, with the result that Macmillan decided to complete the moves before the weekend.

On Thursday, 12 July Kilmuir sat Speaker; at 6 p.m. on the same afternoon Selwyn Lloyd had his interview with Macmillan. 'I did my best—but it was a terribly difficult and emotional scene. It lasted three quarters of an hour.'[4] Selwyn Lloyd refused a peerage and retired (temporarily) to the back-benches. (He does not seem to have been offered the Woolsack.) The interview with Kilmuir seems to have been even more painful. He was summoned from a Cabinet committee to Admiralty House (No. 10 being under repair) at 11.15 a.m. on Friday 13th, and left at noon. 'I once remarked . . . that "loyalty was the Tories' secret weapon." I doubt if it has ever had to endure so severe a strain.'[5] At 11.30 a.m. the Lord Chancellor's Office had received a telephone call from the Principal Private Secretary at Admiralty House. He said simply 'You have a new Lord Chancellor'. So the staff were prepared for the return of a shattered Kilmuir. He went on with the day's programme, which included a

---

drivers, who testified as to what happened in the 130 yds. between the police officer jumping on to the bonnet and being thrown off. The accused drove his car directly at their cars, each of which was damaged by the impact with the policeman's body. The accused's car was undamaged because the body of the police officer acted as a fender. It is not difficult to deduce that the accused must have intended to cause at least grievous bodily harm to the officer. Both Dilhorne, who as Attorney-General had argued the appeal for the Crown, and Lord Denning later complained of misrepresentation: see 287 H.L. Deb. col. 250; R. v. Hyam [1975] AC 55, 59; Lord Denning, The Family Story (1981), pp. 195–97.

² Butler, Art of the Possible, p. 234.
³ H. Evans, Downing Street Diary (1981), p. 202. The last statement shows how ignorant even those at the centre may be.
⁴ H. Macmillan, At the End of the Day (1973), p. 94.
⁵ Kilmuir, Political Adventure (1964), p. 234.

cocktail party at the Land Registry. It was not an occasion remembered with pleasure by anyone who was there. In mid-afternoon Manningham-Buller put in a cheerful appearance at the House of Lords: the Permanent Secretary to the Lord Chancellor, Sir George Coldstream, found him seated behind his desk. Politely, he was asked to return after the weekend. The news was officially released at 7 p.m. that evening. 'And thus ended, at seven hours' notice, the great political adventure on which I had embarked as an undergraduate forty years ago.' Listening to the 9 p.m. news Kilmuir heard what the Prime Minister had forgotten to tell him—that he had been created an Earl. Both Kilmuir and Macmillan spent the weekend in Sussex recovering from nervous exhaustion.

The published accounts left by Kilmuir and Macmillan do not tell a wholly satisfactory story. Kilmuir was dignified, but failed to explain why he should have taken his dismissal quite so hard. Macmillan admitted frankly that he may have made a mistake in trying to mask the replacement of Selwyn Lloyd, an immediate if painful necessity with that of six other Ministers.[6] Some of these accepted the decision and did not complain—Mills, Deputy Leader of the House of Lords, had been brought into public life by Macmillan, and continued his practice of dining *en famille* with the Macmillans once a week.

The unpublished material gives a somewhat clearer picture. On Sunday, 15 July Macmillan sent to Kilmuir a strange personal letter—strange because it can be asserted confidently that it is unique in tone amongst the letters which Prime Ministers have sent to senior Cabinet Ministers whom they have dismissed. Writing in his own hand, the words almost illegible, presumably from exhaustion, Macmillan sent this message.

Dear David:

Of course, it will never be the same fun again. And what fun it has been! From our weekly speeches all over the country in 1945-51; the strange Churchill luncheons at the Savoy; the Shadow Cabinet; the Central Office Committees; right up to the winning of power and Churchill's last Government.

And what we have been through together! From Suez to the Asian seat![7]

Always you have been the best, most trusty, and most loyal friend and colleague.

And what a career you have had and have still before you. For you have never spared yourself and given always of your best.

There is so much for which I have to thank you that I don't know how to finish, now I have begun. I only hope everything between us is will be the same.

As you know, I always felt that Reggie M-B must have a turn before the end. Obviously, it must be a reasonable time before the end—or it would be rather a racket.

---

[6] Macmillan, *At the End of the Day*, pp. 93-5.

[7] 'The Asian seat' was a reference to the question whether the proposed constitution for Northern Rhodesia (now Zambia) should include a special constituency for Asians. Kilmuir had devoted much effort to this question early in 1962.

Events seem to me to make the end much nearer (anyway for me and perhaps for the Government) than I thought (say) six months ago. I feel sure you understand.

That it all had to go so quickly, I regret. For it seemed so discourteous and ungenerous. But, as I expect you realised, it would not have been safe to delay. I had hoped (and tried) [for] a more leisurely approach. But it became impossible. So I thought I could only save the situation by acting quickly.

Let us meet soon.

Your affectionate friend,

Harold Macmillan[8]

It is perhaps hardly surprising that this missive is annotated in one terse word by Kilmuir's hand: 'Thanked—17.7.62'.

The letter certainly reflects the close relationship which had once existed between Macmillan and Kilmuir. The energy and loyalty which Kilmuir gave to the Government and the party had often (as brief letters or minutes in the Kilmuir papers show) evoked Macmillan's admiration. In 1958 Macmillan had offered Kilmuir the post of Lord Chief Justice in succession to Goddard. Only one holder of the office of Lord Chancellor has been appointed Lord Chief Justice (Caldecote in 1940), although some Lord Chief Justices (Jeffreys, Hardwicke, Campbell) have been promoted to the Woolsack. In any event Kilmuir refused—partly on the ground that 'I should prefer to remain by your side so long as you think I am of any use to you and your Government', and partly on the ground that he thought an ex-Lord Chancellor should act 'as elder statesman as well as Law Lord'.[9] (The events of 1962 caused him to change his mind on the second point.)

Macmillan's supporters advanced, in public or in private, some reasons for the dismissal. One was that Kilmuir was more exhausted than he realized, and a change was needed in the public interest. Some of the officials in the Lord Chancellor's Department held this view. For some time they had been concerned at Kilmuir's unwillingness to initiate policy: he simply approved the submissions which came up to him. This argument is bolstered by the assertion that Kilmuir was too old. So one biographer of Macmillan states that Kilmuir and Mills were 'both rising 70'.[1] But, in fact, Mills was aged seventy-two, and Kilmuir had just passed his sixty-second birthday. Nor could it be said that Kilmuir had been replaced by a younger man—for Manningham-Buller was aged fifty-seven, three years older than Kilmuir had been in 1954.

On Kilmuir's side, while it is easy to understand his chagrin that this loyalty to Macmillan and the party should have been rewarded by a sudden dismissal, it is not so easy to understand the depth of his bitter resentment. He admitted that he foresaw a change in 1963. Why should he have been so surprised that the

[8] Kilmuir papers.
[9] Ibid. See also below, pp. 193–5.
[1] A. Sampson, *Macmillan* (1967), p. 197.

change came six or nine months earlier? He had been long enough in politics to know that sudden reversals of fortune are common. Indeed, he had himself requested the premature dismissal of his predecessor. But his family and friends assert that he did not know what was in store for him on the morning of Friday 13th. And he may have taken legitimate offence at being included in a mass dismissal of Ministers, some of whom were not of the first rank. Perhaps his Scottish integrity was offended by the vague popular feeling that it was all a necessary cleansing operation after Profumo. Perhaps his Scottish pride was offended at being so treated by a Macmillan and a Balliol man. It would have been better if Macmillan had treated Kilmuir as Kilmuir had treated Hallett— allowed him to resign quietly at the end of the long vacation. In any event, he, who had been hyper-active all his life, and at the centre of public affairs for eleven years, found the sudden cessation of all activity almost unbearable.

By the autumn it was clear that Kilmuir had decided to cut his links with the law and the Conservative Party. In answer to a parliamentary question, Macmillan stated that Kilmuir had surrendered his pension and gone into the City: 'what he has done is perfectly proper'.[2] Through friends such as Ralph Assheton an invitation to join the Plessey Company as Chairman was arranged, and gladly accepted. But the work proved an unexpected strain, although the income was very welcome. He found it hard to adjust to the interests, values, and conversation of industrialists. He became a member of the boards of various charitable foundations—for example, Wolfson. He sometimes spoke in the Lords on non-party subjects—for example, education and business manage- ment. His opposition to the measure which ultimately became the Sexual Offences Act 1967 was expressed in his old uncompromising way. But the spring which had kept him going without a break for forty years had now unwound. When he was seen at Westminster his friends were shocked to find him looking ill and depressed.

But he found time to supervise the publication of his memoirs, on which he had begun work some years before. It is a volume which stands well in comparison with those written by other twentieth-century Lord Chancellors— Haldane, Maugham, Simon, and Simonds. His style is brisker and his presentation more vigorous—but then, although an exhausted man, he was ten to fifteen years younger at the date of publication than any of them. The opinions expressed about political (as distinct from legal) matters are more interesting and percipient than those of Simon and less self-satisfied than those of Haldane or Maugham. Visitors who commented on the book were informed, sadly, 'That is the only capital I have'!

Kilmuir died at Hardings, Withyham, Sussex, on 27 January 1967. His

---

[2] 677 H.C. Deb. col. 1003. The topic of premature judicial retirement is fully discussed in S. Shetreet, *Judges on Trial* (1976), pp. 374–6.

remains were cremated. There were memorial services at St Margaret's, Westminster, and St Michael and All Angels, Withyham, where he is commemorated by a fine monumental inscription on the north wall of the nave of a church which also contains the splendid tombs of the great Norman family of Sackville. Kilmuir's estate was sworn for probate at £22,202—a modest sum, but still larger than the estates of Loreburn and Caldecote, each of whom left less than £20,000.

LORD DILHORNE

D ILHORNE is a small village four miles east of the city of Stoke-on-Trent, which as the centre of the Potteries is associated in the mind with dirt and depression. In fact the Clean Air Act 1956 has produced an atmosphere which on an autumn day can be sparkling, and, away from the roar of industrial traffic on the Uttoxeter road, the village of Dilhorne, with its good church, looks much as it must have done when Elizabeth, daughter of John Holliday of Lincoln's Inn, brought the property into the Buller family on her marriage in 1793 to Sir Francis Yarde-Buller, though the Victorian Gothic gateway to Dilhorne Hall carries notices prohibiting vandalism to the recreation centre which it has now become. One other feature typical of late-twentieth-century England will be noticed by the visitor. The inhabitants assume that he adopts the 'pronounce as you spell' precept of the teacher's training college, and so will call the place 'Dill-horne'. But amongst themselves the pronunciation is 'Dill-urne', and this is the usage always followed by the Buller family since they moved into Staffordshire from Cornwall. Sir Francis Yarde-Buller was the son of Francis Buller, who had married, at the age of seventeen, Susannah Yarde, a Devonshire heiress.[1] Called to the Bar at the Inner Temple, Francis Buller was appointed a King's Bench judge at the age of thirty-two years and two months. In the previous year he had taken silk. By a happy coincidence, the Lord Chancellor who provided both the silk and the judicial ermine was his mother's brother, Lord Bathurst. (Another ancestor was a daughter of Pollexfen CJ CP (1632–91.) While at the Bar Buller had published a successful treatise on pleading. Entitled *Buller's Trials at Nisi Prius*, it went into seven editions before it was overtaken by the reforms of the 1830s. But in his lifetime it was said that 'as Burke's name in the Senate, is the name of Buller in Westminster Hall'.[2] Mansfield favoured him as a successor in the position of Lord Chief Justice, but when Pitt's choice fell on Kenyon, Buller was consoled with a baronetcy in 1790. Ten years later the youngest man ever to have been made an English judge died at an age (fifty-four) when the modern silk is wondering when he will receive an offer from the Lord Chancellor.

The baronetcy descended to an elder grandson who was made a peer in 1858 with the title of Churston. Eight years later his younger brother, Edward, a Conservative MP, having also married an heiress, the daughter of Maj.-Gen. Coote Manningham, assumed the surname of Manningham-Buller, and was himself made a baronet. Their younger son, Edmund, married Lady Anna

---

[1] Buller was an improving landlord, highly praised by Arthur Young: 'To see a person of ample private fortune, high in rank, and filling an office that requires an almost incessant employment and anxious labour of mind . . . filling his leisure moments with agricultural experiments . . . is a spectacle so uncommon and highly meritorious that too much cannot be said in his praise' (*Annals of Agriculture*, vol. xxxix (1797), pp. 577–8. Charles Abbot, later Lord Tenterden CJKB, went to the Bar because Buller was so impressed by his work as tutor to his son that he advised him to change his career.   [2] (1837) 17 *Law Mag. & Rev.* 29.

Coke, a daughter of the second Earl of Leicester. She was ninth in direct descent from Sir Edward Coke (1552–1634), Attorney-General and later Lord Chief Justice of the King's Bench. The blood of 'Old Sir Edward Coke, a man of the toughest fibre' (in Carlyle's phrase)[3] was now united with that of the Bullers.

One is inevitably reminded of the young lady, who 'had the good luck to captivate Sir Thomas Bertram, of Mansfield Park, in the Country of Northampton, and to be thereby raised to the rank of a baronet's lady, with all the comforts and consequences of an handsome house and large income'. But the Coke family did not regard Lady Anna as having been raised in rank: they were a little inclined to emphasize that each of Lady Anna's six sisters had married a peer (or the heir to a peerage). Doubts were stilled when Lady Anna Manningham-Buller's son Mervyn inherited his uncle's baronetcy and married Lilah Constance Cavendish, a daughter of the third Lord Chesham, whose great-grandfather had been Duke of Devonshire, and whose father-in-law was Duke of Westminster. The eldest of their five children, and only son, Reginald Edward Manningham-Buller, the future Lord Chancellor, was born at Latimer House, Amersham, in Buckinghamshire on 1 August 1905.

The Manningham-Buller parents lived in a style which was familiar in England before 1914—out of doors, field sports; indoors, bridge and conversation about field sports and racing. It was not an intellectual household. After two unsuccessful attempts to find a constituency, Sir Mervyn devoted himself to a military career. He commanded a battalion of the Rifle Brigade throughout the First World War, and in 1924 was elected MP for Kettering. Sir Mervyn was a believer in a boy being able to stand on his own feet. He disliked displays of affection. (He himself had never known his mother, who had died in the year in which he was born.) So Manningham-Buller is recalled by his contemporaries at Eton as giving a faint impression of an unhappy childhood. He was also heavily built and spectacled (weak eyesight had been inherited from his mother), and these characteristics combined in the minds of some to make them believe that Anthony Powell had Manningham-Buller in mind when he created the well-known character of Widmerpool in *A Dance to the Music of Time*. This is not so.

I can definitely state that the main model of Widmerpool, so far as there was a model, or models, was not Manningham-Buller, but someone who was not an Etonian. It is, however, true that Manningham-Buller was a keen wet-bob at a predominantly dry-bob house, and used to go out by himself rowing courses . . . Rowing lonely courses of the river, and getting another boy sacked, simply occurred to me as the sort of characteristics Widmerpool would have. I do recognise, however, that a certain amount of this does fit in with your subject.[4]

[3] T. Carlyle, *Historical Sketches*, 2nd edn. (1898), p. 206.
[4] Mr A. Powell to the author in Apr. 1985.

Chance resemblances of this kind often occur in novels.

Manningham-Buller went up to Magdalen in 1923, and was placed in the Third Class in the Law School in 1926. (In the First Class was Harry Hylton-Foster, an exact contemporary at Eton, who succeeded Manningham-Buller as Solicitor-General in 1954, and became Speaker of the House of Commons in 1959.) As one who was later a judicial colleague, the third Lord Russell of Killowen, wrote, 'he must confess to a Third Class degree in Oxford School of Jurisprudence in the days when a university education left ample room for golf, bridge, and frivolous conversation, and no undergraduate was eager for unpaid participation in the government of university or college.'[5] Manningham-Buller kept up his rowing; he just missed his blue. In later years the physical ability to withstand long hours of work was ascribed to his youthful afternoons on the Thames. Manningham-Buller enjoyed his years at Magdalen. He does not seem to have been affected by any of the doubts which both his near-contemporaries, Gardiner and Denning, occasionally felt. In the twenties the differences between the Oxford colleges were more marked than they were in later years. Manningham-Buller accepted this as part of the natural order of things. He would have agreed with the character in a forgotten novel who remarked that, 'The small fry from the small colleges like Jesus and Pembroke . . . who jostle you in the street don't mean to be disrespectful, but it is a big moment in their drab lives when they see an Eton-and-Magdalen man for the first time.'[6] Magdalen may have been kind to Manningham-Buller in allowing him time to develop in his own way, but in later life he had cause to complain. Neither he nor Gerald Gardiner was elected to an honorary fellowship. Not many Oxford colleges have two living ex-Lord Chancellors amongst their old members, and yet decline to make either an Honorary Fellow—in this respect the Fellows of Wadham on 29 February 1912 showed greater prescience and greater political generosity, when they elected both Simon and F. E. Smith. Magdalen's decision was the more notable since Lord Denning had been so honoured when he was still a puisne judge, and Sir Harry Hylton-Foster when he became Speaker.

Manningham-Buller was called to the Bar at the Inner Temple (the Inn of Coke CJ and Buller J.) on 29 June 1927. Some have recalled him briefly in the chambers of F. T. Barrington-Ward[7] at 2 Harcourt Buildings, along with others who later became famous, such as C. Pearson and B. MacKenna.[8] But by 1930 he had moved to the chambers of F. Beney at 3 Brick Court. He stayed with those chambers until he became a Law Officer in 1951, although various features of life there could not have been congenial to him. While Beney had a good war record, and had been at Harrow and Trinity College, Oxford, he was a

---

[5] Lord Russell of Killowen, *The Lawyer and Justice* (1978), p. 251.
[6] S. McKenna, *Not Necessarily for Publication* (1949), p. 45.
[7] He was not popular at the Bar: see above, p. 68.
[8] See Earl of Birkenhead, *Walter Monckton* (1969), p. 58.

Liberal in politics, and a half-brother of that dubious figure, Sir Alfred Butt. Beney's two marriages ended in divorce. His biographer tersely remarks that he had 'a second-class junior practice'.[9] But life was difficult for a struggling junior in the twenties—especially as Sir Mervyn Manningham-Buller refused to contribute towards his son's expenses—and no opportunity occurred of a change to better chambers.

One who was going through the same experiences was Gerald Gardiner. 'The received mythology is that Reggie and I cordially disliked one another. This is quite untrue. We had an *enormous* amount in common. . . . For years we had lunch at the same table in Hall. The conversation was sparkling. Reggie and I always disagreed about everything.'[1]

Life at the Bar, in the days before legal aid, was certainly hard. In the London area, at least, the judiciary at all levels did not always exhibit the benevolent patience so characteristic of judicial figures today. The lessons which today can be painlessly learned[2] were then all too often rubbed in by sharp and ferocious rebukes administered in public by men who were overworked, underpaid, and sometimes embittered by the belief that their undoubted ability had not received the reward they hoped for in their chosen profession. After a day before a tribunal presided over by such a figure (County Court judge or stipendiary magistrate), there was a long bus ride back to the Temple and then consultations before the next day's work began.

The strains of this life were no worse than those which had to be endured by other young barristers, but they seem to have brought out a certain truculent self-reliance in Manningham-Buller's character, and stories began to circulate about the 'bullying manner'. Some recalled the character in 'Right Royal', of whom John Masefield wrote, 'Perhaps, the thing which he most enjoyed,/Was being rude when he felt annoyed.'[3] One story will be enough. A very young barrister from Gardiner's chambers was briefed to defend some left-wing demonstrators against a charge under the Public Order Act 1936. When he arrived at the police-court (as it was called in those days) he was alarmed to find the prosecution in the hands of Manningham-Buller. But somehow prose-cuting counsel did not gain the ear of the court, and the defence, seeing how the wind was blowing, said as little as possible. Yet afterwards, in the little robing room, Manningham-Buller completely ignored his successful opponent—contrary to all the etiquette of the Bar.

Manningham-Buller built up a small practice on the Midland Circuit, of

[9] I. Adamson, *The Old Fox* (1963), p. 127.
[1] To the author in 1984.
[2] By reading D. Napley, *The Technique of Persuasion* 3rd edn (1983), from the preface to which, by Sir Melford Stevenson, these words have been taken.
[3] John Masefield, *Collected Poems* (1932), p. 682. Manningham-Buller had to resign as Hon. Secretary of the Pegasus Club because the farmers over whose land the Club held its point-to-points objected to his high-handed methods.

which he remained a loyal member. When Lord Chancellor, he dismissed with
scorn a letter from the Leader of the Oxford Circuit, claiming a right to be
considered when the recordership of Birmingham fell vacant.

In December 1930 he married the fourth of the six daughters of the twenty-
seventh Earl of Crawford. Lady Mary's father and her two brothers had been at
Eton and Magdalen. By their marriage there was one son, John Mervyn, and
three daughters, the eldest of whom married a direct descendant of Sir Robert
Brudenell, of Deene, Northamptonshire, Chief Justice of the Common Pleas
(1461-1531). (Sir Robert Brudenell was also the ancestor of the Dukes of
Montagu, the Marquesses of Ailesbury, and the Earls of Cardigan.)

Too old for active service in the Second World War, and in any case
disqualified by poor eyesight, Manningham-Buller served in the Judge
Advocate General's Department. He was also able to enter the House of
Commons in 1943 (unopposed, under the war-time party truce) as Member for
Daventry—a just reward, as he had taken part in every election since 1928. In
1950 the constituency was reorganized as South Northamptonshire, and
Manningham-Buller held it until his appointment as Lord Chancellor,
increasing his majority at each of the four general elections. He was a
conscientious Member, and Lady Mary was all that could be expected of the
wife of a Member, but it was perhaps over-cautious of him to insist that all
questions on agricultural matters should be submitted in writing beforehand.
He acquired a suitable house in the constituency—Green's Norton Court, near
Towcester. He was assiduous in Parliament. The index to Hansard for the
1943/4 session reveals him as active over a wide range of topics—pensions;
servicemen and their problems; food and drugs; and town and country
planning.

In the 1945 Caretaker Government he was Parliamentary Secretary to the
Minister of Works—a position which in the ministerial hierarchy ranked only
just above that of Assistant Postmaster-General. But he was able to persuade the
Prime Minister to take in Towcester on his way to the Midlands and the North
for an election tour in the last week of June. In those days a British Prime
Minister could appear in public in an open motor-car with only an unarmed
driver as escort—though on this occasion the driver showed momentary
apprehension when Lady Mary suddenly thrust a bunch of delphiniums
towards Churchill.[4] In 1946 Manningham-Buller was able to take silk. His
practice had never been other than modest, and some critics (who can always be
found at the Bar) described him as a 'parliamentary silk'. But his formidable
talents as a debater and controversialist were soon appreciated at Westminster.
As in court, he had always read his brief, and could not be easily dismissed as a
glib lawyer-politician.

[4] See Pl. 9.

On 3 November 1951 he was made Solicitor-General, with Lionel Heald, a competent but somewhat colourless patent lawyer, as the senior Law Officer. Manningham-Buller succeeded Heald on 18 October 1954, and remained in that office until he became Lord Chancellor in July 1962. So Manningham-Buller was a Law Officer of the Crown continuously for a period of ten years and nine months. This was a period of five months longer than the achieved by Robert Finlay (1895–1905), but four years shorter than the record span of William Murray (later Lord Mansfield) (1742–56). Manningham-Buller took some time to obtain the respect of the Bar, whose members found it hard to believe that someone from such a background could have the industry and ability necessary to discharge the responsibilities of his position. The Government departments, particularly the Inland Revenue, and the judges were quicker to discern the massive talents hidden under that formidable exterior.

During his term of office first as Solicitor General and then as Attorney General it was not unusual to find him, when all had gone home, working in the small hours in his room just off the central lobby, a pipe firmly in his mouth, alone, and unmoved by the hour of the night or the fatigues of the day, in court and in the House, that would have exhausted a less robust man.[5]

He was known to have left the House at 3 a.m., and by 9. a.m. to be ready for a conference with his devils, at which he showed a detailed knowledge of his brief.

His Revenue work (a chore which tradition assigns to the junior Law Officer) proved unexpectedly satisfying. The complexity of the problems seemed to yield to continuous hard work. But the skills learnt in the police-courts of the metropolis sometimes caused embarrassment to those sitting in the court taking the Revenue list. Defaulting taxpayers and accountants who had devised over-ingenious schemes of tax avoidance were not usually able or willing (or permitted by the judge) to answer the Solicitor-General in his own language. There was one exception. In a case before Danckwerts J.,[6] the taxpayer won a decisive victory, largely due to the expert evidence of an eminent accountant, Henry Benson. Manningham-Buller did not forget: nearly twenty years later the Chairman of the Royal Commission on Legal Services found that the Benson Report evoked a letter from the ex-Lord Chancellor framed in blistering terms.

The Bar learnt how to deal with such letters: the tactic was to ignore them completely and ask for a personal interview, which nearly always went agreeably. Equally, those who were the Attorney-General's devils found, as one

---

[5] *The Times*, 10 Sept. 1980.
[6] *Holt v. Inland Revenue Commissioners* [1953] 1 WLR 1488.

of them later remarked, that 'the only thing was to stand up to him—otherwise he just walked over you. But if you showed that you had solid grounds for differing from him he could be perfectly reasonable—and very charming and helpful to one in one's career. But it took some courage to call him "Reggie" and not "Attorney", as my seniors all advised me to do!'[7] Oddly enough, Manningham-Buller recorded his impressions of Lord Goddard in very much the same language. 'He would take a view and leave you in no doubt as to his view. But if you argued with him and you were persistent, there was always a chance you could persuade him to change his mind—but never more than once! . . . He did not suffer fools gladly—but then why should one?'[8]

Judges could sometimes stand up to the Attorney-General. In one case[9] the Attorney-General argued that an injunction should not be granted because it would interfere with a proceeding in Parliament. 'In the old days', he said, 'those who attempted that kind of thing were dealt with, and one could find instances where counsel and their clients had been summoned to the Bar of the House and dealt with for contempt.' There was a sharp retort by Upjohn J.: 'Are you threatening me, or whom are you threatening?' To which the rather weak reply was, 'I am not threatening anyone, I was merely adverting to what happened in the old days.'

Somehow in the middle and late fifties the impression got abroad that the Attorney-General was an arrogant, rather square-toed individual, not very clever, not even very good at his job.[1] Every week the *Spectator* published a column under the pseudonym 'Taper', in which some Tory politicians, particularly Selwyn Lloyd and Manningham-Buller, were held up to ridicule and contempt. In part this impression may have been due to the unsuccessful prosecution for murder by poisoning of Dr Bodkin Adams. By the early autumn of 1956 the popular Press had begun to spread rumours that a mass poisoner was at work among the population, often elderly and wealthy, of Eastbourne, but it was not until December that Adams was arrested, and put on trial in March 1957 at the Old Bailey before Devlin J. and a jury, charged with the murder in 1950 of Mrs Morrell, an eighty-year-old patient. It was alleged that she had been prescribed and given massive overdoses of heroin and morphia. Adams was also charged with murder in similar circumstances of Mrs Hullett in 1956. As the committal proceedings in both cases took place in public (as the practice was then), there was intense pre-trial speculation,

---

[7] To the author.

[8] F. Bresler, *Lord Goddard* (1977), p. 128.

[9] *Merricks* v. *Heathcoat-Amory* [1975] Ch. 567; *The Times*, 30 Apr. 1955.

[1] Lord Devlin writes that, 'What was almost unique about him and makes his career so fascinating is that what the ordinary careerist achieves by making himself agreeable, falsely or otherwise, Reggie achieved by making himself disagreeable . . . [He was] the last of the careerist lawyers to reach the Woolsack' (Devlin, *Easing the Passing* (1985), pp. 39, 198).

increased by rumours as to the number of cases in which the doctor had obtained a legacy under the will of a patient. (In fact it was 132.) In accordance with the old practice which required the Attorney-General personally to appear for the Crown in a case of poisoning, Manningham-Buller led Melford Stevenson QC and J. Morris. The accused was defended by Geoffrey Lawrence QC (with Edward Clarke), who had acquired a reputation in local-government cases as a cross-examiner. He was to enhance that reputation at the Old Bailey. After the judge had summed up in a way which was generally thought to invite the acquittal which followed ('fraud and murder are poles apart'), there were recriminations in the House of Commons and elsewhere. Bodkin Adams was not a sympathetic character—after the verdict he demanded lunch at the expense of the authorities before returning to Eastbourne in the Rolls-Royce which Mrs Morrell had bequeathed him: 'it is bad luck for him that he has the face of a murderer', wrote George Lyttleton to Rupert Hart-Davis.[2] If so, that was his only piece of bad luck: the Crown's medical witnesses were most unconvincing in the box, and so was a police superintendent; and the nurses who had attended the deceased in her last days were shattered by a brilliant cross-examination, which showed that the drugs administered were not in the same massive amounts as those prescribed. This gave the impression that the Crown's case had been inadequately prepared, and that the prosecution team were insufficiently flexible to deal with an unexpected emergency. 'From the beginning, a weak case was bungled', the judge wrote later.[3] Bodkin Adams was prudent and not lucky in one respect: he did not give evidence, and so escaped a cross-examination, which might not have been brilliant, but would have been pulverizing. If subjected to it, he might have been 'laid open', in Coke's phrase.[4] As it was, the defence were entitled to invoke the ancient principle that it was not the function of the jury to decide whether the accused had committed the crime; rather its function was to decide whether the Crown had proved beyond a reasonable doubt that the accused had committed it. As Devlin J. clearly shared this view an acquittal followed.[5] Immediately afterwards the Attorney-General entered a nolle prosequi on the indictment for the murder of Mrs Hullett. Clearly no conviction could have been obtained from that (or any other) jury: the pendulum of public opinion had in three months swung decisively from the Crown to the accused. But there is some substance in the

---

[2] R. Hart-Davis, *The Hart-Lyttleton Letters* (1982), vol. v, p. 176.

[3] Devlin, *Easing the Passing*, p. 122.

[4] See below, p. 192.

[5] The judge, five years after the death of Manningham-Buller, published a full account of the trial (*Easing the Passing*), in which almost every reference to the Attorney-General is of a patronizing or wounding kind. He is always referred to as 'Reggie', whereas his opponent is always 'Mr Lawrence', or 'Lawrence'. It is, happily, unusual for a judge to describe the Attorney-General and the accused in a murder trial as 'two of the most self-righteous men in England' (p. 183). In a Postscript to the 1986 edition of his book Lord Devlin defends his opinions.

view that in its hour of defeat the Crown might have been magnanimous enough to allow Bodkin Adams whatever satisfaction he might have obtained from a verdict of not guilty on the Hullett charge. This could have been done simply by the arraignment of the accused, his plea of not guilty, and the offering of no evidence by the Crown. There is also substance in the criticism that the Crown had not thought clearly enough about the use it was going to make of the evidence publicly given at the committal in the Hullett case. It should either not have been given at all, or, once given, have been used at the trial of the Morrell case as evidence of system or design on the part of Bodkin Adams, as in the Brides in the Bath case in 1915.

The repercussions of the Bodkin Adams trial were still in the air when in September 1957 there was a steep rise in the Bank Rate. The Leader of the Opposition, Harold Wilson, was sufficiently impressed by some rumours to write to the Prime Minister asking him for a judicial inquiry into the possibility of a leak which might have enabled various individuals to make illicit profits. The name of the Chairman of the Conservative Party Organization, Oliver Poole, was brought into the matter. Macmillan set up a preliminary inquiry under the Lord Chancellor, and in October Kilmuir reported exonerating completely all those against whom allegations had been made. But the pressure continued, and in November a tribunal of inquiry under the Tribunals of Inquiry (Evidence) Act 1921 was established. It sat for three weeks in December, and reported in January 1958 that there was 'no justification for the allegations'.[6]

But the fact that a number of people prominent in the City had, although acquitted of any wrongdoing, found themselves at the receiving end of a severe cross-examination naturally caused comment. The difficulty really arose from the unusual nature of a tribunal of inquiry set up under the 1921 Act. After the unsatisfactory experience in 1936,[7] when the tribunal found itself acting as both prosecution and judge, it had been decided that it was the duty of the Attorney-General to assist the tribunal by examining witnesses—and also by cross-examining them. This was the procedure adopted at the Belcher Inquiry in 1948, and followed by the Bank Rate Inquiry ten years later. It is a difficult task to combine the functions of examining witnesses and cross-examining them, especially when a long interval elapses between the two events. But Simonds thought Manningham-Buller 'did no more than his duty and did it admirably'.[8] Manningham-Buller's behaviour is also praised in the exhaustive account of the matter by the leading authority on the office of Attorney-General.[9]

Still, there were some who thought that the Attorney-General's style was a

[6] *Bank Rate Leak Tribunal of Inquiry Report* (1958), Cmnd. 350.
[7] See above, p. 144.
[8] Lord Simonds, 'Recollections' (unpublished TS).
[9] J. L. Edwards, *The Law Officers of the Crown* (1964), pp. 199-225, 286-308.

little too reminiscent of his ancestor's at the trial of Raleigh. A well-known passage in that cross-examination runs as follows:

ATTORNEY GENERAL : Thou art the most vile and execrable traitor that ever lived.
RALEIGH : You speak indiscreetly, uncivilly, and barbarously.
ATTORNEY GENERAL : Thou art an odious fellow; thy name is hateful to all the realm of England for thy pride. . . . I will now lay you open for the greatest traitor that ever was.[1]

But there followed two major parliamentary successes. The first arose from an issue of privilege. Was a letter from a Member to a responsible Minister 'a proceeding in Parliament' within the Bill of Rights 1689 so as to cover with absolute, as distinct from qualified, privilege any defamatory allegations made in it? The Committee of Privileges decided that it was, but the House, by a narrow majority on a free vote, decided not to accept the report of the committee. A parliamentary question was undoubtedly 'a proceeding in Parliament', but a letter to a Minister could not itself be so classified, although it might be, under modern conditions, the indispensable pre-condition to a question. The committee had taken a high view of the nature of parliamentary privilege, citing with approval a resolution of the House passed in 1837, during the course of the *Stockdale* v. *Hansard*[2] litigation, that the House alone, and not the courts, had 'the sole and exclusive jurisdiction to determine upon the existence and extent of its privileges'. Manningham-Buller advised the House very firmly that it was not competent for it, in the middle of the twentieth century, to create a new privilege or to extend the boundaries of an existing one.[3]

Secondly, in the summer of 1959 the Government had to deal with the deaths in a detention camp of a number of Mau Mau guerillas, and also with the deaths of fifty-two Africans at the hands of the security forces in Nyasaland. A commission of inquiry into the latter incident was appointed with Mr Justice Devlin as chairman. Its report came at an awkward time in the parliamentary year, and contained some difficulties for the Government—in particular, a statement that 'Nyasaland is, no doubt temporarily, a police state'.[4] Devlin's committee had six weeks in which to draft their report; the Government had hardly as many days to draft a reply. But the task was completed by Kilmuir and Manningham-Buller over a weekend as Chequers, and after the debate on 28 July[5] the Prime Minister recorded that 'the Attorney General opened with a

---

[1] (1603) 2 State Trials 1, 25–6.
[2] (1839) 9 A & E 1.
[3] 591 H.C. Deb. col. 811.
[4] *Report of the Nyasaland Commission of Inquiry* (1959), Cmd. 814, s. 2.
[5] 610 H.C. Deb. col. 317.

massive speech, which greatly pleased our party. He was given a great ovation when he finished'.[6]

The members of the Cabinet, and its secretariat, regarded Manningham-Buller as the model of a Law Officer. He knew what the politicians wanted which was firm, clear advice, and not academic disquisitions on pure law. As Simonds wrote:

I remember being told by a senior member of the Cabinet soon after my appointment that the Lord Chancellor and the Law Officers could by giving wrong advice bring down a government quicker than anyone else. That may have been an oblique reference to Sir Patrick Hastings (who, incidentally, was very badly treated) and the Campbell case. I took to heart this formidable warning and will claim the negative credit that no disaster followed any advice of mine. But here let me pay tribute where it is due. Throughout my term of office one of the Law Officers, first as Solicitor under Lionel Heald and then as Attorney, was Reginald Manningham-Buller. To him I owed much. He would not claim to be a monument of erudition such as his great ancestor Sir Edward Coke. But he was the equal of him or any man in bringing to bear a sound commonsense upon the often difficult problems that faced us. Later on it was my fortune to hear him argue many appeals, which he did with equal brevity and clarity.[7]

In September 1958 Lord Goddard, aged 81, resigned the position of Lord Chief Justice, which he had held for twelve years. His strong personality had made a great impact on the public, and there was speculation about his successor. It was 'common gossip in the Temple' that Manningham-Buller would have liked to have been appointed.[8] Goddard himself confided to an old friend that Manningham-Buller had 'come on a lot lately' and would fill the position adequately.[8A]

In any event those immediately concerned with making the appointment did not seriously consider Manningham-Buller—partly because he seemed to be too like Goddard in outlook, and a change in 'image' was thought to be desirable; and partly because his standing within the profession was not, then, sufficiently secure. 'He was an unsaleable product' was the terse comment of one closely involved with the matter. After the position had been refused by Kilmuir,[8B] Macmillan appointed Lord Justice Parker (who took the same title as his father, Lord Parker of Waddington), who was much respected in the profession for his legal learning and calm personality. He was exactly the same age as Manningham-Buller, but had no political experience, and had never taken silk. Manningham-Buller in private confessed that he felt

[6] H. Macmillan, *Riding the Storm* (1971), p. 737. Devlin's reaction was different: 'The speech, when I read it in Hansard, had struck me as flimsy. Then I remembered that the Prime Minister had listened to it while I had only read it. There was no doubt that Reggie could put things across in a massive way' (*Easing the Passing*, p. 189).   [7] Simonds, 'Recollections'.
[8] Bresler, *Lord Goddard*, p. 296.   [8A] Letter to Pilcher J. (11 Aug. 1958).
[8B] See above, p. 178.

disappointed[8C]—and also annoyed that Macmillan should have offered him Parker's place in the Court of Appeal. Such an offer could not with decency have been accepted—not least because no Attorney-General in office had ever accepted such an appointment. In public the Buller family refused to show any disappointment. Manningham-Buller himself later recorded:

I did not raise a finger to assert the Attorney-General's right to the succession. I do not believe in such rights of inheritance. The man for the job is the man who will do the job best. I personally think the Lord Chief Justice's job is one of the most awful jobs in the world. I wouldn't go as a volunteer. The incessant work. The mass of papers. Every weekend having to toil through it all.[9]

The attitude of the Bar, or rather some of its members, towards Manningham-Buller in the forties and fifties is well described in words used by G. M. Trevelyan about the attitudes towards Garibaldi of some English intellectuals. He referred to 'that contempt which clever people of the second order so often feel towards men of great but not strictly intellectual powers'.[1] But all this changed slowly, but very perceptibly, in the sixties and seventies. In particular Manningham-Buller's 'intellectual powers', though not the same kind as those of, say, Denning or Devlin, had their own peculiar quality. The change came slowly, partly because the Bar, like other human institutions, does not quickly alter established prejudices, and partly because the Chancellorship of Dilhorne was so brief (exactly two years and three months), and so much dominated by the political troubles of the Conservative Government, that there was little time for the conventional achievements of a Lord Chancellor.

The circumstances under which Kilmuir was dismissed on Friday, 13 July 1962 have already been fully described.[2] Lord Denning later wrote:

One day I was warned that I would have to swear in a new Lord Chancellor. I was not told who he was. But during that morning the Attorney General, Sir Reginald Manningham-Buller, who was arguing the case himself, asked to be excused for an hour or two. We guessed the reason. He was to be the new Lord Chancellor. So one day he was arguing before us as Attorney General.[3] The next day he was Lord Chancellor above us. We decided in his favour—but on the merits of his argument—not because he had become Lord Chancellor. Things like that make no impact on us.[4]

Manningham-Buller received the Great Seal on Monday, 16 July, and on Tuesday 17th was sworn in before the Master of the Rolls in the morning and introduced as 'Baron Dilhorne of Towcester in our County of Northampton' in

[8C] Letter to Pilcher J. (8 Sept. 1958).   [9] Bresler, *Lord Goddard*, p. 296.
[1] G. M. Trevelyan, *Garibaldi and the Thousand* (1936), p. 189.   [2] See above, pp. 175–78.
[3] The case was *Attorney-General* v. *Butterworth* [1963] 1 QB 696, in which the Court of Appeal held that it might be contempt of court to victimize a witness by depriving him of his office.
[4] Lord Denning, *The Due Process of Law*, p. 20.

the afternoon.[4A] (In 1964 he was promoted to Viscount—the last to be created until Whitelaw (1983).) He was succeeded as Attorney-General by the Solicitor-General, Sir John Hobson,[5] and he by Sir Peter Rawlinson.

In July 1962 Dilhorne was a few weeks short of his fifty-seventh birthday—younger than Halsbury, Loreburn, Finlay, Cave, Hailsham, Sankey, Maugham, or Caldecote, but older than Herschell, Haldane, Buckmaster, or Birkenhead. Dilhorne was amongst the seniors in a Cabinet the average age of which was only fifty-one. One biographer of Macmillan has remarked that the Prime Minister 'was like de Gaulle or Adenauer, an old man in a government of young men'.[6] In the fifteen months which elapsed before his illness and retirement in October 1963 his Government was hit by an exceptional number of crises, which seemed to relate as much to personalities (Profumo, Philby, Vassall, Enahoro) as to issues or events, such as Cuba or entry into the EEC.

In his capacity as Cabinet Minister, Dilhorne was closely involved with most of these problems. So in May 1963 Dilhorne carried out a preliminary investigation into the security aspects of the Profumo affair, and made a report to Macmillan in June. Later, there were many who said that if Dilhorne had been asked to use his formidable powers of cross-examination in March, when at a post-midnight meeting at the House of Commons, Profumo falsely assured the Attorney-General, the Solicitor-General, and the Chief Whip, that there was no truth in the rumours about him, he might have been 'laid open'. Hobson simply could not believe that someone who had come from the same background as himself (Harrow, Brasenose, and the Northamptonshire Yeomanry) would persist in telling lies. Dilhorne had the same simple loyalties; but he could also be ruthless in the pursuit of the truth if he suspected that something was being hidden. In the event the confidential Dilhorne report was overtaken by events. Profumo himself resigned his office and left the House of Commons, and on 20 June Macmillan announced the establishment of an inquiry under Lord Denning, who published his report in September.

Only a month later the country watched with amazement the scenes at Blackpool, where the Conservative Party happened to be holding its annual conference, when Macmillan was obliged by ill health to resign suddenly. From his sick-bed the Prime Minister organized an elaborate electoral process for the succession. The members of the Cabinet were polled by the Lord Chancellor. The interviews took place in a scruffy hotel bedroom, the Lord Chancellor's massive frame perched on a cheap bentwood chair.[7] When Reginald Maudling's turn came he replied that he would vote first for himself and secondly for

[4A] See above, p. 10 n. 1.

[5] 'He was not exciting, but many of his colleagues thought he was the best Law Officer the Conservative Party had produced since the first Viscount Hailsham' (*DNB, 1961–70*, p. 523).

[6] A. Sampson, *Macmillan* (1967), p. 204.

[7] J. Boyd-Carpenter, *Way of Life* (1980), pp. 175–6.

Butler.[8] Dilhorne recorded the answer impassively, and informed Macmillan that a clear majority favoured Lord Home. So the new Prime Minister emerged. When the clamour subsided, Dilhorne wrote to Butler to congratulate him on not having split the party by refusing to serve under Home.[9]

There remained little over a year in which to take up again the normal duties of a Lord Chancellor. The legislative programme was relatively light. Acts relating to London government (and consequential changes in the structure of the courts), legal aid, and Africa duly reached the statute-book. A valuable but highly technical law-reform statute, the Perpetuities and Accumulations Act 1964, was based on the Fourth Report of the Law Reform Commission, published in 1956. Dilhorne was sceptical about the major proposals for law reform which Gardiner was known to have in preparation. There was a debate on the topic in June 1964[1] in which an airing was given to the proposals of Gardiner that the various part-time unofficial bodies—the Law Reform Committee, the Private International Law Committee, and the Criminal Law Revision Committee—should be replaced by a permanent body of Commissioners under a Minister. Dilhorne would have none of this. He assured the House that 'the general shape of our law is good and the task of reform is of a limited character'.

It would be easy, but wrong, to depict Dilhorne as an opponent of reform. He has to his credit several pieces of reform—all conducted by administrative means, without lengthy and expensive meetings of committees. First, he secured the abandonment of the practice whereby the judgments ('speeches') of the Law Lords were read aloud as in a debate.[2] The practice had the charm of tradition, but was wasteful of judicial time. Secondly, he made compulsory training schemes for new magistrates which had been instituted on a voluntary basis by Simonds. It took the officials of the Lord Chancellor's Department some time to convince Dilhorne that the proposal was both wise and necessary, but, once he had been persuaded, he used his considerable influence in Whitehall to secure the necessary funds. Thirdly, in 1963 he gave instructions that the Offical Solicitor should review quarterly all cases of persons committed for contempt of court, and apply for their release if satisfied that the public interest no longer required their imprisonment. A surprising number of such people do not apply for their own release presumably because of ignorance, or obstinacy,[3] or a desire for martyrdom.[4] In the period 1975–80 the Official Solicitor reviewed over 2,000 such cases.

Dilhorne also favoured a wider membership for the Judicial Committee of the Privy Council. Senior judges from Australia, New Zealand, and Nigeria

---

[8] R. Maudling, *Memoirs* (1978), p. 128.   [9] R. A. Butler, *The Art of the Possible* (1973), p. 249.
[1] 258 H.L. Deb. col. 1035.   [2] See above, p. 27.
[3] See *Enfield LBC* v. *Maloney* [1983] 1 WLR 749, 745 ('prepared to stay in prison until Doomsday').
[4] See *Heaton's Transport* v. *TGWU* [1973] AC 15 (six dockers released though no apology tendered).

were duly appointed, but he was less successful with his support for the perennial proposal that the tribunal should go on circuit throughout the Commonwealth.

Under the tactful guidance of Sir George Coldstream, the Lord Chancellor's tendency to write irritable letters was controlled. Indeed, he could when necessary write a very good 'senior partner's letter', conciliatory yet very firm, to a political or judicial colleague in trouble. (One of the differences between solicitors and barristers is that the former must be capable of writing a good letter—i.e. one which will not only seem good to the sender and recipient, but will also sound good if read aloud in court a few years later.)

There were surprisingly few High Court appointments—N. Faulks, J. Stirling, and J. R. Cumming-Bruce to the Family Division; H. Milmo to the Queen's Bench Division; and B. Stamp to the Chancery Division. Cumming-Bruce and Stamp had been Treasury devils; Faulks had a good war record, as had Milmo in Intelligence; Stirling had been in the Judge Advocate General's Department. There were, however, an unusually large number of appointments to inferior courts, of which two may be recorded—the first woman to the County Court Bench (Dame Elizabeth Lane, as she became),[5] and as an Additional Judge at the Central Criminal Court, A. King-Hamilton QC, who caused controversy after his retirement by taking employment on ITV to preside over 'trials'.

As a presiding judge Dilhorne sat in only seven appeals. One is of some interest, because it shows that, contrary to common belief, he was not always in favour of the prosecution: he saw his task as being to ascertain and apply the law. The House unanimously held, in a judgment delivered by Dilhorne, that an undischarged bankrupt does not obtain credit when he receives money in return for a promise to render services or deliver goods in the future. It was conceded that many fraudelent persons might escape justice, but the remedy lay with Parliament.[6]

In the sixties a disturbing constitutional development was the tendency of MPs, sometimes eminent, to attack the judiciary in general or individual judges in particular. The tendency increased in the seventies, and caused much concern to Lord Hailsham of St Marlybone, who, like Dilhorne, thought it the duty of a Lord Chancellor to defend those so attacked. In 1963, while on a visit to West Germany, Dilhorne took the opportunity of an address to Federal Court judges to rebuke Harold Wilson, the Leader of the Opposition, for what Dilhorne described as a suggestion that the British Government was improperly influencing the judiciary. Dilhorne protested that the suggestion was a libel on the judges. He declared that there was no shred of justification in the charge and added:

[5] She later wrote of Dilhorne's 'bold originality' in appointing a woman (E. Lane, *Hear the Other Side* (1985), p. 168).   [6] *Fisher* v. *Raven* [1964] AC 210.

If I were to be asked what I thought was the Lord Chancellor's chief job in life, I should tell you without hesitation that it was to preserve the independence of the judiciary, to make absolutely certain that the judges of the land are completely independent, and to protect them from every attempt, however indirect, to undermine that independence.[7]

When Dilhorne surrendered the Great Seal to Gardiner on 17 October 1964 he was only just past his fifty-ninth birthday. In the same year, and at the same age, Devlin retired from the judicial bench. Dilhorne did not intend to retire. He had had twenty years experience of public life, thirteen of them at the highest level in law and politics. There were only two Tory ex-Lord Chancellors alive, Simonds and Kilmuir: the former was out of affairs by reason of age, the latter by personal choice. So it is not surprising to find Dilhorne active in debate. Although Deputy Leader of the Opposition in the Lords, under Carrington as Leader, he did once give support to the Government. The Bill which became the War Damage Act 1965 proposed to reverse the decision of the majority of the Law Lords in *Burmah Oil Co.* v. *Lord Advocate*[8] that the appellants were entitled to be compensated for property destroyed by the order of the Crown in war-time. There were obvious reasons of policy for such legislation. What aroused the wrath of a formidable body of critics (including the Lord Chief Justice, Parker of Waddington) was that the legislation was expressed to be retrospective in effect. It was a very strong exercise of parliamentary sovereignty to deprive a successful appellant of the fruits of his judgment. The Government defended this on the grounds that Burmah Oil had been warned by the Deputy Treasury Solicitor that such legislation would be introduced 'in the unlikely event of your company succeeding'. It is most improper for the solicitor for one of the parties to a dispute to communicate directly with the party on the other side (as distinct from his solicitor). Dilhorne did not feel able to stand by such a breach of professional etiquette. But otherwise he gave strong support to Gardiner—largely on the ground that 'it was not all that easy' to introduce an indemnity Bill earlier when the prevailing legal view was that there was nothing for the Crown to be indemnified against.[9]

But later in 1965 there was a change in Dilhorne's activities from the political to the judicial. No doubt this was because the Conservatives had replaced Sir Alec Douglas-Home (as he had become in 1963) by Edward Heath. The two men had little in common. Dilhorne must have thought that as he was not a member of Heath's Shadow Cabinet his chances of being reappointed Lord Chancellor were remote. So he gave up his post as Deputy Leader of the Opposition—but told the House very firmly that he was still entitled to sit on the Opposition front bench.[1] Unlike Kilmuir, he did not take refuge in silent

[7] *The Times*, 10 Sept. 1980.
[8] [1965] AC 75.   [9] 264 H.L. Deb. col. 750.
[1] 274 H.L. Deb. col. 472.

abstention. He devoted himself to his judicial functions with such energy that his attendance record for appeals has been truly described as 'phenomenal'.[2] Between October 1964 and July 1968 he sat in no fewer than twenty-four appeals to the Lords. He also caused a little alarm in 1972 by going out on the Western Circuit as Judge of Assize—an unprecedented step for an ex-Lord Chancellor. In the event his sentences were thought to be on the light side. (It has been settled for many years[2A] that it would be unconstitutional for a Lord Chancellor to take any part in a criminal trial, as he is a Minister of the Crown holding office at the pleasure of the Sovereign).

A well-placed parliamentary question in July 1968 made these facts known.[3] In the summer of 1969 Lord Pearce retired. He was only sixty-eight, but he had been a judge for twenty-one years. Gardiner decided that the vacant position should be offered to Dilhorne. A story got abroad that Dilhorne would have been appointed in 1968 to a vacancy filled by Diplock but for his political views. It was at the time believed by Dilhorne himself. But, as Lord Gardiner pointed out, it:

presuppose[d] that someone was trying to make him a Law Lord and that I was opposing it. But who could this someone have been? It was for the Queen to decide. But she was constitutionally bound to accept the advice of the Prime Minister, and in this field the Prime Minister always asked for, and accepted, my advice. There never was anyone else who could have made him a Law Lord, so I have always been hurt by this story.[4]

It is true that when Gardiner's intentions became known, some signs of uneasiness appeared about the chairmanship of the Appellate Committee. The rules were changed to ensure that seniority of appointment as a Law Lord was the only criterion to be applied.[5] Dilhorne never displayed any displeasure at being the junior Law Lord. (The position then carried a salary of £11,0000, compared with a Lord Chancellor's pension of £5,000.)

Then began a period of remarkable judicial activity. Formally it might be regarded as the third stage in Dilhorne's judicial career (first, Chancellor; secondly, an ex-Chancellor; and thirdly, a Law Lord). But neither Dilhorne nor anyone else made the distinction, which certainly need not trouble any reader of the Appeal Cases for the years 1969–80, during which Dilhorne sat in no fewer than 205 appeals, according to the LEXIS computer.

One comment can certainly be made about Dilhorne's judgments; they will not figure in any anthology of English prose. They are not written in what it was once fashionable to call the grand style. Sometimes they read rather like a digest

---

[2] L. Blom-Cooper and G. Drewry, *Final Appeal* (1972), p. 180.
[2A] See Lord Coleridge's opinion cited in (1976) 92 *L.Q.R.* 93, 104.   [3] 769 H.C. Deb. col. 225.
[4] To the author.
[5] See above, p. 278. At first Gardiner sought to solve the problem by telling Dilhorne that at 62 he was too old to preside over appeals. Then the solution of changing the rules occurred to him.

of cases. He made it very plain that his views about the judicial function were conservative.

As I understand the judicial functions of this House, although they involve applying well established principles to new situations, they do not involve adjusting the common law to what are thought to be the social norms of the time. They do not include bowing to the wind of change. We have to declare what the law is, not what we think it should be. If it is clearly established that in certain circumstances there is a right to exemplary damages, this House should not, when sitting judicially, and indeed, in my view, cannot properly abolish or restrict that right ... If the power to award such damages is to be abolished or restricted, that is the task of the legislature.[6]

Dilhorne did not regard it as being part of the duty of an English judge to be committed, purposive, result-oriented, or socially responsive (to use some of the adjectives which can be found in socio-legal writings). When the facts had been found, the law was applied to them, and the result clearly stated. But even a critic has conceded that 'in his hands, "ascertaining the facts" was, at times, an impressive performance'.[7] If this revealed a gap, it was for Parliament to fill it. It was 'not part of the judicial function to alter all this', said Dilhorne, dissenting, when the House was asked to hold the Crown liable for the escapades of Borstal boys.[8] But he was capable of analysing and restating legal doctrines and rules in a way which gave satisfaction. So many authorities on the law of contract think that his opinion in the famous *Suisse Atlantique* case[9] on the scope of exemption clauses is in no way inferior to those of Lords Wilberforce and Reid.

His judgments reflect two qualities. First, negatively, there is no evidence that (despite popular belief) he was unduly kind to the Crown or prosecuting authorities—indeed, he held the unusual view that a judge might stop an oppressive prosecution.[1] In one of his last judgments, dealing with a lottery, there were some strong criticisms of the conduct of the Director of Public Prosecutions.[2] In another case Dilhorne 'had some very salutary remarks as to the considerations which prosecuting organisations ought to bear in mind before instituting proceedings in consumer cases'.[3] Dilhorne had critized the Government for bringing an action for violation of public health legislation when no harm had resulted. 'What this litigation has cost I dread to think. A great deal of the time of the courts had been occupied. I cannot see that any

[6] *Broom* v. *Cassell & Co. Ltd.* [1972] AC 1027, at 1107.
[7] R. Stevens, *Law and Politics* (1979), p. 427.
[8] *Dorset Yacht Co. Ltd.* v. *Home Office* [1970] AC 1004, at 1045.
[9] [1967] AC 361.
[1] J. L. Edwards, *The Attorney General, Politics and the Public Interest* (1984), p. 130.
[2] *Imperial Tobacco Co. Ltd.* v. *Attorney-General* [1981] AC 718.
[3] *Wings Ltd.* v. *Ellis* [1985] AC 272, at 290, per Lord Hailsham of St Marylebone, LC, referring to *Smedleys Ltd.* v. *Breed* [1974] AC 839, 855.

advantage to the general body of consumers has or will result, apart, perhaps from the exposition of the law.' In *Veste* v. *IRC*[4] Dilhorne joined the majority in holding that the Crown's claim to tax income arising from certain settlements failed because it produced injustice in the form of multiple tax—an injustice which was not truly cured by an extra-statutory concession by the Revenue. One should be taxed by law, and not untaxed by discretion. But Dilhorne must have been a little surprised to find his judgment for the majority in a Privy Council appeal[5] criticized by Lord Salmon, dissenting, on the ground that it 'would encourage nationalisation without compensation throughout the Commonwealth'.

Positively, Dilhorne's long experience as a Law Officer was of value in a number of cases in the area of public law—in particular *Gouriet* v. *UPW*,[6] in which the House, reversing the Court of Appeal, held that the Attorney-General had an unfettered discretion to institute or discontinue proceedings for an injunction in public law. Dilhorne's exhaustive examination of the law and practice on the matter covered twelve pages of the Law Reports. There is a judgment of similar length on the issue of whether a US Federal Grand Jury had infringed the sovereignty of the UK by summoning English residents to give evidence.[7] Other characteristic opinions exist on the questions of whether a local valuation tribunal could be protected by contempt of court proceedings,[8] and whether the granting of planning permission extinguished existing use rights.[9]

In the field of criminal law there are a number of authoritative judgments. In *Broome* v. *DPP*[1] Dilhorne considered the law relating to picketing, and in *R.* v. *Scott*[2] the scope of conspiracy to defraud. In *R.* v. *Smith (Roger)*[3] Dilhorne emphasized that it was conduct and not belief which was punishable criminally as distinct from morally. This reflected the traditional view of English criminal law: an evil intention (or gross recklessness) might require to be treated on the psychiatrist's couch, but unless it resulted in some prohibited behaviour it was no concern of the courts. So there could not be a conviction for an attempt to commit a crime when the crime in question could not be committed because of legal or physical impossibilities. For over a century it had been generally

---

[4] [1980] AC 1148.
[5] *Government of Malaysia* v. *Singapore Pilot's Association* [1978] AC 337.
[6] [1978] AC 435. When he was Attorney-General in 1958 Manningham-Buller produced an exhaustive memorandum favouring the right of a private person to institute a prosecution without the leave of a Law Officer. Developments have since been in the other direction: see Edwards, *Attorney General*, pp. 1-36.
[7] *RTZ Corporation* v. *Westinghouse Corporation* [1978] AC 747.
[8] *Attorney-General* v. *BBC* [1981] AC 303.
[9] *Newbury RDC* v. *Environment Secretary* [1981] AC 578.
[1] [1974] AC 587. On 8 Apr. 1975 he wrote to *The Times* to correct what he said was a misinterpretation of his speech. The only other Law Lord known to have done this was Lord Davey on 26 Sept.1904.
[2] [1975] AC 819, on which see *R.* v. *Ayres* [1984] 2 WLR 257.
[3] [1975] AC 476.

accepted that—for example—a man could not be guilty of attempted theft if he took his own umbrella from a stand believing it to be that of another. Then those who believed that dishonest thoughts should be brought within the scope of the criminal law procured the enactment of the Criminal Attempts Act 1981, which abolished the common law and substituted a statutory code governing attempts to commit offences. (The Law Commission had made such a recommendation,[4] but the Commission's draft Bill was not accepted by Parliament.) The proper interpretation of the tortuous phraseology of the 1981 Act required two appeals to be brought to the House of Lords within one year.

In the first case[5] it was held in May 1985 that Mrs Ryan did not commit the offence of attempted handling of stolen goods when she bought a video recorder which she believed to have been stolen when it was not. This seemed to suggest that the Dilhorne view was still law despite the Act of 1981. Three hundred and sixty-one days later Mr Shivpuri was held to have been rightly convicted of attempting to deal with and harbour a substance he believed to be a prohibited drug (heroin or cannabis) when in fact it was harmless vegetable matter.[6] The Ryan case was said to have been wrongly decided. It was remarkable for the House of Lords to use its powers under the 1966 Practice Statement[7] to refuse to follow one of its own previous decisions (made only one year before), especially in the field of criminal law, where certainty is thought to be all important. But the Law Lords said that even if error had crept into the body of the law it should be expelled before prosecutors (and criminals) had time to act on it. It can be said with confidence that Dilhorne would have approved neither of the result nor of the manner of reaching it.

Dilhorne's contributions to English criminal law were not limited to his judgments. Although scrupulously careful to observe the convention which inhibits a Law Lord from taking part in a debate on a purely political subject, he was entitled to, and did, speak on such topics as the rehabilitation of offenders (1974) and standards in public life (1976). He also instituted a major debate (1972) on the Eleventh Report of the Criminal Law Revision Committee on Evidence in Criminal Cases. The report had been in preparation for no less than eight years, and an unprecedented number of Law Lords took part in the debate.[8]

The Criminal Law Act 1977 and the Theft Act 1978 were major statutes which had been preceded by reports from various committees. On the committee stage of the 1978 Theft Bill Dilhorne put down no fewer than twenty-five amendments. The Theft Act 1968, s. 16, had become what the

[4] See Law Com. No. 102 (1979).
[5] *Anderton v. Ryan* [1985] AC 560.
[6] See *R. v. Shivpuri* [1986] 2 WLR 561.
[7] See below p. 219.
[8] 388 H.L. Deb. col. 1546.

Court of Appeal described as 'a judicial nightmare'.[9] The section had produced consequences which were legally and morally absurd. A housewife who spun a hard-luck story in order to persuade the milkman to wait a week for payment of his bill might be criminally liable; whereas the person who entered a restaurant with the intent of obtaining a meal without payment, and did so, was only liable if the waiter was present when he ran away. After titanic efforts of drafting and redrafting the offending section was repealed and replaced by another, which has given rather less trouble. Dilhorne's last significant intervention in debate was in February 1980 on Lord Scarman's Interpretation of Legislation Bill, which in five clauses set out the substance of a Law Commission Report. The sponsor was unlucky in that the Bill was called after the House had been exhausted by a four-hour debate on economic policy, and somehow it did not attract support—indeed, it was known to be opposed by the parliamentary draftsmen. Lord Diplock went so far as to express 'strong dislike' of the measure, and by the time (10 p.m.) that Dilhorne rose to oppose it, its fate had been sealed.[1]

Another activity was that of Treasurer of the Inner Temple for the year 1975. There was much work as a result of the reorganization of the profession which created a body known as the Senate of the Inns of Court and the Bar. It was not admired by Dilhorne, although he conceded that the ancient structure of the Inns did need some reform. But one aspect of the history of the ancient society known as the Inner Temple (so concentrated in space, so spread out in time) was beyond the reach of the reformer. In November 1977 Dilhorne was present in Hall to see his twenty-one-year-old grandson, Thomas Mervyn Brudenell, called to the Bar. He was thirteenth in direct descent from both Sir Robert Brudenell (paternally) and Sir Edward Coke (maternally). It was exactly fifty years after Dilhorne's own call, almost exactly 400 years after that (on 20 April 1578) of Sir Edward Coke (CJ KB), and nearly 500 years after that of Sir Robert Brudenell (CJ CP) (date of call unknown, but in practice by 1490). Such a remarkable event demonstrates the historic continuity of the English Bar. (In November 1979 Dilhorne was again present to witness the call of his son, John Mervyn, who had had careers as a soldier and as an accountant before committing himself to the Bar.)

At the end of the Trinity term 1980 Dilhorne sat on an important appeal on the scope of an order for discovery made against Granada television in an action brought by the British Steel Corporation. The Court of Appeal had refused to accept the argument of Granada that compliance with the order would result in the disclosure of the name of their informant. (This was exactly what the plaintiffs desired in order to discover which of their employees had 'leaked' a

[9] R. v. Royle [1971] 1 WLR 1764, at 1767, per Edmund Davies LJ.
[1] 408 H.L. Deb. col. 295.

confidential document.) Argument concluded on 22 July. On 30 July it was announced that the appeal would be dismissed for reasons to be given later.[2] (Lord Salmon indicated doubts.) Two days later Dilhorne retired from his position as a Law Lord: to all but a few close friends he seemed to be in perfect health, but the Judicial Pensions Act 1959, s. 1, specifically required retirement on the seventy-fifth birthday. (Lord Salmon, two years older than Dilhorne, did not retire until the end of the long vacation, because he had been appointed a judge before the 1959 Act came into force.) But on 7 September Dilhorne died very suddenly at Knoydart in Inverness-shire after a day on the hill. It was characteristic that he had completed his opinion in the Granada case before his death. It was also characteristic that when it was printed it covered nine pages of the Appeal Cases. To Dilhorne retirement would have been no reason for failing to perform conscientiously a public duty.

Dilhorne, whose estate was valued for probate at £120,060, was buried in the graveyard of the parish church at Deene, Northamptonshire. Until it was closed by the ecclesiastical authorities, the visitor could see in the church the magnificent alabaster monument over the remains of Henry VIII's Chief Justice; now all that can be seen (and heard) at Deene are the industrial achievements of the town of Corby on the horizon.

Dilhorne disdained the arts by which a lawyer-politician often seeks popularity. He evoked respect rather than affection; even some of his Cabinet colleagues were a little frightened of him. But the respect was given to qualities which were once thought to be characteristic of his class and his profession—integrity, loyalty, and a desire to do the State some service.

---

[2] [1981] AC 1096. The effect of the judgment has been diminished by the Contempt of Court Act 1981, s. 10.

LORD GARDINER

CHAPTER I

GERALD AUSTIN GARDINER, the second of three sons, was born on 30 May 1900 (one day after David Maxwell Fyfe), at his father's house, 67 Cadogan Square. His parents were an unusual couple. Robert Septimus Gardiner (1856–1939) was one of the nine children of the Revd George Gregory Gardiner, an Anglican clergyman who had become chaplain to the English Church in Paris. The grandfather of the Revd G. G. Gardiner had changed the family name from Webber to Gardiner on inheriting some property in Somerset. The Revd G. G. Gardiner was himself son of a Somersetshire rector, and no fewer than four of his own sons entered the same profession. But the seventh graduated from Grenoble University and emigrated to Quebec; after returning to England he achieved prosperity as chairman of various gas and shipping companies in the area of Newcastle-upon-Tyne. Moving to London he became interested in theatre ownership, was knighted, and painted by de Laszlo, and acquired one house in Cadogan Square and another outside Canterbury. At the age of forty he had married Alice Marie, a daughter of Count (later Baron) Hermann Ludwig Wilhelm Karl Gregory von Ziegesar. Baroness Ziegesar was the granddaughter of Dionysius Lardner, an LLD of Trinity College, Dublin, who later devoted his talents to the popularization of scientific knowledge. (One lecture tour of North America earned him the amazing sum of £40,000.) He was also understood to be the father of the playwright and actor Dion Boucicault. So the great-great-grandfather and great-great-uncle of Gerald Gardiner displayed some qualities of interest to the future Chancellor of the Open University and President of OUDS.

This somewhat exotic background had no real impact on Gardiner. 'I do not feel at all cosmopolitan.'[1] His appearance and conversation were unmistakably those of someone born before the First World War into the English upper classes. Although his mother had been a convert to Roman Catholicism, Gardiner later assured the peers: 'I am a member of the Church of England'.[2] (Contrary to popular belief, he was never a member of the Society of Friends (Quakers), although he served with the Friends' Ambulance Unit in the Second World War.)

Gardiner's education was the conventionally unhappy one of the upper

[1] This remark, together with some others in this Part not otherwise attributed, was made by Lord Gardiner in conversation with the author in 1984.

[2] 352 H.L. Deb. col. 415. The parish churches of Bathealton and Langford Budville, near Kittisford in west Somerset, contain monumental inscriptions to members of the Webber and Gardiner families.

classes, of which so many autobiographical and fictional accounts exist. He was ill-treated at his private school, and then found the bleak atmosphere of war-time Harrow difficult to accept. One member of the staff, H. Kittermaster, was recalled with affection, for he had (for Harrow) radical views. Sir Robert Gardiner was so shocked by the sight of a copy of the *Nation* on the master's desk that he resolved to save his youngest son from temptation by sending him to Eton. (The eldest son had been sent to Wellington.) When Gerald Gardiner had risen to be Chairman of the Statesman and Nation Publishing Company this episode was often recalled with wry amusement.

An ordinary English schoolboy of mildly intellectual tastes with a dislike for organized sport is not likely to become an ensign in the Household Brigade. But Harrow and Cadogan Square carried Gardiner into the Coldstream Guards, in which he was commissioned within a month at the end of the war, and then demobilized.

In Hilary term 1920, he went up to Magdalen College, Oxford. The intervening months had been spent partly at a crammers at Maidenhead to get through the necessary examinations, and partly at Tours to improve his French. Sir Robert said on his son's return that he did not detect any improvement. (It is notable that although both Simonds and Gardiner had French-speaking grand-parents on their maternal side, neither was really fluent in the language; by contrast, in an earlier generation both Cave and Maugham spoke impeccable French.)

There arose at this time in consequence of a friendship with Gerald du Maurier an interest in acting which became more intense at Oxford. Gardiner found Magdalen narrow and self-contained. ('I should have been at the House'.) His tutor, R. Segar, was as uninspiring as A. T. Denning had found him a few years earlier. But OUDS opened up exciting vistas. In his first summer (1920) he played Orlando; in his last (1924), Horatio to the famous Hamlet of Gyles Isham.[3] (Isham was like Gardiner in being President of both OUDS and the Union). In Hilary term 1924 another undergraduate who was taking his academic duties lightly, Evelyn Waugh, wrote to a friend: 'They have elected Gerald Gardiner President this term. Do you remember him? A tall man with a jerky voice.'[4] At Magdalen the news was greeted with pleasant surprise, and no difficulty was made about Gardiner staying up for a fourth year, ostensibly to read for the BCL. Today the Magdalen dons would not extend such a conces-sion to one who had been placed in the Fourth Class of the Final Honour School of Jurisprudence—as Gardiner had been in 1923, along with no less than eighteen others. (In the First Class there were nine names: only one later achieved eminence—J. Harlan of Balliol, a judge of the US Supreme Court.)

---

[3] H. Carpenter *OUDS* (1985), pp. 72–81.
[4] E. Gallagher (ed.) *Essays of Evelyn Waugh* (1983), p. 20.

In the event the fourth year was abruptly terminated by the Proctors when a complaint was made to them about an article written by a Somerville undergraduate, Dilys Powell, and published in pamphlet form by *Isis*. The article was on the theme of what today would be called sexual discrimination. Gardiner was only a sub-editor of *Isis*, but as the editor, Michael Tandy, had not yet taken Schools, Gardiner persuaded the Proctors to allocate to him the major share of the blame. So Gardiner was sent down and Tandy gated for the term.

In those days such decisions were accepted without protests or rancour. Half a century later Dilys Powell, who had had a distinguished career as a film critic, recorded that 'I remember apologising to my College; my article (which I feel sure was silly) ended in a blaze of unwanted publicity. Everyone but me, it seems, behaved in the most gentlemanly way.'[5]

Sir Robert Gardiner was surprisingly tolerant about this development. Indeed, unlike that other Magdalen father, Sir Mervyn Manningham-Buller, he continued his son's allowance in order that he should be called to the Bar, which took place at the Inner Temple on 6 May 1925. Gardiner went into chambers at 2 The Cloisters. The head was St John Field, later a County Court judge, who had succeeded to most of H. A. McCardie's practice when the latter became a judge. There was a stately and formidable clerk, Adam. In later years he and Gardiner came to respect each other, but the early years were miserable. Sixty years later Gardiner said tersely of those chambers: 'They were very bad.' Sharing a room with Hartley Shawcross was not recalled with pleasure. Despite the fact that his professional income was exactly nil for his first two years, Gardiner was able to marry in 1925 Lesly Doris, daughter of Edwin Trounson, of Penzance, later of Southport. The bride was ten years older than her husband, and had a small boy (who died young) by a previous marriage. The Gardiners had one daughter, Carol, who later left home to live in New York.

By 1930 Gerald Gardiner's practice had improved, and his annual income rose to £1,500. But he remained at 2 The Cloisters until 1945, when he moved to 12 King's Bench Walk—which, showing characteristic self-reliance, he redecorated personally. (Skill with his hands was a domestic asset: at his house at Oxshott, in Surrey, a large model railway was constructed in the attic, and clocks, mowing machines, and refrigerators were repaired by the owner.) After 1945 the house at Oxshott was given up, and the Gardiners lived in a succession of rented flats or houses—Montpelier Square, Stanhope Terrace, and Onslow Square (twice).

The demands of an increasing practice left little time for outside activities. Even the stage was given up—in the late thirties Gardiner resigned from the Windsor Strollers and the Canterbury Old Stagers. But in the sixties it was noticed that the Lord Chancellor's sole recreation was attendance at a first night followed by a late dinner in Soho.

[5] Letter to the author in 1985.

CHAPTER II

THE Bar seems to have been the only institution (as distinct from persons or causes) which evoked Gardiner's complete loyalty. He had not been happy at Harrow, and although Magdalen offered opportunities for happiness, that had been found outside the College and not within it. The Coldstream Guards left its mark on his physical appearance—but within a year of being demobilized he had isolated himself from that remarkable institution most decisively by becoming a pacifist. The Bar, however, met some interior need—perhaps because of the slightly theatrical element involved in common-law advocacy. (Later as Lord Chancellor Gardiner confessed frankly that he enjoyed 'the dressing-up side of the business'.) There was something attractive in the self-reliant and robust atmosphere of the Temple—perhaps because its social life was not too demanding; it could be taken or left. The gregarious side of Circuit life was certainly left: after his early years Gardiner was seldom seem in any Bar Mess on the Midland Circuit. This did not diminish the respect of its members for him. In return Gardiner recognized his debt to his profession. The reformer of the English legal system regarded some aspects of it as sacrosanct. To the end he believed fervently in the public value of a divided profession.[1] He was active in the affairs of his Inn, of which he became a Bencher in 1955. He was active on the Bar Council, and defeated Lionel Heald in a contest for the chairmanship in 1958, to which he was re-elected in 1959. There followed much work in obtaining increases in the level of fees, which had been frozen since 1939. It was decided to begin the negotiations with fees payable for work done outside London. Then the London problem was tackled with separate investigations into fees at the Old Bailey, London Sessions, and Middlesex Sessions. Barristers are more secretive than most professional men about their earnings, but the Treasury was impressed by the number who had been persuaded to supply copies of their income-tax returns.

The high esteem in which Gardiner was held by the Bar was not due solely to his activity as Chairman of the Bar Council. The Bar regarded him as a person of complete integrity. He had never to suffer the covert sneers which Jowitt had to endure. There was never any real doubt in the Temple or at Westminster that Gardiner would be Lord Chancellor in a Labour Government—which, after the death of Hugh Gaitskell, would be led by Harold Wilson.

The outbreak of war at first brought little change to Gardiner's position at the Bar. Just young enough for the Kaiser's War, he was too old for Hitler's. In

---

[1] See 'Two Lawyers or One', (1970) 23 *CLP* 1; and below, p. 227.

any event he had for long been an active member of the Peace Pledge Union, which had been formed by an old friend of the family (the Revd) H. R. L. (Dick) Sheppard. Gardiner's revulsion towards physical force as a mode of settling disputes was an intellectual rather than a physical or emotional one. 'War was WRONG', he said emphatically many years later.

In 1943 he joined the Friends' Ambulance Unit. 'I was making a good deal of money at the Bar, which didn't seem right with people away at the War, so I did what seemed logical. I threw up my practice and joined the Friends' Ambulance Unit'.[2] The unit arrived in Europe in June 1944, and saw much action—and its results, including Belsen.

In September 1945 Gardiner returned to a flat in Jubilee Place, Chelsea, to resume his practice. An unfriendly local bank manager refused him a necessary overdraft, so recourse had to be had to a money-lender. Ten years later Gardiner was able to keep his account at Hoare's in Fleet Street.

It is less easy to plot the path by which the son of Sir Robert Gardiner came to join the Labour Party—indeed, the reasons which impel members of the upper, or upper-middle, classes, to support socialism have not been adequately investigated or explained—a distinct gap in English intellectual and social history. Gardiner himself was very reticent on the matter—but so were Attlee, Jowitt, Dalton, Crosland, Cripps, and Gaitskell—all members of Labour Governments. Another, Frank Pakenham (later Lord Longford), was reduced, most uncharacteristically, to silence when asked directly by his sovereign, 'Why did you . . . join them?'[3]

There are few clues—at Harrow a master who subscribed to the *Nation*; at Oxford membership of the New Reform Club, of which he was President in 1922, but which seems to have been as short-lived as most undergraduate bodies; membership of the Oxshott Labour Party (against which must be set acting as a special constable during the General Strike in 1926)—but they do not amount to enough to form a reasoned conclusion.

There does not seem to have been any one political event, such as the suppression of the Social Democratic Party in Vienna in February 1934, which to Elwyn-Jones was 'a watershed in my political experience'—an opinion shared by Gaitskell.[4] Equally there does not seem to have been any personal experience of poverty and unemployment gained through social work in the East End, as with Attlee in Stepney. It is also fairly clear that there was no intellectual influence from socialist literature. Attlee had been much influenced by Ruskin's *Unto This Last*. But when Gardiner was asked whether he had been affected by reading authors such as Harold Laski and G. D. H. Cole, who were fashionable

[2] M. Box, *Rebel Advocate* (1983), p. 59.
[3] F. Pakenham, *Born to Believe* (1953), p. 159.
[4] Lord Elwyn-Jones, *In My Time* (1983), p. 33.

in the twenties and thirties, he looked completely blank. The idea did not seem
to have occurred to him before.

It is only surmise, but it may be that the Christian socialism which is
associated with the writings of F. D. Maurice, Carlyle and Ruskin, and
exemplified by the activities of Dick Sheppard, had more influence than was
openly acknowledged.

In any event there was close connection with, and much activity for, many
bodies—above all, JUSTICE, which first met in 1957 in Gardiner's chambers,
and later developed into the British section of the International Centre of
Jurists. Other bodies with which there were close links were the National
Marriage Guidance Council, the Howard League for Penal Reform, and the
National Advisory Council for the Rehabilitation of Offenders (NACRO).

Gardiner's association with these causes is more easily described in negative
than in positive terms. He was absolutely the reverse of the passionate platform
speaker such as Dick Sheppard or Victor Gollancz. Before Gardiner became
associated with Gollancz in the National Campaign for the Abolition of Capital
Punishment, he 'had been warned, that [Gollancz] was an explosive character,
that he would both sentimentalize and sensationalize the movement, and that
he was not easy to work with'. Nobody would have thought of applying this
description to Gardiner. Nor would he have thought of applying to himself the
ugly Americanism 'civil libertarian'.

From 1945 onwards Gardiner was an assiduous attender at meetings of these,
and other, bodies and causes. No school hall or committee-room in suburban
London was too remote or too dilapidated for him to fail to attend at if invited.
The organization of these well-meaning affairs is often marked by casual
inefficiency. More than once a chairman and a secretary, strolling in late, were
disconcerted to find Gardiner already seated—punctual, impassive, immaculate
in the black cloth and white linen which were then essential for the London
barrister. Gardiner was able to endure functions which were a torture to Harold
Nicolson, who in 1947 went to a meeting of the Haldane Society, the audience
being largely 'young lawyers and their girl-friends'.

I loathed it . . . the atmosphere of comradely fifth-ratedness upset me. Vegetable soup
we had, and liver and onions and beer. There were speeches by the Lord Chancellor, by
Stafford Cripps, by [Sir Frank] Soskice. They spoke about Law Reform. In the end we all
sang the *Red Flag*.

I always knew that I was a theoretical Socialist. I do feel profoundly that we can only
avoid totalitarianism or tyranny by a planned social economy. I believe we can achieve it
in this country without destroying the freedom of the individual. It is for this that I am
prepared to work. But the sham matiness and the *Red Flag* business are to me abhorrent.[5]

⁵ H. Nicolson, *Diaries and Letters 1945-62* (1968), p. 96.

Even Attlee, not a sensitive soul, had flinched at his first sight of the Fabian Society. 'My impression was a blurred one of many bearded men talking and roaring with laughter.'[6]

By the middle of the fifties Gardiner, who had taken silk in 1948, was at the top of the common-law Bar. To use a phrase which had not then become completely obsolete, he was 'a fashionable silk'. The cases which attracted most public attention were those in which there was a jury. In court Gardiner was an impressive sight. No judge ever had to hint that he should stand up straight or take his hands out of his pockets. Completely composed in manner, he still retained the actor's gift for communicating strong emotions without recourse to gesture. (Some jurors found disconcerting his habit of fixing his eyes about a foot above the level of their heads; conversely, others found it intimidating when he did catch their eyes.) A law reporter remembered that 'His only idiosyncrasy is the slow rolling-up and unrolling of the "fee-bag" string which hangs down the front of his gown'.[7] There were at least four big cases in which these talents were displayed—actions for libel involving Evelyn Waugh, the singer Liberace, the Duchess of Argyll, and the American author Leon Uris.

Two other cases may also be mentioned—the ETU case, and the *Lady Chatterly's Lover* case.[8] The former raised the issue of Communist penetration of a major trade union. The trial, before Winn, J. sitting alone, lasted forty-two days, and revealed what Gardiner, for the successful plaintiffs, called 'the biggest fraud in the history of British trade unionism'.

As for *Lady Chatterley's Lover*, the publishers of D. H. Lawrence's novel were prosecuted for obscene libel before Byrne J. and a jury at the Old Bailey. The common law relating to obscene libel had been swept away by an Act of 1959, which also provided a new defence—that the publication was for the public good. The acquittal which Gardiner secured, after calling no fewer than thirty-five witnesses to persuade the jury that the publication was protected by the statutory defence, was generally thought to be a triumph for the right of free speech. Anthony Powell was 'a spectator of some of the scenes of this singular extravaganza, something between a morality play and a pantomime'.[9] As he truly remarked,

Lawrence, capable of an occasional joke in his letters, is consistently without humour in his books, a failing rarely if ever to be found in novelists of the highest class from Petronius to Proust. There was therefore a certain justice in the rights and wrongs of *Lady Chatterley* being hammered out without a vestige of humour on either side.

[6] K. Harris, *Attlee* (1982), p. 25.
[7] M. Hill and L. N. Williams, *Auschwitz in England* (1965), p. 44.
[8] Nothing can be added here to two admirable books by C. H. Rolph, *The Trial of Lady Chatterley* (1961), and *All Those in Favour?* (1962).
[9] A. Powell, *To Keep the Ball Rolling* (1982), p. 366.

Yet it would hardly be reasonable to expect Gardiner to have been able and willing to deflate any of his own witnesses, although counsel for the Crown, Meryn Griffith-Jones, if he had been blessed with the requisite quickness of thought and lightness of touch, was certainly given many opportunities for puncturing balloons of dogmatic self-importance, and as the Crown called no witnesses, Gardiner could not have done so in cross-examination.

In one case[1] Gardiner succeeded in obtaining judgment before Vaisey J. by invoking the simple constitutional principle that the subject could not be taxed without the authority of Parliament. The Post Office had levied a charge on the users of mobile radios, the validity of which was strongly asserted by Manningham-Buller A.-G. even after Gardiner's junior (Raphael Tuck) had made the happy discovery that no regulation authorizing such a fee had ever been made. Gardiner could not resist making the additional point that the plaintiffs had a grievance about the many changes of wavelengths.

It had been publicly stated that the Post Office again proposed to change the frequencies, this time in favour of the powerful financial interests behind commercial television. British citizens were meek and mild and did not in practice tend to question authority unless they had cause to look into the position.

The ATTORNEY-GENERAL.—No question arises as to the frequencies in this action; I do not accept this criticism of the Post Office. The Court should not be used as a forum for advancing political argument.

His LORDSHIP.—I have not understood that these changes were capricious. Try not to be unnecessarily provocative, Mr Gardiner.

Gardiner's name was known to academic lawyers as well as to practitioners. In part this was because he had contributed to each of the two major periodicals—the *Law Quarterly Review* and the *Modern Law Review*. (As Lord Chancellor, he was the co-author, with Nigel Curtis-Raleigh, of an article in the former entitled 'The Judicial Attitude to Penal Reform' and of another entitled 'The role of the Lord Chancellor in the field of Law Reform'.[2] It is unusual for a Lord Chancellor in office to publish anything except perhaps a lecture outlining the duties of his office—as, indeed, Gardiner had done in 1968 with his Holdsworth Lecture entitled 'The Trials of a Lord Chancellor'. The spirit of the times had changed since Jowitt wrote to Denning, LJ, to rebuke him for having delivered the Hamlyn Lectures.)

It is also unusual for a silk in busy practice to find time to contribute a case-note to a learned journal—indeed, this is a form of legal writing usually reserved

---

[1] *Davey Paxman & Co. Ltd.* v. *Post Office* (1957) *The Times*, 15 Nov.

[2] See (1969) 65 *LQR* 196, and (1971) 87 *LQR* 326. Three other periodical articles by Lord Gardiner may be listed here: 'Law Reform and Teachers of Law' (1966) 9 *JSPTL* 190; 'Methods of Law Reform' (1969) 13 *St Louis Univ. L. Jour.* 3; 'Some Aspects of Law Reform' (1969) 47 *NZL* 171.

for junior academics. But Gardiner published an interesting note[3] on a case in which he had been engaged which raised some difficult questions of law and policy. The case was *Lister* v. *Romford Ice Co. Ltd.,*[4] in which the House of Lords had held that an insurance company which had satisfied the claim of a third party under an employer's liability policy was entitled to claim reimbursement from the employee who was the primary wrongdoer. The employer had such a right to claim indemnity from his wrong-doing servant, and the insurance company by virtue of the doctrine of subrogation had the rights of the employer. After the decision 'a gentleman's agreement' was made between some liability insurers and employers' representatives under which the former agreed not to invoke the *Lister* principle except in cases of collusion or wilful misconduct. Gardiner truly remarked that it was doubtful whether 'this rather peculiar method of law reform should be encouraged'.

Such a position at the Bar normally leads to a judicial office. Gardiner

once applied for the Recordership of Warwick but a member of the Circuit with a much larger practice was rightly appointed. I only applied out of a sense of duty and did not feel bound to apply again. I was very happy to have been twice elected Chairman of the Bar Council. I loved my work at the Bar. I had no political ambitions and I never wanted to be a judge or anything grand.[5]

Presumably Gardiner's well-known objections to capital punishment would then have disqualified him from a Queen's Bench judgeship. 'They offered me one in Probate, Divorce and Admiralty. But I should get thoroughly bored dealing with divorce the whole time. Wouldn't feel I'd done a real day's work'.[6] So Gardiner was appointed to the Woolsack direct from the Bar. His political experience was minimal.

Gardiner was as good before an appellate tribunal as he was with a jury—a gift which is not possessed by all advocates. In *Rookes* v. *Barnard*[7] the issue was whether a threat by employees to go on strike, in breach of a no-strike clause in their contract of employment, unless another employee was dismissed, was actionable in tort at the suit of that employee (Rookes) if the employer acceded to the request. The threat in respect of Rookes was made because, although he had once been a member of the same union as the defendants, and indeed a shop steward, he had since left the union and refused to rejoin it. His leading counsel, Neville Faulks, QC, was doubtful about his client's chances on the facts as well as on the law. Apart from the generally accepted view that the Trade Disputes

[3] (1959) 22 *MLR* 652.
[4] [1957] AC 555.
[5] Lord Gardiner to the author in 1985.
[6] Box, *Rebel Advocate*, p. 144. The offer was made by Kilmuir.
[7] [1964] AC 1129.

Act 1906, s. 3, gave immunity to just such threats, the plaintiff did not inspire confidence. 'I don't care for bearded pacifists, and I told him I didn't think an English jury would, either, and I forecast much lower damages than he was later awarded. But the enemy were so unattractive in the witness-box that we easily beat the £1,500 paid into court.'[8] The trial judge, Sachs J., ruled that, although there was a trade dispute, the statutory protection did not apply where the threat to break one's own contract also amounted to the tort of intimidation, and the jury showed their opinion by awarding £7,500. The trade-union interest could not allow this to stand, and Gardiner was brought in to lead Colin Duncan in the Court of Appeal. His opponent recorded that, 'Gardiner opened the case at a tremendous rate of knots, so that he had finished quoting one case and passed on to the next before I had found my place in the first one. How the Court of Appeal kept up with him, I don't know. I certainly couldn't.'[9] Gardiner's argument covers no less than eight pages of the Queen's Bench Reports, and is a mine of information relating to the complexities of economic torts. Gardiner persuaded the Court of Appeal to hold that the statutory protection could not be outflanked by invoking the obscure and unfamiliar tort of intimidation, which was restricted to acts of violence or threats of a criminal nature, and did not extend to threats simply to break one's own contract. This avoided the curious situation that a threat to induce another to break his contract was protected, but a threat to break one's own contract was unprotected.

But the Court of Appeal granted leave to appeal, and argument took place before Lords Reid, Evershed, Hodson, Devlin, and Pearce over ten days in July 1963. (The Lord Chancellor did not sit.) Gardiner's argument in support of the decision covers five pages of the Appeal Cases. Then in November Lord Reid announced that because of the public importance of the case further and broader arguments were desired on the scope of s. 3 of the 1906 Act. Here Gardiner's arguments cover nearly eight pages of the Appeal Cases. A remarkable ability to summarize complex legal history is displayed. Dealing with the well-known trilogy of trade-union cases in the Lords at the turn of the century, Gardiner said: 'The judiciary showed a bias against trade unions and therefore Parliament took the extraordinary course of exempting trade unions from actions in tort altogether, and tried to ensure that judges could not get round the Act by making workmen liable in conspiracy'.[1] This perhaps over-emphasizes the supposed bias of the courts against unions (a subject on which some recent historical revision has resulted in a more balanced view), but can hardly be surpassed as a pithy summary of the reasons for s. 1 of the Trade Disputes Act 1906. Then there were another two pages on the issue of exemplary damages.

---

[8] N. Faulks, *A Law Unto Myself* (1978), p. 96.
[9] Ibid., p. 98.
[1] [1964] AC 1129, 1154.

The result was that the defendants lost on the issue of liability, but won on the issue of damages. On liability, the Lords held unanimously that the tort of intimidation extended to breaches of contract, and so the defendants were not protected by s. 1 or s. 3 of the 1906 Act. But a new trial was ordered on the issue of damages, the Lords considerably restricting the cases in which such damages should be awarded. (In the event, the matter was settled for £4,000.)

The results of *Rookes* v. *Barnard* have not been entirely satisfactory. On the liability issue, the tort of intimidation as revived still exists, but in so far as it affected the right to strike the decision was reversed by the Trade Disputes Act 1965. (It is not often that leading counsel in an unsuccessful appeal to the Lords is able to secure parliamentary approval for his views within a couple of years.) On the damages issue, there has been a marked lack of enthusiasm in courts throughout the common-law world for the restriction of the scope of exemplary damages.

In 1949 Gardiner (at the request of Transport House) had been selected as prospective Labour candidate for Croydon West (a constituency later renamed Croydon South). The general election took place in October 1951. It was not likely that a barrister aged fifty-one would make much impact on such a constituency, especially as the sitting Member (Sir) R. H. M. Thompson, was a younger man with a good war record. But in fact Gardiner obtained 47.8% of the votes in a straight fight against Thompson, who had a majority of 1,950.

No more party political activity is recorded until 1961, when Hugh Jenkins MP asked Gardiner if he would be willing to become an Alderman on the London County Council (as it then was). The offer was accepted, and, as usual with public duties, there was an attendance record of 100 per cent. London government has always been characterized by tight party control. Then it was exercised by Sir Isaac Hayward, whose activities as Chairman of the LCC struck Gardiner as being of an authoritarian nature. Some of the tensions which exploded twenty years later were apparent in 1961-4.

CHAPTER III

WHEN Harold Wilson succeeded Hugh Gaitskell as Leader of the Labour Party he seems to have shared the general belief of the legal profession that Gardiner would be his Lord Chancellor. Yet there were at least two others with respectable claims—Frank Soskice, who had been a Law Officer for six years, and Terence Donovan, who had been on the Bench since 1948. Donovan's parliamentary experience was brief, but Soskice had been in the House since 1946. Each had a high reputation. Wilson hardly knew Gardiner personally. The deficiency was remedied by Wilson's solicitor, Arnold Goodman, who arranged a small dinner party at which the succession to the Woolsack was discussed. It was decided that Gardiner's lack of political experience was to be overcome by the conferment of a life peerage.

In December 1963 it was announced that the Prime Minister, Alec Douglas-Home, had invited Harold Wilson to nominate six life peers to strengthen the Labour Party in the House of Lords. Gardiner was one of the six, and on 15 January 1964 letters patent were issued creating him 'Baron Gardiner, of Kittisford, in our County of Somerset'.[1] (Kittisford is 7 miles west of Wellington and the M5, approached by the deep winding lanes between ploughed fields so characteristic of the west country. There are still only seventy inhabitants in the lonely little parish.)

Gardiner was then the only member of the Lords who owed his peerage to the fact that he was a practising barrister—and indeed remained unique in that respect for ten years, when he was joined by a Liberal, B. T. Wigoder. Only nine months later the general election returned the Labour Party to office with a majority of four. It had been in opposition for thirteen years. Gardiner was in the middle of a case in which Lloyd's were being sued by some Greek shipowners when he received the expected summons to No. 10 at 6 p.m. on Friday, 16 October. It was only the third occasion on which he had met Harold Wilson. Other senior members of Wilson's Cabinet—for example, James Callaghan—were also unknown, or almost unknown, to him.

Those who have spent their political lives at Westminster are apt to regard newly arrived lawyers as 'innocents'. This was Kilmuir's phrase for Simonds, and it was also Richard Crossman's phrase for Gardiner.[2] But Gardiner might

---

[1] The title (and name) of Gardiner should be pronounced as if it contained three distinct syllables. Otherwise it might be confused with the dormant hereditary peerage of Gardner, or the life peerage of Gardner of Parkes.

[2] See, e.g. J. Morgan (ed.), *The Crossman Diaries* (1979), p. 598 ('utterly remote from the realities of politics').

have replied that he evoked a greater degree of personal respect and affection from colleagues and civil servants than was ever given to Crossman.

Gardiner received the Great Seal on Saturday, 17 October, and was sworn in on Tuesday the 20th before the Master of the Rolls and twenty-four other judges. It was thought that the usually imperturbable Gardiner showed a trace of nervousness—his hand seemed to tremble slightly as he held the New Testament. When Parliament was opened by Commission on the 27 th October, the Lord Chancellor was on the Woolsack. As he was already a peer, he needed no introduction. In March 1966 Labour was returned with an increased majority (ninety-six instead of four), and there was never any doubt that Gardiner would continue in office. Thereafter he was accustomed to refer to himself as 'the lucky Chancellor', for, without any previous political experience, he was given six years in which to carry out his programme of reform.

Gardiner gave a high priority to his duties as Speaker of the House of Lords. He was accustomed to sit for hours, silent and motionless, through debates which were often not of the first importance, but which tended to be lengthy because the influx of life peers after 1963 brought to the House some who felt that their selection had to be justified by speeches. The value of this exercise was questionable. It did not lessen the tasks of the Leader of the House (Shackleton), and a personal knowledge of many of the members was not really necessary for the maintenance of order in debate—which in any event was in the hands of the peers themselves. But his attendance record is remarkable—for the sessions 1963–8 it was no less than 98 per cent.[3] Dilhorne came next with 85 per cent.

Gardiner's name is always associated with a major change in the administration of justice—the decision of the Lords in 1966 to free itself from the self-imposed obligation to follow its own previous decisions. Here too the tide had been flowing for some time in favour of a change: 'the innovatory activities of Lords Reid and Denning, taken together with the academic consensus ... had contributed to an atmosphere receptive to the change. It required but a catalyst.'[4] It was decided to make the change at once by issuing what was called a Practice Statement, which outlined the conditions under which the supreme appellate tribunal would exercise its new power. At the time there was some debate whether it was theoretically possible to change a judge-made rule of the common law by a statement not judicially uttered in the course of an appeal *inter partes*. Twenty years later the success of the revolution has dispelled those doubts. But in fact the catalyst for the change was not Gardiner. In the words of the same authority, Gardiner, 'despite his desire for the reform took relatively little part in bringing it about. He did not act until approached by the Law

---

[3] L. Blom-Cooper and G. Drewry, *Final Appeal* (1972), p. 211.
[4] A. Paterson, *The Law Lords* (1982), p. 149.

Commission, and he left the decision as to whether a change should be made, and if so how, to the Law Lords'.[5] In this process Lord Reid took a major part. This self-restraint by Gardiner was entirely sensible. There was no need to dissipate time and energy required for other reforms if others were willing to make the running in respect of this one. A similar change was made in the procedures relating to Privy Council appeals. There the power to refuse to follow previous decisions had always existed, but there was no power to publish dissenting opinions. This was now permitted.

A change which was not pursued, although advocated in *Law Reform NOW*,[6] was the abolition of the two-tier system of appeals. The reason seems to have been simply that there was insufficient public and professional reaction to the suggestion to justify further action at a time when much else was happening.

For each of the other seventeen Chancellors covered by these volumes, one of the main tasks of the biographer has been to provide an assessment of the judicial work of the subject as reflected in his reported judgments in the Appeal Cases. In the case of Gardiner the task is unexpectedly simple, for he sat on only three appeals in his six years on the Woolsack, and delivered judgment in only two—*DPP* v. *Button and Swain*,[7] and (in the Privy Council) *Commissioner for Railways* v. *McDermott*.[8]

In the first case the House of Lords upheld a conviction before MacKenna J. at Somerset Assizes of two men who had been indicted of committing the common-law misdemeanour of affray. In the sixties the problems of gangs of young men fighting each other had not reached the dimensions which it did in the seventies. But it was certainly a problem in the mining districts of north Somerset, and after prosecutions before the local magistrates had failed to solve it, the advice of the Director of Public Prosecutions was sought by the Chief Constable of Somerset. The Director advised that the participants in the next serious fight should be indicted at assizes for committing an affray. As this offence was a common-law misdemeanour the punishment was not limited in the same way as with statutory offences. But the question as to the constituent elements of this obscure offence had to be resolved by MacKenna J. when the accused, Button and Swain, who had fought at a dance in a scout hall, argued that they were entitled to be acquitted as the fight had not occurred in a public place. In an admirable survey of the authorities, MacKenna J. held, reluctantly, that it was indeed an essential ingredient of the offence that it should have occurred in a public place, but that on the facts the jury would be entitled to find that the scout hall was so open. The jury convicted, and Button and Swain appealed unsuccessfully. The Lord Chancellor stated: 'The essence of the offence

---

[5] Ibid., p. 151.
[6] See below, p. 230.   [7] [1966] AC 591.
[8] [1967] AC 169. In *Re Kray* [1965] Ch. 376, Gardiner sitting as a High Court judge, held that he had no power, original or appellate, to consider an application for bail.

is that two or more fight together to the terror of the Queen's subjects'.[9] It was an error, albeit long-established, to suggest that the fight should occur in a public place. For over a century the peaceful citizen had been deprived of the protection of the law: public policy did not require the deprivation to be continued.

In the Privy Council appeal Gardiner delivered the judgment of a board whose members included Lords Morris, Guest, Pearce, and Pearson. The issue was the liability of an occupier of property to a trespasser thereon. The traditional English rule was that the only duty to a trespasser was not to inflict harm on him intentionally, or perhaps recklessly, if he was known to be present.

The Australian courts had developed two techniques for evading this rule— one was to say that the duty was also owed to a trespasser reasonably likely to be present; another was to hold that a second relationship might subsist between the occupier and his unlawful visitor when the occupier was carrying on some dangerous activity, the latter attracting a higher duty of care than the former. In the *Quinlan* case only three years before, an emphatic judgment by a strong board disapproved of these techniques and reasserted the traditional test. So Gardiner had to step very carefully in expressing his evident disapproval of *Quinlan*. He started by uttering an often approved dictum that 'occupation of premises is a ground of liability and is not a ground of exemption from liability'.[1]

He then distinguished *Quinlan* on the ground that it dealt with a trespasser 'who should not be there at all', whereas McDermott was not a trespasser but a licensee, and so was allowed a higher duty. He reasserted the concurrent liability principle, and suggested that there might be liability if the presence of the trespasser was 'extremely likely', as distinct from being actually foreseen. Seven years later another Privy Council appeal from Australia[2] built on Gardiner's judgment to distinguish *Quinlan* again. *Quinlan* is now of no authority.

The Law Reports record a third appeal on which Gardiner sat—a rating appeal from Northern Ireland entitled *Commissioner of Valuation* v. *Fermanagh Protestant Board of Education*.[3] The issue was whether schoolteachers who resided in houses on the premises of Portora Royal School were liable to be rated separately as distinct from sharing in the charitable immunity of an independent school. Gardiner was content to concur in the elaborate opinions of Lords Upjohn and Diplock, which, reversing the Court of Appeal of Northern Ireland, held in favour of the rating authority.

During the hearing Lord Diplock fired a number of somewhat teasing questions at Counsel—not the last time I suffered them—you had to tackle him head on and in

---

[9] [1966] AC 591, at 625.
[1] [1967] 1 AC 169, at 186.
[2] *Southern Portland Cement Ltd.* v. *Cooper* [1974] AC 623.
[3] [1969] 1 WLR 1708; [1970] NI 89.

cricketing terms drive the ball straight back at him as hard as you could. I did wonder if
Gardiner appreciated it very much from the junior Law Lord ... Gardiner was very
courteous and pleasant ... He was rather a good presiding judge, and ran the
proceedings in an exemplary fashion

so one of the respondent's counsel recalled the appeal.[4]

The quality of his two judgments is such as to make one regret that Gardiner
took such a limited view of his judicial function. In length they are just right—
avoiding the perfunctory brevity of Kilmuir and the overloading of argument
of Dilhorne. They show that capacity for analysis of the previous authorities
and ability to state a comprehensive principle in simple English which is more
easily recognized than described but which is characteristic of the greatest
common-law judgments.

After June 1970 Gardiner sat on three appeals but did not deliver judgment
in any one of them. In each a simple concurrence with the majority is recorded.
The cases are *F. E. Callow Ltd.* v. *Johnson*,[5] *Rugby Water Board* v. *Shaw-Fox*,[6] and
Moschi v. *Lep Air Services Ltd*.[7] Despite a few invitations or suggestions of both
Lord Hailsham of St Marylebone and Lord Elwyn-Jones, Gardiner never sat
again judicially. His energies were given to other causes.

The late sixties was the period in which the judicial work of the House of
Lords was dominated by Lord Reid—as a decade earlier it had been dominated
by Simonds. So in each period the fact that the Lord Chancellor adopted a low
profile on the judicial front was obscured by the presence of a judge of
outstanding ability. Yet the interests both of litigants and of the legal system as a
whole require that the Lord Chancellor should be as assiduous as possible in the
discharge of his judicial functions.

Gardiner once remarked that he had 'a scandalous amount' of judicial
patronage,[8] and stated in the Lords that 'It is much more important than
anything else the Lord Chancellor does, more important than his office as
Speaker of this House, and more important than his Cabinet work'.[9] In the same
debate Gardiner recorded that 'The method of appointment is a simple one.
The work is done by the Lord Chancellor himself, and he consults anyone he
thinks fit'. Gardiner also remarked that he kept an open mind on the question of
appointing academic lawyers as judges—and pointed out that he had made R. E.
Megarry QC a judge, and 'he is a first-class academic lawyer who has, perhaps,
divided his time pretty equally between academic work and practising work'.

[4] Letter to the author in 1985.
[5] [1971] AC 335.
[6] [1973] AC 202.
[7] [1973] AC 331.
[8] Gardiner, *The Trials of a Lord Chancellor* (1968), p. 5.
[9] 288 H.L. Deb. cols. 636-8.

When Gardiner was Lord Chancellor he decided to dispel the 'very old Labour Party myth' that the higher judiciary was too old and came from the same public-school background. He discovered, as he later recorded, that the average age of the seventy-eight judges in question was sixty-one, and that they had been educated at fifty-one different schools.[1]

Gardiner filled no fewer than thirty-six High Court vacancies—five of them (Elizabeth Lane, Talbot, Chapman, Crichton, Kilner Brown) by way of promotion from the County Court. The other thirty-one, in chronological order, were: Latey, Cantley, Browne, Waller, Park, Geoffrey Lawrence, James, Blain, Orr, Reginald Goff, Cusack, Willis, Swanwick, O'Connor, Donaldson, Brandon, Geoffrey Lane, Megarry, Cooke, Fisher, Caulfield, Bridge, Shaw, Eveleigh, Dunn, Graham, Mars-Jones, Foster, Bean, Whitford, and Brightman.

Of these, all except one (Nigel Bridge, a former Treasury devil) was in silk at the date of his appointment. It is more significant that not one was, or ever had been, a Member of Parliament. In the two decades since Jowitt's Chancellorship the relationship between the Bar and House of Commons had changed so much that it was no longer an effort for a Chancellor to avoid 'political appointments': there were simply few barristers of the first rank in the House of Commons.

Of Gardiner's appointments, one rose to be Lord Chief Justice (Geoffrey Lane), one to be Vice-Chancellor (Megarry), and three to be Law Lords (Brandon, Bridge, Brightman). Some had other qualities which struck their contemporaries. So Foster J. 'was safe and sound and sensible, and pleasant to appear before . . . In fact everyone liked Peter Foster. He was a good-looking, charming, elegant English gentleman, a member of White's and of the Royal and Ancient.'[2]

In Cabinet Gardiner was somewhat silent—partly because of a natural reserve which inhibited him from interfering in matters of which he knew little, and partly because he was preoccupied with his great measures of legal reform. But three problems lying outside the area of the administration of justice must be mentioned—the Burmah Oil Case, Rhodesia, and House of Lords Reform.

On the first, Gardiner was obliged to defend—with the help of Dilhorne—a governmental case which every lawyer instinctively felt to be unjust: the reversal of a judicial decision with retrospective effect.[3] Rhodesia raised the old problem of how those who have for high-minded reasons renounced the use of force can deal with people who show no sign of obeying the dictates of pure reason. Gardiner detested the Smith regime. When Elwyn-Jones accompanied Wilson and others to meet Smith in December 1966 he was handed a note from Gardiner which read: 'Remember, you are our conscience'.[4] Gardiner and

[1] 389 H.L. Deb. col. 499.
[2] *The Times*, 12 May 1985.
[3] See above, p. 198.
[4] Lord Elwyn-Jones, *In My Time* (1983), pp. 212–13.

others thought that Wilson might be tempted to offer excessively favourable terms to Smith to settle the problem.

The preamble to the Parliament Act 1911 indicated that a thorough reform of the House of Lords was proposed. But in 1917 the Bryce Conference was unable to suggest a satisfactory scheme; and the same happened in 1948. Twenty years later the matter was revived.

It was announced in the Queen's Speech at the opening of Parliament on 30th October 1968 that legislation would be introduced to reform the composition and powers of the House of Lords.

A Conference of representatives of the three main parties was convened, on the initiative of the Government, in the hope that an all-party consensus could be reached about the place, powers and composition of the second chamber in the present day. The conference met first in November 1967 and continued its discussions until June 1968, when they were suspended following the Lords' rejection of the Southern Rhodesia (United Nations Sanctions) Order 1968.

The Inter-Party Conference had by that time reached agreement on the main outlines of a comprehensive scheme for reform, covering both the powers and the composition of the House of Lords, and much constructive work had also been done on the details of its implementation.

The neutral prose of a White Paper[5] concealed some tension behind the scenes. Gardiner and Shackleton for the Lords and Crossman for the Commons had worked immensely hard to secure agreement. At one stage Gardiner had hired Chequers (at his own expense) for the weekend in the hope of finding a solution there. But the Prime Minister had something like a brainstorm after the Lords rejected the Rhodesian Sanctions Order, and cut off all further discussion of the proposal, which then lapsed.

Outside his official engagements Gardiner had little social life. He certainly did not imitate the life-style of the Jowitts—partly from a certain asceticism in his character (he sometimes said that his only extravagance was having his hair cut at the Savoy), and partly because of his wife's health. Although he had some close friends in the theatrical world going back to his days with the OUDS, he did not 'drink champagne with the wits'. So there was little personal, as distinct from official, hospitality.

A vivid picture of the Lord Chancellor's Breakfast on 1 October 1968 was given by Crossman.

This morning I found myself invited, as Lord President, to the Lord Chancellor's annual reception. This is a very curious occasion on which the Lord Chancellor receives in the Royal Gallery behind the House of Lords all the judges down to the rank of

[5] (1968) Cmnd. 3799.

recorder, all the Q.C.'s and a select number of junior counsel. I walked in from the Lords and saw a queue hundreds of yards long winding up the stairs to shake hands with the Chancellor, so I got the servants of the House to take me round the back and push me through the catering tables to an open space. There I found the judges standing about in full fig, their regalia of black, gold or red, and white ermine. They vary enormously in looks. There is a small thin-looking drunken minority but most of them are judges cherubic and all of them are marked with the judicial glare. It struck me once again how separate we keep ourselves in Britain. There is the legal world, the doctor's world, the artistic world, the dramatic world, the political world. We are tremendously separate and here was one world having its annual get-together on beer and sausages.[6]

(Although beer may be available, the traditional drink at this function is mulled wine. At the earliest recorded function, under Charles II, at the Lord Chancellor's home, the menu was 'macaroons and fruit wine'. The Breakfast now takes place immediately after the service at Westminster Abbey to mark the beginning of Michaelmas term—a function which cannot be traced back before 1897.)

Even at the height of his professional success the pessimistic or sad side of Gardiner could appear. Victor Gollancz was visibly shocked, Gardiner recalled, by Gardiner saying

that, having done most of the things I had wanted to do and having seen most of the places I wanted to see, I saw no particular point in living to a much older age. He clearly regarded this as a heresy of the first magnitude and maintained that as long as he lived he would enjoy every minute of it.

Lord Hailsham of St Marylebone once remarked:

I suspect that future biographers of my distinguished, and admired, predecessor in office will not be slow to discern amongst the many ornaments of his character a certain asceticism which not all Lord Chancellors in the past have sought to emulate.[7]

In another place, Lord Hailsham said: 'He reminds me enormously of a 17th-century divine. He's got a high sense of purpose and morality, and very austere morals. He's not without humour, but he's not a warm, approachable man.'[8] The comment might be made that women, as distinct from men, have very different memories of Gardiner. To women he was relaxed and agreeable in conversation.

[6] Morgan, Crossman Diaries, p. 206. The fact that the Lord President of the Council (wearing a livid red tie) evaded the democratic queue did not go unnoticed. For more information about the Breakfast, see R. F. V. Heuston, Lives of the Lord Chancellors 1885-1940 (Oxford, 1964), p. 33.
[7] Lord Hailsham of St Marylebone, The Problems of a Lord Chancellor (1972), p. 1.
[8] Box, Rebel Advocate, p. 227.

CHAPTER IV

I T IS as a law reformer that Gardiner will live in English history. As his successor on the Woolsack, Lord Hailsham of St Marylebone, wrote:

Clearly when the Chancellorships of the latter half of the twentieth century come to be assessed . . . the chief monument which my predecessor, Lord Gardiner, has left behind him will come to be regarded as the Law Commission. I regard this as an institution of the greatest value to the law reformer, both inside and outside government.[1]

It will be convenient to consider first Gardiner's efforts for reform apart from the Law Commission.

Some of the problems which face a reforming Lord Chancellor have already been considered in the life of Jowitt. After Jowitt left office in 1951 there was a period of more than a dozen years in which little of significance occurred in the area of law reform. In part this was due to the personal characteristics of Simonds, Kilmuir, and Dilhorne. But their personalities reflected a deeper problem about the nature of the Lord Chancellorship. It is not easy for a lawyer to make a mark as a reformer when he becomes Chancellor. Nobody has explained the reason for this better than Sir Samuel Romilly (1757–1818), whose eminence as a reformer is undoubted although he never held the Great Seal.

Whenever that day arrives it will be too late to form plans or to trace out a line of conduct. You will find yourself distracted with the hurry, and overcome by the immense labours of your office. Every moment will be occupied with judicial attendances, with measures of temporary expediency, with private solicitations and conferences, with audiences which must be given, with the little intrigues of party which must be counteracted and with all that empty pageantry and solemn trifling which in stations of the highest dignity are the most unavoidable. You will retire every night to rest, having added one day more of splendid but unavailing fatigue to your existence; and if, in the course of it, some reflection should have forced itself on your mind upon the higher duties of that office which remain to be discharged, you will defer the consideration of them to a period of promised leisure, which, however, will not arrive. You will live, like your predecessors, from day to day, and like them, you will descend from your high elevation with no more consoling reflection than that you have filled a great office without impropriety, and that you have decided impartially the causes which came before you, that you have left the condition of your countrymen no

---

[1] *Problems of a Lord Chancellor*, p. 5.

worse than you found it, and that you will be known to future ages as the ancestor of those individuals whom they will see distinguished from the mass of mankind by nothing but vain titles and large possessions.[2]

Gardiner somehow avoided the pitfalls which Romilly had pointed out. He also avoided the charge of being an academic theorist motivated by dogmas and without practical experience. As his close friend, Andrew Martin, wrote twenty years later:

Among Socialist theorists, there have been those who regarded any legal system as an instrument of class oppression, to be replaced in the fullness of time by a fraternal anarchy. Others have regarded all existing systems as so incurably bad that it would be necessary to begin again and construct a new body of laws from different formulations.[3]

As a leading advocate Gardiner did not display these faults.

On one topic relating to the legal profession Gardiner wished to leave things as they were. He did not believe in a fusion of the barrisers' and solicitors' professions. He put forward his arguments in 1970 in a carefully considered paper. In general his arguments were the same as those advanced by (Sir) Robert Megarry in his Hamlyn Lectures (1962). Fusion would not lead to any marked saving of costs or greater efficiency. It would deprive a litigant with a difficult problem in a remote area of access through his local solicitor to the specialized services of the Bar in London. Above all, it would have the great disadvantage of threatening the undisputed integrity of British justice. The independence, honesty and impartiality of the British judge was 'entirely due to our having a divided profession.'[4]

The structure of the profession apart, there was much that Gardiner thought needed to be done.

By the mid-1960s the system of criminal justice was on the verge of breaking down. The Government decided in 1968 to set up a Royal Commission on Assizes and Quarter Sessions. Gardiner thought that the right person to be its chairman was Dr Richard Beeching, who had recently rationalized the antique network of British railways. Gardiner made a special journey to Dr Beeching's home to induce him to accept the invitation. (The Prime Minister did not approve of this procedure: Dr Beeching should have been invited to call on the Lord Chancellor.) But the choice was inspired: with remarkable speed Beeching grasped the essentials of the problem, and with even more remarkable speed, by the standards of the eighties, when the reports of Royal Commissions are

[2] P. Medd, *Romilly* (1968), p. 112.
[3] A. Martin and P. Archer (edd.), *More Law Reform Now* (1983), p. vii.
[4] (1970) 23 *CLP* 1, at 19.

regarded as the basis for a further round of consultations rather than as a prescription for action, produced his report.[5] The changes which were proposed were put into effect by the Courts Act 1970. The Act did for the criminal law what the Judicature Act 1875 had done for the civil law. The 1970 Act merged Quarter Sessions, Assizes, and the Central Criminal Court (Old Bailey) into one Crown Court with two levels of judges sitting in fewer places. It also provided for a unified administration of court services under the Lord Chancellor's Department.

On the civil side of the court structure, Gardiner secured parliamentary approval for the re-establishment of the post of Vice-Chancellor (after a lapse of eighty-five years) by the Administration of Justice Act 1970, s. 5, which came into force on 29 May, just three weeks before the end of Gardiner's Chancellorship. The Lord Chancellor's statutory Presidency of the Chancery Division had long been of a nominal character, and it was desirable to recognize that his administrative responsibilities in the division were in fact discharged by one of the puisne judges. This was usually the senior judge, but in the early sixties this was Lloyd-Jacob J., an authority on patent law, who took little part in the general work of the division. So the position came to be held by the next-senior judge. The Act authorized the Lord Chancellor to nominate one of the judges of the division to be Vice-Chancellor. The Supreme Court Act 1982 made further changes to the office.[6]

At the lower end of the judicial structure, Gardiner dealt with the problem of ex-officio magistrates. There were 2,250 of these, ranging from High Court judges (62) to the mayors of non-county boroughs (276). It was decided to phase them out. But Gardiner, a friend of open government, was obliged to resist a Press campaign for the publication of the names of the advisory committee in Middlesex. The chairman was known to be Lord Denning, but the Press argued that the others should also be known. They themselves settled the matter by informing Gardiner that they would resign *en bloc* if their names were published, as they 'would be lobbied to death'.[7]

The proposal to establish an Ombudsman occupied six hours of debating time before the Bill became law in March 1967. This Swedish term had become popular with commentators in the sixties who wished to establish a public official who would have power to investigate and remedy the complaints of ordinary citizens against the administration. Eventually the term Parliamentary Commissioner for Administration was chosen in order to emphasize that his powers could be activated only on the authority of a Member of Parliament.

---

[5] *Report of the Royal Commission on Assizes and Quarter Sessions* (1969) Cmnd. 4078.
[6] On these (and other) problems, see the magisterial article by Sir R. Megarry, 'The Vice-Chancellors' (1982) 98 *LQR* 370.
[7] Lord Gardiner to the author.

The institution so established is generally regarded as successful. At first limited to maladministration on the part of organs of central government, it has since been extended to local government.

The Law Commission, which is generally considered to be Gardiner's most lasting achievement, may now be considered. When it was established, law reform in the United Kingdom, and later in the whole common law world, entered a new dimension.

During the fifties Gardiner had practical experience of the machinery of law reform through his membership of the Evershed Committee on Supreme Court Practice and Procedure,[8] and also of the Law Reform Committee. He felt deep dissatisfaction with the results achieved by the first and the procedure of the second. He wrote:

I should here perhaps just say for the record that my own interest in law reform has not at all been that of the academic lawyer. It has simply been an instinctive reaction to injustice. Whenever I saw something in the law which seemd to me to be causing injustice, I always wanted to get it put right. So I joined the Medico-Legal Society, the Howard League for Penal Reform and the Institute for the Study and Treatment of Delinquency. I was for a good many years a member of the Executives of the last two. I was a member of the Divorce Law Reform Association and of the Abortion Law Reform Association and was one of the founders of *Justice*. It was perhaps because I made myself such a nuisance about law reform that for eleven years successive Lord Chancellors made me a member of the Lord Chancellor's Law Reform Committee. And I was a member of the Evershed Committee on the Practice and Procedure of the Supreme Court, of which Committee I attended 300 meetings, as I shall never forget. Naturally when elected Chairman of the Bar Council I took particular interest in its law reform work.

It seemed to me during the years that I was in practice at the Bar that the two principal barriers to law reform were first, the absence of specific responsibilities falling upon specific Ministers for the reform of specific branches of our law and, secondly, the absence of any sufficient law reform machinery. The Law Reform Committee did useful work, but the trouble was that it consisted of busy judges, barristers, solicitors and academic lawyers who only met about once a month at 4.30 after a day in court, and at 6 someone would say: 'I am afraid that I have to go now,' and I eventually resigned because I came to the conclusion that you simply cannot reform the law of England in that way.[9]

Yet the Law Reform Committee had a good record. By 1984, of its twenty-two reports, two had recommended no change, and no fewer than eighteen of the remaining twenty had been implemented by legislation—sometimes, it is true, after the lapse of some time. It cost the Treasury almost nothing, as it relied

---

[8] See above, p. 103.
[9] (1971) 87 *LQR* 326, at 328.

on the public spirit of its unpaid members. The quality of their product was not noticeably affected by the fact that they met after a day's work. The committee's weakness was the absence of what by 1975 had become known as support staff. The amount of research which the mid-twentieth century required simply could not be done by the single secretary, however devoted, provided by the Lord Chancellor's Department.

Gardiner made much of the fact that he had written to every Minister of Justice in Europe to ask how much of their states' national income was spent on the administration of justice: the UK was at the bottom of the league. This was true, but hardly gave credit to the once-strong English tradition of unpaid public service by the middle classes.

To some these limitations were welcome. So Simonds, who had revived the Law Reform Committee in 1954, complained that 'these efforts do not satisfy the critics, who would like to see a high-powered and highly paid body in more or less continuous session advising the Lord Chancellor what changes in the law are desirable. Such a suggestion goes much too far.'[1]

Dilhorne supported Simonds when he repeated these views in a significant debate in the House of Lords on 11 June 1964,[2] which was formally initiated by a young Conservative peer, Viscount Colville of Culross. Gardiner had been in the House for only six months, but the debate quite clearly showed that the tide of opinion was moving decisively in his favour inside the Houses of Parliament, as it was outside. In part this was due to the publication (in July 1963) of a book of essays entitled *Law reform NOW* and edited by Andrew Martin and Gerald Gardiner. A second impression appeared in May 1964—and the publisher, Victor Gollancz, was an acknowledged master of the art of achieving the maximum public impact for his products. The problems had been identified, and their solution outlined.

Sometimes the tidal current for reform is flowing so strongly that the task of the innovator is relatively easy. So even if Eldon had not been the man he was, the anti-revolutionary mood of England in the first two decades of the nineteenth century would have made change almost impossible. On the other hand, when Haldane took over the War Office in 1905, and resolved to reform the Army (a British institution as unique and complex as the legal system), events moved with him. So it was with Gardiner in 1964. As Lord Scarman, the first Chairman of the Law Commission, said: 'We got off to a flying start, thanks to a dedicated Lord Chancellor and an interested Parliament.'[3] Scarman might have added that the Prime Minister, Harold Wilson, gave the whole project his personal support. On the eve of the general election in 1964 he had spoken at a

[1] Lord Simonds, 'Recollections' (unpublished TS).
[2] 282 H.L. Deb. col. 1035.
[3] M. Kirby, *Reform the Law* (1983), p. viii.

public meeting in the Temple outlining the government's proposals for law reform. As the speech had been written by Gardiner, its message was familiar to the audience. But Wilson would never (least of all on the eve of an election) have given up an hour of his time to a project unless he could have seen some party advantage in it.

Wilson's support for law reform was intensified by an incident when he was forming his Cabinet. There was no doubt that Elwyn-Jones was to be Attorney-General; but Wilson had it in mind to appoint E. G. M. Fletcher MP as Solicitor-General. Fletcher was a solicitor by profession who had been a member of the Evershed Committee on Supreme Court Practice and Procedure. When it was explained to Wilson that a solicitor could not possibly be Solicitor-General, he reasonably enough displayed some impatience with the legal profession, as he also did when there was successful opposition to a proposal to give Fletcher the title of Queen's Solicitor. So Fletcher became Minister without Portfolio with special responsibility for law reform, and the Solicitor-General was Dingle Foot QC MP.

Gardiner explained his proposals as follows:

What I had to discover when I became Lord Chancellor was how large and effective the role of the Lord Chancellor in the field of law reform could be made to be.

The first thing, obviously, was to create proper machinery for law reform—a whole-time law commission of the right commissioners and with an adequate legal staff, including a number of the parliamentary draftsmen, and on a statutory basis. I contemplated appointing them on my own as a departmental committee, but concluded that a body one Lord Chancellor could appoint, another could abolish—hence the Law Commissions Act.[4]

(There was also a Law Commission for Scotland. It is not considered, solely because the Minister responsible for it was the Secretary of State for Scotland. The Lord Chancellor of Great Britain has no functions in Scotland.)

So in one sense the Commission was removed from the control of the Lord Chancellor. If another Simonds were to hold office, he could not disestablish the Commission, as he could do with one of his own departmental committees, such as the Law Reform Committee. The Commission had become part of the permanent machinery of government. But in another sense the Commission was peculiarly subject to the control of the Lord Chancellor, for he alone appointed its members and approved its programmes for reform. Originally Gardiner had intended that the Commission should formulate and execute its own proposals; but the facts of political life required that there should be a Cabinet Minister responsible for such a body. So the ingenious device of a

---

[4] Lord Gardiner to the author in 1984.

programme subject to ministerial approval combined flexibility and initiative with the doctrine of responsible government.

The Law Commissions Act was composed of only seven brief sections, some of which were drafted in surprisingly wide terms. (Here, at least, the parliamentary draftsmen were not open to criticism.) The central section (s. 5) provided that it should be the duty of the Commission (by s. 1 composed of a chairman and four other members) 'to take and keep under review all the law ... with a view to its systematic development and reform, including in particular the codification of such law, the elimination of anomalies, the repeal of obsolete and unnecessary enactments, the reduction of the number of separate enactments and generally the simplification and modernisation of the law'. A number of subheads gave powers which would be helpful in carrying out these objects—for example, to obtain information about foreign legal systems. Matters might also be referred to the Commission by the Government. Since 1970 the Government has shown an increasing tendency to use this power. As the Commission feels obliged to give a high priority to such requests, and as they are often for reports on highly complex matters (for example, breach of confidence), the result has been a serious degree of interruption of the normal work on the programmes.

On 15 June 1965 the Law Commission Act received the royal assent, and came into force immediately. It was a significant date in the history of English law, and also of the legal systems of the many other countries which imitate or follow it. On 16 June Gardiner appointed the Chairman and the four other Commissioners, and they started work immediately in premises already prepared for them conveniently near the centre of legal London. (It is part of the folk-memory of the Commission that when the Chairman and two of his colleagues arrived at 9.30 they were a little disconcerted to find another Commissioner had been at his desk since 8 a.m.)

The Chairman was Sir Leslie (later Lord) Scarman, a judge of the Probate, Divorce, and Admiralty Division since 1961. His colleagues were Neil Lawson QC, Andrew Martin QC, Norman Marsh (later QC), and Professor L. C. B. Gower (a solicitor). All were under the age of sixty. Scarman and Marsh were graduates of Oxford, where Marsh had been a Fellow of University College between 1948 and 1960 before becoming Director of the British Institute of International and Comparative Law. Before the war he had been a member of Gardiner's chambers. Andrew Martin was a graduate of four universities (Budapest, Paris, Vienna, and London), and held a part-time professorship of international law at a fifth (Southampton). But in deference to the customs of the English Bar, which rigorously exclude all titles with an 'academic' air, he styled himself Mr. English solicitors are not subject to a similar inhibition, so Gower did not need to conceal the fact that he held a full-time professorship at the London School of Economics. On the other hand, the Treasury seems to have shared the views of the Bar about academics. It was revealed in the Commons that the salary structure of the Law Commission was:

Mr Justice Scarman, £8,000 p.a. (paid as a judge); Mr Neil Lawson, Q.C., £7,000 p.a.; Mr Andrew Martin, Q.C. £7,000 p.a.; Mr Norman Marsh, £6,000 p.a.; and Professor Gower, £6,000 p.a.[5]

These differences later disappeared. Opponents of the commission, such as Dilhorne, referred to it as being composed of one practising barrister and three left-wing dons: Gardiner retorted that only one of them was a member of the Society of Labour Lawyers.

Gardiner and Scarman set a cracking pace. On 19 July, one month after their appointment, the Commission submitted its First Programme for the approval of the Lord Chancellor, which was given, with some amendments, on 20 September. The First Programme contained seventeen items, for thirteen of which the Commission itself was to be the examining agency. But one item contained three distinct, though related, topics in family law. Ten years later the Commission thought that 'that was the area in which we have so far made the greatest progress. In that field the emphasis is now changing from matrimonial proceedings to family property law.'[6]

Meanwhile, on 7 July, the Lord Chancellor had requested a special programme on statutory consolidation and revision; this was submitted on 17 November, and approved on 14 January 1966.

The Second Programme, issued in November 1967, was much briefer. But it is important, because it suggested some business which is still unfinished—the codification of criminal law, and the law of evidence, and 'the examination of some aspects of administrative law'. In 1969 a submission to the Lord Chancellor recommended the establishment of a Royal Commission on Administrative Law.[7] But powerful forces intervened. Not only was the submission found unacceptable, but the remit of the Commission was limited to remedies in administrative law. On this topic, a valuable report (Law Com. No. 73) appeared in 1976, which was implemented by changes in the Rules of the Supreme Court in 1977 (now incorporated in the Supreme Court Act 1981). In the fifties it was customary to say that Great Britain had no separate system of public law; two decades later an elaborate system of public law remedies had been created. The Third Programme (1973) contained only one item.

Two features of the Commission's organization and procedure have remained fairly constant since 1965. First, although the full-time support staff is highly qualified, it has never been large, and indeed its numbers have remained surprisingly constant. At the end of five years the staff, legal and non-legal, totalled forty-eight; fourteen years later, after nearly two decades, the number was almost exactly the same—twenty-four legal and twenty-five non-legal. But to some extent the Commission had committed itself to the view that too large a staff was undesirable, as it promoted a tendency to be inward-looking. From the outset the Commission thought that it should be a small, harmonious team; if special skills were required, or special interests represented, then that should be secured by the appointment of consultants. So when there was criticism of the fact that the original appointees did not include a practising solicitor, the Lord Chancellor appointed A. G. Stapleton Cotton to the position of Special Consultant. A small, integrated team had other advantages—it enabled the right balance to be kept between Commissioners and staff, and so prevented waste of public time and money. Again, a small body of Commissioners of high quality was treated with respect in the status-conscious Whitehall community.

Secondly, the Commission early established the procedure of consultation by means of a widely circulated working paper before a report was issued. This process, at first regarded as very successful, originated when Law Com. No. 10, on *Criminal Intent in Murder*, was in the pipeline. As it in effect proposed the reversal of *DPP* v. *Smith*,[8] great caution was required. But in 1985 a former Commissioner doubted whether the processes of consultation were in any real sense successful, and might even be counter-productive by being wasteful of time and money.[9]

Law Com. No. 10 was significant for another reason—it consolidated the bridgehead in the area of criminal law which the Commission had established in its very first report (Law Com. No. 3), entitled *Proposals to Abolish Certain Ancient Criminal Offences*. The report was in substance carried into effect by the Criminal Law Act 1967. Hitherto criminal law, and its reform, was a territory strongly defended by the Home Office. As Gardiner himself said, 'Metaphorically at least, outside the Home Office there are large notices saying "Lord Chancellors keep out".'[1] But by the middle seventies the Commission had produced reports on forgery, conspiracy, and public order offences. In March 1985 major proposals for the codification of criminal law appeared (Law Com. No. 143). But the Home Office seems to have retained jurisdiction over statutory as distinct from common law offences—hardly a logical distinction.

It was, however, in the field of civil law that the main contributions to the Commission were made. The unique respect in which Gardiner was held by the

---

[8] [1960] AC 290.

[9] See P. M. North, 'Law Reform: Processes and Problems' (1985) 101 *LQR* 338. A rather different view of some of the problems is taken in S. Cretney, 'The Politics of Law Reform—A view from the Inside' (1985) 48 *MLR* 493 (which has a useful bibliography).

[1] 428 H.L. Deb. col. 1003.

legal profession and the Civil Service were considerable assets. The goodwill of the profession was essential if the reforms were to work in practical life and not merely exist on paper. Equally the respect of the Whitehall mandarins, so necessary if the departmental legal advisers were not to be obstructive, was, in the early years, readily forthcoming.

The goodwill of the staff of the Lord Chancellor's Department was also forthcoming. In 1966 they had responded enthusiastically to a questionnaire asking for suggestions about topics to be included in the Commission's First Programme. The two most popular subjects for action were divorce law and the disposal of business at Assizes and Quarter Sessions. When the request was repeated two years later, the subject at the top of the list was administrative law—but there were also several warnings to the effect that what was in the pipeline would keep everyone busy for some time.

Wilfrid Bourne, a future head of the department, added the further warning:

... in practice, the courts (from the judges downwards) turn more and more to your office for advice and guidance, while we have grown more and more remote from the realities of forensic practice. The more senior we get, the worse this becomes. I have a good idea of what it was like twelve years ago to conduct a case at Assizes, in the High Court, in a County Court, at Quarter Sessions or in a magistrates' court, but that experience must by now be hopelessly out-of-date. It is like spending all one's time on the staff without ever serving in a fighting battalion since having commanded a platoon in the last war but one.[2]

By July 1970 the Commission had submitted twenty reports, of which fourteen had been implemented. By 1984 no fewer than 140 reports had been published—including three programmes for future action. Legislative effect had been given to eighty-nine proposals; of the remaining fifty-one reports, thirty did not require any legislative action—for example, because they were the Commission's Annual Reports. On the assumption, generally made, that success in the field of law reform is to be measured by legislative action, this is a gratifyingly high success rate.

Some reports had, however, been rejected by the Government (for example, that on *Interest on Debt* (1978)), which caused unexpected political difficulties in the sensitive field of consumer protection. Other reports had fallen into an administrative limbo as a result of the now prevalent habit in Whitehall of regarding a report as the reason for yet another round of consultations. This was the fate of, for example, the *Report on Non-disclosure in Insurance Contracts* (1980). But even former members of the Commission differ amongst themselves on

[2] Communicated to the author by Sir Wilfrid Bourne.

whether the figures show a slowing down of the rate of legislative implementation, and, if so, of the reasons for it.

Gardiner devoted much effort to reform of 'our awful statute book'—and, in particular, to trying to achieve an alphabetical statute-book instead of a chronological one. With remarkable brevity and clarity he set forth his aims.

> I still hope to see my ideal statute. It will be a codification of the statute law in one field (which will already have been consolidated) and the existing case law. It will be written in ordinary simple words and will be accompanied by a commentary explaining what are the things which it is intended to achieve. It will not try to cover every possible eventuality but will leave it to the judges to apply the Act to the circumstances of the case so as best to achieve the objects of the Act. It will prohibit any reference to the pre-existing case law. The first section will be section 3 because when lawyers have got the section numbers of the permanent code into their heads it wastes their time when Parliament alters the numbers: so slots must be left for later additions. It will of course by then be axiomatic that you never have another Act on the subject at the same time. You simply amend the existing code.[3]

One of his first acts, in July 1965, was to request the Commission to prepare for his approval a programme of statutory consolidation. In its annual report the Commission always devoted some paragraphs to progress (if any) in this area. A second stage was to consolidate existing enactments, and present them to the profession and the public in a clear and usable form. Apart from its direct and visible utility, such work was an important basic step in the preparation of other law-reform proposals, which nearly always involved research into the relevant statutory provisions. In the years 1965-84 consolidation accounted for 28.5 per cent of parliamentary time—a higher proportion than is generally supposed.

It was also decided to replace Jowitt's third edition of *Statutes Revised* by a new official edition of the statutes, which would be self-renewing in format. Work on this great project was finally completed in 1981. A few years later there was published at last a chronological *Table of Local and Personal Acts*. Such a table for public Acts had appeared as far back as 1870, but local and personal Acts remained an uncharted jungle.

At the heart of the law-reform process are the parliamentary draftsmen. So Gardiner had to face questions relating to their quality, numbers, and control. Quality was generally recognized to be very high. Numbers were another matter. In 1975 the Renton Committee on the Preparation of Legislation recommended that the existing staff of five draftsmen should be 'increased at the earliest possible moment'.[4] In 1984 there were still five. This shortage has had at least one unfortunate consequence—reports now sometimes lack the

---

[3] (1971) 87 *LQR* 326, at 332.
[4] Cmnd. 6053, s. 8.

draft Bill which used to be regarded as a valuable feature. As Gardiner once said, 'There is no large business in the country whose main work would be allowed to be completely held up by a shortage of half a dozen professional men or skilled craftsmen.'[5] But it is worth noting that, in the words of a former Commissioner, 'legislation is like concrete—very difficult to change or move once it is in place'.[6] The general assumption that the product of the law–reform process must be legislation may be questionable. More might be left to the courts to do.

Control over 'those canny men' (as one Lord Chancellor has described the parliamentary draftsmen) was a perennial problem. It would have been convenient and logical if they had been part of the Lord Chancellor's Department; but all attempts to cut their historic links with the First Lord of the Treasury have so far failed. Control over the draftsmen is allied to the problem of control of the legislative process. Overcrowding of the parliamentary timetable is all too familiar.[7] The Lord Chancellor, like the heads of other departments, has to fight for his bills before the Legislative Committee of the Cabinet. Sometimes a private member can be found to take on a Bill—but although everyone is in theory in favour of law reform, in practice it is not a subject which attracts votes—and so the attention of MPs. The Commission developed the practice of submitting a draft Bill with its report. This had the advantage of evoking discussion in advance of the publication of the Bill itself. As parliamentary protocol deems that a Bill must never be seen by the public before it is seen by MPs, there is no opportunity for discussion in the very brief interval between the first and second readings. Again, legislation must be passed in the parliamentary session in which it was introduced, or the whole process has to start anew.

Twenty years on, some sins of omission and commission can be discovered. The first major failure has been the collapse of the scheme to codify the law of contract, and the comparatively slow progress made with other codification plans. Indeed, there seems to have been some diversion of time and effort to projects of apparently minor utility—for example, chancel repairs, and rent charges.

The second failure has been that 'our awful statute book' is still in an unsatisfactory state, not least in the vital area of tax legislation. The new edition of *Statutes in Force* is indeed an improvement on its predecessors; but despite the improvements made possible by modern technology the ordinary citizen is still presented with a formidable pile of paper, whose comprehensibility is made

[5] 87 *LQR* 326, at 333.
[6] P. M. North (1985) *LS* 119, at 129.
[7] Ten years after Gardiner retired this was still a major problem: see Lord Hailsham of St Marylebone, 'Obstacles to Law Reform' (1981) *CLP* 279.

more difficult by the English draftsman's preference for extensive cross-references. The consequential art of statutory interpretation, despite several reports and a debate in the House of Lords,[8] remains a professional mystery. All the speakers in the debate deplored these problems; none could see any quick or easy solution.

It must be recognized that these (and some other) weaknesses may be due to factors operating outside the framework of the Law Commission—in particular, the complexities of House of Commons procedure. Some failures have been due to governmental interference (administrative law), or the fact that the problem, once identified, has for some reason been remitted to another agency for examination (compensation for personal injuries). It is hard to see how these difficulties can be overcome. The Act specifically contemplates that a Cabinet Minister is to be in ultimate control of the Commission—and in a parliamentary democracy the Cabinet must have the final word in the disposition of public resources. The Act also specifically contemplates that some agency other than the Commission itself might be a more appropriate body to examine some areas of the law in need of reform. This may well be so with a topic like insurance in the field of personal injuries, for which a broadly-based Royal Commission might be better suited to the complex processes of consultation. But the failure to give effect to the major recommendations of the Royal Commission on Liability for Personal Injuries must be one of the disappointments of the reform process of the Commission. Perhaps it would have been better if the parliamentary commmmission had had the benefit of a Law Commission paper on possible options and consequences.

Finally, one should note a major piece of reform which occurred in Gardiner's time, although the need for it was not recognized in *Law Reform NOW*—namely, the almost complete abolition of imprisonment for debt by the Administration of Justice Act 1970. Most people, lawyers as well as laymen, had a vague idea that this had been done in 1869 as a result of Dickens's novels. It came as a real shock to discover that in 1964 civil debtors constituted 14 per cent of the prison population. It was urgently necessary to relieve the prison service of this burden, if it could be done without peril to the vast twentieth-century industry of credit trading. Gardiner appointed Payne J. to be a chairman of the Lord Chancellor's Committee on Enforcement of Judgments, and prompt action followed its report.

Ten years after giving up office Gardiner himself looked back with pardonable pride on the achievements of the Law Commission. The only weakness he detected in its reports was an over-emphasis on substantive law as distinct from procedure.[9] The Commission might have replied that Gardiner's

---

[8]   437 H.L. Deb. col. 606.
[9]   421 H.L. Deb. col. 885.

other creation, the Beeching Report, had dealt thoroughly with procedure. In 1983, following the Benson Report, the Lord Chancellor announced a complete and systematic review of civil procedure. (The memory of those 300 meetings of the Evershed Committee was not forgotten.)

Looking back from a wider Commonwealth perspective, Mr Justice Kirby, President of the Australian Law Reform Commission, wrote:

If some of the enthusiasms of the 1960s have been replaced by a cold-eyed realism in the 1980s, the fact remains that institutional law reform throughout the common law world, especially in the Commonwealth of Nations, is at this moment in full flower. The one jurisdiction which established and terminated its law commission, Sri Lanka, has now even revived it.[1]

What have been the long-term consequences for the English legal system of the establishment of the Law Commission? First, the demand for a Ministry of Justice has almost disappeared, because the Law Commission is part of the ordinary machinery of government, with a full-time staff committed to the central planning of law reform, pooling the resources of policy-makers and draftsmen. It has power to review all the law, and has an impressive record of achievement, at least in the area of substantive law. Secondly, the office of Lord Chancellor has been profoundly affected. A primary duty has been laid upon him by statute to control and supervise the process of law reform. Since 1965 a distinct legal obligation has replaced a vague constitutional convention.

[1] Kirby, *Reform the Law*, p. 30.

CHAPTER V

ON THURSDAY, 18 June 1970 a general election returned the Conservatives to power under Edward Heath. On Monday, 22 June Gardiner surrendered the Great Seal to Mr Quintin Hogg (as he then was), and on the following day moved out of his flat at Westminster to one in the Temple. Henceforth he lived the busy life of a retired Lord Chancellor—although he did not think it necesary to sit on appeals.[1] But, as the index to Hansard shows, he was active in debate. He was well regarded by the Whips as his speeches were always brief,[2] He was surely wise not to put himself in contention for a second turn on the Woolsack when Heath lost the general election in February 1974. In the nature of events, he could hardly have expected to repeat (at the age of seventy-four) the triumphs of his six years as the reforming Chancellor. He devoted himself to other issues in public life.

Gardiner accepted two invitations to help to solve the problems of Northern Ireland. The Heath Government asked him to join a small committee under the Lord Chief Justice (Parker of Waddington) on the methods used to interrogate persons suspected of terrorism.[3] The report of the majority was a bland document which did not really tackle the question whether the alarming techniques employed were lawful in the domestic law of the UK or under its international obligations. Gardiner dissented. He had clearly been astonished and revolted at what had been happening without explicit ministerial approval. His minority report is reminiscent of the forceful closing speech of the advocate rather than the balanced conclusions of the judge. The questioned procedures 'were secret, illegal, not morally justifiable and alien to the traditions of what I believe still to be the greatest democracy in the world'.[4]

In 1974 the Wilson Government asked Gardiner to consider the whole question of countering Irish terrorism 'in the context of civil liberties and human rights'. The 78-page report of the seven-member committee was published early in 1975.[5] It was unanimous, except for a Note of Dissent on one point by Lord MacDermott. The Gardiner Report recommended that detention without trial should be brought to an end, and the usual processes of criminal justice revived. As Gardiner said later,[6] it was to the credit of the

---

[1] See above, pp. 22, 221–2.
[2] 389 H.L. Deb. col. 492.
[3] (1972) Cmnd. 4901.
[4] Ibid., s. 821.
[5] (1975) Cmnd. 5487.
[6] 421 H.L. Deb. col. 866.

Northern Ireland Secretary of State that he accepted this particular recommendation, so unpopular with the Unionist majority. On the other hand, the report
also recommended the abolition of special treatment for those convicted of
terrorist offences. This had not only made parts of prisons almost ungovernable,
but came near to conceding that those offences were of a political nature. The
report also recommended the retention of existing special powers to stop,
search, and question.

In 1981 the IRA made an unsuccessful attempt to assassinate Gardiner while
he was on a visit to Belfast. An unexploded bomb was found beneath his car. It
was a paradox that one who had fought so long in many countries to maintain
human rights should be the target of the mingled cruelty and incompetence of
the modern terrorist.

One successful institution of the Wilson Government with which Gardiner
became closely associated was the Open University. It was set up in 1969 to
provide a university education for people of all ages who had been left outside
the rather rigid structure of English higher education. Full advantage was taken
of modern techniques of communication for the provision of instruction. By
the end of the decade it had nearly 10,000 students. In a House of Lords debate
on higher education in March 1984 each of the forty speakers (including Lord
Hailsham) praised the quality of the work done by the Open University, of
which Gardiner had become Chancellor in 1973, in succession to Lord
Crowther. Characteristically, he also enrolled as a student in the social sciences,
and graduated in 1977. 'He was not himself dismayed by the essays, for he was
used to writing opinions; but the economics course he found extremely tough.'[7]
His services were recognized by the award of the CH in 1975 (a year after
Hailsham of St Marylebone—the first Lord Chancellor to receive this honour—
and a year before Elwyn-Jones).

There were many other activities in England and elsewhere. One may be
cited to show that even a master of the techniques of law reform may find
himself baffled by the machinery of government. In 1972 there was published a
report entitled *Living it Down: the Problem of Old Convictions*. The report was that
of a committee whose chairman was Gardiner; the other members were
representatives of two of his favourite institutions: the Howard League for
Penal reform, and NACRO. The title of the report indicates the problems with
which it dealt. There were said to be over a million people in Great Britain who
had a criminal record, but who had not been reconvicted for at least ten years.
The committee recommended that a person's rehabilitation should be accepted
by society. This was the practice in many European countries. To carry this
simple general principle into law required an extraordinary amount of effort,
all of which was nearly frustrated by two of the built-in hazards to reformers

---

[7] Box, *Rebel Advocate*, p. 214.

presented by the British Constitution—namely, the accidents of Parliamentary procedure, and the complexity of English statutory draftsmanship.

The original Bill, drafted by Mr Paul Sieghart, contained seven sections and thirty-two sub-sections. Gardiner steered it through the Lords, but it was lost when Parliament was prorogued in October 1973. A second Bill, sponsored by a private Member, was also lost when Parliament was dissolved in February 1974. A third Bill, sponsored by another private Member got through the Commons by June 1974. Then opposition developed. The Committee on Defamation under Faulks J. issued a Special Interim Report strongly criticizing the Bill insofar as it permitted a person to lie about the existence of spent convictions and excluded truth as a defence in an action for libel based on the disclosure of such convictions. Gardiner and his supporters had to modify the Bill to meet this point. Then there was an outbreak of acrimonious correspondence about the Bill in *The Times* throughout that summer, and some testing amendments were put down in the Lords. The Government also insisted that the Bill should be redrafted by Parliamentary counsel. A measure of considerable length (eleven sections and sixty sub-sections) was produced, drafted in a style of extraordinary complexity. Extensive use of cross-referencing between sections and subsections produced obscurity on a scale remarkable even in the twentieth century. Gardiner was deeply distressed: this tremendous measure was not what he meant by law reform—but he had to accept it, or lose the Bill completely, and so a worthwhile reform. He made a statement deploring the turn which affairs had taken, but acquiescing in them, and the Bill became law on 31 July 1974.

Almost the only other note critical of Gardiner in the seventies was sounded after he had made a speech in the Lords attacking the Sixteenth Report of the Criminal Law Revision Committee. The committee was a law-reform agency set up by the Home Secretary (R. A. Butler) in 1959 (in the days when the Home Office had exclusive control over criminal law.) Therefore it had always operated outside the framework of the Lord Chancellor's Department and the Law Commission. Its membership was distinguished. Its Sixteenth Report (1971) had two main proposals—to modify the accused's right to silence, and to relax the rules about admitting hearsay evidence. A number of criticisms were made, mainly by the self-appointed bodies who are active in the field of civil liberties. There was also a debate in the Lords in which a number of Law Lords spoke. Some favoured the proposals, but others, including Gardiner were dubious. There was a vigorous response by the Vinerian Professor, Sir Rupert Cross, a member of the committee. He protested against the 'ignorance, self-righteousness and unreason'[8] of the civil-rights activists, and went so far as to describe Gardiner's speech as 'quite unforgivable for a former Lord Chancellor'.

In the eighties Gardiner was a firm supporter of the various agencies and

[8] (1973) *Crim. L. Rev.* 329.

institutions for reform, social and legal, with which he had been connected. In April 1980 he acted as chairman at the opening meeting of the World Disarmament Campaign, attended by over 2,000 persons, at Central Hall, Westminster. In April 1984 he wrote to *The Times* to draw attention to the arguments of *JUSTICE* in favour of an independent prosecuting authority, such as he himself had proposed for Northern Ireland. In 1985 such an authority was set up in England. He also gave full support to Lord Wade's Bill of Rights on each of the occasions when it came (unsuccessfully) before the House of Lords. But Gardiner also recognized that within the Labour Party there were two elements which strongly opposed accepting the jurisdiction of the European Court of Human Rights—the first because it might outlaw the closed shop (as, indeed, it came near to doing soon afterwards in the British Rail case); and the second because it might insist on widening the scope of parental choice in secondary education.

Gardiner remarried in 1970. His wife was Muriel (nee Baker), formerly the second wife of Sydney Box, author and film producer, by whom she had had one daughter. Gardiner moved out of the Temple to live in his wife's house in a secluded part of Mill Hill, in north London—the first time for over thirty years that he had lived within sight of green fields.

APPENDIX OF DOCUMENTS

The Oath of Allegiance

I
do swear by Almighty God that I will be faithful and bear true allegiance to Her Majesty Queen Elizabeth the Second and Her Heirs and Successors according to Law.

The Judicial Oath

I
do swear by Almighty God that I will well and truly serve our Sovereign Lady Queen Elizabeth the Second in the Office of Lord High Chancellor and I will do right to all manner of people after the laws and usages of this Realm without fear or favour affection or ill will.

The Oath of a Privy Counsellor

You do swear by Almighty God to be a true and faithful Servant unto the Queen's Majesty, as one of Her Majesty's Privy Council. You will not know or understand of any manner of thing to be attempted, done, or spoken against Her Majesty's Person, Honour, Crown, or Dignity Royal, but you will lett and withstand the same to the uttermost of your Power, and either cause it to be revealed to Her Majesty Herself, or to such of Her Privy Council as shall advertise Her Majesty of the same. You will, in all things to be moved, treated, and debated in Council, faithfully and truly declare your Mind and Opinion, according to your Heart and Conscience; and will keep secret all Matters committed and revealed unto you, or that shall be treated of secretly in Council. And if any of the said Treaties or Counsels shall touch any of the Counsellors, you will not reveal it unto him, but will keep the same until such time as, by the Consent of Her Majesty, or of the Council, Publication shall be made thereof. You will to your uttermost bear Faith and Allegiance unto the Queen's Majesty; and will assist and defend all Jurisdictions, Pre-eminences, and Authorities, granted to Her Majesty, and annexed to the Crown by Acts of Parliament, or otherwise, against all Foreign Princes, Persons, Prelates, States, or Potentates. And generally in all things you will do as a faithful and true Servant ought to do to Her Majesty.

SO HELP YOU GOD

Letters Patent for the Lord Chancellor's Pension [1]

George the Sixth by the Grace of God of Great Britain Ireland and the British Dominions beyond the seas King Defender of the Faith.

To Our Commmissioners of Our Treasury or Our Lord High Treasurer of Our United Kingdom Chancellor and Under Treasurer of Our Exchequer and to all others whom these Presents may concern Greeting Whereas by the Lord Chancellors Pension Act 1832 authority was given to His late Majesty King William the Fourth and His Heirs and successors by any Letters Patent under the Great Seal of Great Britain to give and grant unto any person executing the office of Lord High Chancellor of Great Britain for the time being or the office of Keeper of the Great Seal of Great Britain an annuity or yearly sum of money not exceeding Five thousand pounds of lawful money of Great Britain to commence and take effect immediately from and after the period whenever the person to whom such annuity or yearly sum of money should be granted should resign the said office of Lord High Chancellor or the office of Keeper of the Great Seal of Great Britain or be removed from the same respectively and to continue from thenceforth for and during the life of the person to whom the same should be granted as aforesaid in the manner therein provided Know Ye therefore that We of Our especial grace Do by these presents for Us Our heirs and successors Give and Grant unto Our right trusty and well beloved Counsellor WILLIAM ALLEN BARON JOWITT now executing the office of Lord High Chancellor of Great Britain an annuity or yearly sum of Five thousand pounds to be payable and paid out of the Consolidated Fund of the United Kingdom To have hold receive and enjoy the said annuity or yearly sum of Five thousand pounds to the said William Allen Baron Jowitt from the day on which he shall resign or be removed from the said office of Lord High Chancellor and to be payable and paid to him quarterly free from all taxes and deductions whatsoever at the four usual days of payment in each year the first payment to be made on such of the said days as shall next happen after such resignation or removal as aforesaid And We Do hereby Authorise Require and Command you Our said Commissioners of Our Treasury or Our Lord High Treasurer of Our United Kingdom Chancellor and Under Treasurer of Our Exchequer and all others therein concerned that you do from time to time pay or cause to be paid unto the said William Allen Baron Jowitt the said annuity or yearly sum of Five thousand pounds at such times and in such manner as the same shall become due or payable according to the true intent and meaning of these Our Letters Patent and his receipt of any sum of money in pursuance of this Our Grant shall be good and sufficient discharge for the payment thereof And We do hereby Direct and Grant that such payments shall be allowed without any further or other Warrant or authority to be had or obtained from Us or from Our Commissioners of Our Treasury or Our Lord High Treasurer for the time being or otherwise howsoever And it is Our Will and Pleasure that the said annuity to be paid and payable to the said William Allen Baron Jowit during such periods of time during his natural life as he shall not be in possession of any office of profit under Us Our heirs or successors of the annual value of Five thousand pounds Provided That if the said William Allen Baron Jowitt shall at any time be in possession of any office of profit under Us Our heirs or successors of less than the annual value of Five thousand pounds the said annuity shall in such case abate so that the annuity together with the salary and profits of such office shall not exceed in the whole the annual sum of Five thousand pounds In Witness whereof We have caused these Our Letters to be made Patent Witness Ourself at Westminster the eighth day of September in the ninth year of our Reign.

By Warrant under the King's Sign Manual
Napier

A Writ of Summons to Parliament[2]

Elizabeth the Second by the Grace of God of the United Kingdom of Great Britain and Northern Ireland and Our other Realms and Territories Queen Head of the Commonwealth Defender of the Faith To Our right trusty and

Greeting Whereas by the advice and assent of our Council for certain arduous and urgent affairs concerning Us the state and defence of Our United Kingdom and the Church We have orderd a certain Parliament to be holden at Our City of Westminster on the   day of   next ensuing And there to treat and have conference with the Prelates Great Men and Peers of Our Realm We strictly enjoining command you upon the faith and allegiance by which you are bound to Us that the weightiness of the said affairs and imminent perils considered (waiving all excuses) you be at the said day and place personally present with Us and with the said Prelates Great Men and Peers to treat and give your counsel upon the affairs aforesaid And this as you regard Us and Our honour and the safety and defence of the said Kingdom and Church and dispatch of the said affairs in nowise and you omit Witness Ourself at Westminster the   day of   in the   year of Our Reign.

Bourne
To   A Writ of Summons to Parliament
Bourne

[1] Crown copyright 1987. Published with the permission of the Controller of HMSO.
[2] Crown copyright. Reproduced with the permission of the Controller of HMSO.

TABLE OF CASES

INDEX